The Making of the Indo-Islamic World

In a new, accessible narrative, André Wink presents his major reinter-pretation of the history of India and the Indian Ocean region from the perspective of world history and geography. Situating the history of the Indianized territories of South Asia and Southeast Asia within the wider history of the Islamic world, he argues that the long-term development and transformation of Indo-Islamic history is best understood as the outcome of a major shift in the relationship between the sedentary peasant societies of the river plains, the nomads of the great Saharasian arid zone, and the seafaring populations of the Indian Ocean. This revisionist work redraws the Asian past as the outcome of the fusion of these different types of settled and mobile societies, placing geography and environment at the center of human history.

André Wink is H. Kern Professor Emeritus of History at the University of Wisconsin–Madison. He is a leading scholar of Indian and Islamic history and is the author of numerous books and articles, including *Land and Sovereignty in India: Agrarian Society and Politics under the Eighteenth-century Maratha Svarajya* (Cambridge, 1986), *Al-Hind: The Making of the Indo-Islamic World, 5 vols.* (Leiden, 1990, 1997, 2004; vols. IV and V forthcoming), and *Akbar* (Oxford, 2009).

T0384810

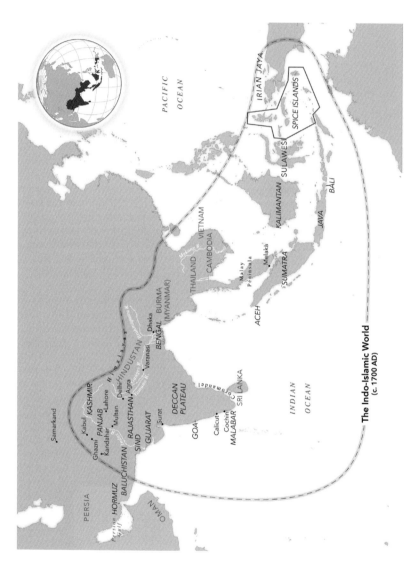

Map of the Indo-Islamic world, c. 1700 CE. Meghan Kelly, University of Wisconsin, Department of Geography, Cartography Laboratory.

The Making of the Indo-Islamic World

c. 700–1800 CE

André Wink

University of Wisconsin–Madison

CAMBRIDGE
UNIVERSITY PRESS

University Printing House, Cambridge CB2 8BS, United Kingdom

One Liberty Plaza, 20th Floor, New York, NY 10006, USA

477 Williamstown Road, Port Melbourne, VIC 3207, Australia

314–321, 3rd Floor, Plot 3, Splendor Forum, Jasola District Centre, New Delhi – 110025, India

79 Anson Road, #06-04/06, Singapore 079906

Cambridge University Press is part of the University of Cambridge.

It furthers the University's mission by disseminating knowledge in the pursuit of education, learning, and research at the highest international levels of excellence.

www.cambridge.org
Information on this title: www.cambridge.org/9781108417747
DOI: 10.1017/9781108278287

© André Wink 2020

First published 2020

Printed in the United Kingdom by TJ International Ltd, Padstow Cornwall

A catalogue record for this publication is available from the British Library.

Library of Congress Cataloging-in-Publication Data
Names: Wink, André, author.
Title: The making of the Indo-Islamic world / André Wink.
Description: New York : Cambridge University Press, 2020. | Includes bibliographical references and index.
Identifiers: LCCN 2020005212 | ISBN 9781108417747 (hardback) | ISBN 9781108405652 (ebook)
Subjects: LCSH: India--History--324 B.C.-1000 A.D. | India--History--1000-1526. | Islamic Empire--History.
Classification: LCC DS451 .W545 2020 | DDC 954--dc23
LC record available at https://lccn.loc.gov/2020005212

ISBN 978-1-108-41774-7 Hardback
ISBN 978-1-108-40565-2 Paperback

Contents

Figures

Preface

My intention with this book is to make the results of my previous and ongoing research more easily accessible to both specialists and a larger audience – all those interested in the fields of world history, Islamic history, South Asian and Southeast Asian history, and Central Asian and Mongol history, as well as European medieval and ancient history. This is a work of synthesis and interpretation, short on footnotes. For a more detailed treatment of all issues covered here and extensive footnotes, acknowledgments, and bibliographies, I refer the reader to my *Al-Hind*, both the three volumes already published and the two final ones that will deal with the sixteenth to eighteenth centuries and are now in the process of being completed.[1] The challenge has always been to strike a compromise between clarity and complexity, not to write a comprehensive work of history. I would like to acknowledge with gratitude the research funds that were put at my disposal during 2017 and 2018 by the Wisconsin Alumni Research Foundation and the History Department at the University of Wisconsin–Madison.

Abbreviations

AN H. Beveridge (trans.), *The Akbarnama of Abu-l-Fazl*, 3 vols. (New Delhi, 1979). With folio pagination.

BN Zahiruddin Muhammad Babur, *Bāburnāma: Chaghatay Turkish Text with Abdul Rahim Khankhanan's Persian Translation, Turkish Transcription, Persian Edition and English Translation*, by W. H. Thackston, Jr., 3 vols. (Department of Near Eastern Languages and Civilizations, Harvard University: Sources of Oriental Languages & Literatures XVIII, edited by S. Tekin & G. A. Tekin, Turkish Sources XVI, 1993). With folio pagination.

ED H. M. Elliot and J. Dowson (trans. and eds.), *The History of India as Told by Its Own Historians*, 8 vols. (London, 1867–1877).

HN A. Beveridge (trans. and ed.), *Humayun-nama by Gulbadan Begum* (Lahore, 1987). With folio pagination.

MA J. Sarkar (trans.), *Maāsir-i-'Ālamgiri: A History of the Emperor Aurangzib-'Ālamgir (Reign 1658–1707 A. D.) of Saqi Must'ad Khan* (Calcutta, 1947).

ML S. Moinul Haq (trans.), *Khafi Khan's History of 'Alamgir (Being an English Translation of the Relevant Portion of Muntakhab al-Lubab with Notes and an Introduction)* (Karachi, 1975).

MT G. S. Ranking (trans.), *Muntakhabu-t-Tawarikh by Abdul-Qadir Ibn-i-Muluk Shah, Known as Al-Badaoni*, 3 vols. (New Delhi, 1990).

MU H. Beveridge (trans.), *The Maathir-ul-Umarā*, 2 vols. (Kolkata, 2003).

SJN *The Shah Jahan Nama of 'Inayat Khan, an Abridged History of the Mughal Emperor Shah Jahan, Compiled by His Royal Librarian; the Nineteenth-Century Manuscript Translation of A. R. Fuller* (British Library Add. 30,777), edited and completed by W. E. Begley and Z. A. Desai (New Delhi, 1990).

TA   B. De (trans.), *The Tabaqāt-i-Akbarī: A History of India from the Early Musalman Invasions to the Thirty-Eighth Year of the Reign of Akbar, by Khwajah Nizamuddin Ahmad*, 3 vols. (New Delhi, 1990).

Introduction

The seven chapters of this book offer a new interpretation of the history of India or, as I prefer to call it, the Indo-Islamic world. It is an interpretation that is rooted in the study of historical geography and a world-historical approach.

Historical geography teaches us that India was not a national state with clearly demarcated boundaries but instead a major world region – extending from Afghanistan and the Makran coast across the subcontinent to the Malay-Indonesian archipelago – with open frontiers. From a world-historical perspective, the long-term development of this major world region is best understood as the outcome of a shift in the relationship between the sedentary peasant societies of the Indian river plains on the one hand and the nomads of the world's great arid zone and seafaring populations of the Indian Ocean on the other. The book thus presents the history of the Indo-Islamic world as the outcome of the fusion of these different types of settled and mobile societies.

It is a history with a clearly defined beginning, middle, and end. The Indo-Islamic world had its beginning in the seventh century CE, then expanded throughout the medieval (seventh to fifteenth) and early modern (sixteenth to eighteenth) centuries, until it fell prey to the superior arms and colonizing ventures of the East India Companies in the later eighteenth and early nineteenth centuries. As defined here, the Indo-Islamic world is a distinctive historical formation that ceased to exist after about 1800 CE and belongs entirely to the past.

Geography remained of fundamental importance throughout the history of the Indo-Islamic world. It was precisely due to the region's geographical conditions that the pre-Islamic heritage of India was radically different from that of Persia and the Mediterranean world, setting it on a different path from the outset. As is well known, the early Arab Caliphate emerged at the heart of the ancient world and took over its prodigious urban life. What has long been obscured, however, is that the Indo-Islamic world arose in a region without such an ancient imperial heritage and with no such continuous tradition of urban life.

1

The ancient past, the heritage of the ancient past, and the transition from the ancient to the medieval past were entirely different here. This "second Islamic world" was disassociated from imperial and urban traditions to a degree not found anywhere in the "first Islamic world." As this book aims to show, it was largely the geographical factors at work in the unstable environment of monsoon India that thwarted the growth of such traditions.

What is more, significant agricultural expansion and the growth of a settled social order did not gain momentum in India until the beginning of the early medieval centuries. This is true everywhere beyond the Indus borderlands – in the Panjab, Kashmir, Gujarat, the Ganges plain, the Bengal delta, the southern peninsula and the Deccan, Sri Lanka, Myanmar, Thailand, Cambodia, and Vietnam, as well as in Java and the other islands of the Malay-Indonesian archipelago. This is not to deny that Indian agriculture and settled civilization *originated* in an ancient and even prehistoric past. But everywhere to the east of the Indus was a region where agriculture took off late and for long remained inadequate to sustain empires.

There were two major reasons for this exceptionally slow expansion of Indian agricultural settlement. One is the wet, monsoon climate that made forest clearing more difficult and laborious than in the Mediterranean, Persia, and the Indus borderlands. The other is the slow population growth associated with the peculiar situation with regard to disease in the hot and humid alluvial plains. Once it gained momentum in the early medieval centuries, agricultural expansion and settlement gave rise to a fragmented landscape of monarchies of varying size and importance in which monumental Hindu temples emerged as the typical architectural expression of a new vertical and hierarchical social order wherein landed elites exercised political power with the Brahman priesthood. Early medieval India thus emerged as a land of kings, priests, peasant societies, and the earliest Hindu temples in rural surroundings – not ancient cities.

Historical geography also provides the conception of a frontier of settled society. All major settled civilizations in world history have known such a frontier, and, without exception, their spokesmen – be they priests or custodians of the law – described the inhabitants of the frontier as barbarians beyond the pale of their respective settled civilizations. Indian civilization was no exception and had its own derogatory conception of the frontier. This was essentially a twofold frontier: There was the great arid zone with its deserts and steppes, of "Saharasia," on one side and the equally immense Indian Ocean on the other. These features formed the pastoral nomadic frontier and the maritime frontier – both with significant extensions into or links with the heartlands of the settled world of India itself. The two frontiers were fundamentally alike and interconnected insofar as both fostered movement outside the control of settled society. Rather than cities, these open and unsettled realms of nomadic and seafaring peoples together represented the frontier of mobile wealth and the major source of change and dynamism in land-based society. Both frontiers gained in importance and flourished simultaneously and in symbiosis with the emerging settled, agricultural world. This book explores the underlying causes of this medieval upsurge of the twofold frontier and finds them in a combination of geographic, climatological, demographic, military, and political-organizational factors that had been absent in ancient India.

It is this conception of a frontier that provides the key to understanding the rise of Islam in India. In the medieval period, the mobile populations on the margins of the settled world of India moved center stage, to a position of dominance under the aegis of Islam. From the outset, Islam had universal aspirations, aiming to supersede what went before, and it soon gave rise to a religious civilization that recognized no boundaries and fostered the unrestrained mobility of men and goods. From the late tenth and eleventh centuries onward, nomadic populations that had converted to Islam conquered much of the Indian subcontinent. They aligned their rule with an idealized and universal history of Islam, which they interpreted as a religion of empire, and extolled the Islamic ideals of religious and political authority of the early Arab Caliphate. But the conquests did not involve the migration of nomads as such. The geographical conditions of the subcontinent did not allow such migration, at least not on a major scale. They did not promote nomadism as a mode of production and did not cause the widespread destruction of settled agriculture. Instead, they were instrumental in expanding the latter. This resulted in post-nomadic states in which horse-riding military elites established their dominance over a largely Hindu population of peasants and integrated them into a wider world.

The resulting fusion of nomadic frontier and settled society that set the parameters of the medieval Indo-Islamic world was successful up to a point. The heritage of horsemanship and mounted warfare on the steppes of the post-nomadic, poly-ethnic military elites among the Turks, Mongols, and Afghans gave their population a decisive military advantage over the settled peasant population, but they were as yet unable to turn their nomadic legacy into a durable institutional framework of political domination. Throughout the medieval centuries, they continued to suffer from rapid turnover, and institutional weakness remained their hallmark, while dynastic succession was in constant jeopardy. As conquest states, they also failed to accommodate the leadership of the majority Hindu population, in particular the great Rajput lineages. The constantly shifting capitals of the conquerors were not historically durable cities but instead mobile camps or garrison towns pitched on the violent and ever-shifting interface of arid zone and settled agriculture. If there were urban elites in the medieval Indo-Islamic world, they consisted largely of fugitives from territories over-run by the nomadic Mongols. The post-nomadic elites themselves were mostly "military converts," recent and often nominal converts to Islam, so-called "new Muslims," and did not see it as their mission to convert the Hindu population to Islam but merely to extend the military fron-tier ever farther eastward and southward.

The situation was similar on the medieval maritime frontier. In con-junction with the rise to power of pastoral nomads, seafaring popula-tions and sea nomads spread out across the medieval Indian Ocean and established maritime empires in their own right. The open and mobile conditions on the maritime frontier brought about an ever more intimate association between sea power and Islam. But the coastal and seafaring populations that converted were as small in numbers as the pastoral nomads. Here again Islam remained the religion of a small minority, and the Indo-Islamic states of the seaboard remained volatile throughout the medieval centuries.

A great transformation followed in the early modern centuries. The sixteenth to eighteenth centuries present themselves as a time of insti-tutional consolidation, further economic expansion and integration, and substantial political change throughout the Indo-Islamic world. The most consequential single factor in this transformation was the rise to power of the Great Mughals (1526–1540, 1556–1707). Among the most powerful and wealthy imperial dynasties of the early modern centuries, the Great Mughals brought Indo-Islamic culture to a bril-liant zenith. In much of the subcontinent, the Great Mughals had the advantage of being able to build on the achievements of their medieval predecessors, including the Afghans. But this was not the only reason for the Great Mughals' unprecedented success. Nor can it plausibly be argued that the success of the Great Mughals was due to their adop-tion of artillery and gunpowder weapons. If in Europe infantry replaced cavalry from the sixteenth century onward in conjunction with new developments in gunpowder warfare, horsemanship and the heritage of the nomadic steppe lands – not artillery or infantry – remained the chief military asset of the Great Mughals. A culture of a horse-riding nobility continued to prevail in the Mughal empire until the age of European colonialism and the closing of the nomadic frontier. The key to the Great Mughals' imperial success, then, was not gunpowder weaponry but rather their successful assumption of leadership of a horse-riding, largely post-nomadic nobility under the conditions of economic growth and monetization that accompanied the early modern expansion of world trade and the influx of American and Japanese silver through sea trade.

The Great Mughals achieved this position of leadership through the successful adaptation of their medieval nomadic heritage to the changing conditions and economic expansion of early modern India. They inherited an entire institutional framework of imperial rule associated with the corporate Turko-Mongol clan and based on the customary practices of rule, dynastic succession, and princely feuding that went back, over many centuries, to Chingiz Khan, Timur, and the early medieval nomadic Turks. This allowed the Great Mughals to consolidate power in ways their medieval predecessors could not. They did so, most importantly, by making critical changes in their dynastic succession practices. The sharing arrangements of the corporate dynastic clan were replaced by a new system of open-ended succession and alliance building. Princely feuding and sedition became the key mechanism that allowed the empire to succeed as a distributive enterprise and increased the power and longevity of the dynasty. Yet another key adaptation of Turko-Mongol customary law was the apparatus of imperial ranks, developed for the imperial service nobility, that accommodated the leadership of the Hindu majority population of the empire and gave it a stake in the continuity and prosperity of their empire along with the Muslim nobility. Within this framework, the Great Mughals developed an extraordinarily sophisticated imperial version of a nomadic band of horse warriors that could successfully operate in an expanding settled society. More than anything else, it is this adaptation of the nomadic heritage that accounts for the success of the dynasty.

If their imperial constitution was founded in Turko-Mongol customary law, the entire system of governance and the administration of justice of the empire of the Great Mughals broadly evolved within the same matrix of customary law, not the canonical or prescriptive matrix of the Sharia, or "Islamic law." Although the Mughal dynasty ostensibly drew closer to Islamic scriptural ideals of justice and legitimation in the course of its extraordinary imperial expansion in the sixteenth and seventeenth centuries, much of the law and the practice of jurisprudence that prevailed in the empire did not follow religion. In the towns and cities of the Mughal empire, the reach of the Sharia was mostly felt in the religious sphere and in the realms of Muslim marriage and divorce. Here Islam informed an entire way of life, a religious belief system, and a set of ritual practices, as well as dietary and dress codes, not to mention art, literature, and architectural styles. But the towns and cities of Mughal India were mostly tiny and only weakly differentiated enclaves in an immense and largely unconverted countryside. Even the largest cities of Mughal India were highly unstable and dependent on the presence of the peripatetic court. In the countryside, conditions were quite different. Everywhere the joint or extended family household was the basic institution of rural society and the characteristic form of property enjoyment and hereditary rights in land. The beneficiaries of hereditary rights in land were "sharers" of these rights – in effect, the political community in any given locality that collectively held landed estates and was able to defend them by force of arms. They, too, were guided by customary rights that had the force of law and by political considerations – not by religious law, be it Islamic or Hindu. At all levels, the arbitration of justice was really politics by other means. Customary law codes associated with some degree of divine justice provided the legal framework for the conduct of a broad range of clan, tribal, ethnic, caste, and religious feuds and conflicts, just as they did for royal dynastic feuds. Thus, these judicial codes were embedded in a negotiated, not a modern, state. Negotiation and compromise rather than "communalism" were the hallmarks of this society, which systematically blurred its religious contours.

Similarly, the age of the Estado da India and the East India Companies brought major changes in trading and navigation patterns in the Indian Ocean as well as concurrent shifts of political power in the sixteenth to eighteenth centuries. But it did not change the fundamental nature of political power. The new developments in naval warfare associated with artillery and other innovations introduced by the Portuguese and the Dutch, British, and French East India Companies notwithstanding, the maritime frontier remained an open frontier. Even though incorporated in more powerful states, it did not close until the eighteenth century. What happened in these centuries is by no means a simple story of Indo-Islamic trade not being able to compete with European trade or being overwhelmed by superior European naval force. For two more centuries Indian Ocean trade flourished, and expanded significantly. New ports emerged and old ones disappeared, trading patterns realigned, and Islam continued to spread on the Malabar coast and elsewhere in the peninsula. New Indo-Islamic states with unprecedented naval power arose in the Malay-Indonesian archipelago: Aceh, Johore, Bantam, Demak, and other pasisir or "coastal" states in Java, later Makassar, and, turning inland, Mataram. The patterns of domination in these new states in the archipelago were very similar to those of Mughal India. They were Islamic states operating on Indic soil, and the urban element was even less significant here than in the subcontinent. They were not founded on the scriptural law of Islam but instead on customary law – the local *adat*. Thus, the law codes of Mataram and the Javanese pasisir, as well as Makassar, owed almost nothing to Islam. What these states took from Islam was the tradition of kingship we also encounter in Mughal India and other features of Islam that had to do with the exercise of political power. They largely confined Islamic law to the religious sphere. When Islam spread beyond the ports in the archipelago, as in the subcontinent, it was mostly as a kind of "holy-man Islam" of the rural hinterlands and still virtually untouched by scriptural religion. The ultimate closing of the maritime frontier in the eighteenth century, and as early as the final two decades of the seventeenth in Java, resulted from the interplay of many different factors. Among these were the inexorable rise to territorial power of the British and Dutch East India Companies; the Anglo-French competition for power and world hegemony; the decline of Safawid Persia; the emergence of a new Indo-Afghan empire on the ruins of the old Mughal dispensation; the expansion of multiple Mughal successor states; and, in the deep south, the rise of Mysore and Travancore. In the archipelago, it was the rise of agrarian Mataran and its willful destruction of the pasisir of Java. The complexities of these developments of the late-seventeenth and eighteenth centuries are such that aspects of some of them remain unclear. What is not in doubt is the outcome: the medieval and early modern patterns of movement and free trade on the maritime frontier came to an end in this century and made way for European colonialism. Without its open frontiers, the Indo-Islamic world was no more. A millennium of history had come to an end.

1   Prehistoric and Ancient Antecedents

In Hindustan the destruction and building of villages and hamlets, even of cities, can be accomplished in an instant.

Zahiruddin Muhammad Babur[1]

L'Inde est le lieu du "non-Empire."

Georges Duby[2]

This first chapter begins by taking a look at the historical geography of South and Southeast Asia.[3] Together, from the early centuries CE these areas constituted a single major world region that encompassed the bulk of the landmasses, peninsulas, islands, and maritime spaces affected by the seasonal monsoon winds of the Indian Ocean. Throughout its fertile and often extensive river plains, its inhabitants adopted recognizably similar patterns of Indian civilization and settled organization.

Early geographers referred to this world region as "India." Thus the geographers who produced the medieval and early-modern European versions of the world map of Ptolemy's *Geographia* (c. 150 CE) depicted a closed Indian Ocean (*Mare Indicum*), which was conceived of as a circular river, with an island called Taprobane (Sri Lanka) in the middle, below the subcontinental landmass of "India this side of the Ganges," and beyond it the peninsular contours of a misshapen "India beyond the Ganges" (Figure 1.1).

The medieval European geographers themselves advanced a similar conception of a closed Indian Ocean with a coastline running from Africa to China, along which they identified three Indias: India Major, the largest part of modern India; India Minor, extending from the north of the Coromandel coast and including the peninsulas and islands of Southeast Asia; and Meridional India, including Ethiopia and the southwest Asian coastal regions. The exact location of these three Indias could shift somewhat, but what we call Southeast Asia today was always unambiguously included in the medieval notion of a tripartite India.

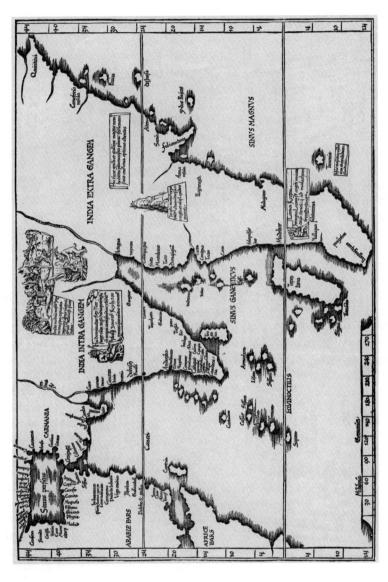

Figure 1.1 Map in Ptolemy's *Geographicae Enarrationis*, 1535 CE. Culture Club/Hulton Archive via Getty Images.

Arabic geographical and navigational works called this entire region *al-Hind*. With some variations, they defined it in broadly the same terms across the centuries – often with remarkable precision – and described a region generally coterminous with the bipartite or tripartite India of medieval European geography. It extended well beyond the Indus River to the west, certainly much further to the west than India today and further than British India in 1893 (the year the Durand Line was drawn, now the border between Pakistan and Afghanistan). By the seventh century, al-Hind extended into the Himalayan valleys of Kashmir and Ladakh and, beyond the Indus, into the Karakorum valleys of Gilgit and Baltistan, as well as into Gandhara, embracing the Kabul River valley and reaching down to Zabul and Zamindawar (the areas of Ghazna and Kandahar, respectively). From this point onward, al-Hind continued to the east of the Bolan Pass, up to Baghwana, and further west, embracing the whole of ancient Gedrosia – i.e., the arid Makran coast and a large part of Baluchistan. Arabic geographical and navigational works, in addition, display their authors' detailed knowledge of the Indian Ocean and identify the maritime boundaries of India with the same precision, tracing the coastlines from the Red Sea all the way to the Java Sea and the South China Sea. Here al-Hind is shown extending much further to the east than India does today or British India did with Burma at any time. It comprised all of the mainland of Southeast Asia, including the major Indianized states of Burma (Myanmar), Cambodia, Thailand, and parts of Vietnam, as well as the "islands of al-Hind" – which is to say the islands of the Malay-Indonesian archipelago, including Java, Sumatra, and the Spice Islands (our "Indies," what is now Indonesia).

A Graveyard of Cities

The settlement ecology of this major world region was quite different from that of the Mediterranean peninsulas, islands, and coasts. The Mediterranean is ecologically a much more marginal environment, characterized by an unusually fragmented topography of agricultural microregions offset by relatively easy seaborne communications. Partly as a result of its unique ecological conditions, the Mediterranean became what was probably the most durably and densely urbanized of all major world regions. Athens and Rome, Alexandria, Cairo, Antioch, Jerusalem, Constantinople (Istanbul), Marseille, Cordoba, Barcelona, Naples, Pisa, Florence, Venice, and numerous other Mediterranean cities have been prominent centers of civilization over many centuries – and in some cases millennia. Across the centuries, the *city* became the privileged locus of Mediterranean, European, and Arab-Islamic civilizations and came to be seen as the source of their dynamism by contemporary and later observers alike. The Mediterranean idea of the city as first formulated by the Greek philosophers has been remarkably consistent. For Aristotle, man was a "political animal," because it was only by being a citizen of the Greek city-state, or polis, that he could pursue the good life and realize the highest aims of human existence. Our entire vocabulary of politics derives from this original conception of the city. In Latin, the very concept of civilization derived from *civilitas*, or "city-ness"; and for the Romans as for the Greeks, political society focused on the cities of the empire. European thinkers have continued to endow the medieval European city with the characteristics of the Greek polis and have looked upon it as the precursor of the city of their own days – still the civilizing agent par excellence and the source of all progress and modernization. No less fundamentally, the Arab-Islamic world was heir to the same ancient and late-antique past of the eastern and southern Mediterranean and conceived of itself as a series of urban islands connected by the threads of commerce and long-distance trade.

In the Indo-Islamic world, by contrast, such a close relationship with an ancient past was lacking. This was due to the absence of a continuous tradition of urbanism. No comparably dense and durable patterns of urban life ever developed in the ecologically unstable environment of the river plains of monsoon Asia. Without taking this different settlement ecology into account, we cannot understand the long-term development of Indian or Indo-Islamic civilization or the reasons why it diverged so radically from the patterns of the ancient Greek-Persian-Roman, medieval European-Byzantine, and Arab-Islamic civilizations that are familiar to historians.

Consider, first, the prehistoric and historic settlement patterns and urbanism of the Indus borderlands – today's Pakistan and adjacent areas in Afghanistan and India. Archaeologists have long looked at the cities that were built in the Indus River valley between 3000 and 1500 BCE as proof of a precocious tradition of city building going back to the very beginnings of Indian civilization – preceding even Greece and Rome – and, in all their obsessive uniformity, representing the world's first planned cities and townships. We have, in effect, incontrovertible evidence of brick-built urban centers scattered across a distance of some nine hundred miles in an area in and adjacent to the valleys of that great river and its extant and defunct tributaries – an area larger than Egypt's Old Kingdom or Mesopotamia's Sumeria. The largest of these archaeological sites are known today as Harappa (in the Panjab)

Figure 1.2 View of the ruins of the prehistoric city, urban structure with streets at right angles, of Mohenjodaro, Sind. Indus valley civilization, 2600 BCE. De Agostini Picture Library via Getty Images.

and Mohenjodaro (in Sind), each of which is estimated to have accommodated at least several tens of thousands of permanent inhabitants (perhaps as many as a hundred thousand) (Figure 1.2).

These cities of the Indus valley civilization, however, do not represent a tradition of urban settlement that in any way remained vital to the borderlands of South Asia, let alone to South and Southeast Asia as a whole. It appears that the Indus cities were obliterated by the combined impact of earthquakes and the shifting of the courses of the Indus River and its tributaries, as well as flooding. Their physical remains were buried under the sand or submerged in water, with no one being aware of their prehistoric existence for thousands of years – until they were more or less accidentally rediscovered in the early twentieth century. There are some archaeological remains dating to later times of brick-built cities to the west of the Indus, but these, too, are not duplicated anywhere to the east of that river at any time in later history.

The Indus borderlands were the site of the earliest urban development in South and Southeast Asia, but they never became a densely and durably urbanized region like the Mediterranean. In ancient times, in the wake of continuing shifts in the courses of the Indus and its Panjab tributaries – a river system that has steadily been moving westward – existing towns and cities continued to be abandoned as new ones arose. The historical cities attributed to the imperial Mauryans (326–184 BCE), the Indo-Greeks (190 BCE–10 CE), the nomadic Kushanas (second century BCE to third century CE), and all subsequent late-antique ruling dynasties suffered the same fate as Harappa and Mohenjodaro. As a result, the Arab conquerors of the eighth century found no ancient cities here resembling the great, walled metropoles of Persia (like Balkh, the Old Persian *Bakhtri*, where Zoroaster preached – *umm al-bilād*, or "mother of cities"). The cities the Arabs themselves built, such as the once-famed seaport of Debal and the capitals of ar-Rūr and Mansūra, were in their turn obliterated by the silting up of the Indus River mouth or by earthquakes and floods, and often left little trace. In medieval times (600–1500 CE), the Indus borderlands boasted remarkably few important cities and towns with anything like an ancient past – and none that became great cultural centers for extended periods of time. The city of Multan (Old Persian *Mūlasthāna*, "frontier land") has ancient antecedents and today is the oldest continuously inhabited site in the Indus borderlands; but we know very little about Multan before it became a capital of Arab Sind and began to thrive on trade with the west. We know that it was repeatedly devastated – like all cities of the Indus borderlands from Kashmir to Sind – by nomadic Mongol hordes in the thirteenth and fourteenth centuries. And between the fourteenth and seventeenth centuries, the city was frequently threatened by the silting and subsequent shifts of the Ravi and Chenab Rivers. As a result, it had to be continuously rebuilt and was much diminished by the seventeenth century. Thatta under the Mughals (1612–1737) was the largest city (built mostly of unburnt, sun-dried brick) ever to arise on the Indus prior to the twentieth century, but its origins go back no further than the eleventh century, and it was likewise repeatedly destroyed by the Mongols in the thirteenth and fourteenth centuries. Thatta recovered in the seventeenth century, when it became an important textile production and trading center and the seat of a Mughal governor, but always remained a city of the desert frontier, surrounded by predatory tribes. It is remarkable how quickly Thatta, which was simply known as *Nagar*, or "The City," lost its economic and political importance, together with 80 percent of its population, in the early decades of the eighteenth century, when its port of Lahori Bandar at the mouth of the Indus declined due to silting, following which the political and economic configuration of lower Sind abruptly changed its contours once again. The three cities that

Figure 1.3 Indus delta, Pakistan, satellite image. The Indus River flows into the Arabian Sea near Pakistan's port city of Karachi (top left of the image). The city of Hyderabad, located on the east bank of the Indus River, is at the top center of the image. The Indian subcontinent extends to the southeast of the Indus delta. Planet Observer/Universal Images Group, via Getty Images.

displaced Thatta were Karachi, Hyderabad, and Shikarpur; until 1828, these do not appear to have reached a population of much more than one hundred thousand combined, and none was founded before the eighteenth – or at most the seventeenth – century. In short, the region of Sind was still overwhelmingly rural by the late eighteenth century, and nowhere in Sind had there been a cumulative development of significant city life in the millennia since the rise of the prehistoric Indus valley civilization (Figure 1.3).

Like those of Sind, the historical cities further north in the Indus borderlands, such as Ghazna, Kabul, Kandahar, and Peshawar, typically had a "citadel" within or outside their walls but otherwise had few or no significant public buildings that could bear comparison with those of the cities of Persia and the Mediterranean lands. Here, too, there is abundant archaeological as well as textual evidence that bears this out. Ghazna in the tenth and eleventh centuries was briefly the capital of the empire of the "Ghaznavids," which stretched from the Tigris to the Ganges, but was badly damaged by earthquakes, floods, and landslides in the eleventh and fourteenth centuries, as a result of which it sank into insignificance. For similar reasons, the city of Kabul had shrunk to a village by the mid-fourteenth century. The Mughal emperor Babur (1483–1530), a century and a half later, restored some of Kabul's commercial importance, but Babur also wrote at length about the city's isolation for almost eight months of every year. In his time, its houses were built of unburnt brick and mud or wood to resist the frequent earthquakes, and the city was remarkably small – probably numbering less than twenty thousand permanent inhabitants. By contrast, the city of Kandahar had antecedents going back to a Persian king of antiquity and to Alexander of Macedonia. But it was really an eighteenth-century city laid out and walled in by Ahmad Shah Abdali, the founder of the Durrani dynasty of Afghanistan, and built to the northwest of the ruins of an earlier one designed by the Persian conqueror Nadir Shah. In turn, the older city had replaced a still-earlier one built by the Ghilzai Afghans, of which only ruins were left some two miles away and which Nadir Shah dismantled. Before that, this was the site of a town founded by the Timurid ruler Husayn Mirza (1438–1506), called Husaynabad. And it was the same with Peshawar, another city in the Indus borderlands with ancient antecedents – going back to Kushana times but itself not ancient and only occasionally mentioned, as *Parshāwar,* in medieval chronicles, while appearing merely as a fortress in Babur's writings. This, too, was a city that does not appear to have really flourished until the advent of the Durrani dynasty in the eighteenth century, and, like Kandahar, it quickly collapsed in the early nineteenth century.

It was not only in the Indus borderlands that the continuity of city life was threatened and difficult to sustain over long periods of time. Everywhere in South and Southeast Asia the shifting mud and water masses of immense river plains hampered urban development and continuity. Throughout the region, city life remained fragile and insignificant, and civilization remained primarily rural in orientation. This was demonstrably the major world region with the most extreme and highest-impact environmental instabilities of all kinds: hydrological, seismic, climatological, meteorological, and volcanic, as well as all possible combinations thereof. Indian cities and towns, and settlement patterns in general, were subject to a much higher degree of disruption than their Mediterranean counterparts. As Chapter 2 will show in more detail, the disruption was not such that it prevented the long-term expansion of agriculture and the overall growth of rural settlement and population increase. Agriculture was often resilient and rural settlement adaptable. But it was different with cities. Subject to a very high degree of disruption, followed by dislocation and abandonment, India became a graveyard of cities.[4]

In sharp contrast to the Mediterranean, settlement throughout South and Southeast Asia spread across the flat alluvial plains of navigable rivers of extraordinary magnitude. Sweeping hydrological and geomorphological change has always been pervasive in these plains as well as in the deltas of the rivers, particularly during the monsoon rains. Because of the erratic nature of the rains, it was impossible to predict the volume and direction of the annual river floods. Innumerable Indian cities and towns, together with their surrounding villages, have been destroyed by such floods or by the resultant changes in the courses of rivers. Others were abandoned because they lost access to water in the wake of such changes or because of other problems associated with water management, the outbreak of malaria, deforestation, and mudslides. There was also geomorphological change associated with soil erosion – common in areas of soft alluvium – and river instability due to the silting up of the deep water channels, often in combination with earthquakes, and delta formation (the retreat of the sea). The resulting digressions were of such magnitude as to have few or no parallels in other parts of the world. Coastlines shifted due to sedimentation and cyclones or tsunamis caused by suboceanic tectonic plate movements (such as happened as recently as 2004).[5] Desiccation and changes in the patterns of settlement resulted from climate change. Earthquakes of great destructive power have always been a common phenomenon in the northern mountains of the subcontinent, and numerous volcanoes in Indonesia have never ceased their devastating eruptions.

If in Sind, in the words of Richard Burton, "deserts spring up, cities, ports and towns fall in the space of time which it takes the Indus to shift its bed for a few miles,"[6] in the Panjab it was no different. Some of the Indus's tributary rivers in the Panjab have been even more erratic than the Indus itself, and abandoned settlements are exceedingly numerous throughout the "Five-River Land." The Panjab's major city of Lahore is not ancient. It was merely a market town with a fortress before the Mughal emperor Humayun moved his court there in the sixteenth century. Located at the confluence of the Indus and Ravi Rivers, Lahore lost a great deal of traffic in the subsequent centuries and declined due to obstructions in these rivers, to reemerge badly damaged by flooding and heavy rainfall. The extreme seismic instability of the northern mountain zone affected the entire Panjab. It is the result of the geologically recent collision between the subcontinent and the Eurasian landmass that created the Himalayan mountain range and the Siwaliks in front of them. The subcontinent is still moving at a pace of a half to two inches per year, and the mountains continue to rise, causing earthquakes in association with mountain building and producing landslides and severe floods in the monsoon season. The resulting combinations of powerful earthquakes and landslides devastated the Panjab in the early fourteenth century and turned vast parts of it into a desert, which reached as far south as Agra. In other parts, agriculture recovered but towns and cities did not.

The plains of the Ganges, and the delta where the Ganges and the Brahmaputra come together, developed into rich agricultural subregions but not without often changing their hydrographic map. Not only the Ganges but also all tributaries of the Ganges displaced themselves during floods or filled up older, dry riverbeds. Throughout these northern plains, the resulting changes were also quite disruptive, particularly in the newer and softer alluvial soils, making it hard to recover the sites of numerous cities and towns. Archaeological research has clearly shown that Hastinapura and Ayudhya, the most famous ancient cities in this subregion, were abandoned due to environmental causes. The early medieval capital of Kanauj suffered a similar fate. There are thousands of dead cities here, for the majority of which even the name has not survived. Varanasi, with its great riverfront display of temples and stone ghats, is practically the only Indian city to survive from ancient into medieval and modern times. The main reason for this city's exceptional longevity is the fact that it was built on a riverbank made of *kankar,* an impure form of limestone occasionally found in nodules in the older alluvium of the plains' nearest approach to rock – hence its relatively high resistance to erosion. Even so, no significant riverfront structure of Varanasi can be dated to before 1600 CE, there are no significant ancient ruins anywhere in its precincts, and the city has yielded nothing from the pre-Gupta period (fourth century CE) in terms of art.[7]

In the Ganges-Brahmaputra delta – now spread over eastern India and Bangladesh – the cities, and even capitals, buried in the marshes cannot be counted (Figure 1.4). None of the ancient cities has been found here. Between the twelfth and seventeenth centuries CE, its entire river system gradually moved eastward, and the older cities of West Bengal were regularly eclipsed by newly rising ones in the eastern delta, which was then opened up for wet rice cultivation. Meanwhile, Bengal's coastline kept advancing outward. All ports mentioned in Portuguese accounts from this period are today much further removed from the sea than they were then: the main ports of Sonargaon and Satgaon thus became inaccessible, while Gaur, the capital of medieval Bengal, regulating

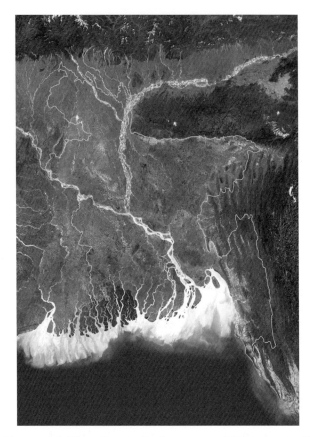

Figure 1.4 The Ganges-Brahmaputra delta, eastern India and Bangladesh, satellite image. Planet Observer/Universal Images Group via Getty Images.

access to Sonargaon and Chittagong, was abandoned in 1575. Written records such as the historical chronicles of the Mughal empire also preserved the memory of the destruction caused by many cyclones hitting these shores.

In every delta of the Indian Ocean, erosion and the heavy silt deposition of rivers in the wet season led to the retreat of the sea and the formation of vast flatlands that caused frequent migration of distributaries, the blockage of harbors, and the abandonment of old channels at every river mouth. On the fringes of the Deccan plateau, this occurred in the lowlands of the major eastward-flowing rivers such as the Godavari, the Krishna, the Kaveri, and the Tamraparni, which were much smaller than those in the north but equally mutable. The sedimentation and migration of the Kaveri River can be traced inland through many sites in Karnataka, where the bed of the river was gradually raised by gravel and sand. There were no ancient cities in the Deccan that have survived. Port towns on the estuaries and deltaic plains of the peninsula – but also Gujarat, the Konkan, and Sri Lanka in medieval times – all suffered the same fate as those of the north: Cranganore and Eli on the Malabar coast, Old Kayal and Korkai opposite Sri Lanka in the extreme south of the peninsula, Kambaya in Gujarat, Chaul in the Konkan, and Mantai in northeast Sri Lanka. In inland Sri Lanka, the decline and abandonment of the northern Buddhist capitals of Anuradhapura and Polonnaruva were associated with problems of water management in the great ancient tanks in the arid zone of the island, which in turn were caused by military invasion and the spread of malaria.

Further east, we again find no ancient cities at all. The land masses surrounding the so-called Sunda platform (the underwater extension of the continental shelf of Southeast Asia) are fringed with huge, flat marshlands, and here, too, every river shows evidence of frequent migration and of riverbed sedimentation in the lower reaches. The Tonle Sap alluvial plain and lake in Cambodia, with its adaptations of marine fish species, are the result of Mekong sedimentation in not-too-distant times. In the thirteenth century CE, the decline and abandonment of the great Khmer capital of Angkor is associated with hydrological disruption, deforestation, climate change, and the spread of malaria in expanding riverine swamps and stagnant backwaters. The distributaries of the Chao Phraya, in Thailand, also changed their courses in medieval times, leaving historic ruins much further to the west. The premier medieval estuary port of Melaka (Malacca) was rendered useless by silting in the early-modern centuries. So was Baruas, once perhaps the second most important port on the Malay Peninsula. The Mekong and the Irrawaddy also added annually to their deltas – at a rate of sixty yards or more – with similar consequences. Everywhere south of Thailand and outside of Java, city-states at the mouths of rivers were the rule, and these rose and fell with striking rapidity as a result of hydrological instability. Shrivijaya, from about the seventh century CE, was the epitome of such river-mouth population centers. Located in the eastern coastal marshes, which take up about half of the island of Sumatra, with rivers flowing eastward from the Barisan Mountains into the shallow sea and mangrove forests, its capital near modern Palembang was destroyed in the thirteenth century by river sedimentation, accompanied by volcanic eruptions in inner Sumatra and mudflows that swept down loose ashes, as well as by forest cutting, heavy rainfall, and tectonic movement. In eastern Sumatra, such sedimentation began at least five thousand years ago and produced very rapid changes in the coastline throughout known history, ruining many other city-states in these amphibious eastern parts of the island, inundated frequently by tides in the rainy season. There is abundant evidence on this coast of dead rivers and of settlements obliterated by mudflows and descending clouds of volcanic ashes or abandoned because of outbreaks of malaria. In Java, too, hydrological instability, aggravated by volcanic eruptions, had a destructive impact everywhere in the alluvial plains of the Solo and the Brantas Rivers, and highly unstable lowland plains are a characteristic feature throughout the Javanese north coast. As a whole, the Indonesian archipelago has had more volcanoes – and more volcanic activity in all of recorded history – than any other part of the world. Krakatoa and Tambora have become bywords of cataclysmic disaster.[8] Numerous cities and small kingdoms throughout Indonesia have been wiped out by volcanoes in a matter of hours – as, for instance, in 1006 CE, when the city of Dharmavamsa in Java was obliterated by what was probably an eruption of the Merapi. Volcanic eruptions in the Opak and Praga basins of Mataram in the tenth and eleventh centuries drove a major population movement from these areas to the eastern parts of Java. As a result of such continuing volcanic activity between the eleventh and fifteenth centuries, the hegemonic centers of Javanese royal authority shifted to the lands of the Brantas River.

Babur's observations on the fragility of the cities of the northern Indian subcontinent, or Hindustan, deserve to be quoted in their entirety, because they are valid not only in Hindustan. As Babur wrote,

In Hindustan the destruction and building of villages and hamlets, even of cities, can be accomplished in an instant [dar hindūstān ābādān-shudan-o-vīrān shudan-i-deh-hā balkī shahr-hā dar ek zamān mī-shūd]. Such large cities [shahr-hāy kalān] in which people have lived for years, if they are going to be abandoned, can be abandoned in a day, even half a day, such that no sign or trace remains. If they have a mind to build a city, there is no necessity for digging irrigation canals or building dams... There is no making of houses or raising of walls. They simply make huts from the plentiful straw and innumerable trees, and instantly there is a village or city [deh yā shahr].[9]

With some variations, we have seen that this was basically true for cities in all parts of India as historically defined. If Indian agriculture was a gamble on the monsoon, the survival of cities was no less so. Dependent on the monsoon, Indian cities are described in the chronicles as subject to sharp seasonally determined demographic fluctuations; alternating patterns of long- and short-distance migration of specialist groups of merchants, soldiers, and priests; and migration and high mortality caused by frequently occurring drought-induced famines or periods of scarcity, with epidemics (in particular cholera) in their wake. Raids by rival states, invasions, and warfare also had a detrimental impact on cities, commonly leading to the evacuation of all their inhabitants or overcrowding with refugees. Elite mobility, as well as the general volatility of political life, aggravated these tendencies. Extremely peripatetic political elites created new cities and towns where often none had existed before, and the fortunes of these places remained intimately tied to the fortunes of the elites themselves. Not only the major Mughal cities of Agra and Lahore but also many of the approximately 205 urban localities in the sixteenth- and seventeenth-century Mughal empire were founded either in Mughal times or just before. Delhi was a city with origins in the early medieval period, but it was ravaged by the Mongols and depopulated in the thirteenth and early fourteenth centuries not just once but on several occasions, when famine raged. Delhi reemerged from all of this as the largest city of India, but its fortunes fluctuated with the frequent relocations of the imperial court. In the mid-fourteenth century, the traveler Ibn Battuta, on his first visit, described Delhi as the "capital of the country of India (*qāʿida bilād al-hind*), a very illustrious city, large, combining beauty and power [and] ... surrounded by a wall which does not have its equal in the universe ... the greatest of the cities of India (*mudun al-hind*) and even of all the cities of the Islamic East."[10] Shortly afterward, however, the same author observed that Delhi was "entirely abandoned without fire, smoke, or torch.... [I]mmense city that it is ... it was empty, abandoned and its population completely scattered."[11] This sudden and dramatic reversal of fortune was due to the ruler Muhammad bin Tughluq's decision to relocate his capital to Daulatabad, in the Deccan. While this decision was soon reversed in its turn and Delhi recovered, the city was destroyed in 1398 by the Turko-Mongol conqueror Timur and then fell prey to devastating famine and pestilence in the wake of that conqueror's withdrawal. Centuries later, the temporary departure of the imperial Mughal court to another capital would still have a comparable impact on the city of Delhi: the French traveler Thevenot reported in 1666 that "Delhi appears to be a desart [sic] when the king is absent."[12]

Unsurprisingly, then, from the demise of the Indus valley cities in the millennia BCE down to the later eighteenth century CE and the beginnings of European colonialism, Indian cities were almost never again built in brick or stone. While many ancient texts, such as the *Ramayana*, the *Saundarananda*, the *Lalitavistara*, the *Divyavadana*, the *Milindapanha*, the *Aupadikasutra*, and the Jaina texts, and even inscriptions of later times would have us believe that well-built and illustrious towns and cities had dotted the land for ages and persistently exaggerate the extent of these population centers, they fail to give a realistic picture of any city and are repetitive, conventional in the extreme, and histori- cally inaccurate. Every city is described in the most extravagant terms, as possessed of "sky-touching mansions," wide streets, high defensive walls, and parks with lotuses and geese. It is only from around 600 BCE, a millennium after the demise of the Indus valley civilization, that archaeology provides material evidence of what has misleadingly been called "India's second urbanization."[13] This evidence makes it perfectly clear that the rulers of the early *janapadas*, or "peopled territories," had their headquarters in places that were at best relatively large rural set- tlements.[14] Earthen ramparts of this period that must have enclosed large settlements or "cities" have been uncovered at Ujjayn (in Malwa), Varanasi, and Kaushambi (the post-Hastinapura capital of the Kuru, on the western periphery of Allahabad), but little is left of these settle- ments themselves.[15] Other sites – like that of Sravasti (the post-Ayudhya capital of Koshala) and Rajgir (the Magadha capital) – seem to have had such ramparts as well but have little else that has survived in the archaeological record. Only in the west, in Taxila and Charsadda, some remnants of stone monuments have survived, belonging mostly to the Indo-Greeks and the Kushanas, but these can hardly be seen as the remains of cities. On the city sites of the Gangetic basin, any kiln-fired brickwork – the Indus valley civilization's specialty – reappears very rarely and not until the last centuries BCE. Even the early stupas, the dome-shaped "shrines" of the Buddhists, in the north Indian towns in this period were simply earthen barrows, while their *caityas*, or sacred spots, were without any significant edifices on them. The endowments of the Mauryan emperor Ashoka (261–226?), apart from the pillars, with their Persian-style (Achaemenid) capitals, were mainly modest stupas and monasteries made of brick or timber. Buildings, including royal residences, were evidently made of timber and mud. Of ancient architecture nothing remains. Later, in medieval times, from about the seventh century CE onward, permanent building materials came to be reserved for religious architecture (temples and, later, mosques), fortresses, palace foundations, and the like – and sometimes for the mansions of a small number of wealthy merchants and nobles – but were not normally used in residential architecture. As a rule, the vast majority of the inhabitants of historical Indian cities lived in dwell- ings made entirely of such perishable materials as dried mud, wood, bamboo, thatch, or palm leaves. In Sind, the common people lived in houses of the poorest description – almost always made of mud – or in huts of grass or twigs, reeds, or tamarind wood covered with mats and boughs or grass and clustered in villages and hamlets that could easily be removed and re-erected elsewhere in a few days and at little expense when floods inundated the land. The perhaps forty thousand inhabitants of late medieval Gaur, in Bengal, all lived in palm-leaf huts except the king, who lived in a well-built adobe house. Agra in the seventeenth century was a city of gardens, and Delhi was mostly a conglomerate of many villages, often rebuilt, consisting largely of thatched cottages.[16] The great port of Surat had no more than ten well-built houses and was surrounded by walls made of earth. Calicut (*Koli Koddai*, the "fortress of the cock"), in the fifteenth century at the very source of pepper production in Malabar, was one of the busiest trading emporia of the world, but it had no wall around it. The city was built on an inhospitable shore and had to rely on neighboring ports at some distance – Calicut itself was without a port of Calicut. Houses that were built closely together extended for about a mile, and then the houses that were separate one from the other extended for another six miles. These houses were generally very poor, the greater part covered with leaves. Because of water logging, no foundations could be built for large houses. There were many empty spaces within the built environment and large lakes of water, and pepper was grown right inside the city, giving it a rural ambience; the palace of the king, in contrast, was about a mile in circumference. Further east, cities like Angkor, Pagan, Sukhothai, and Pakuwan in their heyday were essentially collections of temples, hydraulic works, and rice fields strewn over great distances amid residential quarters consisting of houses or huts that could be built – or rebuilt somewhere else – in a few days if necessary. Archaeologists have been using a technology known as lidar to shoot ultra-quick pulses of light at the ground from lasers mounted on helicopters in order to generate maps that reveal an intricate urban landscape across several provinces of modern-day Cambodia, along with a sophisticated network of canals, earthworks, and dams that the Angkorians used to control the flow of water. But only the great stone monuments have endured, not the residential dwellings of everyday life – made from wood, thatch, and mud – that are identifiable on these maps but have long ago rotted away in the hot and humid tropical climate.

   With little or no infrastructure and without paved roads, Indian cities were often indistinguishable from extended rural villages. They were "rurban" rather than urban centers.[17] Such rurban centers could be built, destroyed, and depopulated with dazzling speed. In effect, labile rurbanism was typical of Indian civilization from prehistoric and ancient times onward. Many of these centers left nothing but complete desolation.

Empire Lite

The important long-term secular development that lay at the foundation of Indian civilization was not urbanization but, rather, agricultural expansion and the rise of peasant villages. Outside the Indus valley, this happened surprisingly late. Much later than the soft soils of the narrow Indus valley and its extensions into Gujarat and the western Panjab, agricultural expansion and settlement of the alluvial plains of the Ganges and its tributaries got under way around 1000 BCE, when the Vedic Aryans mastered the metallurgy of iron and introduced heavy ploughs yoked to oxen and hafted iron axes. The use of this new kind of equipment, apparently in combination with slash-and-burn techniques, allowed land clearance to proceed eastward.[18] The soils were heavier here, the forests ever denser, the climate more humid as one moved further east. It was here that Indian civilization began – not in the Indus valley. In the peninsula, moreover, it began even later. Although pepper appears to have been grown in gardens on the Malabar coast as early as the second millennium BCE, wet rice cultivation did not emerge in the river deltas of the peninsula until the early centuries CE, and only then overtook the Tamil plain. In some parts of the drainage basins of the great rivers of both island and mainland Southeast Asia, we can date the earliest beginnings of agricultural settlement and irrigated rice cultivation, in combination with Indianization (the spread of Indian culture) from around the same time. But, as Chapter 2 will show, it was not until the early medieval centuries that agricultural expansion became truly significant anywhere in South and Southeast Asia. It took many centuries for Indian agriculture to generate the surpluses that could sustain any political formations on the scale of an empire.

If empires existed in ancient India, they were very different in nature from the Roman or Persian-Achaemenid empires.[19] Ancient Indian imperial organization did not extend far beyond the rurban town centers and trade routes, representing a type of horizontal integration that could be far flung but had little coercive power or potential for land revenue mobilization and land control. Empires rose, declined, and fell in an environment that still consisted overwhelmingly of unsubdued forests and jungles and as yet little cultivated and settled land.

However, the Mauryan empire (326–189 BCE) has provided the present-day Indian republic with its most potent symbols of political unity, and it has in fact generally been presented as the greatest of India's ancient empires in such a way that invites comparison with the coeval empires of the Mediterranean and Persia.[20] Founded by Candra Gupta Maurya, this empire was expanded by his sons and successors

Bindusara and Ashoka until – it is generally argued – it comprised virtually the entire subcontinent in the third century BCE. According to British Indologist A. L. Basham's best-selling and still widely read book *The Wonder That Was India*, Ashoka created an imperial order through the use of force and reason of state, built an impressive and centralized bureaucracy, and then converted to the pacifist religion of Buddhism and became devoted to the principles of humanitarianism and "the abandonment of aggressive war" while setting an example of enlightened government for neighboring states in an attempt to "gain the moral leadership of the whole civilized world."[21]

This version of ancient Indian history has been almost universally accepted for decades but, remarkably enough, is not supported by any of the evidence. In effect, the sources of information that were once believed to support the textbook interpretation of the Mauryan empire no longer are today. The manual of statecraft that is known as the *Kautilīya Arthashāstra* ("Kautilya's Treatise on Politics") – the sole source that for many, including A. L. Basham, provided detailed information on the workings of the state and bureaucracy of the Mauryans – is regarded by today's scholarly consensus as an abstract and normative manual of political science produced in the late third or early fourth century CE, more than half a millennium after the end of that empire.[22] A second source of information on the Mauryan empire once deemed authoritative was Megasthenes, a Greek-Seleucid ambassador at the Mauryan court, author of the *Indika*, fragments of which have been preserved in the works of later Greek and Latin authors such as Arrian, Strabo, Diodorus, and Pliny the Elder.[23] But the surviving fragments of the *Indika* today invite mostly skepticism among historians. Megasthenes is regarded as the father of the *Mirabilia Indiae* literature, not the father of Indian history. It was Megasthenes who first presented the world with those legendary gold-digging ants, rivers on which nothing floats, and men who neither eat nor drink that turned ancient India into a land of "wonder." Megasthenes also informs us that the Indians had no written laws and were ignorant of writing. Candra Gupta Maurya's capital of Palibothra (Pataliputra) was a city "girded with a wooden wall, pierced with loopholes for the discharge of arrows, [and with] a ditch in front for defense and for receiving the sewage." A people called the Prasii, in whose country this city was situated, was "the most distinguished in all India." Megasthenes says nothing about imperial unification. Any quantitative information he provided is deemed doubtful by the editors of his work and unreliable and contradictory at best, not being confirmed by any other source. For different reasons, the set of edicts and inscriptions left by the second Mauryan emperor, Ashoka, is now considered by recent scholarship to have been an even more deficient source of historical information on the Mauryan empire than Megasthenes. Engraved on rocks and pillars across the subcontinent, these texts are devoid of political content and do not provide historical descriptions of anything related to imperial administration or military organization.[24] They propagate the "world conquest" of the *dhamma* (dharma), an ethical system particular to Ashoka that is often regarded as embedded in Buddhism but which equally applied to Hinduism, with its notions of karma or ethical causation and metempsychosis, and Jainism, a contemporary salvation religion that was the first to advocate vegetarianism.[25] Ashoka's edicts address the people of India as his "children" and enjoin them to promote goodness and live in accordance with dhammic morality. They address the inhabitants of the entire subcontinent but do not mention a single name of a province or a city or any administrative entity. They provide no serious evidence of political unification or of how the Mauryan empire worked. Only one military campaign of a Mauryan emperor is mentioned in the inscriptions (in the thirteenth of the fourteen Major Rock Edicts): the campaign to neighboring Kalinga, eight years after Ashoka's accession, which made Ashoka express remorse for the bloodshed and mayhem he had perpetrated on that occasion (more than a hundred thousand slain, many more perished, and one hundred fifty thousand deported) and become a lay Buddhist.

Taking the evidence of these inscriptions, Ashoka comes across more as a religious reformer than an empire builder. Some of the Ashokan pillars, to be sure, retained fluted, bell-shaped capitals crowned with an animal image, features derived from the monumental sculptures found at the Achaemenid capital of Persepolis, in Persia. The very idea of these edicts was clearly of Persian derivation. Their aim was perhaps simply the dissemination of a fairly obvious set of humanitarian injunctions. The surviving evidence suggests that the Mauryan empire was at no time very different from the ancient Indian empires that came afterward. All ancient Indian empires were mostly ideological constructions of ritual sovereignty – more often than not vaguely Buddhist – and provided loose, extensive, and horizontal modes of integration of de facto autonomous and localized "circles of kings" along nodal points (rurban centers) and routes of long-distance trade in a period of increased connectivity. Their coercive powers and abilities to raise revenue and tribute beyond their own, still small, core areas of nucleated agricultural settlement always remained very limited. This was true even of the empire of the Guptas (c. 320–550 CE). Founded by Candra Gupta I, the Gupta empire, in the eyes of many generations of historians, brought India's ancient history to another glorious zenith. This idea was almost entirely founded on a single inscription dating to the end of the reign of Candra Gupta I's son and successor Samudra Gupta (c. 335–380 CE), originally located at Kaushambi. It is an inscription that contains long lists of kings and regions allegedly subdued by the Maharajadhiraja, or "Greatest Maharaja," in wars that established Gupta rule throughout the ancient Aryavarta, or Aryan homeland (between west Bengal and the Panjab), and made Samudra Gupta the acknowledged overlord of kings as far away as Sri Lanka and Nepal and Gandhara, "conqueror of the four quarters of the earth," and "a god dwelling on earth."[26] But there is no evidence of direct bureaucratic Gupta rule anywhere in this vast region (to which later Gujarat was added), and instead there appears to have been a network of feudatory arrangements in which the Guptas were merely concerned with some kind of precedence or ritual paramountcy. The great cultural and artistic achievements that they allegedly presided over, such as the poetry of Kalidasa, are now thought to have predated the beginnings of Gupta rule. These triumphs of culture and art are real enough but apparently did not require an imperial context, and political fragmentation or instability did not thwart them. Great achievements in architecture are barely hinted at under Gupta rule and would not come until several centuries later. Ancient India is to be celebrated for its brilliant religious, literary, philosophical, and scientific achievements, but not for successful empire building.

It should be clear, then, that there was no prehistoric or ancient urban and imperial heritage that shaped the historical development of the Indo-Islamic world in medieval and early modern times. It is difficult to decide even whether the emerging civilization of India was Hindu or Buddhist or even Hindu-Buddhist or Jain. It is also difficult to find firm evidence of a Buddhist India that, as has been argued, was in some sense the result of an ancient urban revolution accompanying the rise of regional and long-distance trade. Emerging as a virtuoso religious technique and philosophy of wandering monks and nuns, Buddhism originally had the aim of individual salvation from the suffering that it saw as inherent in human existence. It did not aspire to regulate or transform society, nor did it provide a blueprint for political organization. When in due course the Buddha founded the Sangha, the monastic order of Buddhist monks and nuns, he provided it with virtually no organizational structure or leadership other than seniority from the date of ordination. The Sangha was not organized as a church with the aspiration of attending to the needs of laymen or propping up a polity. Thus, it could not have had much of a positive impact on society or engaged in good work. The Buddhist doctrine stood for an otherworldly renunciation of society, not a reciprocal relationship with it. Ancient Indian Buddhism was not an imperial religion as such but, because of its renunciatory quality, could serve as a legitimating ideology that transcended the use of brute force and feuding in local society. Evidence suggests that it was largely confined to monasteries, whereas Buddhist laymen were an amorphous category of people not necessarily living in towns or cities who adhered to various ancestral belief systems having nothing to do with Buddhism as such and were enjoined to regard the monastic order as "a field of merit" but were hardly instrumental in the development of the Buddhist religion. This was a situation that did not fundamentally change under the Mauryans and the Guptas. Because of its persistently narrow social and elitist base, Buddhism did not survive in its original homeland. The Buddhism that persisted in the northern mountain zones of the subcontinent, in Sri Lanka, and in mainland Southeast Asia was a demotic version of that religion with much broader social underpinnings. In these outlying territories, it was accommodated within the more robust political and religious institutions of what we can broadly conceptualize as medieval Hinduism. This meant that, here, Buddhism was completely transformed and developed social, political, and at times theocratic dimensions that allowed it to transcend its earlier monastic limitations and arguably have the broadest impact. This also meant that the cosmopolitan orientation of Buddhism that we associate with the ancient empires was already a thing of the past by early medieval times. There was no specifically Buddhist or Hindu-Buddhist imperial legacy associated with the ancient dynasties of the Mauryans and the Guptas.

Virtually no cities have survived from ancient India – no roads, no monuments. Indian monumental architecture began in medieval, not ancient, times. The Indian lexicon of politics, religion, and caste organization may have had its earliest origins in ancient times, but, as Chapter 2 will show, its practical implementation had to wait until the conditions of settled society had progressed much further in medieval times. Indian history is radically different in this regard from European-Mediterranean and Near Eastern history. If European history consisted of a series of renaissances of the urban traditions of ancient Athens and Rome, and if the Islamic history of the Mediterranean and Persia was similarly embedded in an ancient and urban heritage (even though it did not preserve its original texts), the medieval civilization of India had to invent its ancient heritage from rare surviving literary sources, and there was no *translatio imperii* of the kind that allowed the establishment of a new order in medieval Europe and the Mediterranean lands. As is well known, these rare surviving Indian literary sources are not precisely dated. Like Kautilya's *Arthashastra*, many were once deemed ancient but now appear to have been medieval in the editions in which they came down to us – or at least of much later date than previously thought. The final composition of the great Indian epics of the *Ramayana* and the *Mahabharata*, on which so much of our interpretation of ancient India has been based, may not have been completed even by Gupta times. As a result, wildly differing dates have been adduced for the great Mahabharata war, and the original core stories of the epics are as hard to isolate as their dates. The *Puranas*, or "ancient legends," hardly compensate for this deficiency, since the most important of these texts, in their turn, date only from around 500 CE, and all the evidence shows that these too, like the epics, have been endlessly reworked and edited for various propaganda and edifying purposes. Equally uncertain is the chronology of the vernacular Pali Buddhist, and even more the Jain literature. It was recently discovered that the Buddha lived between 400 and 350 BCE – some 160 years later than previously assumed – and this new timeframe has potentially dramatic consequences for the chronology of just about the entire first millennium BCE of ancient Indian history.[27] The study of ancient Indian history has been remarkably light on dates.[28] Not only do we not know the precise dates of Ashoka, but we also have not been able to establish those of the ancient Kushana emperor Kanishka. The latter's successors are even more elusive. The second and third centuries CE have been described as "a blind summit" along north India's chronological highway.[29] In the Mediterranean, in sharp contrast, this was the time when Hadrian, Pausanias, and Plutarch fought their "history wars" over the legacy of the Greek city-states – a legacy that seemed all-important to them. In the absence of such a legacy, a great deal of what we once thought we knew about ancient Indian history has in fact vanished into thin air.

2 The Expansion of Agriculture and Settled Society

Le phénomène des moussons, inconnu dans les autres régions, amène, à des époques régulièrement fixes, des pluies périodiques qui fertilisent les terres de toutes les parties de ce pays... De vastes plaines fournissent, sans crainte de les voir s'épuiser, et presque sans frais de culture, par la supériorité des méthodes agricoles, des fleurs suaves, des fruits exquis, et de nombreuses et abondantes récoltes.

Legoux de Flaix (1807)[1]

We have seen that the origins of agriculture and settled life in India take us back to the prehistoric Indus valley civilization and the migrations of the Vedic Aryans but that it was not until the early medieval period that in most parts of India agricultural surpluses were generated that could sustain a settled order of society and government on a wider scale. The Gupta empire of the fourth to sixth centuries CE may well have anticipated the beginning of this transformation, but it was the subsequent medieval expansion of agriculture and settled states, occurring hand in hand with population growth, that led to a new dispensation that, I argue, had little continuity with the prehistoric and ancient past.

The soft alluvial soils of the arid Indus borderlands, the drainage basin of the lower Indus, and the upper basin of the same river where it is joined by the Jhelum, Chenab, Ravi, Sutlej, and Beas – i.e., the westernmost part of the Panjab, or the "Five-River Land" – were the site of the original Neolithic revolution and the most remote agricultural development. Having superseded the marginal agricultural village economy of the Baluchi hills, the Indus civilization was supported by an interconnected and advanced agricultural system based on inundation and irrigation, the annual floods on the river plains allowing for the cultivation of two, sometimes three, crops per year, including grains like wheat and rice, pulses, oilseeds, dye plants, drugs, fruits, sugarcane, and cotton – crops that came to be cultivated across India for millennia. Since the Indus borderlands largely consisted of deserts, they also reached their maximum potential earlier than any other region of India. They were exceptional in both their early agricultural settlement and reaching their maximum potential at an early date. Precociously settled, in the long millennia between the efflorescence of the Indus civilization and the Arab conquest of the seventh and eighth centuries the configuration of agricultural settlement of the Indus borderlands remained broadly similar. The major concentrations of sedentary agriculture remained confined to the same broad regions around the cities of Mansura in the southern delta and Multan at the northern confluence of the Indus and the Panjab Rivers, on a somewhat but not dramatically expanded scale.[2] In the early medieval centuries, the green or cultivated area of the river valley was still quite small. Only Mansura and Multan, respectively replacing Mohenjodaro and Harappa, were situated in fertile country cultivated without discontinuity and dotted with agricultural villages and hamlets. Beyond the spills of the river, the ever-shifting alkaline sand deserts and jungles of lower Sind, and what came to be known as Baluchistan, Rajasthan, and parts of Gujarat and the Panjab remained a barrier to agricultural expansion. Here the population was engaged in pastoralism, with at most subsidiary forms of extensive agriculture. Much of lower Sind still consisted of a land of marshes and reeds. The total number of people living along the lower Indus in the early medieval centuries probably did not exceed several hundred thousand. And it diminished due to a northward migration of many pastoralists.

A great migration of Jat pastoralists from Sind to the Panjab and to areas east of the Panjab – including Bikaner, Jaisalmer, and Jodhpur in Rajasthan – as well as the upper Ganges and Yamuna plains appears to have gained momentum toward the end of the tenth century CE.[3] Sustained over the subsequent centuries and accompanied by the introduction of new irrigation systems associated with the Persian wheel (a mechanical water-lifting device usually operated by draft animals), this migration resulted in the creation of the Jat peasant caste, which contributed greatly to the settlement of the Panjab and adjacent regions (until then patchy). In the fertile alluvial plains of the medieval Panjab, two distinct blocks of cultivation then developed: one extending from the Jhelum River to Ludhiana and comprising the towns of Sialkot and Lahore, the other extending from Multan to Uch and Pakpattan across the area where the numerous channels of the major Panjab rivers come together.

To the east and south of the northernmost curve of the Indus River, legend has it that a total of 66,063 villages dotted the valley of Kashmir from "times immemorial." But the Kashmir historian Kalhana's twelfth-century chronicle, which is known as the *Rājataraṅginī*, or "Stream of Kings," traces the village agriculture of Kashmir to the early medieval period, when the valley was just emerging from a long period of invasions by the Hephthalites, or "White Huns," and other nomadic peoples.[4] It is from the same period that we can date the rise of the *dāmaras* ("landlords") in the valley, while the full development of this new ruling stratum comes into view with the accession of the royal Lohara dynasty in the early eleventh century CE. Its breakthrough into the political history of Kashmir took place in the subsequent two centuries.

In the tenth century CE, the region on the northwest of the coastline of the subcontinent that is now the state of Gujarat was still located at the mouth of a wayward branch of the Indus running east of the Rann of Kachchh, immediately to the northwest of peninsular Gujarat or Kathiawar (the ancient Saurashtra). This region contained settlements of great antiquity in its central and northern parts, and Kachchh shows traces of the Indus civilization as well. But the Gujars (or Gurjaras), after whom the region is named, rose to power in a still overwhelmingly pastoral-nomadic context in the seventh century CE, and they underwent significant sedentarization beginning in the eighth and ninth centuries.[5] This happened at the same time that Gujarat began to acquire significant maritime importance and attract a considerable Zoroastrian or "Parsi" trading diaspora from Persia on its already-Persianized coast. By then there was fairly continuous cultivation in some parts of its extended southern coast, from the port of Kambaya southward. Yet, overall, agricultural development was still limited. In most of Gujarat, the great leap forward in agricultural development appears to have been made under the Caulukyas of Anahilvada (941–1297), the Hindu dynasty that gave some kind of political coherence to Gujarat and presided over the construction of numerous step wells and water reservoirs, while also building a "military road" to connect the Gujarat capital with Kathiawar. Not until the twelfth century CE did the inland territory extending from the north of Anahilvada down to Kambaya become the core area from which Gujarat was ruled and the center of its agricultural production and manufacturing. It was then that cotton became the leading agricultural product of Gujarat, next to indigo, oilseeds, cereals, sugarcane, and hemp. Due to improved irrigation, the cultivation of these crops in Kathiawar, Kachchh, and southern Rajasthan increased sharply at the same time.

Agricultural progress was tantalizingly slow in the northern parts of the subcontinent, throughout the immense Ganges plain and even more so in the eastern delta, where the Ganges comes together with the

Brahmaputra. In due course, these became the agricultural heartlands of India. But, as elsewhere, the research in the archaeology, geography, and settlement history of the northern plain still has to be fully integrated, and we do not possess any detailed and authoritative studies of it as yet. Scant archaeological evidence points to the existence of Neolithic settlements between the northern edge of the Chota Nagpur plateau and the Ganges River, as well as elsewhere on the plain, with monsoon-dependent cultivation of wheat and barley, paddy rice, and legumes as early as the sixth and fifth millennia BCE.[6] This was very different from the rainfall-and-inundation agricultural regime of the Indus River plain. The agricultural settlement of the much heavier soils encountered in the more humid climate of the alluvial plain of the Ganges and its tributaries gained momentum only with the introduction of iron equipment around 1000 BCE, allowing land clearance to proceed eastward in interaction with the preexisting agricultural population. It continued to be slow, however, for at least another millennium. Initially, it just followed the transitional zone between the drier and more humid parts of the plain. This then allowed for the development of a mixed economy of cattle tending and wheat, barley, and rice cultivation. Proceeding along both a "northern route" (*uttarapatha*) from the Panjab and the upper Indus to Bihar and the lower Ganges and a "southern route" (*dakshinapatha*) from the Gangetic settlements to Malwa, Gujarat, and the Deccan, population densities had increased by the middle of the millennium. Simultaneously, migration slowed, the tracts workable with relative ease being cultivated and settled and, first in the northeastern region of Gangetic Bihar, growing into a network of proto-states to become the agricultural nucleus of the ancient Magadha kingdom and subsequently the Mauryan and Gupta empires.[7] Thus, political and monastic centers like Pataliputra, Rajgir, and Bodh Gaya were already dependent on agricultural hinterlands in the times of Ashoka and Candra Gupta II (d. 410 CE). But these backcountry areas did not extend very far. The Tibetan Buddhist pilgrim Dharmasvamin as late as 1234 observed forests beginning just a few miles to the south of Bodh Gaya, where they abutted the heavily wooded Chota Nagpur plateau, and it was not until later in the thirteenth century that a wave of colonizers initiated a decisive new phase, which was to continue over several centuries of agricultural expansion in the South Bihar Plains.[8] Elsewhere in the northern plains, sustained agricultural expansion (primarily the cultivation of wheat, barley, sorghum, and other millets but not rice), the colonization of far-flung territories, increasingly efficient hydraulic management, and sedentarization and settlement of pastoral groups originating in the more arid western parts of the subcontinent largely took place between the seventh and tenth centuries CE – even later than in Gangetic Bihar. These developments were accompanied by the emergence of a host of new landed dynasties that here became known as the ancestors of the Rajputs.[9] They provided the foundation for the rise of the empire of the Gujara-Pratiharas, a "royal" clan of the same tribal and pastoral population that gave its name to Gujarat and in the eighth to eleventh centuries presided over lesser, competing proto-Rajput dynasties. The emergent landed ruling elite network was perhaps India's first empire, with powers of resource mobilization and elite incorporation that went significantly beyond the largely ritual sovereignty of the ancient empires.

Beyond the northern plain and Bihar and the Moghyr bottleneck (with steep hill slopes to the south and numerous tributaries of the Ganges to the north), in the humid Bengal delta, Indo-Aryan expansion followed the course of the combined river systems of the Ganges and the Brahmaputra and began the transformation of scattered aboriginal hunting-and-gathering and fishing societies into a more settled agrarian order based on wet rice cultivation starting in the late centuries BCE. Decisive agricultural development began in Bengal well after Gupta times and for about half a millennium remained confined to the western parts, while the eastern expanses were still densely forested and almost entirely unsettled. The confluence of the Ganges and the Brahmaputra created the alluvial plain and delta that made Bengal the most fertile and densely settled agricultural region of the subcontinent in the millennium between the seventh and seventeenth centuries.[10] In the tenth and eleventh centuries, a gradual eastward movement of the Ganges-Brahmaputra river system first began to create conditions favorable to forest clearing and agricultural further to the east. Agricultural colonization gained momentum in these parts of the region in especially the eleventh and twelfth centuries, under the Pala and Sena dynasties. Extensive embankments that enhanced agricultural productivity in the growing eastern delta did not occur until the arrival of the first Muslim rulers in the thirteenth century. To the north, in the vast, forest-covered hill region of Assam, large-scale deforestation and agricultural expansion began with the arrival of the Tai-Ahoms from Myanmar in the thirteenth and fourteenth centuries.

With the exception of the ancient economy of pepper and spices on the Malabar coast, agriculture in the South Asian peninsula proceeded at a similar pace. The Coromandel plains became a densely populated region of wet rice cultivation with large-scale tank irrigation during the three hundred years of Pallava rule between c. 575 and 900 CE.[11]

This was not much later than similar colonization of the riverine tracts of the southern Tamil plain. The semi-arid Deccan plateau always accommodated relatively more scattered settlement patterns than the northern plains and southern deltas and retained a significant pastoral-nomadic economy. Irrigated agriculture based on water tanks did not become widespread in the Deccan until the centuries after 1000 CE. Tank construction was also undertaken in Sri Lanka as early as the third century CE but mostly between the early medieval centuries and the beginning of the thirteenth century.[12] Wet rice cultivation expanded in the wake of the development of these tanks (which were the size of small lakes) in the arid northern zone of the island, where the successive medieval capitals came to be located, as well as in the wet and forested southern zone.

On the mainland of Southeast Asia, the transition to agricultural colonization of river deltas has been traced to the second century BCE.[13] About four hundred years later, Funan became the first state in Southeast Asia to be supported by an extensive form of lowland rice cultivation, at the same time developing the port of Oc Eo in the Mekong delta, as an entrepôt for the maritime trade of China. When the Chinese trade shifted to the strait of Melaka in the fifth century CE, Funan became almost exclusively dependent on the development of irrigated agriculture in the upper Mekong delta. Its rice economy flourished in what is now Cambodia throughout the seventh century, based on a mixture of shifting cultivation, entrapped rainfall, and irrigation. The agriculture of Cambodia only turned a corner when the Khmer kingdom of Angkor superseded Funan in the first half of the ninth century.[14] By developing a rice economy in the ecological niche of the Tonle Sap region with the aid of extensive tank construction, the Khmer established Angkor as an agrarian state with the power to dominate the south and center of the Southeast Asian peninsula for centuries. To the west of Angkor, the agricultural settlement of the central Irrawaddy plain in Myanmar was taken up by the Pyu at about the same time. Soon thereafter, the Burmans founded the state of Pagan by bringing the central Irrawaddy river network under their sway and incorporating the northern territories of the Pyu. The Burmans brought along their agricultural practices from their northern homelands and also drew heavily on the civilization of the Mon, a people with early contacts in South Asia that had begun to settle in the Menam basin in the seventh century and was eventually absorbed by Pagan. Thanks to its wet rice economy and highly developed hydraulic foundations, Pagan reached the peak of its power in the eleventh, twelfth, and thirteen centuries.[15] As in Myanmar, in Thailand agriculture developed almost entirely in a single south-facing trough, with a focus on the Chao Phraya River valley and delta. This happened when the Thai, or rather their ancestors the Tai, dispersed from their barren homelands in the north (near the current border between China and north Vietnam) and began to settle in areas as far apart as Assam in the west and what became the heartland of Thailand in the south as well as, on the periphery of the Khmer state, the lowland valleys of Laos, from around the beginning of the second millennium.[16] In due course, in Thailand as in Myanmar and Cambodia, paddy rice cultivation came to dominate, and the first Thai states – Sukhothai and Chiangmai – were established in the thirteenth and fourteenth centuries.

Finally, in the Indonesian archipelago, the agricultural development of the plains of the Solo and the Brantas Rivers of Java bore a close resemblance to the pattern of the Southeast Asian mainland.[17] In Java, as elsewhere in Indonesia, volcanic debris kept soils fertile along the coasts and in the plains on the river-transported alluvials as well as in the mountainous interior. Wet rice cultivation thus flourished on a minor scale as early as the beginning of the Christian era in the enclosed inner reaches of rivers of some of the central and eastern parts of the island. *Sawah* agriculture became the characteristic form of wet rice agriculture in these intermontane valleys and was dependent both on rainfall and on river irrigation. Not until medieval times, however, was any part of Java densely settled. Up to the end of the tenth century, dense agricultural settlement was primarily found on the Kedu volcanic plain in central Java. Only later did such settlement spread to the lower Brantas basin of east Java, at the same time becoming supported by further agricultural expansion in the upper Brantas region.

The mountainous landmasses of the major outer islands of Sumatra, Kalimantan, Sulawesi, and Irian Jaya were mostly covered by equatorial rainforest throughout the ancient and medieval centuries. Here, in these centuries, we sometimes find shifting cultivation in isolated pockets. The agricultural potential of the bulging eastern flatlands of Sumatra – the amphibious homeland of the coastal Malay-Buddhist civilization of Shrivijaya in the seventh to thirteenth centuries – was limited. Settled agriculture developed in Sumatra mainly on the fertile volcanic plateaus of the western Bukit Barisan range, among the Minangkabau and Batak, and in the alluvial plains of the rivers of the north coast, but not until after the demise of Shrivijaya in the fourteenth century. In Kalimantan, wet rice and other forms of intensive agriculture were introduced in the thirteenth century by Malay, Chinese, and Arab immigrant populations and remained confined to the coasts and river outlets. Sulawesi resembled Kalimantan and most parts of Sumatra in essential respects. The little agriculture there was in Irian Jaya remained confined principally to the Baliem valley in the central highlands; it had remote origins going back to 7000 BCE but emphasized root and tree crops and hence was more like horticulture, with cereals never cultivated anywhere in Irian Jaya. In Halmahera and its small, offshore islands of the Moluccas, the cultivation of cloves and other spices may well be as old as that of pepper in Malabar, but these famed agricultural products of the so-called Spice Islands, again, did not enter the limelight of world history until medieval times.

Looking at agricultural expansion and settlement in South and Southeast Asia as a whole, it is evident that similar patterns are repeated. Beyond the Indus borderlands, the medieval centuries were the great era of such expansion and settlement. The process occurred late in comparison with other major world regions such as the Mediterranean or Mesopotamia-Persia. Once it did take off, however, it showed greater potential than almost anywhere else.

This medieval success story, of course, had its limitations. There were innumerable reverses: periodic or permanent depopulation of large subregions caused by the failure of the monsoon rains, climate change, and other environmental disruptions, as well as human interference. The Indus borderlands, in particular, suffered all of these reverses serially and sometimes simultaneously throughout much of their medieval history. Substantial portions of the Deccan and Telangana plateaus reverted to pasture or became savanna-like terrain due to overgrazing by goats or went into irreversible decline because of droughts, followed by famine and emigration. In the semiarid parts of northern Sri Lanka, as we have seen, tank irrigation was ruined due to the outbreak of malaria in the wake of Tamil invasions from the subcontinent in the thirteenth century, leading to a relocation of the Sinhalese capitals to the south of the island (cf. p. 19). Much of Angkor's agriculture declined irreversibly in the thirteenth and fourteenth centuries due to deforestation, the spread of malaria, climate change, and hostile Thai and Chams incursions (the latter from Vietnam), as well as probably a reorientation of coastal trade.

The medieval land clearance movement and the demographic growth that accompanied it in this world region occurred slowly in comparison with the same processes in other major world regions. One reason for this was the endemic presence of numerous diseases – including smallpox, cholera, and bubonic plague – among the ever more populous agglomerations of people living in the hot and humid conditions of the monsoon climate. In no other hot and humid climate in this period were human settlements in such close juxtaposition to animal herds, permitting infections to be easily transmitted to humans.[18] The Indian demographic growth rate was probably nowhere more than 10 percent per century, well below the Mediterranean and European average. Around 700 CE, the total population of South and Southeast Asia combined was probably less than that of the Roman republic at its height in the second century BCE – which is estimated to have been around sixty million. The bulk of this total, about 95 percent, lived in South Asia, and 5 percent in Southeast Asia. Between 700 CE and the Black Death pandemic of the mid-fourteenth century, the population of Europe nearly tripled, while the population of South and Southeast Asia combined probably did not even double in that time.[19] In sum, India's population was not dramatically cut down in size by the Black Death, as Europe's was. Indian population growth occurred late, it was steady, and it was slow.

Almost everywhere in South Asia, agricultural production was concerned with textiles and basic food crops such as wheat or millets, with insecure yields, and pulses or barley. Rice was the predominant food crop only in the settled and relatively small enclaves of Southeast Asia, whereas this was the case in South Asia only in the deltas and floodplains of some of the peninsular rivers. In the Ganges delta (now Bangladesh), rice was only beginning to be widely cultivated in the thirteenth century. Within this agricultural economy of monsoon Asia as a whole, the pepper and fine spices originating from the jungles and backwaters of Malabar, parts of Sri Lanka, and some of the islands of Indonesia were of marginal importance for the bulk of the cultivating population of peasants, even though these crops were commercially attractive and in global demand.

Peasants and townspeople everywhere in South and Southeast Asia continued to live in the midst of an immense habitat that was forested, hilly, arid, and uncultivated, as well as sparsely inhabited by unsettled, tribal, and pastoral populations, or almost entirely deserted by humans. No more than 20 to 30 percent of the land surface of this region was settled and densely populated at the beginning of the sixteenth century. There remained plenty of room for further expansion in the subsequent centuries. Medieval Europeans, too, had lived in the midst of vast forests. But by the beginning of the sixteenth century, the forests of Europe were disappearing, and there a nutritional and fuel disaster could only be averted by the introduction of coal burning and the cultivation of New World crops like potatoes and maize. New World crops did not revolutionize Indian agriculture – at least not to the same degree.

Kings and Brahmans

In the early medieval period, between the seventh and eleventh centuries, the expansion of agriculture and settled society was beginning to give rise to a fragmented landscape of monarchies of varying dimensions and importance in the plains of all the great river systems of South and Southeast Asia. The growth of an agrarian economy and peasant society provided the foundation for a new political order, and made possible the rise of a new type of monarchical state that simply had not existed before. Some of the resulting states reached an imperial or quasi-imperial scope and size. Next to the Gujara-Pratiharas of northern India, the early medieval dynasties of the Karkotas of Kashmir, the Rashtrakutas of western India, the Palas of Bengal, the Colas of South India, and, on a smaller scale, the Khmer of Cambodia, the Burmans of the Irrawaddy plain in Myanmar and the Shailendras of Java can properly be regarded as the first truly imperial dynasties in Indian history.

The more vertical and hierarchical political order emerging in the zones of nucleated agricultural settlement of early medieval India superseded the thinly spread empires that integrated the ancient trade routes and were loosely Buddhist in orientation and mostly based on ritualistic forms of suzerainty. Typically, the former was based on a network of Hindu kings ruling jointly with the Brahman priesthood.[20] It must be stressed that this was a virtually new dispensation. The new landed dynasties of the early medieval centuries did not lay claim to an imperial legacy associated with the Mauryans or the Guptas but invented a tradition that they were the reincarnates of the ancient Indian *varna* of *kshatriyas*, or "warrior caste," that had become extinct. It was a tradition that takes us into the realm of mythology, not history. The ancient *kshatriyas* are almost exclusively known from the epic literature (in particular the *Mahabharata* and the *Ramayana*), with a confused and uncertain chronology. There they are depicted as the urbane and highly literate progenitors of the anti-Brahmanical religion of Buddhism who were wiped off the earth by the Brahmans in vengeance for their enmity. The tradition then portrays a political vacuum in which ignorance and infidelity spread over the land, the sacred books were trampled underfoot, and humankind had no refuge from the monstrous brood of asuras or "demons and infidels" of the Indo-Scythian pastoral-nomadic tribes from the northwest.[21] In these circumstances, the mythical sage Viswamitra resolved upon the ritual re-creation of the *kshatriyas* on the summit of a mountain. There he summoned hermits and sages and the deities Indra, Brahma,

Rudra, and Vishnu, with all the inferior deities in their train, to perform expiatory rites and initiate the ritual re-creation of the *kshatriyas* through the medium of a fire fountain. This story became part of the medieval bardic tradition and as such represents an account of a purification ceremony that may have occurred in the eighth century CE on the sacred crest of Mount Abu in Rajasthan and through which the extinct *kshatriyas* of ancient India were virtually "regenerated" by the Brahmans as fire-born Rajputs, or "king's sons." The absence of a clear genealogical link with the ancient past made it all the more urgent for the tradition to invent one.

Rajputs gradually became the generic name for the Hindu ruling elite which consolidated its position in the context of the accelerating expansion of agriculture and settled society in the northern and northwestern parts of the Indian subcontinent. The elite's rise from little-known, and often pastoral, backgrounds, sometimes from outside the subcontinent (from among the maligned Indo-Scythians), can be traced in the historical record, but not even their preeminent and major dynasties can be traced back to a period prior to the seventh century CE. The early medieval Rajputs were the first landed elites in India to closely associate themselves with Brahmans, who propagated a religion that was often antagonistic toward Buddhism and became the recipients of considerable largesse, including land, while gaining considerable political influence at all emerging courts. The preeminent fire-born royal Rajput dynasty of the Gujara-Pratiharas emerged from the wandering population of Gujara pastoralists in the wake of the invasions of the nomadic Hephthalites, or "White Huns" (probably assimilating elements of these as well as others of the earlier so-called Indo-Scythians), and established itself in the capital of Kanauj in the central Ganges plain in the early ninth century. Fire-born Rajput clans subordinate to them included the Cahamanas of Rajasthan; the Gujaras of Gujarat; the Paramaras of Malwa; the Tomaras of Delhi; and the Guhilots of the Panjab, Rajasthan, and Kathiawar – all pastoral nomads of the arid and semiarid frontier zones of western India – before moving into the agricultural plains in the seventh and eighth centuries. Some other Rajput dynasties of the Panjab traced their *kshatriya* genealogies to the Zunbils and their kinsmen the Kabul Shahs of what is now eastern Afghanistan, boasting descent from the ancient Kushana emperor Kanishka although they were almost certainly mere epigoni of the southern Hephthalite rulers of Zabulistan and Zamindawar (also now Afghanistan) of much later times. In western India itself, in lower Sind and Kachchh, we witness the emergence of the Thakurs, or "lords," of such pastoral clan formations as the Sodhas, the Sumras, the Sammas, and the Jharejahs, as well as the so-called "Rāī kings," in the same early medieval centuries. These came to be regarded as so many subdivisions of the fire-born Rajputs as well.[22] Other fire-born Rajput dynasties such as the Candellas of Jejabhukti (Bundelkhand), the Gahadavalas of Varanasi and Kanauj, the Haihayas of Awadh, and the Kachchapaghatas of Rajasthan and central India do not become visible in the historical record until they broke away from Gujara-Pratihara overlordship in the later decades of the tenth century and are of an unknown origin. In Kashmir, the Karkota dynasty, with no realistic pedigree on record, emerged out of the same competitive and often-violent matrix before rising to prominence in the eighth century. In subsequent centuries, this dynasty continued to be propped up by immigrant Rajput warriors, even though it was not advancing claims to Rajput status for itself at any time.[23]

Elsewhere in the subcontinent we find no claims to Rajput status as such – at least not until many centuries later – but rather obscure clans and lineages from the rural and pastoral backwoods promoting themselves to newly created kingships in emerging peasant domains in the same early medieval centuries and, even without a mythical pedigree, transforming themselves into *kshatriyas* through alternative but not fundamentally different paths of upward mobility. To the east, the rulers of the peripatetic Pala dynasty were "not of noble extraction" but sought recognition as the *kshatriyas* of Bengal over the eighth and ninth centuries CE.[24] To the southwest, the Rashtrakuta dynasty, ruling the Deccan and Gujarat from their capital at Mankir between 743 and 974, adopted the title of Vallabha Raja, or "Beloved Lord and Husband" (which became *Ballaharā* in the Arabic geographical literature), from its predecessors the Caulukyas, a dynasty that itself goes back to the early seventh century.[25] In the southeastern peninsula, the Tamil literature of the early centuries CE refers to the Cola dynasty and their Cola-mandalam, or "circle of kings" (which defined the Coromandel plain). However, Prakrit (vernacular) and Sanskrit inscriptions between the fourth and ninth centuries CE record the rise of the *kshatriya* dynasty of the Pallavas, not the Colas, to the first important kingship in Tamil Nadu.[26] It was then that communities of Vellalas, Reddys, and Kammas became landed ruling elites comparable to the Rajputs in the northwestern and northern parts of the subcontinent, providing the backbone of the warrior caste, even though officially they remained *shudras*, or peasants, and *kshatriya* status in the peninsula remained the exclusive preserve of royal dynasties like the Pallavas and later the Colas themselves, and only a few Vellala chieftains. This occurred at approximately the same time that the Pandyas established themselves as a royal dynasty in Madurai, still further to the south, and the Ceras in Malabar. Meanwhile, the Buddhist kings of Sri Lanka consolidated their power in the rice-growing northern half of the island, the Khmer superseded Funan in Cambodia, the Pyu and Burmans created the first kingship in the central Irrawaddy plain of Myanmar, and the Shailendra dynasty (founded 732), claiming to be the representative of the ancestral rulers of Yāvadvīpa, established the first kingship in the Indonesian archipelago, in the Hindu temple complex on the "field of Shiva" of the Dieng plateau.

In conjunction with the new royal dynasties, the rise to prominence of the Brahmans was entirely an early medieval phenomenon. In the ancient empires, the Brahmans did not play much of a role, and it was not until two centuries after the demise of the Guptas that they began to become part of the political establishment. This is especially evident in Kanauj, the early medieval capital of the preeminent dynasty of the Gujara-Pratiharas. Kanauj, or "Kanyakubja" (that is, "the city of hunchbacked maidens"), was situated in the center of the agricultural heartland of the northern subcontinent, on the west bank of the Ganges. It began its rise to prominence in the early seventh century under the Pushpabhuti king Harsha (606–647), to become the sacred center of the Brahmans at the same time that it became the political capital of the Gujara-Pratiharas in the ninth and tenth centuries. Kanauj was clearly the wealthiest city in early medieval India at large.[27] The Kanauj or Kanyakubja Brahmans became the highest-ranking subcaste of Brahmans in the subcontinent and are known to have migrated to and colonized many areas outside their northern preserve. In the process, they created a hierarchy of subdivisions and exceedingly complex rank differentiations that correlated their ritual purity and standing with their position within the emerging sacred landscape of early medieval India inversely to the distance separating them from their capital.[28]

It seems likely that Kanauj and the surrounding *Madhyadesha*, or "Middle Country," was the place of origin of the majority of migrating Brahmans throughout the medieval centuries. There is good evidence, however, that Brahmans were on the move everywhere, in considerable numbers, and that they had multiple places of origin. In the Indus borderlands of Sind, the mass immigration of thirty thousand Brahmans "from all parts of India" is recorded to have predated the Arab conquest of 711–712 by one century or at most one-and-a-half.[29] The Anavil Brahmans of southern Gujarat, by contrast, regard themselves as descendants of the Brahmans of Kanauj and do not seem to have arrived until the eighth century CE, when, in the agricultural parts of Gujarat, Brahman immigration was just beginning a centuries-long process.[30] In Kashmir, it is evident that Brahmans became predominant

in the wake of the Karkota ruler Lalitaditya Muktapida's conquest of
Kanauj in 733, and especially under his grandson Jayapida, who collected them from around the subcontinent. They further increased in
number in Kashmir in the early eleventh century, during the conquest
of the Panjab by the Turks.[31] In Bengal, the immigration and settlement
of Brahmans began in the fifth century CE, gained great momentum
under the Pala dynasty between the mid-eighth and eleventh centuries
in the western Ganges delta, and then peaked under the Senas and
Varmans in the twelfth century, when it also began to reach the eastern
and southeastern parts of the delta created in the wake of the beginning
of a gradual eastward swing of the river system.[32] The inscriptions of
all of these dynasties indicate that in Bengal many Brahman immigrant
settlers arrived from Madhyadesha, Pañcaladesha (Uttar Pradesh),
and southern Gujarat, or from other parts of Bengal itself, and that
there were many among them who moved on to Assam and Orissa and
into the Telugu-speaking part of the peninsula. In Malabar, it was the
Kulashekara kings who sponsored Brahman immigration on a perhaps
unparalleled scale from the beginning of the ninth century, and here, in
the subsequent centuries, they came to constitute part of the influential
Nambutiri caste that ruled in condominium with the Nayar military
caste.[33] On the Coromandel coast, both the Pallavas and the later Colas
sponsored Brahman immigration and settlement; many, if not most,
of the Brahmans here traced their origins to the Gangetic heartland,
while in fact the vast majority was of local peninsular origin.[34] Although
Brahmans never played the same role of moral and religious guardians
in Sinhalese Buddhist society, they did maintain a persistent presence
in medieval Sri Lanka as well, accumulating lands and villages, with
many of them coming from the subcontinent, and increasingly so in
the fourteenth and fifteenth centuries, when their influence grew as a
result of the breakup of the unitary Buddhist monarchies of the north
and the shift to a series of temporary capitals in the southern parts of the
island.[35] Finally, the presence of Brahmans of both local and overseas
provenance is also attested in the emerging kingdoms of the wet rice-
cultivating plains of Southeast Asia.[36] We find them in Funan, Chenla,
and Angkor, as well as in Champa, where kings not only employed
Brahmans in prominent sacerdotal and secular functions but generally claimed a brahmanical origin in the subcontinent for themselves
as well. The kings of Pagan Burma and the Buddhist Mon country of
lower Burma continued to attract such numbers of Brahmans to their
courts that Chinese records referred to the Pagan ruler as "the sovereign of the Brahmans." Medieval Javanese kings patronized Brahmans
in the same way throughout the medieval centuries. With the rise of a

new medieval Buddhism, of the conservative Theravada variety, among the peasantries of the mainland of Southeast Asia from the thirteenth century onward, there was a gradual decline in the numbers and influence of Brahmans here, although they never entirely disappeared. In the archipelago, this did not happen until the rise of Islam in the sixteenth century.

As an abundance of inscriptions shows, the Brahmans played multiple roles. Most conspicuously, the newly emerging nexus of regional kingdoms became closely associated with the sacerdotal power of a Brahman priesthood, which became the privileged recipient of "great gifts," including donations of land and in some areas, not uncommonly, the revenue of entire villages or clusters of villages. The medieval Brahman priesthood ritually integrated the expanding agricultural domains. Sponsored by the emerging regional kingdoms, it produced a religious and scholastic literature in the form of Puranas, digests on Hindu law, ritual, iconography, speculative philosophy, and much more besides. From around the eighth century onward, Brahman philosopher-theologians such as Bhattacharya and Shankaracharya spearheaded a new polemical drive of Hindu orthodoxy and an institutional overhaul of Hindu monasticism in an effort to undermine monastic Buddhism. This new Hindu orthodoxy spread across the subcontinent and was quite dominant in some parts of it (Malabar and Mysore in particular), while in other regions (Sind, Sri Lanka, Myanmar, Cambodia, Thailand, Java) more hybrid Hindu-Buddhist forms of religious, social, and political life continued to prevail, with Brahmans and the Buddhist laity and monkhood in complementary ritualistic or secular administrative roles. Everywhere the cult of tirthas, or sacred centers, became important at the same time, while bhakti devotional cults spread in conjunction with the new Brahmanical theistic conceptions and proliferating Hindu sects and subsects.[37]

Perhaps the most arresting and visual dimension of early medieval Hinduism was the rise of monumental temple complexes in rural settings (Figures 2.1–2.3). The Hindu temples beginning to be built enshrined for worship icons of Vishnu and Shiva, among other gods of the Hindu pantheon.[38] Such temples provided the setting for elaborate Brahmanical cults and rituals. Rurally dispersed, these massive architectural structures of stone or brick expressed the new vertical linkages that came to characterize the regional Hindu kingdoms that were being established in the nucleated zones of agricultural settlement in the aftermath of the dissolution of the loose, horizontal organization of the empires of the ancient period. In sum, the early

Figure 2.1 Khajuraho temple, Madhya Pradesh, tenth to eleventh centuries. Braunger/ullstein bild via Getty Images.

Figure 2.2 Angkor Wat temple complex, Siem Reap, Cambodia, twelfth century. iStock via Getty Images.

Figure 2.3 Prambanan temple, Indonesia, tenth century. Hermes Images/AGF/Universal Images Group via Getty Images.

medieval pattern was one of agricultural expansion and settlement, emerging landed elites and royal dynasties patronizing Brahmans and their theistic cults of Vishnu and Shiva, and monumental temple architecture. This does not mean that Brahmans were always priests. In fact, most of the Brahmans played secular-administrative or political and agricultural-pioneering rather than sacerdotal or purely ritual roles. If Brahmans virtually monopolized the sacerdotal functions and literacy – especially in Sanskrit – at all medieval courts, a great number of them, indeed most of them, were not highly literate court Brahmans. The general run of Brahmans in all probability, more often than not, could neither read nor write.

Sanskrit texts reveal and highlight, above all, how the agrarian reorientation of the early medieval centuries gave rise to monarchical states and lordships of varying dimensions, importance, and durability, but almost universally in close association with the hieratic, not the administrative, power of the Brahmans. Among the newly settled populations, we find secular and religious resources inextricably intertwined. The Brahmans produced an almost-limitless corpus of Sanskrit texts that made the absorption of the secular into the religious realm their central concern. Kings were the dharmic protectors of creation and presented as gods in human form or "gods on earth," divine incarnates (or descendants) of Shiva or Vishnu, and, according to the idea of plural incarnation, of both Shiva and Vishnu simultaneously or any combination of Hindu divinities or guardian gods of the world.[39] The Majapahit kings of fourteenth-century Java and their predecessors were not only "revered like gods" but regarded as incarnations of "Shiva-Buddha" or Vishnu.[40] In Cambodia and Champa, the divinity of the kings was evident in the cult of the lingam – the phallic symbol of the *devarāja*, or "god king." The idea of divine incarnation was in theory incompatible with the Theravada Buddhism of Sri Lanka and mainland Southeast Asia, but in practice the Theravada Buddhist ideas of rebirth and religious merit did not exclude the notion of a hereditary and quasi-divine right to the throne, and powerful elements of the belief in divine incarnation of either Shiva or Vishnu have in fact survived in the coronation rituals of the Buddhist kings of Sri Lanka, as well as those of Myanmar, Thailand, and Cambodia (Figure 2.4).

The idea of divine kingship, then, was more or less universally found throughout the settled parts of medieval India. But the Sanskrit texts are equally insistent that the ultimate religious authority of the dharma, or religious law, was not vested in divine kings but instead in the Brahman priests.[41] For this reason, the Brahmans were, in a sense, "superior" to kings. Since Brahmans had entrusted kingship and the duty of maintaining order and protecting the earth to kings, as well as to the warrior caste of the *kshatriyas*, they could avoid being tainted by it. Moreover, the temporal order of the king being inherently defective, the king remained dependent on the spiritual power of the "superior" Brahmans. The cooperation of kings and Brahmans was the essential condition for the realization of the moral order of the dharma.

But this most basic ideational configuration of what Sheldon Pollock has termed the "Sanskrit cosmopolis" takes us no further back than the fourth century CE, and it is really medieval in inspiration, not ancient.[42] Sanskrit, in effect, was an ancient language, but its discursive formations emancipated only slowly and reluctantly from the religious into the political domain. If it became the universal language

Figure 2.4 Reclining Buddha, Polonnaruva, Sri Lanka, twelfth century.
Eye Ubiquitous/Universal Images Group via Getty Images.

of medieval India, it did not play the role Latin played in medieval
Europe. Sanskrit was diffused by Brahmans through a wide variety of
competing religious denominations or sects – Shaiva, Vaishnava, and
Buddhist, among others – jostling for position in a kaleidoscopic wel-
ter of constantly realigning and ill-defined medieval states that could
reach an imperial size but did not represent a single centralized political
power such as the Roman empire. Unlike Latin, Sanskrit was a sacred
language and never used as an everyday medium of communication or
practical administration. The literary emancipation of the Indian vernaculars (such as Hindi, Bengali, Marathi) for this reason took much
longer than that of the European vernaculars. Since Latin was not a
sacred or absolute language, the European vernacular languages could
develop their own great literature merely by proving their title to legitimacy in relationship to Latin. Indian vernaculars, by contrast, had to
prevail over a language that had the prestige of a sacred or absolute
language – Sanskrit. The linguistic situation in medieval India was
more like that of the medieval eastern Mediterranean, where Greek
remained unchallenged and where resolutely "modern" vernaculars,
even Demotic Greek, could not attain the status of literary languages
until relatively late.

Settled Society

We should not overstate the religious or otherworldly dimension of the medieval transformation under discussion. The aristocratic prowess and dignity as well as the ideals of noble comportment of medieval ruling elites in India, as everywhere, in practice set clear limits to deference for priestly and clerical cadres. As a result of the social transformation associated with the expansion of agriculture and the rise of settled society, wealth increased and distinctly secular and noble ideals of chivalry, heroism, and aesthetic sensibilities in addition to codes of etiquette and elegance that were specifically courtly in nature gradually spread among medieval Hindu rulers between Rajasthan and Bali.[43] The rhetoric of divine kingship notwithstanding, in this context the deference for the Brahmans reveals itself as highly context-specific, limited in scope, and contested at all levels.

Providing further evidence of significant religious as well as secular change, the spread and consolidation of a Hindu caste ideology occurred in conjunction with an increasingly minute division of labor in the emerging settled societies of medieval India. Although it has sometimes been argued otherwise, the Hindu caste order is neither an Orientalist fiction of British colonial administrators nor an institution of great antiquity. Even though it can be traced back to mythological representations of the Vedas, it can be shown that the caste system's strictly defined hierarchical orderings of rank and status did not come to prevail widely until early medieval times. In effect, a caste-inflected order of society can be seen as highly characteristic of this politically fragmented world of early medieval India. Caste was a form of hereditary occupational specialization that grew in importance wherever economic activity took place in richer, more settled, and more populated places. Originating in a minute division of labor, the hierarchic implications of caste encouraged social actors to constantly seek status distinctions among themselves, and these tended to acquire unambiguously religious aspects of purity and pollution that could render the distinctions quite insidious. India's medieval caste order was an exceedingly complex and differentiated social-religious phenomenon that defies comparison with those of other regions of the world yet can hardly be regarded as uniquely Indian in inspiration. Medieval Europe was rife with the types of blood taboos as well as those about dirt or impurity that were institutionalized in the Indian caste system, and here, too, every mode of life, guild, social estate, and occupation found itself circumscribed by ideals of an ethical and religious nature.[44] The morbid obsession with genealogical purity is found in Europe also. Even the

practice of widow burning known as *sati*, which was widespread among
caste Hindus, has a counterpart in medieval (and early modern) Europe
in the burning of witches – these, after all, were most commonly either
widows or women who never married.[45]

We find unmistakable evidence of a caste order in virtually all settled parts of medieval India. Contemporary descriptions highlight the
large number of professional and endogamous castes in existence that
"when eating must form a group together" in the agricultural villages
of the subcontinent, as well as the presence of outcastes living outside
the perimeters of such villages and towns, who are most often called
Candālas.[46] These outcastes were beef-eating minorities, "low people,"
"foul men," hunters and butchers, sweepers, and the like, who had to
announce their approach by drums or other forms of warning – the
severely ostracized untouchables – and first enter the historical record
in the early fifth century CE. How exactly the caste order evolved in
different parts of the medieval Indian subcontinent is still poorly understood, but we can trace its diffusion to the peninsula. In the agricultural
villages of Malabar, the most severe ritual separation and restrictions
on commensality among the numerous castes, as well as the physical
avoidance of low castes and "outcastes" or untouchables on open roads,
was increasingly enforced under the special custodianship of the military caste of the Nayars from the eighth to the twelfth century CE and
still further afterward. The seaboard always remained beyond the pale
of the Hindu caste system, and women of both the Nayar and sacerdotal
Brahman castes were expressly prohibited from entering the seaports
for fear of ritual pollution.[47] Tamil migrants brought caste to Sri Lanka,
but not until the Polonnaruva period – around the eleventh century.[48]
In Buddhist Sri Lanka, religious notions of purity and pollution did not
arise, nor did untouchability, and caste was much less rigid here than
in the subcontinent itself. Caste in Sri Lanka became the customary
law of the Buddhist laity, a secular code of conduct inseparable from
the system of government put in place by the kings in cooperation with
the Brahmans, but more importantly with that of the Buddhist Sangha,
and defined by its relationship to the dominant caste of landowners. In
the settled parts of medieval Southeast Asia, conceptions of caste and
hierarchical order developed in parallel with the Indian subcontinent,
but, as in Sri Lanka, in attenuated form. A caste-like classification and
the practice of widow burning, juxtaposed to allusions of a tribal and
untouchable population outside the proper caste order, is found in the
Nagarakertagama, an epic poem and chronicle composed in 1365 by a
Buddhist monk for the glorification of the Hindu Majapahit kings of
Java.[49] Caste is still today a familiar concept in Bali, where it dates back

to the fourteenth-century interlude when Majapahit ruled the island.[50]
In Java itself, a weakly developed caste system, restricted to the nuclei
around courtly capitals, was largely erased by Islam once it spread in
the interior of the island in the sixteenth century, while it was absorbed
in the mainland by Theravada Buddhism. Until then, it was part of the
settled order of society throughout South and Southeast Asia. If the
outward forms were different, the substance was not: invariably it was
the product of the expansion of agriculture and settled society. Hindu
law books condemned and imposed severe restrictions on the movements, in particular maritime travel (with the neglect of purification
rites that it entailed), of the high castes and prescribed the avoidance
of those who had undertaken such travel. These kinds of restrictions
were in force throughout medieval and early modern India, mostly
as the customary law of the Brahmans. For Brahmanical Hinduism,
movement meant relocation, not a mobile lifestyle. The same was
true for Jainism – an originally renunciatory sect with close affinity to
Buddhism that developed social dimensions, including caste, effectively
making it a Hindu sect during its successful expansion, particularly in
residential trade and banking but also in agriculture. Hindu and Jain
merchants and moneylenders living abroad in the medieval and early
modern Muslim world and elsewhere were almost always sojourners
and almost exclusively male, rotating in and out of a diaspora, taking
up merely communal residencies in caravanserais, and virtually never
intermarrying with the local populations that hosted them.[51] Caste was
fundamentally an order of settled society.

3   Geography and the World-Historical Context

> The ideal, then, is the preservation of the existing order. Everyone should remain within the bounds of the rights and duties laid upon him by the caste into which he is born.... [Hindu-Javanese] society...cherished no other ideal than to remain as it was, shunning all change. This is not to deny that in the course of time changes did take place as a result of influences from outside. Such changes, however, were not sought after as representing "progress"; rather they were condemned as deviations from the tradition, the primary factors which determined the structure of Javanese society remaining unchanged.
>
> Bernard Schrieke (1957)[1]

The peasant economy of the settled river plains was by no means static. It was mostly characterized by small circles of local consumption. Peasant society, weighed down by its stone and brick monuments in rural surroundings, was sedentary and closely regulated. Its dense and complex networks of ties of interdependence and ritual organization offered little room for innovation and extraneous movement. Change occurred, but it was imperceptibly slow, much of it driven by population growth and the long-term expansion of agriculture and settled civilization. Or it came in the form of disruption – invasion, war, drought, famine, flood, or earthquake – inviting only slow recovery. Whenever possible, the normal rhythms of peasant life reemerged unchanged in their cyclical regularity.

The historical development of India, however, was driven not only by the long-term expansion of agriculture and settled civilization but as much by the proximity of the vast open spaces of the great Saharasian arid zone and the Indian Ocean – the pastoral nomadic frontier and the maritime frontier. Together, these open and unsettled realms of nomadic and seafaring peoples represented the frontier of mobile wealth and the major external source of change and dynamism in land-based society. The pastoral nomadic and maritime frontiers were alike insofar as both fostered movement and were intractably resistant to the principles of sociopolitical and ideological control at work in the settled world. Openness, fluidity, and movement were characteristic of both realms. What mattered geographically was not the opposition of land and sea but of settled society on the one side and the unsettled nomadic and maritime frontiers on the other. In this chapter we will look at these frontiers one by one.

The Nomadic Frontier

South Asia is ecologically positioned at the southeastern end of the world's largest continuous arid zone. This Saharasian arid zone runs from Morocco and the Sahara across Suez to Arabia and the Levant; on to the Persian plateau and Afghanistan; and then northward into Central Asia, Mongolia, and parts of northern China; and it extends deep into South Asia itself.[2] Everywhere, the Saharasian arid zone receives less than 3.28 feet of rainfall per year, and by that measure the size of this (semi-) arid zone increased significantly over the past two or three millennia, especially in the medieval era. By the nineteenth century CE, nearly half of South Asia was an extension of the great arid zone. From the Indus borderlands of Sind, Makran, Baluchistan, Afghanistan, Rajasthan, and the Thar (or the Great Indian Desert, with less than 3 inches of rainfall, the lowest in all of India), the arid zone extended in an eastern and southern direction. Eastward it ran up to the southern banks of the Ganges near Varanasi until it reached the humid eastern parts of the subcontinent. Southward it ran across the Aravalli mountains into Malwa and down the lee side of the Western Ghats into the Deccan plateau. There it turned southeastward onto the Telangana Plateau, extending from Golkonda to the Tungabhadra and Krishna Rivers, thereafter into Kurnool, Anantapur, and Cuddapah – the area known as Rayalsima, or "frontier of the kingdom" – and Chittoor, and finally to the southwest, to the Mysore plateau and into northern Sri Lanka.

By far the largest part of the great Saharasian arid zone could not sustain intensive settled agriculture because of its poor soils and lack of irrigation facilities. It did, however, produce good grasslands for grazing livestock, camels, and horses, and for this reason its characteristic mode of production has traditionally been pastoral nomadism or pastoralism of some other variety (Figures 3.1–3.4).

There were numerous semiarid areas within the arid zone and valleys in some of its mountain ranges where agriculture was possible, but these broadly fell within the same category in terms of their suitability for pastoral nomadism and stock breeding. There were no clear and precise

Figure 3.1 Mongol horseman running his flock of sheep on the steppe outside of Ulaanbaatar, Mongolia. John S. Lander/LightRocket via Getty Images.

Figure 3.2 Nomadic horsemen in the Wakhan corridor, Afghanistan. Scott Wallace/Hulton Archive via Getty Images.

Figure 3.3 Wakhi shepherd with his sheep and goats, Wakhan corridor, Afghanistan. Eric Lafforgue/Art in All of Us/Corbis News via Getty Images.

Figure 3.4 Baluch camel caravan, Baluchistan, c. 1965. Archive Photos/ Stringer via Getty Images.

demarcation lines between the different ecosystems in this part of the world, nor between those populations that practiced pastoral nomadism and those that engaged in agriculture. The inhabitants of the arid zone who practiced pastoral nomadism and other forms of pastoralism also cannot be too sharply distinguished from the scattered forest populations who practiced hunting and gathering and various forms of shifting cultivation while moving from place to place. Forests and jungle lands have been put to human use in numerous ways, and some of these (e.g., elephant breeding) resemble pastoralism. Historically, however, forest people have not been very noticeable. We know little, for example, about the people who lived in small numbers in the forested interiors of Sumatra, Kalimantan, Irian Jaya, Malaya, Myanmar, Cambodia, and Thailand until the latter part of the eighteenth century. In the Indian subcontinent, the area that was covered by either tropical rainforest or other types of wild forest and jungle gradually shrank to smaller and smaller proportions so that here, over time, forest people and shifting cultivators were marginalized in an expanding agricultural society, to whose infectious crowd diseases they were especially vulnerable. While their history remains mostly unknown, forest people did not play a major role in the peasant societies of the plains as military entrepreneurs, or as conquerors and rulers, anywhere in India. In this regard they could not be more different from the inhabitants of deserts, steppes, and other lands characterized by aridity. Unlike the hunter-gatherers of the forests, the pastoral nomadic inhabitants of the arid zone benefitted from the raising of livestock, including war horses, oxen, and camels, and acquired a set of attributes that allowed them to play an important historical role in the settled societies of the plains. What is more, the pastoral nomadic population of the great arid zone continued to expand over time, in conjunction with its expanding habitat. It also became ever more effectively militarized, and its historical role correspondingly more dominant.

Just as there were no clear and precise demarcation lines between ecosystems anywhere, South Asia as a whole was a zone of transition between the Saharasian arid zone and the wet, equatorial habitats of Southeast Asia, where intensive, irrigated agriculture – mainly rice – predominated in river plains and deltas enclosed by evergreen rain forests or hilly jungles. This situation ensured that South Asia was exposed to the great historical nomadic conquests and tribal migrations that occurred across the arid zone, but not Southeast Asia. As has been emphasized by Victor Lieberman, Southeast Asia – with Japan and Europe – has been part of the "protected zone" or "protected rim lands" and differed from the "exposed zone" (including China, most of

South Asia, and Persia, and Southwest Asia) by being exempted from repeated conquest and long-term occupation by nomadic peoples originating in the Saharasian arid zone.[3]

The earliest archaeological evidence of the movement of horse-riding pastoral nomads across the Hindu Kush are the ancient *tumuli*, or earth mounds containing ashes and arms, which have been found in Rajasthan. These are reminiscent of the royal tombs of the "nomad Scythians" of other parts of Asia described by the Greek historian Herodotus (c. 484–425/413 BCE).[4] The presence of Scythian nomads in India was not recorded by Herodotus in his lifetime, only by other ancient Greek writers of later centuries. The anonymous author of the *Periplus Maris Erythraei* of the first century CE and the geographer Ptolemy of the second century CE refer to the Indus borderlands as being part of "Scythia" and, more specifically, "Indo-Scythia."[5] But the nomads whom the Greek authors identified as the inhabitants of Scythia (i.e., the Scythians) are identical to the *Shakas* of the ancient Sanskrit texts and the *Sakas* of the ancient Persian ones – an appellation that has been derived by some scholars from the Old Persian root *sak-*, "to go, flow, run," and hence *saka*, "running, swift, vagrant, nomadic."[6] We know that this "wandering nation" of the Sakas had moved westward at an early stage and southward as well: an inscription of the third Achaemenid emperor Darius (550–486 BCE) describes the Persian province of Sistan as "Sakastana."[7] India does not seem to have been much affected by the movements of the Sakas/Shakas until the third and second centuries BCE, and the nomad tombs of Rajasthan referred to earlier almost certainly date from around that time.[8] The earliest Shakas to move across the Kabul valley into the Panjab were probably part of a Parthian invasion led by the king of kings Mithradates (173–138 BCE); they may well have been Hellenized, possibly Greek speaking, like the Scythians of the Pontic steppes, or they may have adopted an Old Persian dialect. There were other Shakas who moved into India via the Bolan Pass somewhat later, as well as into Bactria, where they overran the Greek kingdoms, and then into the lower Indus valley. Shaka-Parthian satrapies, building on the remnants of the Indo-Greek kingdoms, provided conditions conducive to trade between Bactria, Kashmir, lower Sind, and Rajasthan, while passing on Persian and possibly Roman-Hellenistic cultural elements to the subcontinent.

A new phase of nomadic expansion began in the latter part of the first century CE, when the Shaka (Indo-Scythian) territories were absorbed into the dominion of the Kushana "royal horde," an offshoot of the nomadic Yeh-chih of Kansu. The Yeh-chih headed a heterogeneous assortment of tribes that included one or two hundred thousand mounted archers and reached much deeper into the subcontinent in the subsequent centuries, creating a nexus between nomadic power and trade that eventually came to embrace the entire mountainous divide between the Oxus and the Ganges, Kashmir included. Kushana rule reached its peak under Kanishka, in all probability sometime after 128 CE. Underscoring the importance of trade to their realm, the Kushanas under Kanishka widely patronized Buddhism, and they had their capital at Purushapura (in the area of modern Peshawar), but Mathura, on the Indian plains, achieved the status of an important secondary capital. Still later, in the fifth century CE, much the same territory that was ruled by the Kushanas and was called "Indo-Scythia" by the Greeks was absorbed into the dominion of the nomadic Hephthalites (or "White Huns") – yet another nomadic people with origins across the Hindu Kush who were possibly an offshoot of the later Kushanas but also related to the Shakas. The Hephthalites were allied to the Huns, an ethnic group that by that time had emerged as the nomadic power between Kashghar and Bactria. They were able to occupy the countries immediately to the south of the Hindu Kush, including Zamindawar, Zabulistan, and Kabul (ancient Gandhara, as far as the Indus), and here they became the successors of the Kushanas and the Shakas, establishing control over the important trade routes running from the Indian subcontinent to the cities north of the Hindu Kush, where the Soghdian merchants held sway. The Hephthalites broke through to the Indian plains around 465 CE and had subjected the Panjab to their rule by the end of the fifth century – together with parts of Rajasthan and Kashmir, and later the more central parts of the subcontinent – for a short while growing into a formidable power under Mihirakula. But the power of the Hephthalites, like that of the Shakas and Kushanas, also did not last for long. To the north of the Hindu Kush, the Hephthalites, and the Huns backing them, were subverted between 563 and 568 by the Sasanids, in alliance with the newly rising power of the nomadic Turks. Not much remained thereafter of their power in Zamindawar, Zabulistan, and Kabul either – regions traditionally part of South Asia – and by the eighth and ninth centuries, the Hephthalites had largely vanished. Like the other ancient nomads in the region, they were important facilitators of trade relations across the Hindu Kush, but they were unable to establish empires beyond Indo-Scythia.

The relationship between pastoral nomads and the sedentary world changed, however, in medieval times. In the later part of the first millennium and the first half of the second millennium CE, the great arid zone gained significantly in importance as a conduit of people and

animals, and hence in political importance as well. The primary beneficiaries of this change were the nomadic Turks and Mongols of the
eastern steppe lands and, within their expanded orbit, the Afghans.
What allowed the medieval Turks and Mongols to overcome the limitations of their predecessors was a combination of geographic, climatological, demographic, military, and political-organizational factors that
had been absent in ancient times.

One factor was global warming. A medieval warming period affecting the entire globe was identified over a half century ago, and thanks
to tree-ring research, we know enough about this phenomenon to be
able to conclude that it probably played a role of particular importance
in the great arid zone.[9] Average temperatures never rose more than a
few degrees Fahrenheit anywhere in the vast area, but arid zone envi-
ronments are extraordinarily sensitive to even the smallest variations
in temperature and rainfall. There is evidence to suggest that, between
the eighth/ninth and thirteenth centuries, an unusual pattern of cycles
of colder and wetter winters and warmer and drier summers damaged
and shrunk steppe pastures. These changes particularly affected horse-
breeding nomads, because horses have an exceptionally inefficient
digestive system: they assimilate as little as 25 percent of the protein
they consume and have great difficulty surviving on dried-out, low-
protein grass, in a way that cattle does not. When grasslands were reduced
or fresh grass killed, the resulting protein scarcity triggered nomadic
movements to places with better grazing on the margins of agricultural
lands and even onto those lands themselves. A warming climate appears
to have aggravated already-existing conditions of overpopulation on the
steppes. Together, global warming and demographic pressure provided
part of the drive behind the movements and empire-building efforts of
the steppe nomads in medieval times. Possibly they had a similar but
lesser impact on population movements in other parts of the arid zone
as well; the Bedouin of the Arabian Peninsula and the previously mentioned Gujaras and other proto-Rajput clans of India (pp. 40–1) come
to mind, but with these we are on more speculative ground.

Also important were key innovations in nomadic military technology
that were beginning to be diffused around the same time. The steppe
nomads, to be sure, had always enjoyed significant military advantages over sedentary townspeople and peasants: mobility and virtually
unrestricted access to horses, a near-universal male participation in
organized violence, and the unparalleled stamina and toughness engen-
dered by life in a wild and inhospitable environment – long-standing
attributes of the nomadic life that had already been highlighted by
Herodotus. With the dissemination of the new technology of the stirrup,

the improved compound bow of the steppe, and iron body armor in the early medieval centuries, however, nomadic power came to dominate the entire continental landmass between Hungary and Mongolia.

Global warming and technological change were, in their turn, accompanied by the introduction and diffusion of new modes of military and political organization that allowed the horse-riding steppe nomads to overcome some of the most serious limitations of their ancient tribal cultures. The pastoral nomads of ancient times had tribal cultures in the sense that kinship and descent groups were the basic building blocks of their political organization. This does not mean that ancient nomads were in any sense primitive. As Thomas Barfield has pointed out, having a tribal culture merely means that their basic political structures employed a model of kinship to build corporate groups that acted in concert to organize economic production, preserve internal political order, and defend the group against outsiders.[10] In any such tribal political culture, relationships among individuals and groups were mapped through social space rather than geographic territory. To identify people as members of a defined social group rather than residents of a particular place was particularly useful for people who regularly moved in physical space, as pastoral nomads always did. But the limitations of such a tribal political organization are as obvious as its advantages: it was difficult or even impossible to create larger states and empires out of mere tribal constituents. Ancient nomads lived in an egalitarian society based on the strong but narrow tribal solidarities of kinship and descent groups. The political dynamics of egalitarian lineage systems in such ancient nomadic societies were segmentary, and this meant that cooperation or hostility between groups was determined by the scope of the contingencies of the day. The maximum size of such groups as operational units, according to anthropological studies, rarely exceeded ten thousand people. Small in scale, rejecting the legitimacy of hereditary leadership, especially kingship, as a rule the tribal political system remained open and fluid: prejudiced against ranks, titles, and hierarchy and difficult to overcome in supra-tribal units. In effect, among many historical pastoral nomadic populations, like for example the Afghans and Indo-Afghans, this remained a debilitating condition until as late as the eighteenth century CE.[11] This was not so, however, among the Turks.

The change in military and political organization that occurred in the later part of the first millennium is that one nomadic polity – that of the Turks – successfully overcame the unreconstructed tribalism of its ancient predecessors. As is often the case with momentous change, there was little, if anything, that was absolutely novel in it. Some early versions of the notions of the divine origin of ruling clans, the divine right to rule, heavenly ordained charisma, domination and vassalage, and the joint sovereignty of the ruling clan can already be found in the ancient Scythian kingdoms. Certain ancient nomad leaders – such as Kanishka of the Kushanas and Mihirakula of the Hephthalites – had been able to mobilize far greater followings than the typical ten thousand of their average tribal competitors, at least for a short time, by sheer force of personality if nothing else. With the ethnogenesis and rise of the Turks in the sixth century CE, however, the authority of the ruler acquired dimensions of absolutism that it lacked in ancient times. And this became a permanent legacy passed on to the entire Turko-Mongol world.

The Turks were the first ethnic group to emerge from the Mongol or Hunnic (Chinese: *Hiung-nu*) nomadic populations of the eastern steppes and to begin replacing the Scythians/Shakas, Kushanas, Hephthalites, and other groups speaking Indo-European languages that had until then dominated the western steppes.[12] We first encounter the Turks when they were still a small tribe whose name meant "the strong one" and was semantically associated with a whole range of tribal names connoting "force," "violence," "ferociousness," and the like. These earliest Turks were headed by their own charismatic and divinely endowed Ashina clan and lived primarily in the Altaic mountains but as yet were subordinate to the Juan-juan, another ethnic group of eastern nomads whose empire had arisen a century earlier in the territories between the watersheds of the Orkhon and Selenga Rivers, the northern edge of the Tien Shan mountains, and the Ordos steppe.[13] Already at that point in time, the Turkish pastoral nomads were horse-riding warriors equipped with the compound bow, "singing arrows," and the stirrup. Their unique metallurgical skills and industry provided them with iron swords (which they also passed around as currency), coats of chain mail, and then, when they finally rid themselves of Juan-juan overlordship between 545 and 556, the "iron gates" that demarcated the first Turkish empire recognized independently by the Chinese. The ethnonym "Turks" passed into the medieval era as a generic denomination for all people nomadizing within these iron gates. But soon enough, after their military victories over the Hephthalites between 563 and 568, the Turks became the rulers of the entire steppe between the Great Wall of China and Sasanid Persia far to the north.[14] This first successful unification of the entire steppe by a single ethnic group was clearly a moment of world-historical importance. In due course the Turks were to become so dominant that the ancient Shakas, Kushanas, and Hephthalites began retroactively to be referred to as Turks as well. As a result of the cooperation between the charismatic Turkish nomadic leadership and capital-providing merchants with an almost-global reach, especially the Soghdians, there was also a great upsurge of trade between Byzantium and China.[15] But the decisive difference between the medieval Turkish empire and the ancient nomadic tribal and at best proto-imperial polities lay in its more complex and structured political and administrative system.[16] In the Turkish-Altaic world, the charisma of the ruling Ashina clan led to the idea of legitimacy by descent and a full-blown ideology of heavenly mandated rule by a *Qaghan* (an appellation introduced by the Juan-juan in 402), who formed the basic tribal union and established the *Törü*, or customary code of law, of this union. The Qaghanate, in its universalist aspiration, was closely aligned with the monarchical political system as it had come to exist in China, and much earlier in Egypt, Persia, and Mesopotamia, the Hellenistic empires that were created in the Mediterranean world between 350 and 100 BCE, and the Roman empire. Below the Ashina clan, the Turkic Qaghanate consisted of a tiered system of confederate and "in-law" tribes and clans as well as "subject tribes," nomadic and non-nomadic tribute-paying vassals, and even slave tribes as well as individual slaves. These various categories of tribes and other constituent elements of the polity did not disappear as such but merely subsumed their identity under the broader political identity of the ruling tribe. In this way the Turk Qaghanate provided a broad formula that became the blueprint for all later nomadic polities and empires of the Turko-Mongol world.[17] From these roots the pan-nomadic Turkish imperial forms were further developed in the direction of a tight military organization and centralized absolutism by the Manchurian Khitans in the tenth century, and through them they were subsequently transmitted to the Mongols, the dominant tribe of one of the confederations of the Mongolian steppe in the twelfth century. Mongol imperialism and its later offshoots were basically a modification of a continuous nomadic customary tradition initiated by the Turks some six hundred years earlier. The Turko-Mongol *Törü* and the different strands of earlier monarchical traditions of the sedentary world would come together and reinforce each other in myriad forms in the subsequent centuries of nomadic conquest and domination.

It is no coincidence that we can trace the medieval expansion of Turkish power across the Hindu Kush in much more detail than the ancient expansion of Shaka, Kushana, and Hephthalite power. We can clearly see that the first Turks to arrive in the Indus borderlands were the successors of the earlier Shakas, Kushanas, and Hephthalites rather than the Arab conquerors of that area of the early eighth century. The Arabs who established the early Islamic Caliphate as far as the Indus borderlands favored infantry in their pitched battles, supported by archers, and mostly came from the sedentary population of the towns and oases of the Arabian Peninsula and neighboring parts of the great arid zone.[18] Insofar as there was a nomadic element in the Arab armies, it was mostly put to tactical use as light cavalry and in raiding. The superior mobility of camels was crucial in the Arab conquests but mostly because it allowed rapid troop concentration over great distances. The Arabs did not fight from camelback, nor did they deploy horse-mounted archers as steppe nomads always did. And in the Indus borderlands they did not bring along a significant tribal following of pastoral nomads, accompanied by women and children, for relocation in the conquered territories. Here the Arabs were merely a new military and ruling elite and as such held on to power for about three centuries. Throughout these centuries of Arab rule, it appears that the Turks did not independently take over any part of the Indus borderlands.[19] Using the designation Turks in a loose and inaccurate way, the Arab geographers of the tenth century refer to some of the pastoral nomads on the plateau of Kabul and Bust in eastern Afghanistan as "Khalaj Turks," but it is virtually certain that these were the ethnic debris of the earlier Shaka, Kushana, and Hephthalite invasions, not Turks. And the so-called Turk-Shahi rulers of Kabul – who held on to power until the late ninth century, like the Zunbils of Zabulistan – were probably also descendants of the Hephthalites rather than Turks. All we know for certain is that the Turk-Shahi rulers of Kabul, as well as the Hindu rulers of Kashmir and some petty Hephthalite rulers in the valleys of the tributaries of the Kabul River and the upper Indus, began employing Turkish nomads as mercenary horsemen as early as the mid-eighth century and continued to do so in the ninth century, but still on a small scale. This situation did not change until the tenth century, when the Turkish conquest of India and the Islamic world began in earnest.

Yet the Turkish conquest of India was not a nomadic conquest in the strict sense.[20] The Indian subcontinent was ecologically unsuitable for extensive pastoral nomadism, and this is the reason it never allowed, let alone invited, the massive migrations of nomadic peoples, complete with herds, that were characteristic of large parts of Central Asia, Persia, Iraq, and places such as Anatolia and northwest China. In the extensions of the arid zone in the Indian subcontinent, pastoral nomadism as such quickly reached its natural limits, because here it came to be closely associated with agriculture and settled society. There was a great deal of pastoral variability in India, and the distribution of Indian pastoralists varied according to the type of pastoralism, animals, and environment, but most commonly there was just a kind of herdsman husbandry. Arid and humid areas that served as summer and winter pastures were within relatively short distances of each other, and most herds in India, in effect, consisted of cattle, sheep, and goats moving vertically up and down hills or back and forth between river beds – many of which turned dry seasonally – or from monsoon grazing on the seasonal grasses of the open lands to the foliage and herbage on the rim of forest tracts. Horse breeding was even more restricted, although there were some good breeding grounds in places like Kachchh, Kathiawar, and Bikaner, and the subcontinent always remained dependent on horse imports from beyond the frontier. Indian grasslands suffered from the extreme difference between rainy and dry seasons; this made the soil swampy at one time and hard and parched at another, with the result that the grazing season was comparatively short. Genuine pastoral nomadism existed in India, but it was always closely associated with the agriculture of sedentary society and in all its variety represented a kind of enclosed nomadism. It never constituted an autonomous mode of production and involved distances that were relatively short in comparison with those traversed by Turkish nomads in the arid zone to the north. Beyond the Indus borderlands, the Turkish conquest therefore at no time involved the migration of nomads, or nomadization, on a significant scale. The Turks in India had to leave their nomadism behind. Here they did not create nomadic, but rather post-nomadic, empires under the dynasties of the Ghaznavids (977–1186), the Ghurids (1186–1206), and successive dynasties of the Sultanate of Delhi up to the invasion by Timur (1206–1398) and afterward. Effectively, pastoral nomads turned themselves into post-nomadic conquest elites in a society of settled peasants.

Post-nomadic expansion into the Indian subcontinent was a far more controlled process than nomadic expansion in the arid zone generally. It did not lead to nomadization but instead boosted the importance of the arid parts of the subcontinent by giving more power to populations living on the peripheries of the old nuclear zones of settled cultivation. Post-nomadic expansion facilitated the mobilization of agrarian resources and fiscal extraction within the framework of post-nomadic empires upheld by powerful horse-riding military elites of nomadic extraction, both from without and within the subcontinent – which, collectively, brought about a horse-warrior revolution. The expansion enhanced the use of precious metals (the essence of mobile wealth) and created a more globalized economy, giving a much higher profile to commercial and financial groups. Post-nomadic Turks, Mongols, and Afghans, while abandoning their pastoral-nomadic life, brought new military, political, and commercial networks of unprecedented intensity into play at the interface of arid zone and settled agriculture, thereby opening up increasingly important corridors for traffic and movement and initiating innovation of all sorts, in an ecosystem that was otherwise primarily geared to settled agriculture and the preservation of a hierarchical caste order and tradition. Unlike nomadic expansion, post-nomadic expansion did not put an end to agricultural growth but instead accelerated it over the long term. Many of the capitals of the post-nomadic dynasties of the second millennium CE – Delhi, Devagiri, Dvarasamudram, Warangal, Bijapur, Golkonda, and Vijayanagara – were not situated in the nuclear agricultural zones like the Hindu monuments and cultic centers; rather, they were located at the interface of the arid and settled worlds. It was their raison d'être to mediate between sedentary investment and the mobilization of the resources of pastoralists, military entrepreneurs, and merchants.

We see this pattern everywhere in the subcontinent except in the Indus borderlands. With their deserts and mountains, the Indus borderlands were geographically, and to a large extent climatically, an extension of the Persian plateau, and in some respects the later medieval development of these areas resembled that of Persia and Anatolia rather than that of the Indian plains to the east. Whereas the Arab conquest of the eighth century did not bring a large tribal migration in its wake, the Turko-Mongol nomads of the thirteenth and fourteenth centuries devastated these lands and even turned agricultural areas into grazing lands for horses, while bringing to them a large population of practicing pastoral nomads. Here nomadic expansion largely overturned the Hindu-Buddhist religious and sociopolitical infrastructure, putting the Indus borderlands on a trajectory that diverged radically from the rest of the subcontinent.[21]

The Maritime Frontier

Friar William of Rubruck described the lands he traversed as papal envoy to the Mongolian court of the thirteenth-century's Great Khan Möngke as a "vast wilderness, which is like a sea."[22] The comparison has often been drawn, and the similarity often observed. Like the desert of the great arid zone, the ocean was ultimately a wilderness, a place where there was no community, the individual was free from the constraints of community life, and the ranking order of settled society broke down.[23] Just as invading Shakas, Kushanas, Hephthalites, and Turks were denounced in the Sanskrit literature as "impure" *mlecchas*, the "people of the sea" and "sea nomads" were held in contempt as a "low, vile people" prone to piracy and slave raiding. Like the desert, the ocean was depicted as a place of heresy and sedition. In the *Prabodhacandrodaya*, the Jain religion is described as *tāmasika*, the outcome of darkness; and according to the same eleventh-century Sanskrit work, Jainism, together with other "heretical" sects such as Buddhism, had retreated to countries that were "rich in vulgar people," by which was meant the arid realm of Rajasthan and Malwa and more particularly the "places on the seashore" of southeast Gujarat and Saurashtra.[24]

The negative attitude was present from the beginning. In ancient times, when seafaring was just beginning to show its potential, Sanskrit texts portrayed maritime enterprise as a possible source of immense wealth and the Indian Ocean itself as "a mine of jewels," but never a source of social status.[25] In medieval Indian writings, the ocean was frequently associated with a chaotic malevolence that contrasted sharply with the order and quietude of the land.[26] Such an attitude of mistrust and ambivalence toward the sea was by no means uniquely Indian, and we find it widely expressed among the literate peoples of settled civilizations around the world.[27] But medieval Hindu law, as we have seen, went much further in its condemnation of seafaring (p. 51). It imposed severe restrictions in particular on sea travel, even prohibiting it for certain high castes, and warned against the interaction with overseas *mlecchas* and the ritual neglect and defilement that such interaction inevitably entailed. These restrictions were taken seriously by many high-caste Hindus, especially Brahmans, and from early medieval times onward, deeply entrenched maritime taboos and *thalassophobia* are in evidence among, for example, the caste Hindus of Malabar. The taboos did not prevent Hindus of all castes in other parts of coastal India from making overseas voyages, and for Buddhists this kind of ritual purity played no role – neither did prohibitions against sea travel – but Indian texts, whether Hindu or Buddhist, offer no passages praising life at sea, and the implicit attitude toward the sea among Hindu scholars has always remained one of fear and distaste. Everywhere the seaboard was seen as a place of ambiguity and extraordinary license, its meat- and fish-eating, liquor-drinking, and promiscuous inhabitants occupying an ill-defined place at the bottom of the caste hierarchy, if they were not downright outcastes. Thus, the Mohanna fishermen and the bird hunters of the Indus delta; the various Konkani castes of fishermen, such as the Bhois, Kharvis, Machhis, Mangelas, and Kolis; the Kharwas and Sanghars of Gujarat; the numerous Mukkuvan fishermen of Malabar; the Mukkuvar and Machuas of the Coromandel coast; and innumerable others were universally shunned by the higher

castes. The social status of the people who lived off the sea – and especially all true nomads of the sea – between East Africa and Socotra, the
Arabian Peninsula, and India and the Malay-Indonesian archipelago,
was low, or at least marginal, regardless of their numbers and actual
importance. In the Old Javanese literature, the sea generally kept the
repulsive aspect of the south coast, as in the myths of the Goddess of
the Southern Ocean, and there are no themes of maritime adventure,
even though the Javanese have been committed to maritime navigation
for centuries.[28] In the popular *Wayang* repertory there are no references
to the sea. And agrarian Mataram has always insisted on regarding the
pasisir, or "coastal," oligarchies as rebels. A more positive maritime orientation did not emerge until the fourteenth and fifteenth centuries, in
the great epic *La Galigo* of the Buginese on Sulawesi, and not until the
rise of the great maritime powers of Aceh, Johore, and Melaka in the
early modern centuries do we encounter any literary affirmation of the
superiority of man navigating the ocean that begins to replace the old
obsession with the settled order of society. Significantly enough, this
happened entirely outside the orbit of agrarian Java.

Comparable in its sheer immensity to the great Saharasian arid zone,
what the Arab geographers called the *Bahr al-Hind* or "Indian Sea"
was an almost equally vast "wilderness" and a second, almost equally
dangerous frontier of settled society where unrestrained and rapid
movement, long-distance trade, and the violent appropriation of mobile
wealth by raiding were part of the normal adaptation to an ecosystem
that was desolate, open, and mostly unsettled, or even uninhabited,
by humans. The Indian Sea was also known as the *Bahr al-Kabir*, or
"Great Sea," and believed to be the largest in the inhabited world yet
part of an even larger body of water known as the *Bahr al-Muhīt*, or
"Encompassing Sea" (the Greek *Okeanos*), which was in practice a
complex of seas, peninsulas, and islands extending southward from the
Red Sea in the west to the Java Sea and South China Sea in the east.
The bulk of navigational movement in these inner seas of the great
Indian Sea was coastwise, with small vessels, but transoceanic travel,
in larger vessels making use of the seasonal monsoon winds, was frequently undertaken as well. The Indian Sea had been an integrated
conduit of trade, migration, and precious metal flows ever since people
had learned to navigate the monsoon winds – from around the first
century CE – and ever more so afterward. With its long-distance trade
and communications, its islands and ports were its oases. Movement
was even more decisive here, and water navigation with dhows was
generally faster and cheaper than overland transportation in the arid
zone. An Indian Ocean dhow could travel the same distance as a camel

Figure 3.5 Indian Ocean dhow, 1909. Science & Society Picture Library via Getty Images.

caravan in one-third of the time, while an average dhow could carry the equivalent of a thousand camel loads, and merely one crew member was needed for several tons of cargo as compared with two or more men for each ton in a camel caravan (Figure 3.5).[29]

There is a further similarity too, in that the people of the sea were a clearly recognizable category but were generally, like pastoral nomads, not very specialized and depended on animals, not agriculture, for their basic subsistence. They were fishermen, just as pastoral nomads were stock breeders and animal herders, but also marine foragers, mollusk gatherers, coral divers, pearl fishers, coastal salt makers, boatbuilders, rope makers, net menders, and sailors, as well as coastal, maritime, and interisland traffickers and traders. Fishing pursuits in the winter would routinely alternate with piracy in the summer. Marco Polo observed seafaring people off the west coast of India who were fishermen in winter but went to sea every year with over a hundred "corsair vessels," taking along with them their wives and children and staying out the whole summer. Their method was to join twenty or thirty of their ships in a sea cordon, with intervals of five to six miles between ships, so that they could cover long stretches of water, sending smoke and fire signals to each other when any one of them spotted a merchant ship.[30] Amid the confusing proliferation of ethnonyms, our sources do not draw sharp distinctions between the "people of the sea," "sea nomads," "corsairs," "robbers," and "pirates."

Historically, the people of the sea wielded great naval power in their medieval heyday, and their mobility and naval capabilities allowed them to organize themselves in great maritime trading networks that were completely integrated with the political and economic life of land-based states. Indian Ocean trade and navigation increased dramatically in importance in the later part of the first millennium and the first half of the second millennium. It first began to increase significantly during the rise of the Islamic Caliphate under the Umayyad and early Abbasid dynasties between the seventh and tenth centuries and then gained further momentum in the context of the almost-global expansion of Turko-Mongol power in the eleventh to fifteenth centuries. An extremely dense, volatile, and ever realigning network of interconnected and often short-lived ports rimmed the Indian Ocean throughout this entire period. These included the ports of the Red Sea and the Swahili coast such as Malindi, Kilwa, Manda, Sofala, Mogadishu, Sawakin, Mombasa, Zanzibar, Aydhab, Berbera, Zayla, Dahlak, Merca, Brava, and Jiddah in the Hijaz; Aden in the Yemen; Shihr in the Hadramaut; the island of Socotra off the Horn of Africa; Hormuz, extending its maritime power across the "land of coasts" (sawāhil) between Ra's al-Hadd and Basra and Abadan in the Persian Gulf; "the noble kingdom of Kambaya" and the Gujarati seaports of Surat, Rander, Diu, Mahim, Daman, Patan, Gogha, Gandhar, Bassein, and Thana, whose mercantile networks spanned almost the entire Indian Ocean; the "sea havens" of the Deccan – Chaul, Danda, Dabhol, Goa, Honawar, Bhatkal, Bacanor, Bracalor, Mangalore, and Cumbola; the few dozen port monarchies of Malabar, including Calicut, Cannanore, Ponnani, Veleankode, Chetwayi, Cranganore, Eli, Cochin, Kayankulam, Kollam, Travancore, and Comorin; a smaller number on the Coromandel coast, including Nagapattinam, Mahabalipuram, Old Kayal, Korkai, and Pulicat; Mantai in Sri Lanka; ports like Visakhapatanam and Mottupalli on the Andhra coast to the north; Sonargaon and Satgaon as well as Chittagong and Mrauku in the Bay of Bengal; the ports of Pegu in the Irrawaddy delta of Burma (Myanmar) and Ayudhya, Tenasserim, and Phuket in Thailand; Phnom Penh in the Mekong delta; Melaka (the most important trading port in the eastern Indian Ocean) and Baruas, both on the Malay Peninsula; the ports of Aru, Perlak, and Samudra-Pasai that preceded Aceh on the north coast of Sumatra and Shrivijaya on the east coast; the pasisir states of Sunda an Java, such as Bantam, Tjimanoek and Sunda Kalapa, and Cirebon, Demak, Japara, Semarang, Tadana, Tuban, Gresik, and Surabaya; Brunei on

Kalimantan; Makassar on Sulawesi; Jolo in the Sulu archipelago; and the small Maluku "spice islands" of Ternate, Tidore, Motir, Makian, and Bacan, as well as the Banda islands.[31] These ports, and innumerable others, were all near or on the seaboard, and even though they sometimes turned their backs on their own hinterlands (as commonly happened on the east coast of Africa), they were open in physical and economic terms, while pluralistic in political terms, and thus characterized by a high degree of unregulated and open competition. Trading diasporas originated and proliferated everywhere on these coasts. There was, at the same time, a slow reinforcement of overseas Chinese communities, especially in the eastern Indian Ocean. As yet, the trade with China in the medieval centuries was far more important than that with the Mediterranean.[32] This was especially so after 1277, when the Mongol emperor Kublai Khan established his power over the coastal provinces of southeastern and southern China and the drain of China's precious metals toward the Indian Ocean accelerated.

No Mongol emperor ever conquered any part of Southeast Asia. Apart from some incidental Mongol raids in the Indianized states of the mainland and Kublai Khan's maritime expedition to Java, Southeast Asia as a whole was and always remained, by and large, part of the "protected" rim lands of the continent (cf. pp. 56–57). In the Malay-Indonesian archipelago, however, the people of the sea and sea nomads known as *Orang Laut* assumed a more important role than anywhere on the mainland or even in the Indian subcontinent. Here they were an exceptionally large proportion of the population and played centrally important roles in the development of naval power and communicative links on which the hegemony of successive Malay-Indonesian states was based – in a zone of otherwise sparse population and settlement. Southeast Asia, for this reason, was as much a frontier zone as South Asia.

4   Medieval India and the Rise of Islam

He it is Who hath sent His messenger with the guidance and the
Religion of Truth, that He may cause it to prevail over all religion,
however much the idolaters may be averse.

Qur'ān[1]

In the medieval period, the twofold frontier of mobile wealth, nomadic
and maritime, largely developed under the aegis of a new religious
civilization – that of Islam. This was a militant and expansionist civilization of conquest, proselytization, migration, overseas settlement, and
assimilation by marriage, not just temporary relocation accompanied
by exclusiveness. From the beginning, and unlike preceding ancient or
coeval medieval civilizations, Islam had global aspirations to supersede
everything that went before it, recognized no boundaries, and fostered
the unrestrained mobility of people and goods.[2] Emerging from the barren yet strategically best situated parts of the great arid zone, the Arabs,
making use of the camel, succeeded in linking the Mediterranean and
the Indian Ocean in a single economic exchange network that came to
dominate all important maritime and caravan trade routes, with the
exception only of the northern silk route and one major trade center,
Byzantium. The Arabs' unique ability to mobilize men and goods in
their first great expansionist surge was matched by the monetary capacity they derived from the systematic exploitation of all known sources
of gold and silver.[3] Gold seized from the Sasanid palaces of Persia, the
Byzantine churches and monasteries of Syria, and the Pharaonic tombs
of Egypt – as well as booty and newly minted gold and silver obtained
from locations as far afield as the Sudan (West Africa), the Caucasus,
Armenia, the Ponto-Caspian steppe, Central Asia and Tibet, Sofala,
Nubia, and northern Ethiopia – was brought into circulation in a new
and unified Islamic currency system based on the gold dinar and the
silver dirham that set the standard for world trade. Between the Iberian
Peninsula and the Indus, the development of the institutions of the
early Islamic world – from its extensive system of trade routes to its

fiscal system and modes of government – reflected, above all, the over-riding importance of its cash nexus, the free circulation (*rawāj*) of pre-cious metals, and the mercantilist preoccupation with mobile wealth.[4]

What the Arabs called *al-Hind*, or medieval India, remained largely outside that world. The Arabs conquered large parts of the "frontier of al-Hind" (*thaghr al-Hind*) in the seventh, eighth, and ninth centu-ries but were unable to mobilize the military resources and manpower needed to extend Islamic dominion beyond the Indus. In the end, only the barren and thinly inhabited Makran coast and Baluchistan, Sind, Zamindawar, Kabul, and Zabul were incorporated in the Umayyad Caliphate (661–750) and the early Abbasid Caliphate (750–c. 1000). Beyond this frontier of early Arab conquest, the Indo-Islamic world was largely the making of the Turks and their contemporaries in the subsequent centuries.

The Beginning of the Days of the Turks

The eleventh-century Khwarazmian polymath Abu Rayhan al-Biruni (973–1048), in his *Kitāb al-Hind*, or "Book of India," dates the begin-ning of "the days of the Turks" (*'ayyām at-Turk*) from "the time when they seized power in Ghazna under the Samani dynasty, and sover-eignty fell to Nasir ad-Daula Sabuktigin."[5]

Nasir ad-Daula Sabuktigin was a Turkish slave officer of the Samani dynasty (819–1005) of Khurasan and Mā warā' an-nahr ("What is beyond the river [Amu Darya]," the ancient Transoxania) who, in the year 977, broke away from its overlordship and then founded his own dynasty – the Ghaznavids (977–1186) – at Ghazna, in what is now eastern Afghanistan. Between 977 and 1030, Sabuktigin and his son Mahmud went on to extend Ghaznavid power as far afield as western Persia and the Ganges plain and, at the latter's death, left the most extensive empire the eastern Islamic world had seen since the frag-mentation of the Abbasid Caliphate. This was the beginning of the Turkish millennium in Islamic history. From the Ghaznavids onward, it was principally the ruling dynasties of Turkish and – a largely spuri-ous distinction – Turko-Mongol origin that shaped the destiny of the Islamic world.

The Ghaznavids, in effect, became the first truly Indo-Islamic dynasty to straddle the divide between the nomadic realm of the arid zone and the settled Indian river plains.[6] In the armies of the Ghaznavids that invaded India, the numerically most important ethnic component was that of Turkish horsemen of nomadic origin, the mounted archers. Next to them in number were smaller contingents of other ethnic groups of nomadic or, more broadly, arid zone origin. These groups included Afghans, "Khalaj Turks of the low-lying deserts," Arabs of Khurasan (a semi-nomadic, horse-riding population of Arabs that came from Basra to Khurasan in the first century of Islam), Dailamis (infantry from the Caspian mountains), and "Indians" from unspecified areas (most likely from the Indus frontier) – many if not most of whom were, at least nominally, recent converts to Islam, so-called new Muslims or what we might call "military converts."[7] Neither the Turks nor any of the other ethnic groups then arriving in India were practicing nomads. They all were essentially mobile but post-nomadic military recruits in armies built around a small core of elite slave soldiers (*mamluks*) obtained from within the vast realm of the Ghaznavid empire or beyond. These Ghaznavid armies were massive in comparison with the small, overextended Arab armies that conquered the Indus borderlands three centuries earlier. The number of horsemen in the Ghaznavid armies ran in the thousands (not the usual hundreds of the Arabs) at the very least, and, with the large numbers of irregulars (living on plunder) included, often reached into the tens of thousands. They were highly mobile over long distances and, until the second half of the twelfth century, always returned from their annual jihad raids into the subcontinent to their eponymous capital of Ghazna. In 1163, the rival Guzz Turks, retiring before the Qarlugh Turkmans from the north, ousted the reigning Ghaznavid Sultan Khusrau Malik from Ghazna and surrounding territories and forced him to shift his capital to Lahore, in the Panjab. The Guzz Turks were still nomads when they spread out in some of the districts along the lower route from Ghazna to Lahore, most notably in Sanquran and Karman, in an area where pastoral nomadism had always existed.[8] These were real nomadic inroads, but they remained exceptional and confined to a small area until the arrival of the Mongols in the thirteenth century. The pattern of twelfth-century Ghaznavid-Turkish invasions remained one of fast-moving armies of horse-mounted archers under slave officer (mamluk) leadership conducting lightning raids sometimes deep into "infidel" country and then returning to the home base of Lahore in the west. The impact of these invasions was manifold and varied over time, and nomadization was not part of it. In the Panjab in the early eleventh century, existing political networks were severely disrupted, and there was an exodus of Brahmans to Kashmir, while in 1033 a severe famine and epidemic raged "between Isfahan and Hindustan" that appears to have been at least partly the result of incessant warfare and raiding by the Ghaznavid armies over several decades and was the cause of significant, even catastrophic, population losses in some areas.

The number of enslaved captives taken out of the subcontinent during the Ghaznavid conquests was very high, and, for all we know, much higher than during the Arab conquests. Amid the slaughter and pillage of wealth accompanying the continuing raids outside the Panjab, there was a good deal of iconoclastic destruction of Hindu temples. Severely damaging as the early Turkish invasions often were, however, there was no permanent disruption of the deeper fabric of society over broad contiguous areas as would have resulted from a genuinely nomadic conquest and a major influx of nomads accompanying these military and plunder endeavors. There was no attempt to convert agricultural land into pasture for horses. Overall, the demographic losses and shifts were small in proportion to the enduringly large settled population of these areas.

The Sultans of Delhi

The Ghaznavids were succeeded by the Shansabanis of Ghur, or "Ghurids" (1186–1206), the "Slave Kings" (1206–1290), the Khalajis (1290–1320), the Tughluqs (1320–1414), the Sayyids (1414–1451), and the Lodi Afghans (1451–1526). These were the medieval dynasties – without exception of Turkish origin or with numerically decisive Turkish or Turko-Mongol militaries – that understood it to be their historic mission to extend and consolidate Islamic rule in India and made Delhi their capital. They are known as the Sultans of Delhi.

Their capital city of Delhi was the key to their dominion in India because it was ecologically situated in a broad transitional area between the arid zone of Rajasthan and the west and the more humid settled zone to the east, so that, in effect, the decisive battles for the control of the Indian plains were all fought in the wastes facing Delhi to the west, in the medieval and the early modern periods alike (Tarain 1191, 1192; Panipat 1526, 1556, 1761).[9] Historians of the time aligned the rule of the Sultans of Delhi with an idealized and universal history of Islam, which was interpreted as a religion of empire, and extolled Islamic ideals of religious and political authority and the concept of jihad above all others (Figure 4.1).[10]

Releasing the vast wealth of plundered and destroyed Hindu temples and the treasure obtained through tribute levies from subjugated Hindu rulers into an expanding money economy, the medieval Indo-Islamic states of the Sultans of Delhi exhibited a capacity to mobilize land revenue and commercial resources far exceeding that of their Hindu predecessors but did not set out to convert the "infidels" whose "idols" they attacked. The changes they effected were not primarily

Figure 4.1 Verses of the Qur'ān on the Qutub Minar (completed 1197), Delhi. Majority World/Universal Images Group via Getty Images.

intended to be religious. Perhaps most fundamentally, the Sultans of Delhi, in the course of the medieval centuries, put the Indian subcontinent through a horse warrior revolution, driving out or marginalizing the use of war elephants. Administered by post-nomadic, polyethnic military elites of Turks, Mongols, and Afghans without formal criteria of admission – many of slave origin or recent military converts to Islam, "new Muslims," and as yet without formal ranking systems and permanent hierarchies of offices – the medieval Indo-Islamic states inherited horsemanship and mounted warfare from the nomadic steppe tradition of the Turks. They also adopted the institution of an absolute, dynastic monarchy. This institution now took on its Indo-Persian trappings and acquired some kind of Islamic sanction but continued to be in a condition of flux and volatility, with dynastic succession in constant jeopardy. The worst disruptions were caused by immigrant Mongols and dissident fringe groups of Mongols such as the Nögödaris, the Jurmā'īs, and the Qarā'ūnas. Substantial numbers of these groups were eager to take up military service under the Sultans of Delhi and convert to Islam but remained a badly assimilated element in the Indo-Islamic body politic because of their unsubdued predatory inclinations, the rapidity of their uncontrolled movements, and their extraordinary cruelty and general lack of discipline. But the

post-nomadic polities of the Sultans of Delhi always were characterized by a very high degree of militarization and disruption everywhere,
even in the absence of such groups.

Politically, these Indo-Islamic states revolved around strife and sedition (*fitna*) and ad hoc contests of strength among competing horse
warrior elites, and for a long time they had few formal and enduring features that can be regarded as characteristic of an emerging but distinctive Indo-Islamic form of dominion in a religious sense. This situation
changed only gradually when Muslim scholars, jurists, and theologians
began coming in from the lands devastated by the Mongols in the thirteenth and fourteenth centuries. These new immigrants were absorbed
by the ruling elites of the medieval Indo-Islamic states as fugitive sed-
entaries rather than nomads. It was largely as a result of this influx
of Muslim literati, 'ulamā', and shaykhs that the Sultanate of Delhi
obtained a more formal Islamic character and received legitimation
from the Caliph of Baghdad in 1228. From around that time onward,
the sanctification of a new Indo-Islamic homeland proceeded apace.
More mosques were now beginning to be erected (often still from the
rubble of destroyed Hindu temples), Islamic prayer was introduced by
cadres of religious clergy, Islamic law was beginning to be dispatched
in towns and cities by jurists, madrasas or theological seminaries were
founded, and by the first decades of the fourteenth century the dynastic
fortunes of the Sultans of Delhi came to be closely associated with the
homegrown Sufi order of the Chishtis. Increasingly in the fourteenth
century, and especially after the great Turko-Mongol warlord Amir
Timur ("Tamerlane") raided and sacked Delhi in 1398, the Sultans of
Delhi had to cede power to a number of provincial Indo-Islamic successor dynasties. These dynasties had more regional constituencies, but
they were not essentially different from the Sultans of Delhi in their
basic characteristics. Muslims remained a significant but very small
minority almost everywhere. Moreover, outside the small elite of literati
of mostly immigrant fugitives and their descendants in enclaves wide
apart, Islam was the religion of a military and ruling elite of nomadic,
mostly Turko-Mongol, origin without a literate religious tradition and
elaborately organized religious hierarchy of its own; nomads produced
none of the great world religions and only adopted them. But we know
little about the actual religious commitments and attitudes, as well as
practices, of these "new Muslims" of the Indo-Islamic community in
the making. It can safely be assumed that the "new Muslims" were and
remained almost all illiterate, and their understanding of Islam was
not primarily a scriptural one – inevitably deficient in many ways or
of a very basic kind – but this would not necessarily have come at the

cost of commitment or religious fervor. Islamic attitudes appear to have fluctuated widely.

It is striking, however, that among the Indo-Islamic rulers and ruling elites of these centuries, we generally find an overwhelmingly worldly orientation even if they were literate. Muhammad bin Tughluq (1324–1351), for instance, was by all accounts the most accomplished ruler of his time for his knowledge of Arabic and Persian literature, philosophy, history, and science, as well as for his handwriting and composition, but he had no interest in "holy books" and was openly scornful of the religious clergy, putting political expediency before divine law to enhance the royal dignity.[11] ʿAlāʾ ad-Din Khalaji (1296–1316), by contrast, could not read or write, knew little of Islam, and frequently resorted to the most barbaric tortures and executions and on this account had a deserved reputation for cruelty but, according to Ibn Battuta, came to be regarded as "one of the best of Sultans … whom the *ahl al-Hind* praise a lot" because of the way he maintained order.[12] By the same token, Jalal ad-Din Khalaji (1290–1296) was actually condemned by his nobles when, appealing to the Sharia, he abolished ordeals by fire and the torture of revenue officials, while releasing thugs from prison instead of depriving them of sight.[13]

It was certainly not the case that Islam regulated the minutiae of daily life for many rulers or for the Muslim community at large. The Islamic prohibition against wine and other intoxicants was commonly violated, often openly. If some rulers implemented draconian measures to enforce this prohibition, it appears to have been most often (although not always) for political reasons, since wine was one of the main triggers of sedition. In flagrant violation of the Sharia, the nobles often devoted much time to large, cosmopolitan harems, with women extracted from "all nations" or demanded as tribute from subjugated Hindu rulers, in numbers running into the hundreds and thousands. Harem politics and matrimonial alliance building were decisive where religious policies were not. Most medieval Indo-Islamic rulers, committed to the view that those whose authority was not feared were despised, resorted to methods of intimidation that would not be condoned by the Sharia. Some of the most brutal and ghastly tortures, such as flaying alive and impaling, appear to have been phased out, or at least disappeared from the record, from Firuz Shah Tughluq's reign (1351–1388) onward. The latter ruler carved regulations on a mosque in Firuzabad that announced the end of the practice of mutilating prisoners, Hindu or Muslim, and other forms of torture. Many forms of mutilation and brutal punishment, however, remained common throughout the medieval subcontinent.

It is at the same time undeniable that, in these early "days of the Turks," a sense of belonging to a Muslim community was taking root in India. The medieval Indo-Islamic chronicles do express strong sentiments that Muslims, because of their adherence to the true religion, were to be treated differently from nonbelievers and that in fact the whole purpose of the imperial endeavor was to make the world safe for Islam, which was also presented as a civilizing mission of sorts. The result was a theory of dual citizenship. It was deemed contrary to the law of Islam and against humanity to invade without reason a country already ruled by Muslims, or for a Muslim ruler to shed the blood of Muslims without reason, or for Muslims to conduct wars among themselves. The learned opinion of "death or Islam" for the pagan Hindus was never meant to be translated into practice, but the Hindus had to be made *kharājguzār*, "revenue paying," by threat and humiliation, their "idols" destroyed – and these aims were diligently pursued. Even if forced conversion was not normally condoned by the Indo-Islamic dynasties and was rarely practiced, the distinction between Muslims and "infidels" is always emphasized in the literature as the most fundamental among mankind.

It was the Ghurids who laid the foundation of Indo-Islamic imperial dominion across the northern plains in the twelfth century. This foundation was later extended, deepened, and consolidated in innumerable and regionally varying ways, but what stands out over the long term everywhere is that it retained its essentially post-nomadic character under all subsequent medieval dynasties. The immediate successors of the Ghaznavids, the twelfth-century dynasty of the Ghurids, originally came from Ghur – the almost inaccessible, arid, and mountainous center of what is now Afghanistan, and they were not Turkish nomads but instead of sedentary Tajik origin.[14] The Ghurids absorbed the Guzz Turks and other nomadic peoples from principalities neighboring or nearby Ghur in their dominion of the second half of the twelfth century, and this is what allowed them to break out of their narrow mountainous confines. It was from Ghazna and the adjacent Guzz-occupied areas to the east of it that the Ghurids initiated the conquest of India. At first, almost all of the Ghurid cavalry was recruited from among the Guzz Turks, to a minor extent from the Seljuq Turks (who had made the Abbasid capital of Baghdad the seat of power of their nomadic empire in 1055), the misnamed "Khalaj Turks" of the Garmsir and Zamindawar, Afghans, and Tajiks, as well as the Damghanis of northern Persia. In the later twelfth century, however, the expanding Ghurid dominion came under the leadership of Turkish elite slaves (mamluks) purchased much farther afield, in such remote areas as the Qipchak steppe (the Dasht-i-Qipchaq, north of the Black Sea and the Caucasus, subsequently the steppe of the Golden Horde), and more and more Turks were recruited in their armies. Like the Turkish recruits of the preceding Ghaznavids, these Turks of the Ghurid armies were no longer practicing nomads when they broke through to Multan, Peshawar, Sialkot, Lahore, then into Sind as far as Debal and the Makran, and, after 1192, into the northern plains and ultimately, in the early years of the thirteenth century, into Awadh, Bihar, and Bengal. As with the Ghaznavids, nomadization did not accompany the conquests of the Ghurids anywhere. Furthermore, there is evidence that by the late twelfth century the nature of the conquests was beginning to change and that they became better organized. The roving bands of grain dealers with their bullock trains that later came to be known as Banjaras made their first appearance in Multan at this time and began replacing the marauding bands of irregulars in search of food and plunder. These grain dealers soon turned into the regular supply corps or commissariats that served the seasonal demand for grain of the still ceaselessly moving armies, now less dependent on plunder.

In due course, the Ghurids were almost imperceptibly replaced by their own slave officers, who became known (inaccurately in some cases) as the "Slave Kings" of Delhi between 1206 and 1290.[15] The Turkish slave elite in India of that time was never larger than a few hundred men, possibly considerably less. There was a core of "forty Turkish slaves" (*chihil banda' turk*) – the essential power base of the thirteenth-century Delhi Sultanate – with the majority coming from the Qipchak steppe, and they shared power with other groups of slave origin, more specifically Indian Muslims and Habshis (Africans), but mostly freeborn Turks and other immigrants from Persia, Khurasan, and Māwarā' an-nahr, as well as thousands of "new Muslim" Mongols (especially after 1260), next to unconverted Indians, Afghans, and the Khalaj tribesmen – the latter of whom ultimately supplanted the Turkish Slave Kings by establishing their own dynasty.

Coming after a long period of Turkish rule, the accession to power of the Khalajis provoked a legitimacy crisis even though they had been part of the Turkish dispensation, and built on it.[16] The background of this crisis was the controversial ethnic identity of the Khalajis. Arab geographers identified them as "Khalaj Turks" who were pastoral nomads of eastern Afghanistan living on both sides of the Helmand River in an area called Khalaj, their original eponymous homeland, where they appear to have converted to Islam long before the thirteenth century. Later historians have sometimes presented the founder of the Khalaji dynasty of Delhi as a descendant of Qalij Khan, vulgarly called

Khalij Khan, the son-in-law of Chingiz Khan, but this genealogy is entirely spurious. To be sure, the Khalaj moved beyond their early habitat on the Helmand River during the great Mongol upheavals of the thirteenth and fourteenth centuries, and they then became mixed up with the other nomadic populations of a much wider region. Charles Masson, in the early nineteenth century, writes that by his time they were "exceedingly numerous" to the east of Ghazna, in the province of Zurmat, and he also found them between Kandahar and Ghazna, as well as between Farrah and Herat and between Kabul and Jalalabad.[17] The generally reliable Masson describes them as "a great Turki tribe" and "a mixed race," observing that the Khalajis were both an agricultural and a pastoral nomadic people dwelling in villages and castles as well as in tents, that they were "'wealthy in flocks," and that some of them assimilated with the Ghilzai Afghans and adopted Pashtu. In fact, the Khalajis of the thirteenth century were probably ethnic remnants of the earlier nomadic Shaka, Kushana, and Hephthalite invaders that were to some extent Turkicized, but the problem was that at that time they were not perceived as Turks or Mongols. Contemporary historians clearly distinguish the Khalajis from the Turks. These historians describe the Khalajis as a distinctive ethnic population that became participants in the Ghaznavid and Ghurid campaigns in Hind, and they highlight how one Khalaji officer, Muhammad bin Bakhtyar, established a short-lived and pseudo-independent Khalaji principality in Bengal between 1204 and 1227, within the orbit of the dominion of the Slave Kings of Delhi. They also insist that, in general, the Khalajis had been undistinguished and had produced no royal dynasties until Firuz Khalaji, the later Jalal ad-Din, became the founder of the Khalaji dynasty of Delhi. From then on, throughout its thirty-year career, the Khalaji dynasty of Delhi massively promoted its fellow Khalaji tribesmen, particularly family members, while promoting Afghans as well. The dynasty became best known for the exploits by 'Alā' ad-Din Khalaji (1296–1316) against the Rajputs of Chitor, for subjugating Hindustan "up to the sea" and putting in place a more effective revenue collection system that allowed them to deal militarily with the undiminished Mongol attacks on the Indus frontier. Mongol pressure was also deflected by the dynasty's heavy recruitment of Mongol military converts, "new Muslims," who proved however very fickle in their loyalties and prone to apostasy. Many went back "to their own country," as the climate did not agree with them. Yet some four thousand of these "new Muslim" Mongol recruits stayed on in Delhi, with their families, and more of them continued to operate in tumans, or military units of ten thousand, in these years throughout the expanding Khalaji empire of Delhi, as far south as the Coromandel coast. In addition, the Khalaji dynasty relied on a heterogeneous following of obscure pastoral origin outside the subcontinent, and in their drive to the south relied above all on Indian mamluks and eunuchs, who were given key positions. The latter were not necessarily converts to Islam at all, proved even more unreliable than the "new Muslims," and in the end brought about the undoing of the dynasty.

Like the Khalajis, the succeeding dynasty of the Tughluqs (1320–1414) had a typically nomadic origin.[18] Its founder, Ghiyath ad-Din Tughluq (1320–1325), is variously described by near-contemporary authors as "a nomad (*āwāra marde*) who arrived in the reign of Jalal ad-Din Khalaji (1290–1296)," as one of two brothers who came "from the country of Khurasan to Delhi" in the reign of ʿAlāʾ ad-Din Khalaji, or as having come from "among the Turks known as *al-qarāʾūna*, who inhabited the mountains between Sind and the country of the Turks." In his rise to the throne, Ghiyath ad-Din Tughluq was supported by his own kinsmen and people from the *iqlīm-i-bālā*, or "upper country": "Guzz, Turks, and Mongols of Rūm [Anatolia] and Rūs...Tajiks from Khurasan of pure stock." His successor, Muhammad bin Tughluq (1325–1351), consolidated previously made territorial gains and extended the conquests to the south, to Bengal and Orissa, and "up to the Sea of Oman," while presiding over an unprecedented expansion of the imperial governing and military apparatus. In Delhi itself, Indian nobles were vastly outnumbered by people denoted as "foreigners" or "Khurasanians," the procurement of which became the sultan's highest priority. Khurasanians were treated with great liberality, which caused resentment among the Indians, but they were not allowed to leave al-Hind, on pain of death. They did not come just from Khurasan but from virtually all parts of the Islamic world: Ghazna, Badakhshan, Samarkand, Bukhara, Tirmidh, Khwarazm, Rum, Khurasan, Iraq, Syria, Egypt, the Maghreb, Yemen, Persia, Granada, and Arabia are mentioned among their homelands. This (in name) Khurasanian immigrant nobility, for its part, was a mere trickle of small groups compared to the "waves" of mountain Afghans and Turkish and Mongol military converts who operated under their own "new amirs" in units of several tumans throughout the empire. To command the garrisons of his enlarged empire, Muhammad bin Tughluq relied on the same people from the "upper country" as the founder of the dynasty, and on the Khalajis, but he also resorted again to the widescale use of elite slaves (mamluks), especially Turkish ones, and to a lesser extent Habshis and Indians as well – none of whom could prevent the beginning of provincial disintegration of the empire. In his recruitment efforts, the Tughluq ruler was eventually outdone by newly emerging provincial dynasties from among the "new amirs" who "sent emissaries to the Turks, Afghans and Khurasanians and recruited them in very great numbers" on their own account. In the south, Madurai briefly became an independent sultanate in 1333, Bengal broke away in 1338 under its own Ilyas Shahi dynasty, and the Deccan seceded in 1348 under the Bahmani dynasty. Further fragmentation occurred under Firuz Shah Tughluq (1351–1388) and his successors, especially after the destruction of Delhi by Timur in 1398.[19] By the late fourteenth century, Delhi had *two* kings residing within its walls, both virtually powerless, and then lost many of its remaining nobles and a large part of its military to the emerging Sharqi or "Eastern" Sultanate (1394–1479). With its capital at Jaunpur, the Sharqi Sultanate became Delhi's greatest rival, embracing Awadh and the Antarved plain south of Delhi, the area between Delhi and Bengal. These so-called Sharqis or "Easterners" took over a large army of Mongols, Afghans, and Tajiks from the Tughluqs, but, in contrast to the Tughluqs, also relied heavily on the Rajputs and innumerable *zamindars*, or "landholders," in many places. The fragmentation of the Delhi Sultanate, meanwhile, proved unstoppable. By the early fourteenth century, other independent or practically independent Indo-Islamic provincial dynasties had emerged not only in Bengal and the Deccan, but also in Kashmir, Sind and Thatta, Gujarat, Malwa, and Khandesh.

Upon the death of the last Tughluq ruler in 1414, Delhi fell from "the dynasty of the Turks" (*az silsila' turkān*) into the hands of the Sayyid dynasty (1414–1451).[20] The founder, Khizr Khan, advanced Sayyid status by claiming descent from the Prophet Muhammad. He is further distinguished by the equally fictitious tradition indicating that he received the sovereignty of Delhi directly from Timur. He did, in fact, rule Delhi in the name of Timur, and, for forty years after the latter's death, his descendants presumed to derive their authority from Timur's son Shah Rukh and occasionally sent tribute to the Timurid capitals of Samarkand and Herat. Khizr Khan effectively ruled over a very small territory around Delhi and, for some of the time, parts of the Panjab and Sind.

The first half of the fifteenth century, however, saw the rise to political and military ascendancy of the Afghans in Delhi.[21] Already Khizr Khan recruited numerous Afghan warlords with large retinues, and by 1440 the Afghans had become the real foundation of the Sayyids' power in Delhi, at a time when they rose to much greater importance in the provinces of Gujarat, Malwa, Bengal, Jaunpur, Multan, the Panjab, and parts of the Doab as well. This was a new departure for the Afghans. In their homeland of the Sulayman mountains, the Afghans had been nomads, and statehood had been aborted by their parochial focus on tribal loyalty and the blood feud. Afghan chiefs were normally no more than first among equals, unwilling to submit to kings, and too proud to tolerate any higher authority above themselves for long. In Hind they had been serving in the military since the Ghaznavids, rising to official positions by the fourteenth century, and many Afghans by that time had converted to Islam. But by the 1440s, they had acquired influence in Delhi through their increasingly important role as intermediaries in the horse trade. The trade in horses from Turan, or Central Asia, was the one way for Afghans to accumulate wealth and one of the few sources of inequality in their pastoral and semi-pastoral society (which was only beginning to sedentarize), since tolls and booty collected in raids were supposed to be divided in equal shares among tribesmen, but not profits made in the trade in horses. When nomadic Afghan tribesmen engaged in the horse trade, discrepancies in wealth could become pronounced, and these did have the potential of breaking down the tribal structure predicated on the kinship of equals. Significantly, the first Afghans to combine nomadism and the horse trade in a major way were the Lodi Afghans living along the trade routes of the Tochi and Gomal valleys, and these included the immediate ancestors of Bahlul Lodi, the founder of the Afghan dynasty that was to rule in Delhi in the second half of the fifteenth century and had frequented Hind for many years. In addition, under pressure from the growing power of the Ghilzai Afghans on the Ghazna plateau, some chiefs of the Lodis had come out of their mountain valleys and, on the banks of the Indus, had taken the opportunity to join Timur, providing him with contingents of horse-mounted warriors as well as supplies of horses for his expedition to Delhi in 1398. They and other Lodis began amassing large numbers of horsemen – as many as twelve thousand – from among their own tribe in the reign of Khizr Khan (1414–1421). With his support group of Lodi tribesmen and another contingent of twenty thousand Afghan, Mongol, and Indian soldiers, Bahlul Lodi then brought the entire Panjab under his sway and emerged as the most powerful noble in Delhi in 1441. He seized the throne in 1451 and proclaimed himself king of "the whole of Hind" (*tamām Hind*). In effect, under the new dynasty of the Lodis, the first Indo-Afghan empire (1451–1526) restored the authority of Delhi over much of the northwestern and northern subcontinent. Bahlul Lodi and, for a while, his successor Sikandar Lodi (1489–1517) still tried to govern this first Indo-Afghan empire as much as possible by maintaining some kind of tribal organization among their supporters, but this became increasingly difficult when non-Afghan elements, both Muslim and non-Muslim, entered the state on different terms. Already Bahlul

Lodi employed nearly twenty thousand Mongols in his service. And by 1479, the Lodis had destroyed the Sharqi Sultanate of Jaunpur by absorbing a large part of its Mongol, Tajik, and Rajput elites. It became clear by the 1490s that tribal sharing arrangements were not going to work in Hind. The challenge was to find a new imperial authority structure that could accommodate not only Afghans but also Mongols and the Hindu Rajputs. Gradually, therefore, a more centralized organization was imposed on the still-prevailing Afghan tribal system under the more absolute monarchical rule of Sikandar Lodi. The latter's son and successor, Ibrahim Lodi (1517–1526), officially abandoned tribal politics altogether in an attempt to make all Afghans subjects and servants of his state by introducing a formal *mansab*, or ranking system, among his Afghan and other supporters. Jealous of the claims to royal privilege of the Lodi Sahukhail clan to which Ibrahim Lodi belonged, the other Afghans then solicited the Timurid ruler Babur to restore their power. But Babur made a clean sweep of the Afghan presence in Delhi. He dispersed them to Bengal, where in due course they established a new Afghan dominion, out of which eventually came the second Indo-Afghan empire of the Surs (1540–1556), with its capital in Delhi again. This empire, in its turn, was absorbed by the Great Mughals – the Turko-Mongol dynasty that came to dominate in later centuries (1526–1540, 1556–1857).[22]

The Provincial Indo-Islamic Dynasties

In addition to the Sharqi dynasty of the "Eastern" Sultanate, a number of other provincial Indo-Islamic dynasties arose in the fourteenth and early fifteenth centuries. As in the Sharqi Sultanate, the ruling elites of these dynasties accommodated Indian converts to Islam and nonconverted Indians, in particular Rajputs, in greater numbers than the Sultans of Delhi themselves. But almost everywhere specifically post-nomadic groups such as the Turks, Mongols, and Afghans, and to a lesser extent the Khalajis, continued to dominate even here. We see this in the provinces of Bengal, Kashmir, Sind and Thatta, Gujarat, and Malwa and Khandesh, as well as the Deccan. What is more, in the provincial Indo-Islamic states with important maritime connections, significant numbers of Habshis were imported from overseas, mostly as slaves, and these could enter the ruling elites and in some cases even create Indo-Islamic dynasties of their own. The Habshis, of whom there were tens of thousands in medieval India, are often simplistically identified as "Abyssinians" or "Ethiopians." However, if they were from Ethiopia at all, they usually came from

Figure 4.2 Bara Sona mosque (completed 1526), Gaur, West Bengal, India. IndiaPictures/Universal Images Group via Getty Images.

tribute-paying subjugated populations on the Ethiopian frontier, and they could come from as far north as the Nubian Desert or from Somalia or from yet other regions of Africa further to the south, such as Zanzibar. It has even been suggested that most of the Habshis of the Deccan and Gujarat actually came from the arid region of present-day Tanzania.[23] In the Deccan, significantly enough, the Habshis were no longer distinguished from the Zanjis – formerly the people of the east coast of Africa and Zanzibar proper – although they were always sharply distinguished from the elite "Khurasanians," even though they were all Muslims. They can all loosely be designated as post-nomadic groups.

Bengal was in the hands of Turks, Khalajis, and other Muslim immigrants from Khurasan (in the broad sense, meaning the entire great arid zone outside the subcontinent) under the independent Ilyas Shahi dynasty between 1338 and 1414.[24]

Later in the fourteenth century and in the fifteenth, Bengali Muslim society expanded significantly through conversion among a newly emerging peasantry when the active part of the Bengal delta shifted eastward and political control passed into the hands of the Indian convert dynasty of Raja Ganesh between 1414 and 1436, and then back to the restored Ilyas Shahi dynasty between 1436 and 1487. From around 1458, the restored Ilyas Shahi dynasty began importing thousands of Habshi slaves for its military and then began to rely on Bengali footmen and eunuchs of local origin as a counterweight to the former group's overweening influence. Yet in 1486, the Habshis were able to seize the throne of Bengal by toppling what remained of the old Turkish ruling elite and its Bengali footmen and eunuchs, ruling at Gaur for seven years as the Purbiya dynasty and dragging Bengal into an orgy of violence. The subsequent Husayn Shahi dynasty between 1494 and 1538 again favored "Muslim amirs of old lineage" – the descendants of Turkish, Khalaji, and other Khurasanian immigrants of an earlier age – many of whom were invited back to the capital, while the Bengali footmen corps were disbanded and many, if not most, of the Habshis expelled to Gujarat and the Deccan (Figure 4.2). Under the new dynasty there was, again, an increase of Indian participation in the government and political life of Bengal. The annexation of parts of Bihar and the influx of disbanded Jaunpur troops that followed the collapse of the Sharqi Sultanate also drove Bengal in this direction, prior to its becoming an Afghan dominion in 1538.

Kashmir was never part of the Sultanate of Delhi and instead ruled by way of its own Indo-Islamic dynasty of the Shah Mirs (1324–1561). The founder of this dynasty was probably either an Afghan warrior from Swat or a Qarā'ūna Turk who rebuilt the kingdom after it had been devastated by nomadic Mongol invasions.[25] Under the iconoclastic Sultan Sikandar Butshikan ("the idol smasher," 1394–1416), Kashmir absorbed a large and rather sudden influx of Muslim fugitives from the territories of Iraq, Khurasan, and Mā warā'an-nahr devastated by Timur. These refugees became known collectively as "the Sayyids" and opened the door to an element of Islamic bigotry in Kashmir that seems to have been largely absent in the Delhi Sultanate and its provincial outgrowths. Most of the peasant population had probably already converted to a demotic version of Islam under the early rulers of the dynasty, but the once-powerful Brahman elites continued to resist. In the persecution of Brahmans, Sultan Sikandar was only outdone by his Brahman minister Suha, who, with the excessive zeal of a convert to Islam – known in Kashmir as "the religion of the Turushkas [Turks]" – drove many Brahmans into fleeing the valley or committing suicide. Sultan Zayn al-'Abidin (1416–1470) subsequently tried to put an end to such "Turushka" oppression, only to be succeeded by Sultans Hasan (1472–1484) and Muhammad Shah (1489–1499), who restored power to the Sayyids – "eager for the kingdom as vultures are for meat" – and reverted to a pattern of intermittent persecution of whatever was left of a nonconverted Brahman population in Kashmir that continued up to the end of the dynasty and beyond.

Sind and Thatta, Gujarat, Malwa, and Khandesh broke away from the Sultanate of Delhi under their own Indo-Islamic dynasties around the turn of the fourteenth century.[26] Sind and Thatta, as well as the Little and Great Rann of Kachchh, came under the rule of the indigenous Sumras and Sammas and their offshoots after the death of Sultan Firuz Shah Tughluq in 1388. They returned briefly to the Sultanate of the Sayyids of Delhi in the early fourteenth century, were intermittently ruled by the Lodi Afghans, and then in 1520 came under the successive Turko-Mongol dynasties of the Arghuns and Tarkhans until the Mughal conquest of 1591.

An independent Sultanate of Gujarat was founded in 1407 by Zafar Khan Muzaffar, a Khatri convert born in Delhi. His Muzaffarid dynasty ruled until the Mughal conquest of 1583 and drew heavily on the exodus of nobles and military personnel from Delhi occasioned by Timur's attack on the city in 1398. Mamluk slaves of a variety of origins also played a significant role in Gujarat in the fifteenth century, as did Habshis, who arrived through Gujarat's seaports. The adjacent Sultanate of Malwa was ruled between 1401 and 1436 by the Ghuris, formerly of Delhi and originally of Ghur, and between 1436 and 1531 by a Khalaji dynasty that relied on a Khalaji following as well as Habshis and by the latter fifteenth century was able to count some 12,000 Afghans and Rajputs among its military. Khandesh, in the Tapti valley to the south of Malwa, came under its own Faruqi dynasty in the fifteenth century, of which we know little more than that Habshis propped it up and that it continued to pay tribute to Gujarat until 1497.

Finally, and more importantly, the independent Bahmani dynasty of the Deccan was founded in 1348 by Zafar Khan, probably an Afghan who broke away from Delhi with the support of Afghan and Mongol "new Muslims," and ruled first from Gulbarga and, after 1425, from Bidar. The Bahmanis pledged allegiance to Timur and came up against the peninsular Hindu kingdoms of Warangal and Vijayanagara, both of which subordinated themselves to the Tughluq dynasty of Delhi. They overthrew Warangal in 1425, at which point the Bahmani Deccan came to follow almost exactly the geographical contours of the central peninsula, and Bidar became their new capital.[27] Even after reaching this maximum extent in 1425, the Bahmani Sultanate was inferior to the great peninsular Hindu kingdom of Vijayanagara in wealth, territory, population, and revenue. But the Bahmanis' continued ability to recruit large contingents of Turko-Mongol mounted archers ("new Muslims") and obtain the largest number of horses from beyond the subcontinent made them militarily superior to Vijayanagara. It was the Hindu dynasty, with its center at Hampi, on the Tungabhadra River, that had to pay tribute and cede daughters to the Bahmanis, not the other way around. In the end, however, due in part to the persistent rivalry with Vijayanagara, the Deccan itself proved to be too large for the Bahmani dynasty and by the final decade of the fifteenth century was partitioned among five successor states: the Imad Shahis of Berar (1490–1574), the Barid Shahis of Bidar (1492–1619), the Adil Shahis of Bijapur (1490–1686), the Nizam Shahis of Ahmadnagar (1491–1633), and the Qutub Shahis of Golkonda (1512–1687). The ruling elites of these states retained broadly the same generic composition. Both the Bahmanis and the five Indo-Islamic successor states of the Deccan distinguished two classes among their politico-military elites. The first included the Dakkanis on the one hand and the Āfāqīs, or Gharībān (i.e., "foreigners"), on the other. Among the first group we find northern immigrants from the Tughluq realm who participated in the founding of the Bahmani state, such as the Afghan and Turko-Mongol "new Muslims"; Arabs whose ancestors had come to the Deccan from about the tenth century onward through its ports; other Muslims, including Hindu converts to Islam; unconverted Hindus, such as the Marathas, who were indigenous to the Deccan; and Habshis, who were from Africa but so numerous and dominant in the Deccan armies as well as the Konkan navies that they came to be regarded as an indigenous Indo-Islamic ethnicity. The second, more elitist class of Āfāqīs or Gharībān were "foreigners" who often originated from or came via the Persian Gulf and from further north around the Caspian Sea and beyond – the same category of people that the fifteenth-century Russian merchant and traveler Nikitin and others referred to as "Khurasanians," which included many Turks. They were nobles, soldiers, merchants, scholars, and literati, as well as religious figures, and they began migrating to the Deccan, mostly via the sea routes, as early as the final decades of the fourteenth century and regarded themselves superior even to the representatives of the Tughluq tradition. Particularly Sultan ʿAlāʾ ad-Din Mujahid Bahmani (1375–1378) was instrumental in recruiting such "Turks and Persians" for his court, while he himself chose to speak Turkish. After him, Sultan Firuz Shah Bahmani (1397–1422) exerted himself in recruiting foreign Muslims and sent ships from Goa and Chaul to fetch them from as many nations as possible. The final break with the Tughluqid tradition came when Warangal was conquered and the capital moved to Bidar under Sultan Ahmad Shah Bahmani (1422–1436). The latter presided over a virtual colonization of the Deccan by Muslim foreigners. Entire armies, in which mounted archers predominated, were recruited from Iraq, Mā warā' an-nahr, Turkistan, and Arabia. Innumerable Mongol officers – among which were two lineal descendants of Chingiz Khan – and Mongol bowmen (*mughal-i-tīrāndāz*) were recruited by both Firuz Shah Bahmani and Ahmad Shah Bahmani. Particularly the latter gave precedence to Mongols over Dakkanis, and not a year went by when he did not recruit Mongol mounted archers, sometimes by the thousands. In the Deccan, the role of "new Muslim" Mongols had been crucial from the beginning and remained so prominent that the name "Mughal" (i.e., Mongol) was sometimes used for all foreign Muslims, including Turkish, Georgian, Circassian, and Qalmuq military slaves (mamluks) and other recruits, as well as "Tartars" (who had a very substantial presence in the Deccan), the thousands of Arabian cavalry, and even the Afghans and Rajputs. These patterns of elite recruitment persisted in the Deccan throughout the fifteenth century.

The Last Hindu Dynasties

Around the turn of the thirteenth century, it was 'Alā' ad-Din Khalaji and his commanders who made the first incursions into the peninsula. Here they came up against four major independent Hindu dynasties of the subcontinent: the Yadavas of Deogir, ruling the western Deccan and the Maratha country as far south as the Krishna River; the Hoysalas of Dvarasamudram, in Karnataka, the country running from the Krishna River to the deep south, between the Kanara coast and Telangana; the Kakatiyas of Warangal, in Telangana ("Tilang"); and the Pandyas of the Tamil country, which included the Coromandel.[28] These dynasties represented patterns of political domination closely resembling those of the emerging Indo-Islamic states to their north. Inscriptions show that they originated in the twelfth and thirteenth centuries in the ecologically marginal arid zone of the interior of the peninsula, where pastoral nomadism (of sheep, goats, and buffalo, rather than horses) was widespread and levels of physical and social mobility not found elsewhere in the peninsula prevailed – comparable to that of the steppe lands, albeit on a much smaller scale. Around the same time that the Ghurids and their Turkish slave officers established the first post-nomadic Indo-Islamic states in the northern plains, the pastoral-nomadic peoples of the upland arid zone of the peninsula increasingly began gaining control over the fertile, densely populated kingdoms of the peninsular plains. Across the peninsula, the new ruling dynasties came out of a relatively nonhierarchical and individualistic society of great dynamism

Figure 4.3 Virupaksha temple in Hampi, Vijayanagara. Aaron Geddes
Photography/Moment Open via Getty Images.

and high-risk tolerance sharply at odds with the conservatism of settled
caste society. Rather than converting to Islam, these dynasties adopted
militant forms of Hindu devotionalism such as Virashaivism.[29] The rise
of the great Hindu empire of Vijayanagara on the ruins of the Kampili
successors of the Hoysalas in the Karnataka in the fourteenth and fifteenth centuries epitomizes the new importance of the arid upland of
the inland southern Deccan and upland Andhra (Figure 4.3).[30]

The Vijayanagara deities typically had the attributes of the fierce
warriors of the pastoral communities of the region, and mobile Telugu
warriors of upland Andhra carried this martial tradition across the peninsula. Furthermore, throughout much of the peninsula the recruitment of large contingents of Turkish and Mongol mounted archers
from the north, which had started among the Hoysalas as early as the
1140s, reached a peak in the fourteenth and fifteenth centuries and was
accompanied by stepped-up imports of horses through the seaports.
An entirely new peninsular imperial order arose – with a horse warrior revolution at its center and new forms of monetization and fiscal-
ism closely resembling those of the medieval Indo-Islamic states of the
Deccan and the north – condemning the older areas of settlement in the
plains to complete subordination. This imperial order of Vijayanagara

in the peninsula perpetuated itself well beyond the middle of the sixteenth century, when it, too, was brought under the aegis of the Islamic
states of the Deccan.

Religious Conversion

The new Indo-Islamic order did not only impose itself through military
conquest by mobile Turko-Mongol and Afghan elites. There was also
conversion. But this is far more difficult to trace. Conversion to Islam
poses what is probably the most intractable problem in Indian history. It
is intractable because it was often far from clear what conversion meant,
because it was partial, and because, except in a few isolated and individual cases, it was a combined process of religious and social transformation that often happened with imperceptible slowness, over the course
of centuries, and as such did not draw much attention from contemporary historians focused on discrete events. We know little about why it
happened. Furthermore, the pre-Islamic heritage of specific population
groups does not offer obvious clues to their later conversion, nor do the
numerous traditions assiduously fostered by Muslims themselves. As
elsewhere in the Islamic world, current traditions among convert as
well as immigrant Muslim populations of India not only tend to oblit-
erate their "infidel" past but routinely advance claims of descent from
the Companions of the Prophet or the early Caliphs, or other claims
of conversion in the earliest centuries of Islamic history and, indeed,
any number of pious lies regarding the rise of Islam among them. Not
only are few of these claims supported by verifiable evidence, but most
of them are demonstrably false. Most of the religious conversion that
happened in India is of a much later date than claimed by the converts
and, like the military conquests, is not associated with the Arab past.

Modern European and Muslim explanations of conversion to Islam
in India have varied widely over time but cannot be dismissed so easily.[31] Prior to the nineteenth century, it was often maintained that
Indian Muslims were all immigrants or descendants of immigrants and
that there had been no conversion to Islam in India itself. Subsequently,
however, it was at times argued that such conversion was forced or the
result of material, fiscal, social, and political incentives (like "military
conversion") or had come about through missionary efforts by charismatic saints. There is at least some evidence for all of these arguments.
But it is often fragmentary evidence.

We thus read sometimes about various forms of pressure, and even
the threat of deadly force, that were deployed to make vanquished or
besieged Hindu rulers or chiefs convert to Islam, commonly with their

families. More rarely we read of fiscal exemptions motivating some Hindus living under the Delhi Sultanate in the fourteenth century to convert to Islam. Some records show how individual conversions to Islam, out of religious conviction, were welcomed at the court. What stands out during much of the medieval period is the conversion of "Hindu infidels" enslaved during military campaigns, especially women and children, although any quantitative assessment in this regard is hazardous. Slaves had to be obtained "among infidels" (*min al-kuffār*) since there was a prohibition against enslaving Muslims – a prohibition that was enforced, albeit imperfectly. An unknown but significant number of Indian slaves were taken out of the subcontinent throughout the medieval centuries (Timur still carried off great numbers of enslaved Indian captives to his capital of Samarkand), but it is recorded that within the medieval Indo-Islamic world there were numerous specialized markets (*bāzār-i-burda*) where such captive slaves were sold. By all accounts, slavery was ubiquitous in a variety of contexts (military as well as domestic), and there can equally be no doubt that it increased dramatically under the Turks.[32] The recorded (but not necessarily accurate) numbers are staggering: there were allegedly twelve thousand slaves at the court of Muhammad bin Tughluq alone, no fewer than one hundred eighty thousand in the entire Delhi Sultanate under Firuz Shah Tughluq, and sixty or seventy thousand captives from Vijayanagara, mostly women, in the Bahmani empire. Such figures are scattered throughout much of the written historical record. How many of such slaves or captives converted to Islam is not explicitly stated, but there are indications that conversion occurred in this context. It is stated, for instance, that of Muhammad bin Tughluq's slave girls, "many knew the Qur'ān by heart." Of Firuz Shah Tughluq it is said that during his forty-year reign he ordered all of his military fief holders (*iqtā'dārs*) to collect slaves wherever they were at war and send them to his court, where, we are told, many learned to read, some entered into religious studies, memorizing the Qur'ān, and some even went on pilgrimage to Mecca, while they were employed in all sorts of occupations and married off to each other and often sent back into the provinces. At times, village chiefs and headmen "were torn from their old lands" and carried off to Delhi; here they were converted, with their wives and children.[33] When Timur conquered Sarsatti, "all infidel Hindus were slain, their wives and children made prisoners ... [and] the soldiers then returned, bringing with them several thousand Hindu women and children who became Muslims, and repeated the creed."[34] If this indeed happened on a large scale, as seems to be the case, the conclusion can only be that the high degree of militarization of the post-nomadic empires of the medieval Indo-Islamic world was a significant factor in the conversion of Indians to Islam. This may well have been a more important factor than the proselytizing efforts of charismatic Muslim saints. But the two channels probably complemented each other.

It has proven equally difficult to explain a striking peculiarity of the demography of mass conversion to Islam in India, which is that the largest numbers of Muslim converts are found in the rural peripheries of the subcontinent. To explain this peculiarity, today the most widely invoked theory of mass conversion in India is one that relates it to the sedentarization of mobile populations. This theory is largely derived from observations of the historical development of rural Islam in east Bengal (now Bangladesh) and the western Panjab, as well as in the Afghan tribal lands. Here conversion to Islam is linked with processes of agricultural sedentarization of mobile or unsettled groups such as forest people and pastoralists on the peripheries of the Indian subcontinent who were not much influenced by Hinduism. This theory is not entirely new, and there are modern European and Muslim antecedents of it in the literature of the nineteenth and twentieth centuries. In its most elaborated form, however, it is above all associated with the name of Richard M. Eaton, an American scholar who relates it to notions of the "frontier" reminiscent of those advanced by Frederick Jackson Turner and the Wisconsin school of American history, in a forceful attempt to refute the earlier European explanations deemed Orientalist.[35] Eaton speaks of the theory of "the religion of the plough": "Much more in keeping with the geography and chronology of Muslim conversions in India," he summarizes, "would be an understanding of mass conversion as a process whereby preliterate peoples on the ecological and political frontier of an expanding agrarian society became absorbed into the religious ideology of that society."[36] According to Eaton, it was not caste Hindus who most readily converted to Islam, but nonagrarian pastoral and forest peoples whose contact with Brahmanism and caste had been perfunctory at best and who were becoming integrated into a sedentary agrarian society. In the frontier regions, Islam was more a "religion of the plough" than a "religion of the sword." In East Bengal, this came about when nonagrarian forest people were becoming integrated into an agrarian society emerging in the wake of the eastward shift of the Ganges River system and converted to Islam in the context of expanding Muslim rule in the area. The proliferation of rural mosques indicates that this process was well under way in the fifteenth century and gained further momentum in the sixteenth and seventeenth centuries. This process of Islamization, in Eaton's view, was fundamentally the same as what happened (somewhat earlier) among the pastoral population in the western Panjab and Sind. While most, indeed almost all, of the evidence for it derives from East Bengal, the theory of Islam as a "religion of the plough" applies, in his view, to both the eastern and western peripheries. And it is, like the earlier explanations, a theory that cannot be easily dismissed. As opposed to some of the earlier theories of religious conversion, this one has the merit that it relates religious change to broader processes of social and economic transformation. It also serves as a corrective to the view that Islam is necessarily a religion of military elites or the inhabitants of cities by calling attention to the fact that in the Indo-Islamic world the majority of Muslims were rural people living in East Bengal and the Indus borderlands. Its major drawback remains that it is largely a theory designed to fit the evidence from East Bengal. It has a good deal of validity there. As will be seen in the following discussion, however, the sedentarization or "religion of the plough" theory of Islam does not work for the Indus borderlands. The reasons that the vast majority of the inhabitants of those lands converted to Islam have nothing to do with sedentarization as such.

The Rise of Islam in the Indus Borderlands

The Indus borderlands comprised six different parts: Baluchistan, Sind, the Afghan tribal areas and Kabul, Kafiristan (the later Nuristan), the western Panjab, and, to the east and south of the northernmost curve of the Indus River, the Kashmir valley and its surrounding mountain zone. With the exception of about half of the Afghan tribal lands, which are now part of Afghanistan, and the valley of Kashmir, which is part of India, the Indus borderlands are broadly coterminous with Pakistan minus Lahore. Their population is almost entirely Muslim today and numbers well over two hundred million.

Since they largely belonged to the great arid zone and were mostly desert or mountainous, however, the Indus borderlands were historically among the least populated geographical spaces of India. The British census of 1911 estimated the population of the entire area of what is now Pakistan at no more than nineteen million, a tenth of today's. At the time of British annexation – between 1820 and 1850 – it was no more than approximately twelve million. As Masson observed at the time, "entire marches may be made in the country without a solitary human being presenting himself to the observation of the traveller."[37] The further we go back in time, the more these lands offered a spectacle of desolation. Comparing his own observations with those made by Babur in the *Baburnama* in the early sixteenth century, Masson concludes that "there is nothing more evident from all Babur's details than the fact, that the countries of Kabul, Nangarhar, Laghman, & c. were in his days *infinitely less populous* than they are at present" (my emphasis).[38] In the absence of any earlier observations, let alone statistics, we can speculate that the Indus borderlands probably had a population of no more than a few million on the eve of the Mongol conquests.

Thinly inhabited, the Indus borderlands boasted few important historical towns and cities at any time. As we have seen (pp. 11–15), urbanization was precocious in the Indus valley but disrupted. Urbanization cannot have been the driving force of Islamization here. There were no cities with an ancient past, and none that became centers of Islamic culture over extended periods of time. What cities and towns the British found here in the first half of the nineteenth century were mostly Hindu-dominated bazaar and banking centers, and these were generally small, of recent origin, and short-lived to boot. There were no towns or cities that played or could have played a major role in the religious transformation – the conversion to Islam – of the largely rural and pastoral Indus borderlands. Admittedly, in their overwhelmingly rural aspect, the Indus borderlands were similar to East Bengal, but the two regions were different in other, fundamental respects. In East Bengal, an almost entirely new peasant society was created at a very late date (indeed, later than anywhere else in the region) when the Ganges River system shifted eastward into a forested area where there had been little or no agricultural settlement before, whereas the Indus borderlands were the site of the earliest and most precocious agricultural development in the whole of India (cf. pp. 30–31). In the Indus borderlands, in short, sedentarization preceded Islamization by millennia.

What is more, key agricultural parts of these peripheral borderlands were not lightly Hinduized but, rather, deeply integrated into a religious and social framework of medieval Hinduism that was in no way fundamentally different from that of the heartlands of Indian culture for centuries prior to their conversion. It is only in the geographically remote and almost-inaccessible mountains of the Hindu Kush which were called Kafiristan ("Land of infidels") that, until the late nineteenth century, we find a tribal culture with an ill-defined mixture of polytheism and animism and without a written language and much internal differentiation (although possessing an economy of sedentary agriculture) that perpetuated itself over many centuries in virtual immunity from the traditions of the surrounding Indo-Persian and Hellenic worlds. Ironically, Kafiristan converted last.[39] Centered on the Kabul River valley to the south of it, by contrast, Greater Gandhara was closely associated with Shiva in the early medieval period, and ever-larger monumental stone temples were built on a Greater Gandharan foundation that housed Buddhist, Jain, and Shaivite images of worship simultaneously; these stood like towers along the ridges of the escarpments and plateau of the Salt Range, between the Indus and the Jhelum Rivers on the southern Potwar tableland in the western Panjab and in the Kishor range of hills along the west bank of the Indus. The agricultural valley of Kashmir, with some of the earliest, truly massive stone temples in the subcontinent, like Martanda, was the special refuge of Brahmans and a core area of medieval Hinduism. Sind comprised an area on both sides of the Indus much further to the north and west than modern Sind today, including Multan and much of the western Panjab as well as varying portions of the rocky uplands adjoining Baluchistan and the sand hills of the Thar, and developed a composite religious culture of both Persian-Zoroastrian and Hindu-Buddhist elements throughout this area. Hiuen Tsang in the seventh century CE describes in detail the distribution of hundreds of Buddhist monasteries and an equal number of Hindu temples in Sind. There is written evidence, as mentioned before (pp. 42), of the migration of tens of thousands of Brahmans to Sind in the one or one-and-a-half centuries prior to the Arab conquest, as well as the widespread influence of Brahman priests and officials in Sind at a time when it was to become politically subordinate to Kashmir.

Finally, the sedentarization theory of Islamic conversion does not work in the Indus borderlands because, outside their settled parts, there continued to be, at least until the dawn of the twentieth century, important groups of nomadic pastoralists, including many Jats, who never sedentarized but who did convert to Islam and had a more-than-nominal commitment to Islam. In this regard, the Indus borderlands were no different from other parts of the arid zone with nomadic convert populations that may have been unorthodox and nonscriptural but not necessarily less committed – indeed, not uncommonly more so.

In effect, the historical and religious transformation that occurred in the Indus borderlands finds its closest parallel not in East Bengal, but rather in medieval Anatolia and parts of the Persian plateau. In all three cases, an existing religious culture and society unraveled under the impact of protracted nomadic conquest and migration, and the widespread destruction of the old preceded the conversion to the new.

In medieval Anatolia, according to Speros Vryonis, Jr., the invasions and raids of the Turks and similar nomadic groups like the Turkmans over more than four centuries played a crucial role in its evolution.[40] As Vryonis put it, "the impact of this nomadic-pastoral society, which was at the height of its heroic age, upon the stability of the highly developed sedentary society of the Byzantine Christians was one of the principal factors in the cultural transformation of Asia Minor [Anatolia]."[41] What mattered in the evolution of Anatolia were "the repeated shocks and dislocations" it suffered at the hands of its mostly nomadic conquerors over a protracted period of centuries; these undermined the foundations of Byzantine society and its dominant Christian ecclesiastical structure and paved the way for its subsequent Islamization.[42] The Turkish conquest of Anatolia, in other words, was a genuine nomadic conquest, the final completion of which, resulting in settlement and political unification, was not achieved until four centuries after the battle of Manzikert (1071). The towns and villages of Anatolia were besieged, conquered in piecemeal fashion, and raided innumerable times. In this regard, "the Turkish subjugation of Asia Minor [Anatolia] differed from the Arab conquest of the eastern Byzantine provinces in the seventh century wherein the regions of Syria, Palestine, and Egypt... fell rapidly and definitively to the Arabs in less than a decade, the issue having been decided by a few key battles."[43] What set the Turkish conquest apart was the great number of nomadic tribesmen – often accompanied by women, children, and livestock – who were involved in the armies at war.

Similarly, the Persian plateau was exposed for over a century to the conquests of still-pagan Mongols, who brought along very large and genuinely nomadic military forces – of which the rank and file were Turkish – with their women and children in tow, as well as large herds of horses (at least two or three for each soldier) and enormous numbers of sheep and sometimes other animals to sustain the throng of people during their extensive migratory movements. The devastation wrought by the Mongols in Persia during numerous incursions and two major invasions – the first led by Chingiz Khan in 1219 and the second by his grandson Hülegü in the 1250s – and continuing after the establishment of the Muslim Ilkhanate was unprecedented in scale and horror.[44] In Khurasan, entire cities, such as Balkh, Herat, and Nishapur, were left depopulated, with their inhabitants either killed or dispersed as fugitives. Another significant consequence of the Mongol invasions and the occupation of the Persian plateau was the disruption of the equilibrium between settled and nomadic populations due to the large influx of new nomads and the concomitant decline of the settled population in rural areas as well as in the cities and towns. Much of the agricultural land was now turned over to pasture. Persia's demography was deeply affected by these nomadic conquests. The two processes, of mass killing and dispersal on the one hand and of nomadic immigration on the other, radically altered the ethnic composition of Persia and its subsequent religious evolution.

At the easternmost end of the Persian plateau, the Indus borderlands followed broadly the same pattern of historical development as
Anatolia and much of Persia. These areas had retained the substance
of their Hindu-Buddhist and Persian-Zoroastrian identity under the
three centuries of Arab conquest and occupation. The Arab conquest had been swift and was not accompanied by major migrations
of nomads, resulting in the military occupation of a number of towns
and some control of the countryside but no major demographic dislocations. There is no evidence of any extensive Islamization or conversion to Islam of the native Hindu-Buddhist population under the
Arabs. Whatever evidence we have points to the contrary. A Persian
geographical work of 982 CE confirms that the Baluchi nomads of the
hot pastoral deserts between Kirman and the Indus were all Muslims
(they had converted to the faith even before their arrival from Persia)
but claims that in Sind only the Arab capital of Mansura had "Muslim
inhabitants."[45] The earliest Turkish raids and conquests under the
Ghaznavids in the late tenth and eleventh/twelfth centuries resulted
in more significant demographic dislocations, especially in the western Panjab, but these too were restricted. Like the subsequent military endeavors of the Ghurids and their Turkish slave generals in the
twelfth and thirteenth centuries, these were post-nomadic rather than
nomadic conquests. There was some conversion to Islam among some
specific populations in these centuries, but it was mostly sporadic. In
short, when the Mongol nomadic hordes began pouring into the Indus
borderlands in the thirteenth century, they came to a region of the subcontinent that had been under Muslim rule for more than half a millennium but where as yet no significant conversion to Islam had occurred.
However, the social breakdown resulting from the incessant Mongol
warfare, raiding, and nomadic migration that occurred throughout the
thirteenth and fourteenth centuries was far worse than that resulting
from the relatively quick conquests that, at an earlier stage, had led
to the establishment of the Ghaznavid and Ghurid dynasties across
much of the northern subcontinent. It is equally significant that the
Mongol nomads did not penetrate anywhere beyond the Indus borderlands – at least not often and not for long. For ecological reasons,
Mongol nomads could not sustain themselves in these other parts of
the subcontinent. And correspondingly, there was no destruction of
the deeper fabric of Indian society in these parts, and subsequently no
mass conversion to Islam.

It is well documented that Mongol expansion into the Indus borderlands between 1221 and 1398 was extremely destructive.[46] "Surging
like the sea," in the words of Amir Khusrau, sprawling hordes of

warlike nomads, incessantly in search of pasture for their innumerable horses and accompanied by sheep, poured into the Indus borderlands everywhere – the valley of Kashmir included – and effectively turned them, like so much of the Persian plateau, into an extension of Central Asia. Amir Khusrau observed firsthand from Multan the Mongols who came "from Khurasan in serried ranks like storks, with owlish wings and ominous faces." He describes them as clad in cotton, wearing caps of sheepskin on their shaven heads, and having steel-like bodies, faces like fire with narrow piercing eyes, flat noses, broad nostrils, long mouths, sullen cheeks, overgrown moustaches and scanty beards, bodies covered with lice, skin rough as leather, and (a fair indication of their paganism) "devouring dogs and pigs with their nasty teeth."[47] The only part of the Indus borderlands that the Mongols did not overrun was Kafiristan, which is inaccessible for horses (Timur led a largely unsuccessful expedition into this area). Everywhere else, much of the agricultural land was reduced to grassland pasture, and a scene of almost continuous warfare and devastation ensued, which lasted for almost two centuries and decimated the already-sparse populations. These nomadic invasions undermined and destroyed the very basis of the social order and completely delegitimated and dismantled the existing religious infrastructure. They thus proved to be a turning point in the historical development of the Indus borderlands. What is more, they set off a widespread and general migration and dispersal of tribal populations of nomadic Mongols, Turks, Afghans, and Baluchis, among others, over wide areas, that did not really subside until as late as the sixteenth century.[48] It is under these conditions that the gradual conversion to Islam began to take place.

What stands out in the early sources is that the two core agricultural areas of Sind and the southern Panjab – the one around Multan in the north and the other around Mansura in the south – were among the areas that suffered the worst fate. Multan was in the path of many, if not most, Mongol invaders from the beginning and was intermittently attacked, its agricultural districts laid waste repeatedly, by Mongol nomads throughout the thirteenth, fourteenth, and even early fifteenth centuries.[49] Chingiz Khan first appeared on the Indus in 1221 and detached the military commander or noyan Turti with two tumans of horsemen for the pursuit of the Khwarazm Shah, while he himself did not cross the river and instead moved westward against Kalat – which, if tradition can be relied on, he left in desolation. The entire Multan region was plundered and left devastated by Turti in 1224, before he was forced to abandon it on account of the excessive heat of the summer and return to Ghazna (a city that the Mongols seem to have occupied or ruled indirectly through the Kurats of Herat, a dynasty of Shansabani Tajik Ghurids, until Timur brought it into submission in 1383). Later, after Chingiz Khan's death in 1227, the Indus borderlands became part of the patrimony of his son Chaghatay; he and another son, Ogedai, who succeeded Chingiz Khan as the Great Khan of the Mongol empire, continuously ravaged Multan and the southern Panjab for many years (Chaghatay himself spent a winter in Kalanjar). Two decades later, there still appear to have been almost annual raids on Multan, throughout Sind, and in the western Panjab, and there were still large-scale invasions occurring in the area. Another notorious Mongol noyan, "the accursed Manguta" of Indo-Persian sources, led a vast horde of Mongol nomads from the borders of Talqan and Qunduz into Sind in 1245, laying waste the city of Uch, as well as the entire country of Mansura, over a period of two years. In 1258 yet another huge army of Mongols raided Multan and again the nearby city of Uch; on that occasion, again, according to the historian ʿIsāmī, "the [defending] troops [of the Sultan of Delhi] forti-fied themselves in every fortress and cried for help against the violent raids of those accursed invaders, while the whole area, including the countryside, was overrun and the peasant holdings were ruined."[50] A Mongol shahna, or "governor," was then imposed on Multan and Sind, and he dismantled the defenses of the citadel of the city but evacuated it again soon afterward. Still, it was in 1285 when Amir Khusrau wrote from Multan that the Mongols coming from Khurasan "imparted a new splendor to the dust of the city *each year*" (my emphasis).[51] We get glimpses of bands of Mongol nomads marauding in the Multan area as late as 1423, 1430, and 1433.

In addition to these invaders who followed the Multan route, Mongol nomads frequently passed through the extreme northern Panjab fol-lowing the caravan route from Ghazna to Lahore through the Binban and Koh-i-Jud areas (which included Kurraman). These strategically well-located areas belonged to two successive Qarlugh Turkish warlords who were left behind there by the Khwarazm Shah in 1221 and alter-nately pledged allegiance to and served the Mongols and the Sultans of Delhi, sometimes both simultaneously. Most of the time they joined in Mongol raids in the Panjab and Sind undertaken from the north, until they were supplanted in 1266 by the Mongols themselves and their ter-ritories came to be ruled directly by the Khanate of the Chaghatays. Still entirely nomadic and surrounded by their more powerful cous-ins, and having consolidated their power in Ghazna, Kabul, Kandahar, and Afghanistan and then having seized Binban and the Koh-i-Jud, the Chaghatays were the Mongol *ulus* that was least assimilated to settled life and could only project its power eastward. In both Binban and the Koh-i-Jud, vast tracts of agricultural land were now turned into pasture to sustain Mongol contingents of "thousands" that kept pouring in from Khurasan. In these parts of the northern Panjab, the Mongol nomads were thus able to acquire strategic control over areas that could serve as a base for incessant raiding of the plains below. In the second half of the thirteenth century, then, these Mongol invasions from the north brought in the nomadic Chaghatays and also notably large bands of free-booting nomadic war bands under a leader called Nögödar, a nephew of Chaghatay, with devastating impact on large areas of the Indus borderlands as far as Lahore and its surrounding *qasbas* and agricultural villages. Variously known as Nögödaris, Jurmāʾīs, or Qarāʾūnas, the origins of these freebooters within the Mongol empire at large are obscure. But they were the most predatory and warlike as well as undisciplined element in the kingdom (cf. p. 75), and they appear to have become especially numerous in the Indus borderlands under the Chaghatays in the final third of the thirteenth century. Many of them crossed over to the Sultans of Delhi, to serve there as ill-assimilated "new Muslims." But very destructive Chaghatay raids in which the Nögödaris played a central role continued well into the second decade of the fourteenth century, when the Mongol bases in Binban and the Koh-i-Jud were at long last destroyed by Ghazi Malik, the future founder of the Tughluq dynasty of Delhi. Around the turn of the thirteenth century, they seem to have affected Sind in particular. Between 1292 and 1316, Mongol hordes crossed the Indus from the north at least eight times, moving into areas as far away as Sind. In those years, they also surrounded and besieged Delhi twice with huge forces but in the end always withdrew from it in great haste, plundering towns and villages, with indiscriminate slaughter all around.

After the Chaghatay occupation of Binban and the Koh-i-Jud was brought to an end late in the second decade of the fourteenth century, some of the largest nomadic invasions were initiated from across the Hindu Kush, and the scale of Mongol invasions appears to have peaked by the third decade of the fourteenth century. These and some of the other invasions were conducted, the sources explain, under the leadership of descendants of Chingiz Khan and other Mongol princes of "Khurasan," "Turkistan," "Mā warāʾ ʿan-nahr," or "Mughalistan." Again, it is striking that these invading Turko-Mongol hordes were recruited from populations that would return to a pastoral lifestyle between invasions. The nomadic hordes, "resembling ants and locusts," were counted in tumans – two or three tumans in this year, ten or fifteen in another, sometimes twenty, and more during the largest nomadic invasion of the Indus borderlands ever undertaken, in 1328 or 1329, under the Chaghatay Khan Tarmashirin, when "the whole area from Siri to the Jud hills became a military camp."[52] Increasingly effective frontier defense by the Sultans of Delhi, and the strengthening of fortifications, combined with the outbreak of internecine warfare among the Chaghatay Mongols of Mā warā' an-nahr, for the most part put an end to such large-scale invasions for the next sixty years – until Timur repeated them for a final time in 1398. Until the 1330s, however, the northern route opened the western Panjab to Mongol nomadic devastation at its worst. Beyond Multan and Lahore, places such as Bhatnair, Sirhind, Dipalpur, and all other parts of the Panjab were exposed to these constant incursions and more incidental large-scale invasions of the Chaghatay Khans and their freebooter allies. It was the Chaghatay Khans who established a more-or-less permanent nomadic presence on the Beas River in the Panjab. And in between their major invasions there was the other evil of violent raids by the local Khokhar tribes of the Salt Range, which had become unhinged in the pervasive turmoil, bringing death and enslavement to countless people. The Sultans of Delhi made intermittent and often-unsuccessful efforts to stop the slaughter and destruction, as well as attempts to repair the damage done to towns and villages alike. Delhi troops were sent to the Beas to keep the Mongols in check and to secure Uch and Multan, but these troops could transfer their allegiance to the Mongols as easily as the Qarlugh rulers had done. Early fourteenth-century letters from the Sultans of Delhi contain orders to meet "the Mongol menace" (*tashwīsh-i-mughal*) in Thatta, Lahore, and elsewhere. Other such letters of that time are preoccupied with restoring peace and prosperity in areas that had suffered from the depredations of the Mongols, in the Panjab and Sind, and punishing people who had helped bring them into the Panjab.[53]

Turko-Mongol nomads devastated not only the outlying territories of the Delhi Sultanate but the valley of Kashmir as well.[54] Although it was surrounded by mountains, Kashmir had always been closely connected with the nomadic world of the steppe lands because it offered excellent grazing opportunities both inside the valley and outside. The early penetration of Kashmir by nomads had been on a relatively small scale, however, and more often than not led to the assimilation of the nomads rather than the destruction of the valley's agriculture. By contrast, the Mongol invasions of the thirteenth and fourteenth centuries were as destructive in Kashmir as they were elsewhere in the Indus borderlands.

The Mongols invaded Kashmir three times in the thirteenth century, and once again in the early fourteenth century. Each time they entered the valley, they not only appropriated lands that were normally used for the grazing of sheep but turned grain-producing fields into pasture for their horses. The first invasion occurred during the reign of King Ramadeva (1212–1235). The Mongol army that conducted it, under the orders of Ogedai but led by the noyan Ukutu, entered Kashmir through the southern route from the Panjab, took over and looted the capital, and appointed a governor, who was not expelled until seven years later. In the time of the Great Khan Möngke (1251–1259), another Mongol army invaded the valley, again from the Panjab, under the noyans Sali and Takudar. Kashmir was again looted, the chief inhabitants of the capital killed, and much of the rest carried away, including women and children, into slavery in Persia. Marco Polo refers to a third Mongol invasion of Kashmir in the thirteenth century, in 1272–1273, under Nögödar, the nephew of Chaghatay, that went through the Mandal pass, which splits off from the Panjshir in Afghanistan, to Bashgal on the outskirts of Kafiristan, and then down the Panjkora valley and through lower Swat and Buner to the Indus near Amb. From there the route led to the Hazara district, the valley of the Jhelum at what is now Muzaffarabad, and then into the valley and through the "gate" at Baramula. In or around 1323, the country was entered, a final time, by a Mongol army of six or seven tumans under Dalacha (Diljū), who was probably a noyan of the Chaghatays again, through Ladakh and the Zojī La pass. Dalacha spent eight months in the valley, burning down its villages and towns, massacring its people, and again selling off numerous of its inhabitants as slaves. Jonaraja wrote that on that occasion "Kashmir became almost like a region before the creation, a vast field with few men, without food, and full of grass."[55]

Amir Timur, the last of the great nomadic conquerors of the Indus borderlands in the Chingisid tradition, began in 1383 by bringing to heel the Kurat dynasty of the Gazna region, while one of his generals destroyed Kalat at the same time.[56] Fifteen years later, he made his notorious raid on Delhi. Using a pass between the Bolan and the Khyber, Timur entered the Indus valley opposite Multan or somewhat to the north. Departing from Mongol practice, he appears to have broken up his army of ninety thousand horsemen in three separate columns in the Panjab, in order to be better able to deal with the problem of provisions. Again, entire towns were ransacked, their populations massacred or dispersed. Reuniting his forces just northwest of Delhi, Timur's forces then looted the city for five days, killing large numbers of "infidel" prisoners here too.[57] With the accumulated booty and captives, he marched back along the Ganges and the foothills of the Himalayas, everywhere leaving chaos and pestilence in his wake. Having come close to losing his army to fatigue and exhaustion, Timur then returned to his capital of Samarkand and bestowed Kandahar, together with Ghazna, Kabul, Kunduz, and Baghlan on his grandson Mirza Pir Muhammad. Upon the latter's death in 1407, Timur's son and successor Sultan Shah Rukh conferred these territories on Pir Muhammad's son Mirza Kaidu, who made Kandahar his capital.

By now the medieval age of nomadic Mongol conquerors was drawing to a close. The Mongol inroads into the Indus borderlands in the early decades of the fifteenth century were relatively minor ones and did not go beyond Lahore. The mid-fifteenth century still witnessed the rise of the Arghuns, a future rival dynasty of the Timurids or Mughals. Tracing its origin through Arghun Khan to Chingiz Khan, the Arghun dynasty attained preeminence among the Mongol tribes in 1451, the year in which Timur's great-grandson and Babur's grandfather, Sultan Abu Sa'id Mirza, ascended the throne in Samarkand. The progenitor of the Arghun dynasty, Zun Zun Misri, started his career under Sultan Abu Sayyid Mirza (1451–1469) and subsequently, in 1479–1480, under Sultan Husayn Bayqara Mirza (1468–1506), a fourth cousin of Babur and ruler of Herat, received the governorship of Ghur and Zamindawar.[58] Here he brought unprecedented numbers of nomadic Nögödari Mongols under his control (*zabt*), together with a great quantity of Hazara Mongols. The latter were yet another nomadic population that is often mentioned together with the Nögödaris and may have been the descendants of a Chaghatay army sent by the Great Khan Möngke to assist his brother Hülegü under the command of Nögödar. At first, they appear to have been all over what is now Afghanistan and the Indus borderlands, but in the end they gravitated, with their sheep and other animals, into an area that was named after them – the Hazarajāt, around Bamiyan, to the west of Kabul, which was, according to some historians, an area that was almost entirely depopulated by Chingiz Khan. Back in the fifteenth century, Zun Zun Misri was elevated to become viceroy of Kandahar, Zamindawar, and Ghur, attaining a position that allowed him to extend his sway still further during the next few years, with the support of his nomadic Nögödari and Hazara Mongols, over the territories of Shal (Quetta), Mastung, and Siwi.[59] It was his younger brother Muhammad Muqim who, toward the end of 1502, installed himself as the ruler of Kabul with the aid of his own Nögödari and Hazara Mongol supporters but was then ousted by Babur in 1504. Taking refuge in Kandahar, the Arghuns were subsequently besieged by Babur several times and ultimately expelled to Sind in 1522. The Arghuns appear to have fled, along with their nomadic Mongol supporters, to their recently acquired possessions on the northwestern marches of the Samma kingdom and from that time until 1543 expanded and consolidated their rule over Sind, to be succeeded by their Tarkhan kinsmen in 1545, who held out until the Mughal conquest of Sind in 1591.

The rise of Islam in the Indus borderlands, then, took place in an age of anxiety that began with the prolonged turmoil and disruption that accompanied the Mongol invasions in the thirteenth century and ended with the subsequent reordering of the entire political structure and recovery within the context of expanding Indo-Islamic states after the Mongols withdrew. Islamization has nothing to do with sedentarization as such, even if many pastoral nomads did sedentarize during these centuries. Islam came to these regions through the institutionalized cult of *pirs*, or saints, also known as "holy men" (and sometimes as Sufis), and the shrines built over their tombs.[60] These pirs took on multiple roles, including that of rebuilders of communities that had been shattered.

The fundamental raison d'être of the pirs and their shrines was religious. It was through them and their rituals that Islam was made accessible to nonliterate peasants and pastoral nomadic tribesmen alike. It was believed that saints enjoyed a closer relationship with God than did common devotees and that the saints' spiritual power and their ability to intercede with God on the devotees' behalf outlasted the saints' mortal lifetime and adhered to their burial places, which became centers of pilgrimage and worship. Over time, saintly charisma became increasingly disassociated from personal piety. Unlike Christian saints (and post-eleventh-century Catholic priests and bishops), most Muslim saints married and had children. Their spiritual power was hereditary and became distributed among all their offspring, with special provisions made for the few who fulfilled religious obligations and became guardians of tombs. Inherited saintliness came to legitimize acquired wealth, including land and social position, with the result that many saints gained almost regal power. As shrines grew wealthy, so did the proliferating saintly families who succeeded the original saints over many generations (Figure 4.4).

On a religious level, the saints were as much sought after for their miraculous and healing powers as for their knowledge of Islam. Visitors to their shrines would ask for a cure for a disease, sons, wealth, or forgiveness of sins. Just like Christian saints, the Muslim saints reputedly performed miracles. At the same time, shrines became centers of an entire medieval mental health industry, where drugs would be used and emotionally troubled people, especially women, could find therapeutic relief. At the *'urs* or annual death pilgrimages and festivals associated

Figure 4.4 Shrine (built 1494) of Bibi Jaiwandi, granddaughter of Sufi saint Jahaniyan Jahangasht (1307–1383), Uch Sharif, Panjab, Pakistan. Nadeem Khawar/Moment via Getty Images.

with the saints' death anniversaries, people would indulge in ecstatic dancing, screaming prayers or demon-induced obscenities or otherwise giving themselves license to temporarily defy the normal rules of social behavior. And the religious managers of Muslim shrines, like Christian ones, abrogated and at the same time perpetuated pagan cults and pantheistic nature worship. Numerous Muslim shrines, or *ziyarats*, in the Indus borderlands are found to have been erected on religious sites that were originally those of the former "idolatrous" inhabitants. Digging up the soil in the precincts of shrines often brought to light large quantities of buried "idols." To a large extent, the Muslim saints replaced the numerous gods of the Hindus, their shrines replaced the temples, and their festivals superseded the old Hindu celebrations.

But, as previously mentioned, the saints were also community builders in a medieval society that had been shattered. The shrines and holy lineages of Muslim saints brought stability and defined rights and entitlements by political arbitration: they evolved into a "hagiarchy" of hereditary saints in a near-anarchic tribal environment.[61] In the arbitration of disputes, the saints could serve as "professional neutrals" because their lineage connected them to the founder of the religion shared by both sides involved in the dispute but excluded them from identification with either party. The innumerable smaller shrines that were built along roads and on hilltops served as demarcation points for pastoral tribes, or they separated the pastoral from the agricultural realm. The saints themselves would mediate disputes between pastoral and agricultural clans or between competing pastoral clans. This was especially important in Sind and the western Panjab, where, in the wake of the Mongol invasions, the social and economic structure changed radically as tribes increasingly settled on the irrigated plains of the Indus valley and more and more land was opened up through the use of the Persian wheel and later by digging artificial canals. Such profound demographic restructuring was accompanied by constant conflicts about land in which the saints played a critical role. Moreover, in these circumstances, visiting and becoming clients or devotees of a shrine resulted in or formalized rights to pass along a route or graze livestock. The saints could also back up their arbitration by the use of force and often went to war with thousands of troops, interceded with rulers, and served as diplomatic envoys. Furthermore, the 'urs festivals promoted peaceful contact between normally hostile or alien tribes and other population groups, because violence was prohibited during the pilgrimage and the pilgrims traveled under the protection of the saints, while the tombs themselves were at all times exempted from tribal violence and were places of *haram*. And during the 'urs there would be extensive trade in marketable goods, while sporting events brought the diverse tribes together within a religiously organized framework. Markets would be held in these conflict-free zones, and the saints thus controlled trade as well. A situation developed in which saints not only played a very important role in political conflict resolution and the control of markets, while providing places of *haram*, but also played a vital role in bridging sectarian divides and, as a consequence, in religious conflict resolution.

It was in these various ways that Muslim saints and their shrines became part of an entirely reconfigured religious landscape throughout the Indus borderlands and became instrumental in the gradual conversion of their inhabitants to Islam. Historical chronicles of the Delhi Sultanate around the mid-fourteenth century begin to describe the rural and pastoral populations in Sind, the western Panjab, Afghanistan, and other parts of the Indus borderlands as Muslims, and we can deduce from the fragmentary information these chronicles provide that conversion to Islam was by then well on its way. Such conversion was, of course, never complete anywhere, or uniform. There were still numerous Zoroastrians in the Kabul *wilayat* in the seventeenth century, while at least a quarter of the population of Sind remained Hindu even as late as the nineteenth century (there are still millions of Hindus there today), and most of the people of Kafiristan did not convert to Islam until under severe pressure by the Iron Amir, Abdur Rahman Khan, in the late nineteenth century. Outside the orbit of the Delhi Sultanate, the conversion to Islam of the greater part of the population of the Kashmir valley was achieved in the reign of the militant Sultan Sikandar Butshikan (1389–1413), who was not averse to the persecution of Brahmans. Saints and their shrines, however, were to become the central elements of religious life everywhere in the Indus borderlands between the thirteenth and sixteenth centuries, and kept proliferating afterward, marginalizing almost everything else that we normally associate with the urban and literate traditions of Islam to a degree found hardly anywhere else in the Islamic world. Early British travelers recorded that along the Indus the shrines were almost innumerable and opined that the people there had abandoned essentially the religion of Islam, and had become the votaries of a new worship, that of shrines. Towns like Rohri, Sehwan, Nasarpur, and Thatta claimed to have *sawa lakh,* or one hundred twenty-five thousand saints, buried in their graveyards, with the Makli Hills near Thatta acquiring the reputation of being the largest necropolis in the Islamic world. Exaggerated as these claims may be, it is probably true that by the end of the eighteenth century it had become almost impossible to travel more than a few miles almost anywhere in the Indus borderlands without coming across the shrine of one saint or another.

It was not until the nineteenth century that reformist movements began to oppose the culture of saints and shrines, their extravagant pageantry, and above all the claims that they were intermediaries between man and God. This happened for the first time in 1826, when Peshawar and the Yusufzai territories became the center of a formidable Islamic challenge to Sikh dominance under Sayyid Ahmad Shah of Rai Bareli (1786–1831). He rallied the Afghans in a jihad against the Sikhs, in an attempt to create an Islamic state with fundamentalist Wahhabite credentials. He was the first of a number of outsiders – of whom Osama bin Laden and Al-Qaida and ISIS were the most recent ones – to migrate to the Indus borderlands from elsewhere and create jihadist movements that were, and still are, sharply at odds with the religious culture of the local saints and their shrines. Contrary to common belief, these agitators are not a throwback to medieval times but instead a modern phenomenon.

Alla Ripa Del Mare Indico

In sharp contrast to the Indian subcontinent, there were no ecological niches for pastoral nomads, let alone those with horses, in the mainland of Southeast Asia or the Malay-Indonesian archipelago. The Mongol campaigns in Southeast Asia, for this reason, were mostly failures. In the 1280s there were brief Mongol incursions into Burma, Vietnam, and Champa, but the principal beneficiaries of these incursions were the Tai (Thai), not the Mongols themselves. In 1292, the Yuan-Mongol emperor of China sent a large expedition to eastern Java, allegedly consisting of a force of twenty thousand soldiers and a thousand Chinese ships. In 1293 this Chinese-Mongol force advanced on Majapahit, the capital of the Lord of Java, who submitted to it in order to secure Mongol aid against the neighboring state of Ko-lang (Singhosari) but turned against it as soon as Ko-lang was defeated, forcing the troops to return to China with heavy losses. The results of this unprecedented military intervention in the archipelago were, thus, largely political. In addition, there is evidence that a type of sailing vessel or junk "such as was made in the land of the Tartars" began to make its appearance in Java in the 1290s, and that, in the long term, diplomatic and commercial relations between Southeast Asia and China remained close. Chinese copper coins, or *picis*, began to drive out Javanese weights or coins entirely starting at around 1300. Mongolian horses were imported to Java, and these continued to be bred on the grasslands of islands like Sumbawa. Other than that, however, Southeast Asia fell outside the orbit of the Turko-Mongol nomadic world, and it did not go through a medieval horse warrior revolution and the accompanying military-fiscalist transformation characteristic of the Indo-Islamic states and their militant Hindu counterparts in the subcontinent. Here the war elephant appears to have retained a much more central role down to early modern times. The late medieval development was characterized by the territorial consolidation of settled states – most importantly Ayudhya – around the Buddhist Sangha, through the north–south segmentation of the mainland, while the archipelago came to be ruled by Hindu Majapahit from the agricultural core lands of Java, the terraced rice fields of the thickly peopled eastern interior of the island.

There was, however, the maritime frontier, which was wide open: an almost endless coastline – with its indented harbors, peninsulas, and vast island archipelagos – along the full length and breadth of the Indian Ocean and its inner seas (cf. pp. 65–70). In the fifteenth century, the first Italians to arrive *alla ripa del Mare Indico*, "on the shore of the Indian Sea," imagined that they would find Christians here and specifically a Christian emperor known as Prester John, whose aid could be mobilized in "extirpating the Sarracenes."[62] The illusion of a Christian India was still alive when the Portuguese navigator Vasco da Gama set foot in Calicut in 1498 and did not die until after the return to Portugal of Cabral in 1501. It was largely left to the successors of these two men to discover that Christians played a merely subordinate role in the trade of India. Instead of a Christian ally, they found an intensely commercial society that had turned the qibla to

Mecca. Prester John was none other than the Christian emperor of Ethiopia and was himself threatened by the rising tide of Islam, his external trade relations and his port towns already mostly in the hands of Muslims. It became apparent that Muslim commercial interests and Muslim power were supreme throughout the late medieval Indian Ocean. The Islamic pilgrimage dominated the traffic of the Red Sea. Most of the revenue of the Mamluk Sultans of Egypt came, in effect, "from the pilgrimage to the Holy Sepulchre and the duties on spice passing through Cairo."[63]

The rise of Islam in the littoral regions and island archipelagos of the Indian Ocean took place in the context of the steadily expanding maritime trade and increased commercial dynamism of the medieval centuries. This was possible because these regions constituted a frontier zone between land and sea that was permeable and served not to separate or isolate but rather to facilitate the exchange of trade goods and precious metals. Littoral regimes were primarily geared to that end. The port towns were normally not favored with much infrastructure and investment but remained primarily relay stations – in other words, transmission points. In social and religious terms, the situation in the port towns was one of an indeterminacy and openness that was largely beyond the pale of the caste hierarchies of settled society. In comparative terms, the "people of the sea" and "sea nomads" that made a living around the Indian Ocean were the counterpart of the Greek "nautical mob" (*nautiko ochlo*) that was instrumental in the partial turning to the sea of Athens in the fifth century BCE, under the leadership of Themistocles. The difference was that in the Indian Ocean they emerged much later and did not play a crucial role until the medieval era – when they converted to Islam. At no time, not even in its medieval heyday, was this maritime population very large in absolute numbers. Like the arid zone, the littoral was sparsely inhabited, and the port towns were remarkably small. At the beginning of the sixteenth century, Jiddah, the port of Mecca, was "a great trading city" but had no more than five thousand inhabitants.[64] Few of the Swahili ports were larger than forty acres, and Kilwa, with its twelve thousand inhabitants, was the largest port of East Africa.[65] Hormuz, "the most debauched place in the world," had a population of about forty thousand and was the largest agglomeration in the Persian Gulf.[66] Muscat, in Oman, had seven thousand inhabitants.[67] Calicut was a city of about fifteen thousand Muslim inhabitants, mostly converted natives of the country.[68] Demak had eight or ten thousand inhabitants and was the largest port of the Javanese and Sundanese pasisir; it could collect some tens of thousands of fighting men from its lands.[69] Samudra-Pasai, after which Sumatra is named, had twenty thousand inhabitants.[70] The number of converts to Islam on the coasts of the Indian Ocean cannot have been more than one or two million at most – quite small in comparison with the unconverted Hindu agricultural population of the hinterlands.

It is important to point out that Arab influence was generally more significant on the coasts than elsewhere in the Indo-Islamic world and, although hard to date, definitely present from the early centuries of Islam. Instead of conquest memorials built by the Turks, on the coasts we have fragmented evidence of a process of slow and peaceful penetration of traders and religious clergy from the Arabian Peninsula and the Persian Gulf, which was followed by local conversion. It is likely that Muslims from the Yemen and the Hadramaut have been settling on the Malabar coast from the beginning of Islam, and it is from about 1200 that the number of emigrants from the southern Arabian Peninsula to many parts of the Indian Ocean littoral – especially South India and, slightly later, the Malay-Indonesian archipelago and East Africa – became significant. This increased flow of Muslim migrants was in all likelihood caused by a shortage of good arable land in both Yemen and Hadramaut – in other words, by the kind of demographic pressure that was likely to be aggravated by the same medieval global-warming process that played a role in the movements of the Turko-Mongol peoples on the pastoral-nomadic frontier (cf. p. 110). The resulting migration movements carried Hadramis to South India after 1200, to East Africa after 1250, and to the Malay-Indonesian archipelago after 1300. Some of the migrants, who bore no arms and generally paid no taxes, were local Sayyids and Sharifs learned in Shafi'i jurisprudence and Islamic theology or members of Sufi *ta'ifas* – and many of these, inevitably, claimed descent from the Prophet Muhammad. As a result of the Hadramis' widespread influence, their ancestral home, the Wadi Hadramaut, gained a reputation for sanctity that attracted students of Islam from the Arab colonies and Arabicized regions of other parts of the Indian Ocean, and this played a role over many centuries in the further Islamization and conversion of the littoral. However, from observations made in later times we know there was an important difference between the so-called *Samudri* Arabs, or "Ocean Arabs," and their compatriots in the Hadramaut. There were no women in India who were born in the Hadramaut or Arabia, and not even any women of mixed blood who received their education in the Hadramaut. It was probably also the case earlier that the members of the overseas communities of Arabs were married either to indigenous women or to the daughters of their compatriots who had never left the country. The consequence of this predicament was that all Samudri Arabs were more or less of mixed blood. Samudri Arab families, therefore, tended to assimilate themselves in several generations into the indigenous populations, in the Indian peninsula as much as in the Malay-Indonesian archipelago. What disappeared first was the Arabic language, then dress, and finally the family name – never the focus on trade and small industries – and this is one reason that Arab influence must be de-emphasized even on the coasts.

Another reason for de-emphasizing such Arab influence must be the marked tendency displayed by many of the great Muslim trading families of the ports of South India and the archipelago in the era of European colonialism – partly as a result of their increased prosperity – to assert a rigorously purist version of Arab Islam that they purportedly derived from their history of direct links with Arabia but was in fact a novel phenomenon. This tendency is fairly universal among Indian Ocean communities but particularly well documented among the Tamil Muslims of the great ports of Kayalpatanam, Kilakarai, and Adirampatanam on the Coromandel coast. These Tamil-speaking coastal Muslims were known as *Ilappai* or "Labbai," a term said to be a corruption of *arabī*. In the nineteenth century, their Maraikkayar shipping elites put ever-more emphasis on their religious, linguistic, and ethnic distinctiveness and became the custodians of a special Islamic port orthodoxy that banned the folk rites and concomitant animal sacrifice of the inland Tamil Muslims, whose knowledge of Arabic was always very limited and who were heavily influenced by Tamil Hinduism. Their opposition to the syncretic, "degenerate" Islam of the converts of the Tamil countryside produced greatly distorted accounts of the foundations of these communities.[71] The Tamil Muslims of the coast revived the tradition that they were the descendants of the earliest Muslim settlers in India, who were Arabian traders in the tenth and eleventh centuries. Like so many of the other coastal Muslims of al-Hind, the coastal Labbai thus stressed their religious heritage of Qur'ānic scholarship, their mosque-oriented observance, and their Shafiʿi legal orientation, as well as direct and early links with Arabia, as opposed to the Islam of the Turko-Mongol and Afghan northerners of Hanafi persuasion, who were deemed much-later converts, and above all as opposed to rural Tamil Muslims. Participating in maritime trade, they have always cherished a tradition of physical mobility, but the reality is that at no time were any of the coastal Labbai really isolated from the beliefs and practices of the wider Hindu society and free from the popular Islam of the Tamil Muslim majority. Quite early, a sacred geography developed that linked Hindu and Muslim sacred sites in a single network. Instead of Arabic, the medium of worship and religious scholarship became the hybrid Arabic-Tamil. The Samudri Arabs, in other words, were never as Arab as they later claimed to be.

What is irrefutable is the correlation between commercial expansion and the rise of Islam everywhere around the Indian Ocean. Among the foreign Muslims coming to East Africa to trade, many were sojourn-ers, and there was also a small number who settled on the coast on a permanent basis. Among the latter, a majority probably came from the Hadramaut.[72] Some of these were Sayyids or Sharifs who married into local ruling elites or founded entirely new Muslim dominions. But the vast majority of Swahili or "coastal" Muslims of East Africa are really a mestizo population of coastal African converts mixed with other Muslim elements from around the Indian Ocean coming not just from the Hadramaut but also from the Yemen, Oman, the Red Sea and the Persian Gulf, Kachchh, Gujarat, Sind, Malabar, and even beyond, from as early as the ninth century but mostly during the great upsurge of trade between the thirteenth and late-fifteenth centuries. Farming and fishing villages of the East African littoral were thus absorbed into complex, multiethnic networks of trading communities in some thirty-seven entrepôts linked by interrelated families of Muslims, of which Kilwa was the most prominent, from the fourteenth century onward – largely on account of the trade in gold they conducted through Sofala to the central Islamic lands and Hind.

Beyond the Hadramaut and the Ra's al-Hadd, at the entrance of the Gulf of Oman and the Persian Gulf, another maritime and coastal con-figuration began – "the kingdom and seignory of Ormuz [Hormuz]" – in what was variously known as the "land of coasts" (*sawāhil*), "the coasts and the islands" (*sawāhil-o-jazāyir*) or "the maritime land" (*nāhiyat-i-daryā*) in the "hot countries" (*garmsīrāt*), or, more rarely, "the passage" (*ma'bar*). This coastal region had reached a significant level of urbaniza-tion already under the Sasanids from the fourth century CE onward but came into real prominence under the Abbasids in the eighth century, after the conquest of Sind, and converted to Islam at an early stage.[73] Hormuz itself was founded in 1300 on the waterless island of Jarun, replacing the city of Old Hormuz on the mainland and becoming one of the "ports of India." In the fourteenth and fifteenth centuries, (New) Hormuz and the "land of coasts" between Ra's al-Hadd and Basra and Abadan found itself under the suzerainty of the Ilkhanids, and later Turko-Mongol khans of the Timurids, the Turkoman Qara-qoyunlu and the Aq-quyunlu, but it was a monarchy in its own right with ori-gins in the southern Arabian peninsula and political ties to the Persian world; with its own army of Turkish, Persian, and Habshi mercenaries; and with trading links to Sind, Gujarat, and the Deccan rather than the

Indian peninsula. The Sunni-Muslim majority of Hormuz tolerated the presence among its numbers of a Sh'ite minority as well as colonies of Indian *"kuffār"* from Gujarat and Sind, provided that they held their cultic gatherings outside the actual town.

The coasts of Gujarat and the Konkan were drawn into the orbit of this interconnected and flourishing Muslim trading network – mostly through Arab Sind – as early as the eighth, ninth, and tenth centuries but lost much of their Arab imprint after the Turkish conquest.[74] In the three centuries preceding the Turkish conquest of Gujarat in 1298, these coasts became studded with colonies of traders from the Arabian Peninsula and the Persian Gulf, but with the increase of trade, they drew in more and more local people through intermarriage and conversion. These coastal Muslim communities came to comprise not merely wealthy Arab and Persian traders and shipowners but all sorts of indigenous people of the sea, including fishermen and menial workers, who converted in quite sizable numbers. As the Portuguese accounts show, converts were proportionally important in all "coastal towns with Moors" of Gujarat, the Konkan, and the Deccan. In particular, the Isma'ili Muslim communities of Bohras and Khojas became more numerous in Gujarat than anywhere else in India, largely through conversion. By the early sixteenth century, then, Kambaya and the many smaller seaports of Gujarat had a mixed population of "Moors and Heathen" (in the Portuguese descriptions) and together constituted an Indo-Islamic thalassocracy, or "maritime empire," that spanned almost the entire Indian Ocean.

Further south, on the Malabar coast of the peninsula, the Muslim population may have reached as much as a fifth of the total population of Malabar by the late fifteenth century.[75] Typically, it consisted of a "creole" element known as *Paradeshis* or "Foreigners," who were either sojourners or permanent residents and were also known among the Portuguese as "Mouros da Meca" (from any part of the Indian Ocean between Cairo and Sumatra and Java), as well as a much larger "mestizo" category of "Mappillas" or "Mouros da Terra," the offspring of Muslims who had intermarried with Malabari low-caste women or other converts and their descendants. Neither category was able to acquire independent political power on the Malabar coast. What is more, their roots are surprisingly obscure (Figure 4.5).

The Muslims of Malabar did not become highly visible until the thirteenth century, when the Hadramaut Arabs began to arrive in numbers. Subsequently, after the fall of Baghdad to the Mongols, the Karimi traders of Cairo began sailing directly to Calicut and there assisted the Samudri Raja, or Zamorin (i.e., the "Ocean King"), in

MOPLAH MOSQUE, MALABAR

Figure 4.5 Mappilla mosque, Malabar, South India. Print Collector/ Hulton Archive via Getty Images.

his rise to dominance. For several centuries prior to that turnaround, all coastal Muslims of Malabar lived in relatively obscure conditions within the fold of Jewish and Christian trading groups. But in the thirteenth century, other Malabari port rulers followed Calicut, allying themselves with Muslim traders from overseas. Malabar then came to consist of a few dozen small port monarchies of more or less the same type. The Zamorin remained the wealthiest of a fractious congeries of these coastal Hindu rulers who all based their power on the control of the pepper and spice trade and had considerable navies but were unable to project their power far inland; on land the Zamorin could only defer to the Vijayanagara emperor. On these coasts, there was also some Chinese involvement prior to the sixteenth century. The Chinese had a factory in Calicut, and the Ming government briefly reduced the Zamorin to tributary status in 1406, but it abandoned the city several decades later for Melaka, after which date the maritime trade of Malabar was almost entirely in the hands of Muslims who were for the most part natives of the country. These might have seized power if the Portuguese had not prevented them in the sixteenth century, but in Malabar the situation always remained that "the king is pagan; the merchants are Moors." The Muslims of Calicut merely had a Muslim governor of their own, and other Malabari Muslims had their own shahbandars or "port authorities" who regulated succession and inheritance. Such Muslim notables maintained close relations with the dominant landholding caste of the Nayars and took part in the royal councils, and they were protected as well as patronized by the Hindu kings. The Mappillas in particular followed Hindu customs in many ways. They found their closest collaborators at the extreme low end of the social scale, among the Moger and Mukkuvan and others who, like them, were people of the sea, mariners and fishermen, performing multiple tasks of ship maintenance and so on. In Malabar, the Mappillas and other Muslim traders and preachers were generally shunned by the high-caste, landowning population, which did not eat with them and denied them access to their houses. Having multiplied through intermarriage with local women and keeping concubines of low caste, the Mappillas were ethnically quite diverse, spoke Malayalam, dressed like Nayars, and adopted matrilineality but continued to stress their Arab roots and their coastal affiliations with other Muslim communities in Arabia, the Persian Gulf, the Coromandel, and the Malay-Indonesian archipelago, who, like them, adhered to the Shafi'i school of Islamic law. Within the wider community of Muslims in Malabar, the hierarchy of social ranks was always determined by the tradition of physical mobility and participation in trade. They shared these characteristics with the other, smaller coastal Muslim communities of South India – notably the Navayats of the Kanara coast and the Ilappai of the Coromandel (who later became known as the Maraikkayar or Kayalar), as well as some Muslim populations of Sri Lanka. All of these coastal Muslims emerged from obscure conditions in the great upsurge of trade in the thirteenth century and largely assimilated with coastal groups at the lower end of the social scale through conversion. Here, too, political subordination to Hindu kings, and even recognition of Vijayanagara authority, remained the norm.

Bengal, by contrast, became a wealthy Indo-Islamic kingdom in its own right, with "wide and thickly peopled lands" and important port towns – Sonargaon and Satgaon being the most important among them – inhabited by the "Moors and Heathen."[76] There were many wealthy Muslim merchants and shipbuilders in the seaports of Bengal, and Parsis as well, dominating the trade with many countries in large and small ships.[77] Barbosa draws attention to the luxurious lifestyle and great wealth of the Muslim mercantile elite of the seaports of Bengal and also to the large number of Bengalis, both men and women, who were found in Melaka, most of them "fishers and sailors" who were "heathen" but converting to Islam on a daily basis "to gain the favour of their rulers."[78] In Bengal, the relationship with political power was therefore reversed. The Muslims lorded it over the Hindus, and in the fifteenth century the Muslims of Bengal, with their vast resources and trading networks, were able to project their political power as far south as Chittagong. They were instrumental in the founding of the port of Mrauk-U on the relatively poor Arakan coast of Burma. In the kingdom of "Berma" itself, according to Barbosa, there were "no Moors therein inasmuch as it has no seaport which they can use for their traffic."[79] Pegu, to the south, by contrast, had three or four ports that were "inhabited as well by Moors as by Heathen who possess it" and had trading links with Melaka, Pulicat, and Kambaya.[80] As in the other states of mainland Southeast Asia, however, the importance of such overseas trading links within the overall agrarian economy of Pegu and Burma should not be exaggerated.[81] None of these states ever abandoned their essentially agrarian underpinnings. Foreign Muslim traders were not "liked" here, not even in Ayudhya (Siam), which conducted more overseas trade, especially with China (in Chinese ships), than any other mainland state and did have a significant Muslim and Chinese presence in its seaports, all the way down to Tenasserim and Phuket. Muslims of these ports were often not permitted to travel inland, let alone settle there permanently, and were not permitted to bear arms. Correspondingly, there was little or no religious conversion here.

Over the course of the fifteenth century, it was Melaka that became the most important seaport and Muslim emporium in the eastern Indian Ocean.[82] Founded by a fugitive prince of Palembang and his retinue of *Orang Laut*, it was located at the narrowest part of the strait between Sumatra and the Malay Peninsula, through which passed almost all the trade between the South China Sea and the Bay of Bengal, and it was at the end of the monsoon from two directions. Melaka's dynasty of kings converted to Islam at the beginning of its rise and boasted "that Melaka was to be made into Mecca."[83] A considerable proportion of Melaka's wealthy traders and "mollahs and priests learned in the sect of Mohammed" came from Samudra-Pasai across the strait – the first and most prestigious but obscure Indonesian coastal state to be

ruled by a convert to Islam more than a century before the founding
of Melaka.[84] The Melakan Sultan Muhammad Iskandar Shah (1414–
1423) was married to the king of Pase's daughter for eight years, "surrounded by mollahs," and apparently converted his entire court.[85] On
their part, his successors insisted on conversion when passing off their
daughters to tributary rulers in the strait, eastern Sumatra, and the
Malay Peninsula, over which they successfully asserted claims of suzerainty. Muslim women in Melaka in general could marry "heathens"
and thus have them convert to Islam. The reverse was also common.
There always remained in Melaka an unconverted population of merchants from China, the Coromandel, and elsewhere – most of them
sojourners – but by 1433 the Chinese scholar Ma Huan reported that
"the king of the country and the people of the country [of Melaka] all
follow the Muslim religion, fasting, doing penance, and chanting litur-
gies."[86] At that time, the Melakan rulers were already making sustained
attempts to speed up the conversion of the coastal people of northern Java by sending religious emissaries, while drawing them more and
more into their commercial orbit. Islamization and commercial growth
went hand in hand with the expansion of Melaka's tributary relations in
its own immediate neighborhood and the recruitment of manpower for
its growing naval forces. Melaka claimed rights over the Riau Daratan,
an amphibious region comprising the watersheds of the four important
river systems of eastern Sumatra – those of the Rokan, the Kampar,
the Siak, and the Indragiri – along with the island of Siantan. The
latter three rivers gave access to the Minangkabau highlands, whose
gold supplies became an important factor in the city's commercial
success. There were regular military campaigns in the Riau Daratan,
and after the middle of the fifteenth century the kings of Kampar and
Indragiri "and the people nearest to them" converted to Islam, while
receiving two daughters of the Melakan king's brother in marriage.
Subsequently, the king of Minangkabau also became a Muslim and
married the sister of the Melakan sultan Mansur Shah. The conversion and tributary subjection of these three kings appear to have gained
the Melakan sultan Muzaffar Shah high praise from the rulers of the
Yemen, Hormuz, Cambay, and Bengal, all of whom sent him congrat-
ulatory messages, bestowed on him the title "Sultan" (which was to
replace "Raja'), and "sent many merchants from their regions to live in
Melaka."[87] Meanwhile, the Riau Daratan, together with the numerous
islands of the Riau-Lingga archipelago, provided the essential naval
strength. The warlike Orang Laut (which included the Suku Galang
pirates) of the four large islands of the Riau-Linga archipelago became
the most important source of naval fighters and rowers to serve, without

pay, under the Lasemana ("admiral") of Melaka when called upon. As an Indian Ocean port, Melaka thus became an important regional trading center for domestic products and also an entrepôt for the exchange of a virtually infinite number of nondomestic products. Having grown strong through the force of expanding commerce, Melaka broke with the Hindu state of Majapahit in Java. Although the early rulers of Melaka had been more than eager to marry into the Javanese landed nobility and send ambassadors to the island with elephants and other gifts, when the Javanese seaports established their independence from Majapahit and, aided by "priests" sent by Melaka, turned to Islam, that relationship came to an end. Melaka also broke with China. Although China's role in the rise of Melaka had been crucial at first, when in 1435 the Ming emperors withdrew from the Indian Ocean, Melaka secured its position as an independent maritime power and no longer needed or asked for Chinese support, even though its trade with China continued to increase throughout the fifteenth century. Melaka remained under the formal sovereignty of Ayudhya, and thus indirectly backed by China, for much longer. Not until 1488 did the Melakan ruler withdraw all allegiance to Ayudhya, refusing even to send ambassadors, and in an ensuing military confrontation "destroyed the Siamese on the open sea." In practical terms, this meant that Melaka was liberated by the sea, decades before the Portuguese conquest of 1511. It then reached its commercial zenith. According to Pires, in the port of Melaka "very often eighty-four languages have been found spoken."[88] There were thousands of Muslim traders ("Moors") from every part of the Indian Ocean, Parsis, Gujaratis, and Chettis, as well as Chinese and local Malay Muslims. Barbosa looked on Melaka as "the richest seaport with the greatest number of wholesale merchants and abundance of shipping and trade that can be found in the whole world."[89]

Melaka was preceded, however, by Samudra-Pasai, the small coastal realm whose kings had been the first to convert and from where "the religion of Islam took its rise" in the Malay-Indonesian archipelago.[90] Muslim traders had been present in colonies in the archipelago both within the orbit of the maritime empire of Shrivijaya, with its capital at Palembang, and beyond for centuries before any conversion to Islam began to occur in the second half of the thirteenth century. On the northeastern coast of Sumatra we find the sites of the earliest Islamic kingdoms in the Indonesian archipelago, at the mouths of a number of short, fast-flowing rivers that descend from the Bukit Barisan. Ports that developed here – like Samudra-Pasai, Langsa, Perlak, Aru, Samalangan, and Pidie (Sigli) – all converted to Islam in the thirteenth and fourteenth centuries, long before Melaka. Samudra-Pasai retained a certain unique distinction among them. The great island of Sumatra, known as "Jawa Minor" prior to its rise, took its name from the city that was named *Samudra*, or "Ocean" in Sanskrit. It is generally accepted that Islam was its major religion for about three decades before its first Muslim ruler died in 1297, but in fact Samudra-Pasai was not the first state in north Sumatra to adopt Islam. All sources agree that Perlak and Aru preceded it by a few years. The city acquired its unique status when it was incorporated into the great Islamic maritime empire of Aceh in the sixteenth century. Under Acehnese government, Samudra-Pasai was a royal domain administered by a "bentara blang kubur," or "superintendent of the distinguished tombs." The tombstones of Pasai (the city's Muslim name), which included those of the first Islamic rulers of the archipelago and dated back to the late thirteenth century, became the object of a royal Acehnese pilgrimage in 1638–1639. Their presence legitimized the sovereignty of Aceh, the gateway to Mecca of the entire archipelago, over Sumatra and the strait.

There can be no doubt that the growth of trade and trading ports provided the initial spur to the Islamization of the Malay-Indonesian archipelago. After the rise of Samudra-Pasai and other ports on the northeast coast of Sumatra – especially during the so-called spice orgy that began in the late fourteenth century (when the world was recovering from the Black Death) and coincided with increased Ming-Chinese involvement in the region – there were other Islamic ports developing, not only on the Malay Peninsula but also on the north coast of Java and beyond. This largely happened within the orbit of the Javanese state of Majapahit ("Bitter Fruit"), established with Mongol aid in the Brantas valley, in "the core lands of Java in the country of Hind (mūl chāwa az bilād-i-hind)," in the last decade of the thirteenth century.[91] Majapahit was both an agrarian and a maritime realm. It was deeply associated with the Javanese wet rice tradition and the old Indian religious tradition of Vishnu and Shiva-Buddha, which it accommodated in a realmwide network of stone and brick temples administered by royal priests. The foundations of Majapahit's maritime hegemony in the archipelago were laid by Kertanagara, the king who in 1275 sent a naval expedition to Jambi Malayu, the Sumatran port that had also been Shrivijaya's first conquest. The conquest of eastern Java began after the new capital of Majapahit was founded in 1292 with the aid of Kublai Khan. It took several decades to secure eastern Java, then Madura, Bali, and ports to the north and east of Java, as far as the southern Philippines and Irian Jaya. Throughout this period, Majapahit maintained a naval force in the ports on Java's north coast, and in the second half of the fourteenth century it exercised significant coercive power as far as Palembang and

Samudra-Pasai and the islands to the east. There were overseas linkages with as many as ninety-eight different places in the archipelago
and, further away, with the Yemen, the Coromandel, and Bengal. As
early as the fourteenth century, such overseas relations could not have
been maintained without at least some Muslim commercial involvement. Some of Majapahit's tributary states had Muslim rulers, including Aru, Perlak, and Samudra-Pasai. Islam gained a foothold at the
court of Majapahit itself by matrimonial connections, particularly with
Champa. Chinese seamen and traders migrated to and colonized local
ports on the northeast coast of Java and blended with the Muslim population, often converting to Islam in large numbers, and were absorbed
in the navies that Majapahit put together to dominate the east. By the
early fifteenth century, Majapahit was a great power across the archipelago in which Muslims had not yet taken over the maritime trade.
But with the continued dramatic increase of overseas trade in the fourteenth and fifteenth centuries, Majapahit's hegemony in Java and the
archipelago was progressively undermined. With its unwieldy peasant
armies recruited through soccage and with relatively small cavalries,
Majapahit's control of agrarian Java had, in fact, always been tenuous.
If Java was a "sponge country" for precious metals, its growing commercial prosperity brought about an increase of monetization on all
levels, giving rise to an ever-more-important class of intermediaries
(tax farmers and the like) who could not be accommodated in the old
agrarian hierarchy and caste order. The rise of Melaka and Ayudhya
and the aggressive overseas policies of Ming China first reduced, then
destroyed the Hindu-Javanese kraton's control of its outer possessions.
In the early fifteenth century, Majapahit lost its ascendancy over the
islands beyond Java; by 1428, it had lost control over the western part of
Java itself; and by the middle of the fifteenth century, the Javanese pasisir, or "coast," had slipped out of its hands. Then, in 1513 or 1514, the
final phase of the conflict between the pasisir and the Hindu-Javanese
state in the interior began. In 1528, a coalition of coastal states, under
the leadership of Demak, forced the Majapahit royal family to flee and
take refuge in Bali – the island to the east of Java that had long been a
dependency of Majapahit. It was the end of the Hindu-Javanese period
in Indonesian history.

   The crucial factor in the decline of Majapahit was the relentless rise
to power of the pasisir states. In the fourteenth and fifteenth centuries, these were converting to Islam one by one and repudiated the
control of the Hindu-Javanese agrarian state. The pasisir was by no
means completely Islamized in the fifteenth century, particularly not
in the Sunda realm of the western part of the island. Pires describes

the realm of Sunda, which he thought took up a little more than a third
of the island, ending at the river Tjimanoek, as a "heathen" state of
chivalrous, seafaring warriors who practiced widow burning and did
not allow Muslims into it, except a few, for fear that they would do
what they had done in the rest of Java and make themselves masters
of the country.[92] By the early sixteenth century, then, the Tjimanoek
River was the western frontier of Islamic expansion on the island of
Java. It was not until the later sixteenth century that large numbers
of Javanese Muslims would move from the pasisir districts of middle
Java to the west and occupy Kapala (which they renamed "Jakarta")
and Bantam, thereby cutting the Sundanese off from the sea. Pires
explains, further, that the powerful Muslim lords ("patis") who had
"all the trade" of the seacoast were actually not Javanese of long standing but mostly descendants of Chinese, Parsi, Kalinga (South Indian),
and other immigrants who were "slaves and merchants a couple of days
ago" and, being socially insecure and nouveaux riches, were even more
proud and boastful than the Javanese nobility of the agrarian interior.[93]
In the fourth decade of the fifteenth century, Ma Huan divided the
population of the pasisir trading cities into three groups: the Muslims
from many countries; the Chinese, many of whom were also Muslims;
and the unconverted Javanese.[94] The Chinese of the Javanese pasisir
thus appear to have become assimilated within the local Muslim population in the way they were in Melaka. Mystic brotherhoods of Sufis
do not appear to have come to Java until after the rise of these communities. In Java, as elsewhere in the Malay-Indonesian archipelago,
Islam was brought by traders and became a political factor in the rapidly rising ports of the pasisir when the scale of the spice trade began to
increase in the later fourteenth century. Java's ports grew rich in part
because the Javanese were involved in this trade with the Moluccas, or
Maluku islands, and used their ports as transshipment points. They
also exported increasing amounts of pepper and rice and other foodstuffs from their own hinterlands. The Chinese played a major role in
this. Javanese traditions reflect the infusion of Chinese blood, wealth,
and technology into the ruling dynasties of the pasisir. The Chinese
presence was much more significant in fifteenth-century Java than in
Sumatra (let alone South India), and since most of the Chinese of Java
converted to Islam, the controversial claim was advanced that Islam
was brought to Java by them. The grandfather of Raden Patah, who
founded Demak in 1477 and ruled until 1519, was probably a Chinese
Muslim trader, although others maintained that he was a slave from
Gresik, the oldest center in East Java to have a Muslim ruler. At the turn
of the sixteenth century, the land of Gamda – possibly at the mouth of the

Kali Brantas River (the southernmost branch of the Brantas delta) – was
still ruled by a Hindu king, a son of the Majapahit ruling house in its
final days, and was the easternmost place reached by the *"orang slam."*[95]
"From here onwards," writes Pires, "there are no Moors except in
the Moluccas, and those of Banda."[96] But, according to a Portuguese
observer who visited Java in the 1540s, Raden Patah's warlike successor Trenggana, who had assumed the title of sultan around 1524 with
authorization from Mecca, four years before destroying the remnants
of Hindu-Majapahit, aimed "to Islamicize all the surrounding peoples,
so that he himself will become another Sultan of Turkey besides whom
[Portuguese] Melaka is nothing."[97]

5   From the Mongols to the Great Mughals

The Great Mogul descends in direct line from Tamerlan, whose suc-
cessours that settled in the Indies, took to themselves the name of
Moguls, that they might be distinguished from those to whom that
Prince left Zagatay, Corassan, Persia, and other countries to be
governed after him. They thought that that name might contribute
much to the glory of their family, because by taking it they would
more easily perswade men that they are of the race of Cinguis Khan,
the first emperor of the ancient Moguls, who had carried it above
twelve ages before them, and who under that title began the greatest
and most powerful empire in the world.

Jean de Thévenot (1666)[1]

When Babur invaded Hindustan in 1526, his major opponents and
rivals were not the Indian landed elite of the Rajputs but instead the
Afghans – other invaders of nomadic origin.[2] The Afghans were a
nomadic and tribal people who became prominent in the context of
the almost worldwide Turko-Mongol expansion in the medieval era, to
emerge by the mid-fifteenth century as the preeminent Indo-Islamic
rulers of the subcontinent. They twice attempted to create an Indo-
Afghan empire – first under the Lodis (1451–1526) and next under the
Surs (1540–1556) – but the Afghans essentially remained tribal in their
organization and failed to develop durable institutions of dynastic kingship and imperial rule. Nothing explains better the uniquely successful
imperialism of the dynasty of the Great Mughals in India than the failure
of the Afghans to overcome their tribal origins in the same arena.

On the Road of Failure: The Afghans in Hind

In the centuries before they began migrating to Hind, the Afghans were
an almost entirely nomadic people – or so it appears, because we actually
do not know much about the earliest origins of the Afghans.[3] The ethnogenesis of the Afghans was an obscure and entangled process that took

place over the early medieval centuries and involved successive waves
of nomadic migrations into and through the original Afghan homeland
on both sides of the Sulayman mountain range, an area to the south of
Kabul. Even the origin of the name *Afghans* is obscure; it is known to the
Afghans only through the medium of the Persian language. Their own
name for themselves was *Pashtuns* or *Pakhtuns*, while in India they have
generally been known as *Pathans* or *Rohillas* – the latter after *Roh*, the
"hill country" of their origin. Not until the later medieval centuries did
their homeland in the Sulayman mountains in the southern part of Roh
become widely known as Afghanistan. That original habitat of medieval
Afghanistan was a (semi) arid and in many places cold country with a
wild assemblage of hills, mountains covered with perennial snow, and
wastes unmarked by enclosures. It was destitute of roads or navigable
rivers and canals, had only a few towns, and was, above all, overwhelmingly poor. This (semi) arid and mountainous region to the west of the
Indus and south of the Hindu Kush contained only a modest amount
of cultivable land but was eminently suitable for pasturing large flocks
of sheep and goats – not horses – and was part of the genuinely pastoral
nomadic "frontier" (*sarhadd*) of the Indus borderlands.

The medieval Afghan inhabitants of this country shared a common
nomadic culture – called *kūchī* or *powinda* – supplemented with rudi-
mentary agriculture, hunting and gathering, highway robbery, and a
long-distance peddling trade between India and Khurasan along the
routes of their annual migrations. They migrated between their summer pastures in the Sulayman mountains and their winter pastures
at lower altitudes in the valleys of the Indus River, the Kabul River,
and the Arghandab, Tarnak, and Arghastan Rivers in the Kandahar
area. Theirs was a fundamentally pastoral-nomadic society in which
kinship was the main organizing principle of tribes – not territory –
and in which there was no place for chiefs or kings. Medieval
Afghanistan was, in other words, not a kingdom. Its tribal customary
law of the *Pashtunwali* valued kinship solidarity above all else. Each
tribe was independent and a complete commonwealth within itself,
consisting of segmentary lineages that were theoretically all descended
from a single ancestor. It was an egalitarian society – a kinship of
equals. Leadership was in the hands of maliks or khans – the natural
elders or heads of lineages and tribes – but effective power and authority rested with *jirgas*, or tribal councils. The saying was that it was the
blessing and the curse of the Afghan tribes that they should always be
free but never united.

Afghan tribes, in effect, failed to develop kingdoms or chieftaincies in
Afghanistan itself until as late as the mid-eighteenth century. The tribes

always cooperated at the lowest level necessary to meet an outside challenge, while tribal alliances remained ad hoc, with tribal confederations continuing to be the exception in Afghan history and disintegrating at the first opportunity. Afghan nomads rarely paid taxes in kind or in services, let alone in cash – not even when they sedentarized. Moreover, the adoption of Islam by the majority of the Afghans in and after the thirteenth century, which predates the sedentarization of some of the tribes, did not fundamentally change their tribal politics and culture. To the contrary, the Afghans retained no memory of a pre-Islamic past and claimed descent from Qais, a Companion of the Prophet and a direct descendant of King Saul, the first king of the Israelites, and thus proclaimed not only their essential identity as a people but having been Muslims from the very beginning of Islam. And not only did Islam never replace the tribal culture, but, insofar as Afghan tribesmen were aware of the precise nature of Islamic piety, many were conscious of being "bad Muslims" and considered upholding their tribal order of higher importance than being "good Muslims." Ostensibly followers of the Abu Hanifa law school, in practice the Afghans did not follow many precepts of the Sharia. They demanded a high bride price, did not allow women to inherit property, refused to intermarry with non-Afghans, killed fellow Muslims, and refused to pay the religious *zakat* ("alms") and *'ushr* ("tithe"). Moreover, Afghan tribesmen generally regarded pirs and religious professionals from outside the tribe as a threat to tribal solidarity because religious loyalties between pirs and murids cut across kinship lines and thus corroded the basic organizing principle of Afghan society.

Similarly, the Afghans' attempts at empire building outside Afghanistan were always thwarted sooner or later by their inability to overcome their tribal organization. Afghans rose to prominence in the medieval Indo-Islamic states, and in Hind there is evidence of some intermarriage between Afghans and Turks, Mongols, Khalaj, and Indians. But it was not until the mid-fifteenth century that an independent Afghan dynasty tried to build an empire of its own. The reason no such attempt was made earlier is that up to that time there were no significant changes in Afghan society that had the potential to undermine its tribal structures. Ultimately, that kind of change could only be brought about by the increase of commercial traffic through Afghan territories. This is where the origins of Indo-Afghan empire building can be found.

In the thirteenth, fourteenth, and fifteenth centuries, in the wake of the late medieval upsurge of trade that followed the Mongol conquests and migrations, Afghan pastoral-nomadic tribesmen became the primary carriers of a huge volume of merchandise of all kinds (textiles, spices, and horses, among many others), operating in caravans of ten, fifteen, or twenty thousand pack animals. They maintained a very extensive trading network. The roads traveled by the Afghan caravans, at about eight to ten miles per twenty-four-hour day, were among the most discouraging imaginable. One lead northward from Kabul through the Panjshir, Parwan, and Ghurband valleys; on to the passes of the Hindu Kush; to Qunduz and Baglan. Another eastward through Nangrahar, the Khyber Pass, and then the Peshawar plain; crossing the Indus at Hazro, almost fifteen miles above Atak, or at Nilab, ten miles below Atak. Or they went through the Logar valley toward Ghazna or Gardiz and through the Gomal, Tochi, and Kurram river valleys, to the Derajat and Bannu. Beyond this mountainous hub, the Afghan trading nomads, with or without their families, reached out to the furthest regions of the subcontinent and went as far as Bihar, Bengal, the Deccan, and Gujarat, whereas in the other direction they traveled to Kandahar, from there as far as Persia, and, with horses and ponies, across the Hindu Kush to Bukhara. The trade as such did not bring any fundamental changes to the Afghans' tribal politics. But the horse trade, like nothing else, gave Afghan trading nomads access to the courts of the Indo-Islamic kings, providing extraordinary influence and privileges and, as importantly, political intelligence and an initiation into a more sophisticated court life that the purely pastoral tribes missed out on. Moreover, when nomadic Afghan tribesmen engaged in the horse trade, discrepancies in wealth could become pronounced, and these did have the potential of breaking down the tribal social structure predicated on the kinship of equals.

It was in this way that the Lodis rose to wealth and power and set out to create the first Indo-Afghan empire in the second half of the fifteenth century. The Lodis still made use, as much as they could, of the tribal organization of their Afghan supporters, but they recognized that in Hind they had to overcome the limitations of this organization at the same time and, under pressure of their non-Afghan supporters in particular, made serious efforts to do so by introducing a monarchical form of centralized government and a formal ranking system of their supporters that was unrelated to the tribal divisions. Yet these efforts were ultimately unsuccessful, and the Lodi empire proved to be short lived; after about seventy years, it seemingly inevitably ran aground on persistent tribalism. No less inevitably, the subsequent history of the Afghans continued to be marred by the same limitations inherent in their tribal organization and provides only some episodes in which similar but equally unsuccessful attempts were made to overcome these limitations. This was the case not only among the Afghans who lived to the west of the Indus, in the properly pastoral-nomadic and tribal belt, but also to the east of the river, in the settled plains of Hind.

Among the expanding population of pastoral-nomadic Afghan tribes to the west of the Indus, those who lost out in the competition for land moved in every direction except south into Baluchi territory. Such migrations of pastoral-nomadic Afghan tribes are in evidence especially during the chaotic conditions, devastations, and misgovernment that accompanied the Mongol-Timurid conquests of the region. Throughout this time, Afghan tribes continued to expand their power in the arid and semiarid subregions of Kandahar and Ghazna. These Afghans maintained their nomadic way of life and in most cases became even more dependent on it. They retained the same tribal organization they had always had and essentially made Kandahar an extension of medieval Afghanistan.

Afghan migration and conquest to the west of the Indus in the northern direction – in the Kabul River basin, the Lamghanat, and the Peshawar subregion – largely took place between the late fourteenth century and 1580 and was not different from their tribal movements elsewhere. For the Afghan nomads, these regions, with their intensively irrigated agriculture in many river valleys, were difficult to penetrate. There were no unclaimed lands here, the limited grazing land that existed was jealously guarded by Turkish and Mongol nomads, and Kabul and the tributary valleys of the Kabul River were well fortified and defended against nomadic attack. The Afghans moved into these northern regions in tribal formations and, encountering stratified agricultural societies of an Indian type, transformed their tribal structure while doing so, but they never abandoned it. In the Kabul River basin and the Peshawar subregion, Afghans again emphatically failed to create an imperial structure that transcended their tribal ties and, in the end, here too lost their independence – to the Mughals. In this subregion, Afghan expansion is above all associated with the reign of the Timurid ruler Ulugh Beg Kabuli (1460–1502) and subsequently with that of his nephew Babur. The latter's concerns with Central Asia and India left the process of Afghan tribal migration and conquest in the Peshawar subregion, especially in the isolated valleys in the north, relatively unchecked. Complicating this picture, Babur pressured many Afghan tribesmen to enlist in his army. In Babur's campaigns against the Lodis, there were Afghans and Hazaras, next to Arabs, Baluchis, Turks, and Mongols. After the defeat of Sultan Ibrahim Lodi in 1526, the Khalil and Mohmand tribes living on both sides of the

road from Kabul to the Indus via the Khyber Pass were generally more
loyal to the Timurids than the Yusufzai tribes who lived to the north of
this road in the isolated valleys of Swat, Bajaur, Panjkorah, and Buner
and often continued to oppose the Timurids from their mountain
fastnesses and fortresses. But between 1526 and 1530, Babur's main
concern was not the Yusufzai Afghans but the suppression of the "one
hundred thousand" Afghans who, after the defeat of the Lodi emperor,
still held out in the region east of Kanauj and the Ganges, seeking to
restore a Lodi to the throne. It was this preoccupation with the "eastern Afghans" that gave a free hand to the Yusufzai in Swat, allowing
them to expand their tribal dominion. And subsequently, after Babur's
death, Afghan tribal expansion and rivalry in the Peshawar subregion
took place within the broader context of the competition for power
in the Kabul Wilayat between Babur's sons and grandsons and the
wider struggle between the Afghans and the Mughals for empire in
Hindustan under Akbar. The northern boundary of Afghan tribal
expansion became the ecological boundary between double and single
cropping at an altitude of about 5,000 feet and was reached by 1580.
The Indus remained the boundary to the east. But, again, this successful expansion – accompanied by sedentarization and changes in
the patterns of transhumance, land use, and settlement – did not lead
to the abandonment anywhere of the Afghan tribal organization in
these northern agricultural regions. It was merely transformed or, as
in Swat, "feudalized." For tribes like the Yusufzai, even when sedentarized, the ideal of kinship solidarity remained vital, as did their
peculiar attachment to a patriarchal form of government, despite the
inadequacies of this situation becoming painfully obvious and later
inducing them, at times, to put themselves under the receivership of
outsiders. It did not allow them to fend off the Mughals in the sixteenth and seventeenth centuries, or the Sikhs in the nineteenth. They
and other Afghans superimposed their tribal society on the preexisting
stratified peasant societies of Lamghanat, the Peshawar area, Swat,
Bajaur, Buner, and Panjkorah by replacing the landholding elites of
these places and integrating their peasant societies into an overarching
tribal structure. Over the centuries this resulted in the peculiar tribal
patron-client or tribal "caste" societies that are still found in the region
today. What prevented the evolution of a state structure in Swat and
Peshawar was a characteristically tribal system of land holding called
wesh. Based on a periodic redistribution of land (itself not of nomadic
origin), this system ensured tribal cohesion throughout the sixteenth
century – and in the Peshawar plains for three and in Swat for as much
as four centuries afterward.

Thus, in all the territories they occupied to the west of the Indus, the Afghans were unable to overcome the limitations of their tribal institutions and did not create states or empires. In Hind, to the east of the Indus, Afghan empire building got under way but was ultimately aborted in the sixteenth century. The empire of the Lodis had already ceased to exist when Babur invaded Hindustan in 1526, leaving many Afghans adrift. "These Afghans," wrote the historian Ahmad Yadgar, "after being absolute rulers for seventy years, left their habitations, their goods, and their wealth behind, and proceeded to Bengal, and [there] they were completely dispersed."[4] One of them, a soldier by the name of Dattu Sarwani who participated in the defeat of the Afghan army, wrote an unique account in which he provides an evocative picture of the tribal hordes of Lodis, Luhanis, Surs, and Niazis, as well as his own Afghan tribe of Sarwanis, moving incessantly across the plains with their women, children, and even some sheep and how they did so in considerable numbers, setting up temporary camping grounds (*maydān-i-bāshish*), while still speaking Pashto among themselves.[5] The symbolism of his account is still entirely pastoral-nomadic. Dattu describes a vision of the world spread out before him that was not one of a city but of a great encampment with many tents on a broad plain – an encampment from which one day one must pack up and go away. The portable darbar tent, or *barga*, was the visible symbol of sovereignty for this Afghan soldier, not the monumental mosques, tombs, fortresses, and caravanserais left behind by the Lodi emperors. And Dattu dreamt of Babur's invasion as a "fierce wind with much dust and darkness from the west." "When I saw that dream," he wrote, "I was very much afraid whether... we would be preserved from that wind of wrath, and I was still awed by this when I learnt... that the wind had descended on account of the weakness of spirit of the Afghans, and that the battle line of the Afghans would be curled up, and that of the Turks stretched out, and there would be a crowding together."[6] When Babur defeated and killed Sultan Ibrahim Lodi and took the province of Delhi, the Afghan tribes "set off towards the east," crossing the river Saru in boats and then going in "whatever direction each thought fit," with Dattu and the Sarwanis moving into Bihar. Dattu's pir and helper appeared in a dream. "Dattu," he said, "you really have cause to worry. Although the Afghans have gathered in great numbers, they are prisoners of the demoralization of their spirits and are not yet firm. Victory is Babur's and the Afghans will be defeated."[7]

What Dattu Sarwani did not know is that there would be a remarkable resurgence of Afghan power soon after he wrote this account. A second and final attempt to transform the Afghan tribal structure into an empire was undertaken by the formidable Sher Shah Sur between 1540 and 1545, after defeating the Mughals in battle in his turn. Determined to overcome the deficiencies of his Lodi predecessors, Sher Shah Sur introduced important changes in the constitution of the Afghan polity, followed by fiscal and revenue reforms, and he might have succeeded in his aim of getting the Mughals out of Hindustan for good if he had not died prematurely from a gunpowder explosion in his own arsenal. As it happened, the Sur empire did not survive Sher Shah for very long, and it, too, fell prey to the customary Afghan tribal disunion, thus creating the conditions for the Mughal reconquest of 1555–1556 under Babur's son and successor Humayun (r. 1530–1556) and grandson Akbar (r. 1556–1605). Under Sher Shah's son and successor Islam Shah (r. 1545–1554) and the latter's own bickering successors, the second Afghan empire, in its turn, quickly unraveled. Ironically, Sher Shah left his important legacy of state-building efforts and administrative measures to his long-term Mughal rivals, not his own fellow Afghan tribesmen.

The events of Sher Shah's reign are narrated by Abbas Khan Sarwani, an Indo-Muslim historian of Afghan origin who wrote around 1580 CE. As a witness to Akbar's success, Abbas Khan Sarwani, like no other historian of his time, was concerned with the historic failure of the Afghans. An almost Gibbonian sense of melancholy pervades the pages of his *Tā'rīkh-i- Sher Shāhī* as it belabors the decline and fall of the Afghan empire.[8] Tracing the origins of their immigration from the earliest centuries, Sarwani begins by observing that the Afghans ruled Hindustan from 1451 to 1555, with an interruption of only fourteen years between 1526 and 1540 during the early conquests of the Mughal emperors Babur and Humayun. Success and failure during this Afghan century, he says, depended on unity and disunity, respectively. The Afghans succeeded in Hindustan under Sultan Bahlul Lodi because they were cooperating and were unified in their endeavors. They lost their empire under Sultan Ibrahim Lodi because of their internal dissensions. According to Sarwani, "the Mughals did not conquer the country from Sultan Ibrahim [Lodi] by the sword but due to the discord of the Afghans (mukhālafat-i-afghānān)."[9] This observation about "discord" among the Afghans – which the author attributes to the great Sher Shah himself – is repeated throughout Sarwani's work. "The Afghans lost the country of Hind on account of their internal strife."[10] "The greatest cause of the defeat of the Afghans has been the disunity in their own army."[11] "We lost every battle against the Mughals because of our disunity."[12] Statements like these culminate in the author's major insight that discord and quarrelsomeness were part of the very temper of the Afghans as a tribal people.[13] It is this theme that sets the stage for the narration of events of Sher Shah Sur's reign.

Sher Shah Sur was exceptional in Afghan history, according to Sarwani, for three reasons: first, because Sher Shah, born Farid and known merely as Sher Khan until 1539, was an exceptional personality, distinguished by greatness from childhood; second, because he was a relatively marginal figure on account of his obscure tribal genealogy and therefore less interested in a potential restoration of Lodi authority and more inclined to overhaul the very fundamentals of the tribal constitution; and third, because Sher Shah was born and raised in Hind and, like most Indo-Afghans, relatively unaware of "Afghan custom" (*rawish-i-afghānī*) and the notions of tribe and clan that informed the sense of honor of the inhabitants of Roh, or, as Sarwani habitually calls them, the "Rohillas." An assimilated Afghan, Sher Shah's genealogy from his mother's side is possibly also a contributing factor. Most Afghan historians hold that his mother was a Sarwani Afghan, but the bardic traditions of Hind surmise that his mother had been a daughter of the Qaimkhani Rajput family of Shekhawat and thus regard him as half Indian.

However that may be, long before he became sultan in 1539, Farid (the later Sher Shah) began his career in the Sahsaram *jagir* ("revenue assignment") of his father, in what are now the Rohtas and Bhojpur districts of southern Bihar, by challenging Afghan tribal sharing arrangements and claiming the inheritance for himself alone. He then entered Babur's service as a soldier. But, while in the Mughal camp, it became Sher Khan's overriding goal and ambition in life to bring together the Afghans and undertake a joint effort to expel the Mughals from Hind and reestablish Afghan rule there. In 1529 he resolutely left the Mughal camp and entered the service of the newly established Luhani Afghan Sultanate of southern Bihar. The following decade, between 1529 and 1539 – which preceded his successful overthrow of Babur's son and successor Humayun – is noteworthy for his dogged and successful pursuit of independent wealth by a series of efforts. These included multiple marriages with wealthy widows of the Luhani and other Afghan clans, to possess himself of the hoarded wealth and treasure of some of the most important remaining amirs of the defunct Lodi Sultanate; the acquisition of booty and spoils in many places, especially Bengal; and even subsidies from the Sultan of Gujarat, who hoped to use him against their common Mughal enemy. Characteristically, Sher Khan did not share these resources with the Luhanis but used them solely to aggrandize himself, recruit men directly into his service, train them, and thus, again, attack the tribal basis of the realm. Everywhere, the powerful Afghan warlords, observing Sher Khan's daily increasing power, "put their pride aside."[14] "Putting aside every bond of friendship and respect for the honor of the Afghans (nāmūs-i-afghānān), they all bowed down without hesitation and delay before his irresistible farman."[15] Fixed salaries, equal opportunity employment, and discipline replaced clan loyalty. By the end of the 1530s, says Abbas Khan Sarwani, "Sher Khan was known for his qualities of generosity and benevolence; throughout the day he was occupied in scattering gold like the sun and shedding pearls like clouds and this was the reason that the Afghans gathered around him and the kingdom of Hind fell into his hands."[16] When Sher Khan became convinced that all Afghans had united with him and were eager to fight the Mughals, he came out of the hills of Rohtas and marched to engage Humayun, routing him at Chausa in 1539, then at Kanauj in 1540. This was when Sher Khan ascended the throne as Sher Shah. Like Bahlul and Sikandar Lodi before him, he did so after overcoming considerable hesitation. He almost had to be dragged to the throne, if we can believe Abbas Khan Sarwani. In fact, however, the flight of the Mughal emperor Humayun left Sher Shah the unchallenged ruler at Agra between 1540 and 1545. During these years his sustained attempt at imperial centralization and military reform went well beyond the measures taken by his Lodi predecessors. Extending his policies of the preceding decade, Sher Shah emphasized hierarchical subordination to and direct employment by the center instead of horizontal linkages with tribal leaders and warlords. A whole new political economy was devised and implemented to recruit, pay, train, and discipline a professional army. Sher Shah had spies everywhere to watch his nobles. The ranking system of mansabs that the Lodis had introduced was again implemented among Sher Shah's nobility, but much more systematically and in combination with more closely audited revenue assignments. Like his Lodi predecessors but even more so, Sher Shah associated himself with Turks and Rajputs in order to expand the non-Afghan base of his empire. Making use of more-or-less powerful non-Afghan middlemen, he recruited substantial contingents among the agrarian gentry of the zamindars and numerous peasant soldiers in his military. These, too, were accommodated within the new Afghan imperial system under his own aggressive leadership. The second Afghan empire, in short, owed little to ethnic and tribal loyalties and segmentary politics but instead was founded on direct recruitment and individual enterprise.

Within five years it all unraveled. Sher Shah was succeeded on the imperial throne by his son Islam Shah in 1545. The son resembled his father in his desire for dominion and conquest and began his reign by bringing the entire country under his personal control by appointing his own men and perpetuating many of his father's civil and military regulations, including the branding system and the mansabs. Like his father, he assembled an immense army, consisting of cavalry, elephant battalions, and possibly as many as sixty large guns. However, having garrisoned the entire country between Kabul and Bengal with his own troops and retainers, he then tried to destroy his father's nobles. Immense opposition resulted, and tribal factionalism and the intemperate Afghan blood feuds and revenge killings resurfaced with a vengeance. An epidemic of bubonic plague ravaged the whole of Hindustan in 1550. Two years later, Islam Shah followed his father to the family grave in Sahsaram. The fall of the second Afghan empire now at hand, immediately after Islam Shah's death, the Sur domains were partitioned among several sons and relatives of Sher Shah. By 1554, three different Friday prayers were read in Hindustan and three kings, openly declaring war on each other, issued their own sikka coinage. This became known as the time of the "kings of the clans." In the ensuing free-for-all, some two hundred aspiring Afghan amirs obtained royal tents, standards, and kettle drums, while any Afghan who brought with him ten or fifteen horsemen was given a makeshift flagstaff with a bit of red rag wrapped around it, with some other dignities and a revenue assignment. Among the old Afghan nobility of Lodi times, extreme demoralization set in, aggravated in 1555 by the outbreak of severe famine conditions (caused by drought) in eastern Hindustan. When Humayun "received intelligence of the dissensions of the [Afghan] nobles, and the partition of the territories of Hind, he felt persuaded that the discordance of the Afghans (nāsāzī' afghānān) would enable him to take easy possession of the country."[17] And thus, as the Mughal historian Badauni put it, "the kingdom fell away from the race of the Afghans and returned to its original holders."[18]

With the Mughals reestablishing their hegemony in Hindustan, a second dispersal of Afghans now occurred that was not unlike the one following the Lodi defeat thirty years earlier. Many Afghans and other men of Roh returned to their ancestral homelands, either to settle down or to resume a nomadic or trading existence. A great variety of Afghan clans profitably turned themselves into zamindars or landlords and agrarian colonizers, in the way the Yusufzai had in Swat and the Peshawar plain. Everywhere in Mughal India during that time we see Afghan colonies of traders-cum-mercenaries spring up along the traditional routes of the horse trade. Perhaps the majority of Afghans, however, retreated eastward again. Bengal, because of its fragmented topography of waterways and forests, was their last best hope. Fighting tenaciously, these second-issue eastern Afghans were driven ever further toward the sea, in a long and checkered confrontation with Mughal imperialism that took up all of Akbar's reign and did not come to an end until the seventh year of Jahangir's reign (1611). Over the course of these decades, many eastern Afghans surrendered and again took up service with the Mughals, as they did with the Sultans of Gujarat or the Deccan or Arakan. But they never regained the upper hand, and Akbar excluded them from the higher ranks of power, while they continued to stand apart from all other ethnic groups. Scattered across the subcontinent, their leaders employed their own tribal followings and maintained a volatile presence everywhere. They continued to speak Pashto and displayed a remarkably strong sense of ethnic identity, remaining ever hopeful for a return to power and perpetually arousing mistrust, even if their support was frequently sought and obtained in the succession struggles of the subsequent Great Mughals. In the seventeenth century, the Afghans did eventually find their rightful place among the Mughal nobility in considerable numbers. Afghan migration to Hind also picked up again, and by the early eighteenth century the Afghans began to assume a role of importance in Persia as well. But the Great Mughal emperors always remained on their guard against a possible revival of Afghan power. On their part, the Afghans hated the Mughals and generally did not intermarry with them.

Beginning in the 1580s, Akbar also stepped up efforts to increase imperial control among the tribal Afghans beyond the Indus River. Because these efforts coincided with the beginning of the second Islamic millennium in the year 1000 AH (1591–1592 CE) and because, in the words of Akbar's court historian Abul Fazl, the Afghans were "on the road of failure," with their imperial prospects in irreversible decline, the Afghan tribes turned to millenarian Islam. The renewed expectations of a new social order and the restoration of piety by a Mahdi, or "Messiah," fueled a tribal insurrection against Mughal imperialism under the leadership of Bayazid Ansari, the *Pīr-i-Roshān* ("Saint of Light"), and his sons and successors. The resulting *Roshānīya* movement did succeed in unifying some of the most important and numerous Afghan tribes against the Mughals, but the resulting unity, again, did not last long. It is doubtful even that Bayazid Ansari's message would have developed mass appeal if it had not, through the exploitation of its millenarian qualities, been turned into the legitimation of an anti-Mughal insurrection. In any case, the demise of the movement in 1632 clearly demonstrated that Afghan tribalism was ineradicable even by millenarian Islam. Afghan imperialism did not revive until the rise of the Durrani dynasty in Afghanistan in the mid-eighteenth century, when the Mughal dynasty was in full decline. Even then, among the

Afghans themselves, the legitimacy of the Durrani empire still derived to a large extent from a compromise with tribal authority on all levels, despite the fact that it was based on different premises everywhere else among the non-Afghan subjugated population.

Origins of the Mughal Dynasty

If Afghan nomads remained wedded to their tribal politics and culture, the Turko-Mongol nomads of the Eurasian steppelands successfully adopted the institutions of dynastic kingship and imperial statehood requisite for overcoming these.[19] In contrast to mountainous Afghanistan, the Eurasian steppelands are a huge flat saucer and provided an ideal environment for horse nomadism, horse-borne warriors, and the emergence of great empires.[20] Paradoxically, this environment facilitated the introduction of a broad range of hierarchical and ranked distinctions among the nomadic horse-breeding Turko-Mongol lineages, clans, and tribes. Such distinctions gave rise to a conception of leadership – unknown among Afghan tribes – that was the hereditary, legitimate, and exclusive prerogative of specific charismatic dynasties. To be sure, violence was often the final arbiter of rightful succession among rival brothers, uncles, and cousins of such dynasties. But there were strict limitations on who could participate in the process of succession: in practice it was confined to the male descendants of the charismatic founder of a steppe empire or a subgroup thereof. At no time was there a formal system of succession, and because the succession process itself tended to be violent and protracted, usually involving war, it held the potential for the dissolution of the empire. Steppe empires, therefore, were inherently unstable. The institution of the corporate dynastic clan, however, was never abandoned and always remained the foundation of Turko-Mongol empires in spite of the constraints and limitations it imposed.

Historians have found traditions of supra-tribal unity among the steppe nomads from ancient times. For long periods afterward, the tribes could again become the largest effective political units on the Eurasian steppes, but the traditions of unity persisted even through such periods.[21] Turko-Mongol tribesmen thought of themselves as belonging to nations, or *ūlūs*, that came into existence at some remote point in their history and could reemerge with a new or old name in supra-tribal polities, confederations, or steppe empires through the efforts of individual aspirants for the office of supra-tribal ruler. However, if notions of the divine origin of ruling clans and historical nomadic confederations or empires are in evidence on the Eurasian steppes from the centuries BCE, in these early centuries the tribes as yet gave up very little of their autonomy.

With the rise of the Turks in the sixth century CE, the authority of the charismatic ruling clan acquired a dimension of absolutism within a much more complex and structured political and administrative system. The tribes as such did not disappear but submerged their tribal identity under the larger political identity of the ruling dynasty. Subsequently, in the tenth century, the Manchurian Khitans transformed the pan nomadic Turk imperial forms into more centralized and absolutist forms of military rule, which were then passed on to the Mongols, the dominant tribe of a federation of tribes of the Mongolian steppes in the twelfth century that was soon to be unified under Chingiz Khan.[22]

Chingiz Khan and his successors thus conducted their military ventures under an order received from Tängri – none other than the deified sky, the supreme sky god of the shamanistic Turk nomads. They ruled as universal sovereigns by their "good fortune" and the power of heaven, absorbing nations that were still de facto outside Mongol control as de jure potential members of a divinely inspired imperial Mongol order in the making and treating those who failed to accept their rule as rebels against that order. Just like the tribal name *Turk*, the tribal name *Mongol*, which became "Mughal" in Persian, was transformed from an ethnonym into a political designation and disseminated throughout the nomadic world, coming to be borne by peoples with no direct ethnic Mongol affiliations.[23]

In practice, Chingiz Khan created his original power base from his personal following and from the household officers he placed at the head of many of the larger units put together under a decimal military organization with which he broke up the tribal structure of the nomads. Subjugated peoples, whether nomadic tribes, city dwellers, or peasants, were enlisted as auxiliary troops under the same decimal system. By such methods, from 1209 onward, Chingiz Khan gained control of an ever-growing population of Turko-Mongol nomads and settled populations in Persia and northern China. He made use of the expertise of Persian and Chinese bureaucrats in his administration and moved numerous individuals and entire population groups, including nomads, thousands of miles from their places of origin. He also stationed Mongol militias under military governors in the cities of all conquered regions and garrisoned the settled regions with separate elite units drawn from a number of different tribes and areas and the whole of his army. In the wake of his early conquests, Chingiz Khan's immediate successors then developed an imperial taxation system that combined traditional Chinese, Islamic, and Turkish systems with levies imposed by the Mongols themselves. In sum, the Mongols under Chingiz Khan and his successors succeeded in creating the largest contiguous land-based empire in human history because of their ability to effectively mobilize and control the free-floating human and material resources of all areas under their dynastic control – not as commanders of tribal armies.[24]

Chingiz Khan also took special measures to deal with the threat of the dissolution of his empire in a war of succession among his sons.[25] At his death in 1227, he divided his empire into four great territories, or *uluses*, which he assigned in hereditary tenure to his four sons, along with parts of the army. To his eldest son, Jochi, and his descendants he assigned the western part of the empire, the southern Russian steppelands of what later became the territory of the Golden Horde. To his second son, Chaghatay, and his descendants he assigned the central part of the empire: Mā warā' an-nahr and Khwarazm; the pastoral realm to the north that became known as Mughalistan; the lands of the Uyghur; Kashgar; and all the lands that constitute modern Afghanistan – Badakhshan, Balkh, Qunduz, Baghlan, Kabul, Kandahar, and Ghazna up to the Indus River. To his third son, Ogedei, and his descendants he assigned the territory east of Lake Balkash (Zungaria). And to his youngest son, Tolui, and his descendants he assigned the original center of his power in Mongolia, along with his personal contingent of a thousand and the greater part of his army. At the same time, Chingiz Khan appointed Ogedei as his own successor as Great Khan of the Mongol Empire as a whole. A war among the princes was thus averted and did not destroy the Mongol Empire after its founder's death. A significant measure of imperial unity was preserved, and everywhere decimal military divisions continued to be maintained instead of tribal ones, even though the tribes continued to exist independently of the empire at the same time. Under Ogedei and the two succeeding Great Khans, Güyüg (d. 1248) and Möngke (d. 1259), the Mongol Empire not only maintained this unity and coherence but kept expanding until it comprised, at least formally, all steppelands from Russia to Mongolia; Persia, Khurasan, the Indus borderlands; and China and Korea as well. In effect, it was in this period between 1227 and 1259 that the Chingisids acquired their unique distinction as the ruling dynasty of most of the known world and established the foundation of a new political culture that came to be shared throughout the steppelands and the neighboring settled lands.[26] This Chingisid tradition of government and legitimacy was founded on Mongol customary law, which included the decrees of Chingiz Khan and was maintained into the nineteenth century – for as long as nomads or former nomads held power anywhere in this vast realm. It was this set of Mongol customary practices and regulations that governed all Mongol successor polities and became known as the Yasa, or, as it was called more often in Mughal India, the *Tora* or "Code" of Chingiz Khan (after the original Turkish customary law of the *Törü*).[27]

By the second half of the thirteenth century, however, the unity of the Mongol Empire could no longer be preserved. When the Great Khan Möngke died in 1259, a belated succession struggle did break out among a number of Chingisid contestants. Chingiz Khan's grandson, the Toluid Kublai Khan, seized control of China, where he founded the new dynasty of the Yuan. Kublai Khan and his successors still claimed the title of Great Khan, but it was recognized only by the Ilkhanids of Persia, an independent Chingisid dynasty created by the descendants of Kublai Khan's brother Hülegü. The other territories also became independent under their own offshoots of the Chingisid dynasty. By 1309 there were again four Chingisid uluses, or great dynastic realms, but in a configuration that was considerably different from the original fourfold division effected by Chingiz Khan. There was the Yuan dynasty in China; the Chaghatay dynasty ruled Mā warā' an-nahr, Khurasan, the Indus borderlands, and Mughalistan; the Ilkhanid dynasty was in power in Persia. And, long independent under the descendants of Jochi, the dynasty of the Golden Horde ruled the western steppe and southern Russia. These four Chingisid uluses of the early fourteenth century were, in practice, quite separate and independent. They were also usually at war with each other.

In all of the uluses, the contact with settled cultures (not sedentarization) brought about the first formal conversion of the pagan Mongols to the religions of their subjects – around the same time. The Ulus Chaghatay, however, stood out because it preserved the pastoral-nomadic pagan traditions of the steppe longer, and to a greater degree, than the other three Chingisid uluses. Although the nomadic tribes of the Ulus Chaghatay shared a common loyalty to the dynasty of Chaghatay, they remained relatively autonomous in a mixed agricultural and pastoral environment, and the Ulus Chaghatay was, as a result, the least centralized of all Mongol dynastic realms, especially in its most unsettled, eastern part of Mughalistan. The Chaghatay Khan Tarmashirin (1326–1334) converted to Islam and pursued an Islamic assimilation policy in an attempt to overcome this situation. Tarmashirin also gave up the customary annual journey of the Chaghatay ruling house to Mughalistan – an ill-calculated breach with "eastern" tradition that deprived the Chaghatay dynasty of much of its legitimacy as nomadic steppe rulers. Unwilling to cede more power to Tarmashirin, the tribes of Mughalistan deposed him.[28] By the mid-fourteenth century it was again tribal chiefs or amirs that controlled the Ulus Chaghatay and had taken back much that had previously been the domain of the central government and of members of the royal Chingisid dynasty of the Chaghatays, although most of these tribal chiefs maintained puppet Chaghatay Khans. Moreover, while the Chaghatay Khans were rapidly losing power to their tribal constituents even in the relatively wealthy and settled parts of their realm in Mā warā᾽ an-nahr, in 1346–1347 the nomadic eastern division of Mughalistan formally seceded under an eastern branch of the Ulus Chaghatay. These latter Khans of Mughalistan ruled the region of the Talas and Chu Rivers, Issyk Kul, the Ili, Ebi Nor, and Manas, a land of moderate altitudes that is invariably described as extremely pleasant and beautiful and occupied by a sparse population of nomads who bred camels, sheep, and horses but never cultivated agricultural crops.[29] It appears that Mughalistan at this time no longer had fortresses or towns or any kind of unmovable property.[30] Towns that had been built here in earlier times by the Uyghurs and the Qarakhitai – with names like Taraz, Balasaghun, Aimal, Bishbalik, and Almalik – and other sites that once boasted fine buildings, domes, minarets, and arches but whose names had been forgotten, were devastated by the Mongols in the thirteenth century and remained in ruins (*wīrān*) and without cultivation, while the whole population reverted to nomadism and lived in *auls*, or nomadic encampments. When, later in the fourteenth century, the Khans of Mughalistan converted to Islam, most of their subjects became Muslims in name only – indeed, not even in name, insofar as they enslaved and sold their own people like infidels.[31] They were called "Mughals" by the Persian-speaking population of Mā warā᾽ an-nahr, the more settled and urbanized part of the Ulus Chaghatay to the west, because they consisted of Mongolized Turks who, clinging to a quasi-Buddhist, quasi-shamanistic past, still seemed half pagan to them, and wild, "like beasts of the mountains."[32] Originally branches of the same Chingisid dynasty, the western and eastern Chaghatays thus became separate ruling dynasties within the Ulus Chaghatay as a whole, due to their diverging relationships with their common nomadic and tribal past. The western branch, by the later fourteenth century, had to some extent assimilated the sedentary Muslim culture of its realm and was for this reason regarded as *qarā᾽ūnas*, or "half breeds," no longer true Mongols, by the eastern branch. Meanwhile, the eastern branch saw itself as the custodians of the steppe heritage of Chingiz Khan and the last genuine representatives of the dynastic line established by

Chingiz Khan's son Chaghatay in the thirteenth century but were regarded as *jätä*, or "bandits," by the western branch.[33]

The Ulus Chaghatay of Timur's time, then, was a confederation of Turkish and Turko-Mongol nomadic tribes as well as nontribal nomadic groupings that were mostly remnants of armies created by the Chaghatay dynasty. Its political system derived much of its cohesion and identity from political practices that depended on tribes rather than central leadership.[34] It did not have a structured administration, and Timur, when he began his career of conquest in 1360, was merely a non-Chingisid amir who propped up the western Chaghatays by installing a puppet king and becoming a royal son-in-law (*güregen*) married to a Chingisid princess, while in the eastern Chaghatay lands of Mughalistan he had no authority at all. Timur subsequently invoked Chingisid steppe traditions of universal rule as well as Islamic traditions of the marches to justify his conquests and rule – both in the domains of the Ulus Chaghatay and Mughalistan as well as in the adjacent sedentary lands – but did not establish himself as the founder of a new dynasty. In 1370 he had his government formally confirmed by members of the Ulus Chaghatay.[35] In practice, however, Timur's career was that of the founder of a conquest dynasty who was to deliver the death blow to the original line of Chaghatay. Timur may have maintained the facade of the Ulus Chaghatay, but he changed its political system in the most radical way possible. Relying on members of his own family and his personal following (men who owed their position to Timur, including slaves and prisoners of war) and increasingly putting the forces held by tribal leaders under their control, he transformed the Ulus Chaghatay from a tribal confederation into a conquest army in which tribes played a strictly subordinate part.[36] By 1380 the transfer of power in Timur's army was far advanced, and around 1390 it was complete. Most of his followers then led large numbers of troops, and they passed them on to their descendants. Since many of his followers had at least several sons and grandsons, Timur went on to have more and more men at his disposal who were personally loyal to him. His own sons and grandsons also multiplied markedly, and these offspring, too, acquired their own armies. An entirely new but closed and self-perpetuating ruling elite, strengthened by intermarriage between followers and family, thus took control of the Ulus Chaghatay. It was very different from the former tribal aristocracy, whose position had steadily eroded, and it derived its power from a political order exclusively maintained by Timur himself. Most importantly, the new political system allowed Timur to suppress tribal power without having to destroy the actual tribes. During Timur's reign, the nomadic tribes remained intact and unchanged in structure, and they retained their own tribal armies, but they lost control of the armies and the governance of the lands of the Ulus Chaghatay. Avoiding violence in this way, Timur did not break up the tribes but rather pushed them aside. Even Timur's own tribe of the Barlas Turks did not receive an important position in the new political dispensation, and those members of the tribe who did were connected to Timur by personal loyalties. In the final analysis, Timur created his conquest army by a method that was similar to that of Chingiz Khan. Both leaders transformed a decentralized and tribally organized society into a unified army subservient to themselves only. And both kept their armies constantly on campaign or settled them as garrison forces in newly conquered territories, scattering and mixing the members of families and tribal groups, frequently reassigning provincial governorships, and conscripting conquered peoples.

Likewise, but to an even greater extent than Chingiz Khan, the succession to Timur's position remained insecure. Timur was extremely jealous of his power and unwilling to share it with any members of even his own family during his life. His entire imperial system was built on personal loyalty to himself only. But, after Timur's death in 1405, the great empire he had forged and partitioned among his sons fell prey to internal rivalries.[37] By the middle of the fifteenth century even its central provinces of Mā warā᾽ an-nahr and Khurasan had entered an era of extreme fragmentation. By the end of that century, the rivalries and conflicts in these former core provinces of Timur's empire involved not only the Timurid *Mirzas* or *Amirzadas* – i.e., "Offspring of the Amir [Timur]" – but also the nomadic Uzbeks, who had entered Mā warā᾽ an-nahr from the Qipchaq steppe under their Chingisid leader Shaybani Khan, and the nomadic tribes of Mughalistan, who encroached upon the Tashkent area on its frontier. Last but not least, in the first decade of the sixteenth century, the Safawid ruler Shah Ismaʿil of Persia, supported by his Qizilbash Turkish tribesmen, began his move into Khurasan from Azerbaijan in the west.

The age of the Timurids, then, presents us with a kaleidoscopic and ever-widening struggle for the control of the cities and resources of the sedentary Perso-Islamic civilization of Mā warā᾽ an-nahr and Khurasan between competing Turkish and Turko-Mongol dynastic clans and between various members of the same ruling clans, not between tribes or ethnic groups. Among the competing Timurid military elites, agnatic ties were important, but cognatic ones, too – especially since there was a marked preference for matrilineal cross-cousin marriage, or marriage with the mother's brother's children. As a result of the extended nature of the patriarchal clan and extensive intermarriage between Timurids,

Uzbeks, and Mughals, the paradoxical situation arose that each clan's most ardent foes were often its closest blood relations, making Timurid politics even more volatile. Timurid cities, with their splendid architecture, changed hands with a frequency that reminds us of corporate mergers and acquisitions rather than warfare between states in our own time.[38] Remarkably, in the fifteenth century, the civilian populations of the cities of Khurasan, which had borne the brunt of Mongol aggression three centuries earlier, were barely affected by these struggles. In the late fifteenth and early sixteenth centuries, two or three generations of Timurids and Chingisids simultaneously struggled for power in the same area, but only with each other. The nature of these struggles was and remained essentially dynastic. It was strictly a competition for control among rival Turko-Mongol dynastic clans that viewed their sedentary subjects as economic assets rather than political or military actors in what was for them foreign territory.

The Mughal Dynasty from Babur to Alamgir

In 1494, at the young age of twelve, Babur inherited from his father the Timurid "kingdom" of Fergana.[39] It consisted of no more than seven towns and their hinterlands. It was a modest beginning for the future founder of the Mughal empire of India. In this world of rapid territorial mergers and acquisitions, however, it was not the size of Babur's inherited domain but his genealogy that mattered and provided him with his most enduring asset. Through his father, Babur was a descendant and heir of Timur in the fifth generation, while through his mother, the second daughter of the ruler of Mughalistan, he was a direct descendant of Chingiz Khan's son Chaghatay. Female parentage was not sufficient to make Babur a true Chingisid, and he considered himself to have been primarily a Timurid Turk. Babur and his descendants, whom we call the Great Mughals of India, referred to themselves as the "Gurkanid dynasty" (silsila-i-gūrkānīya) – after Timur's title of Gūrkān, the Persianized form of the Mongolian güregen, which was the title he assumed after his marriage to a Chingisid princess – even though the Timurids no longer felt dependent on Chingisid legitimation and ruled in their own right and had in fact reversed the relationship between Timurids and Chingisids. Babur, in effect, never identifies himself as a Mongol ruler. In his memoirs he cast his Mongol ancestors in a negative light, emphasizing their destructiveness. He publicly identified with the courtly culture of the sophisticated Timurid Turks of the urban centers of Mā warā' an-nahr and Khurasan rather than with the still-nomadic and rude "Mughal" tribesmen further to the north and east.

Modern historians have followed suit and overwhelmingly stressed Babur's paternal heritage and ties with the numerous descendants of Timur (the grandfather of his great-grandfather) in terms of genealogy, political style, cultural heritage, and even his personal psychology, at the expense of his other extensive kinship ties, especially his Chaghatay kin, the descendants of Chingiz Khan. Yet the competing tugs of his Timurid and Mongol inheritances in actual fact seem to have produced a more hybrid personality that is often at odds with the adulatory portrayal of Babur as a "steppe humanist" in the Timurid tradition.[40] Because he came of age with his maternal uncles (since his father died while he was still young), he often appears to have been closer to his Mongol relatives and their austere, militaristic Chingisid steppe traditions than to the more urbane Timurid Mirzas. Even more significant in practical terms was the fact that the mainstay of Babur's armies in his subsequent years of wandering in Mā warāʾ an-nahr and Khurasan were nomadic Mongols. It was due to a surge of Mongol troops under his command that Babur was able to take Kabul in 1504 and resuscitate his fortunes as the last remaining Timurid padshah. When the *Baburnama* resumes its narrative in 1519, we read there that it was with the assistance of his maternal relatives that Babur could step up recruiting efforts for a second surge of Mongol *nökärdin*, which became pivotal in Babur's victories in Hindustan.

Babur's career of conquest was still entirely conducted within the context of the corporate Turko-Mongol dynastic clan. The conquest of Kabul provided Babur with a larger dominion, safety from Uzbek attacks, and an end to his years of wandering, but Babur never saw Kabul as anything but a well-protected base for the conquest of Hindustan. He had lost any prospects in the Timurid homelands to the Uzbeks, due largely to the lack of cooperation and assistance, and indeed obstruction, of his two brothers. But even the conquest of Hindustan was delayed by the obstructionism and outright rebellions of the same two brothers in the Kabul wilayat. This situation lasted until 1515, after both brothers had died. The campaign in Hindustan then went ahead without them, but soon Babur began giving away the important appanages in this expanding realm to his sons instead of his brothers or maternal relatives. In the five years that Babur spent campaigning in Hindustan against Afghan sultans and Indian rajas, between 1525 and 1530, his oldest son Humayun received the most important appanages and played a more prominent role than the three younger ones. Humayun appears to have emerged as the designated heir almost from the beginning, even amid constant disputes with the other sons, in particular about the control of the royal demesne of Kabul, the strategically crucial wilayat. When Babur died in 1530, Humayun almost immediately mounted the throne in the dynasty's new Indian capital of Agra. We read in the *Humayun-nama* that Babur had decided "to give the kingship to Humayun."[41] But the Timurid throne in 1530 did not simply pass from one king to another. According to Turko-Mongol customary law, kingship was still the shared possession or property of a corporate clan – of Humayun and his three younger brothers as well as a fluctuating pool of collateral members of the family. It allowed any male of the extended family to compete for political power and entitled each adult male family member to share in his patrimony as well as the enjoyment of a significant measure of political independence.

As emperor, Humayun to a large extent still accommodated himself in these customary sharing arrangements of the steppe nomads, even while attempting at the same time to craft a new imperial dispensation by transforming his court life and making it more exclusively focused on the person of the emperor himself. Humayun's reign, in consequence, is a long, almost uninterrupted narrative of dramatic scenes in which his brothers, next to a number of Timurid relatives, "rose in indignation," "read the Friday prayers in their own name," "set up their own sovereign dominions," nearly succeeded in making him "abdicate," or were "captured in rebellion" and then "begged forgiveness," in most cases only to be appointed to new commands, appanages, or governorships.[42] Driven out of India by the Afghans under Sher Shah in 1540 and prevented from resorting to Kabul and Kandahar by the continued opposition of his brothers – in cahoots with the Afghans – and with yet another Timurid, Babur's cousin Haydar Dughlat, openly defying him in Kashmir, Humayun spent some three years in royal exile in Persia. Once reinforced by the Safawid ruler Shah Tahmasp with an auxiliary force of twelve thousand Qizilbash Turkish horsemen, he reconquered Kandahar in 1545 and, through yet another decade of struggle and competition for retainers with his brothers, Kabul and Ghazna in 1555. He remounted the throne of his father in Hindustan in 1555, when the death of Islam Shah and the disintegration of the Indo-Afghan empire of the Sur dynasty reopened the door for his final return. But the second emperor of the Mughal dynasty died less than a year later, from a fall in his library. His premature death did not allow Humayun to bring Hindustan back into subjection. This task was left to his eldest son, Akbar, who, at the age of fourteen, succeeded him in 1556.

Akbar came up against the powerful Rajput rulers of Rajasthan and Hindustan and innumerable lesser Hindu kings everywhere, as well as, mostly ensconced in the hills, major tribal confederacies such as the Gakkars of the Panjab or the Gonds of Gondwana. He also met with

opposition from one major Indo-Islamic state that had been created in
the early fifteenth century in the wake of Timur's destruction of Delhi
and survived intact into the sixteenth century – this was the powerful
Sultanate of Gujarat, with its capital at Ahmadabad. But, more fundamentally, at the time of the accession of Akbar, the authority of the
Mughal dynasty was still contested on all levels.[43] The nobles were only
loosely attached and frequently offered opposition to Akbar, either
in open rebellion or in more covert ways. Among the Mughal nobles
who rebelled against Akbar were Timurids such as his half-brother
Mirza Muhammad Hakim in Kabul and other Mirzas in Hindustan
and Gujarat. Prominent among those who opposed Akbar were also
the Uzbek nobles, belonging to the Turko-Mongol tribe that had been
Babur's nemesis half a century earlier and was still powerful in Balkh,
Khurasan, Bukhara, and Fergana, numbers of which group had entered
Akbar's service, albeit half-heartedly. Akbar's opponents included
numerous Afghan warlords with their Indian soldiers, who remained
powerful in large parts of Hindustan, Malwa, and Gujarat, as well as in
Bihar and Bengal and other places – the leftovers of the ancien regime,
now hopelessly fragmented but often successfully conspiring with disaffected elements within the Mughal nobility itself.

Under these circumstances, Akbar's dominion increased slowly and
with difficulty. Among the most celebrated of Akbar's early dominion-
building efforts was that of allying himself with the major Rajput rulers.
It was undoubtedly more through the Rajputs' political agency than
their sheer military might that Akbar was able to increase his dominion
in the greater part of Hindustan and well beyond. The Rajputs also provided, at all times, an invaluable counterweight against the overweening power of Akbar's immigrant Perso-Turanian nobilities.

With Akbar's dominion increasing in Hindustan, in Gujarat, too,
the efforts to recruit as well as retain nobles, amirs, and military men
reached a feverish pitch. The contest for power between Akbar and
the Gujarati dynasty would continue until the final years of the century, when it was finally decided in Akbar's favor. Throughout these
decades, the struggle was complicated by the fact that the Uzbeks in
Akbar's service and a number of Timurid princes who were known to
contemporary historians as "the Mirzas" and were led by a descendant of Timur's second son (while Akbar descended from the third
son) would switch sides at opportune moments, bringing Afghan warlords of the ancien regime along with them. These treacherous trans-
actions of Akbar's Uzbek nobility, in their turn, were partly inspired
by Akbar's inability to secure control over Kabul and the Indus
borderlands. Because it was situated beyond the Khyber Pass and

surrounded by mountains, Kabul has always been difficult to reach
from the Indian plains. Yet Kabul – with Kandahar or Zabulistan –
belonged to the Mughal dominion of India from its inception, whereas
the lands beyond the Panjshir pass across the Hindu Kush mountains, including Balkh and often Badakhshan, belonged to the Uzbek
dominion of Turan or Central Asia. Until 1585, Akbar's brother Mirza
Muhammad Hakim retained the Kabul throne with the help of the
Mughal troops of the Panjab. His position was ambivalent in that he
now supported Akbar, now conspired with the Uzbeks against his
more powerful brother – and intermittently also with the Timurid rulers of Badakhshan and even the Mughal commanders of the Panjab in
Akbar's service. Geography ensured that whoever ruled Kabul was the
major resource for all the disaffected Muslim elements in India. Akbar
had the greatest difficulty keeping it under control. He had to go to
Kabul in person to prevent the empire from being subverted from there
by Mirza Muhammad Hakim. After the latter's death in 1585, Akbar
had to protect it from the Uzbeks in Balkh, who, he feared, would use it
as their base for an invasion of Hindustan. The Uzbeks never ceased to
be a danger. Until the end of his reign, Akbar remained tied up on the
northwest frontier against the local Afghan tribesmen. The threat was
aggravated by the lingering presence of the eastern Afghans in Bengal.
And that, again, was the reason that Akbar's conquest of Bengal – and
its adjacent provinces of Bihar and Orissa – was, like that of Gujarat,
not a single event but a long, drawn-out effort that Akbar was involved
in for most of his life, here to subdue the Afghans retaining power in
these eastern provinces. In 1580, Akbar's officers in Bihar joined the
Afghans in Bengal in the greatest rebellion of his reign. They distributed territories, honors, titles, and appointments in the name of Mirza
Muhammad Hakim – the ruler of Kabul – and threatened to collude
with the trans-Indus Afghan tribes once more. The eastern Afghans
were not driven into "the forests near the sea" until the last decade of
the sixteenth century. But this happened at about the same time that
the conquest of Gujarat was nearing completion and the Uzbeks on
the northwest frontier, left without support, were effectively contained
beyond the Hindu Kush.

For all these achievements and more, Akbar is often regarded as the
real founder of the Mughal empire. But Akbar's success also brought
into the open a new dispensation of Mughal succession politics, putting the dynasty itself on an entirely different footing. In as much as
Turko-Mongol customary law still invested power throughout the
Mughal family under the first two Mughal emperors, attempts were
made to narrow down the number of potential aspirants to the throne;

yet no decisive changes occurred. There always remained many adult male members of the extended family of a ruler who were entitled to semi-independent and semipermanent princely appanages or territorial holdings and could even contest the throne. Akbar, over the course of his reign, effected a clear shift away from the idea of an extended ruling family cosharing imperial power, by conclusively excluding all but those in his direct line from competing for the throne.[44] The demise of Mirza Muhammad Hakim allowed Akbar to incorporate the Kabul appanage into the empire in 1585, while imprisoning the latter's young sons, Kaikobad and Afrasiyab, in India. From that date onward, the Mughal dynasty abandoned the custom of granting individual appanages to adult princes and instead granted them formal ranks (*mansabs*) with access to jagir revenues that were reassigned every few years. Equally importantly, subsequent succession struggles involved only the emperor's sons and grandsons. Within that narrowed framework, the Mughal princes' lives now became almost entirely oriented toward an eventual and inevitable war of succession, and for them it was "either the throne or the tomb" (*yā takht yā tābūt*).

This new dispensation did not so much signal a break with the customary law of the Turko-Mongol steppe nomads or the Code of Chingiz Khan as a transformation of it. Instead of undermining the consolidation and extension of the empire over generations by competing for loyalties within a single, delimited, fixed, and semipermanent territorial appanage, in the seventeenth century the princes were challenged to build up a support network of allies on a stage that spanned the entire empire. This new dispensation of open-ended succession and alliance building, instituted by Akbar, became a crucial mechanism for augmenting the reach of the empire. Through intensely competitive and relentless contests, which could never lose momentum and are elaborately detailed in the chronicles, the political, social, and monetary resources of the empire were kept in constant circulation, ultimately resulting in powerful and widespread investment in the dynasty as a whole and enhancing its potential for survival. Rather than weakening the dynasty, princely feuding and sedition became an incorporative mechanism that allowed the empire to succeed as a distributive enterprise. It permitted the Mughal nobility to have infusions of fresh blood every few decades. As princes pursued alliances and built up their own political networks, they drew groups already subject to Mughal power into deeper relations with the dynasty. Competition between members of the "stem dynasty" also fostered ties to powerful individuals and groups who were on the political margins or even opposed to the dynasty. Such efforts only gained further momentum in the course of princely rebellions. Throughout the seventeenth century, it was precisely the capacity of princes to co-opt nonimperial sources of sedition and conflict that enabled the Mughal dynasty to parry the many threats to its rule. The new system played a crucial role in deepening the hold of the Mughal dynasty across its territories. Most importantly, the system of open competition and rivalry among great households that the Mughal dynasty adapted from the steppe nomads successfully captured the momentum of Indian economic growth and expansion associated with the influx of New World silver as much as it allowed the mobilization and absorption of upwardly mobile elites that sustained rather than undermined the dynastic continuity of the empire.[45] It was this transformation of Turko-Mongol succession practices that set the Mughal dynasty apart not only from its Indo-Afghan predecessors but from the medieval dynasties of the Sultanate of Delhi and all other Indo-Islamic states as well. It made the Mughal empire unique among all the empires – Islamic and otherwise – of the early modern world.

Akbar's eldest son, Salim, the future emperor Jahangir, was the first Mughal prince to emerge from the new dispensation of open competition and political rivalry or feuding among princely households that replaced the earlier corporate-style appanage system of the nomadic clan dynasty.[46] In spite of half-hearted and unsustained attempts to move toward a system of quasi-designated heirs – a status that did not guarantee the throne and merely expressed the momentary preference of the incumbent emperor – this was the system that remained in place throughout the reigns of Jahangir and his successors Shah Jahan and Alamgir until the accession of Bahadur Shah I in 1707. Salim, in effect, moved against his father, Akbar, almost immediately when he was granted full adult status and permitted to have his own household in 1585, at the age of sixteen, about twenty years before he would ascend the throne, and he did so even though he was (and remained until 1594) the quasi-designated heir and even though his two brothers had not reached adulthood and were not yet in open competition with him. From the beginning, he vigorously capitalized on political dissent across the empire and built alliances with political opponents of Akbar, including, among others, the numerous supporters of the late Mirza Muhammad Hakim unmoored by Akbar's annexation of Kabul and Afghans marginalized by Akbar. When Akbar counteracted these subversive activities of his son by degrading Salim's supporters and, in 1594, elevating Salim's eleven-year-old son Khusrau to high imperial rank and making him the quasi-designated heir to the Mughal throne, Salim started a rebellion in Allahabad, a turbulent area of northern and eastern India extending over territories between Kanauj and Patna, which had thus far been staunchly anti-Mughal but which he success-fully leveraged into a power bid of his own.[47]

In 1605, Salim ascended the Gūrgānī throne in Agra as Jahangir. As his memoirs reveal, Jahangir moved without delay to crush, like his father, the political ambitions of the collateral branches of the Mughal dynasty – by imprisoning, banishing, and publicly degrading the sons and grandsons of his late uncle Mirza Muhammad Hakim and by converting his three minor nephews to Christianity.[48] Jahangir's reign, after this, is best described as an extended family feud in all its basic characteristics, continuing without interruption for over two decades.[49] The entire empire was convulsed by the successive rebel-lions and feuds of four sons and one grandson. Khusrau's rebellion in the Panjab, which occurred at the very beginning of Jahangir's reign, on the threshold of the Uzbek and Persian lands, quickly metastasized to Rajasthan, Gujarat, the Deccan, and as far as Bengal but ended with his capture and blinding and ultimately his assassination by Khurram, his younger brother. Khurram then for a time replaced him as the quasi-designated heir but later rebelled against the emperor, in his turn, and was pursued over thousands of miles across the subcontinent in a mad scramble for support and resources that on one occasion brought him close to Agra and on another prompted him to arrogate to himself imperial prerogatives and read the Friday prayers in his own name in Bengal, where he gained the support of the resurging eastern Afghans. In the end, with the additional man-power and financial resources of the Deccan, Khurram outmaneu-vered the increasingly debilitated emperor's wife and de facto regent, Nur Jahan, and her Indo-Persian faction, his elder brother Parwiz, and his half-brother Shahryar, to ascend to the throne in 1628 as Shah Jahan. The late Khusrau's son, and also the latter's younger brother, the blinded Shahryar, and his uncle's two surviving sons were all put to death within days, on Khurram's orders, early in 1628.

The chronicles then continue to describe in detail how Shah Jahan began his thirty-year reign by settling scores with and purging the vari-ous parties and factions that had opposed his rise or been implicated in the suppression of his princely revolt, by attacking and degrading key networks of Afghans, moving against the Portuguese in Bengal, intervening in succession struggles among the Bundela Rajputs, and cultivating a broad range of local loyalties everywhere.[50] Then, by the mid-to-late 1630s, the attention shifts ever more exclusively to develop-ments within the Mughal dynasty itself. Both Shah Jahan's mother and his grandmother had been Hindu Rajput princesses of distinguished

lineage, but his great seal, stamped on all the royal farmans and commands, only mentions him as the tenth ruler in direct descent from
Timur, listing the name of each ancestor of the Gurgani dynasty, while
calling the emperor himself the Second Lord of the Conjunction, bor-
rowing Timur's title of the First Lord of the Conjunction. What is more,
the historical record of this emperor's reign is virtually silent about the
living grandsons of Khusrau, the descendants of Mirza Muhammad
Hakim, or any other collateral lines of the Mughal family, while lav-
ishing attention on the four sons and four daughters Shah Jahan had
with his wife Mumtaz Mahal, and also underscoring that he married no
Hindu wives. Shah Jahan deliberately restricted the number of his children and only preserved four sons and four daughters, apparently by
aborting other pregnancies, a practice of which his sons and grandsons
also made use. Equally significant is the fact that Shah Jahan upheld
the regulation introduced by Akbar that daughters should not be married, for fear that their husbands would thereby be rendered too exalted
and powerful and possibly aspire to the throne (Figure 5.1).

Over the course of his first regnal decade, all four of Shah Jahan's
sons – who were full brothers and all sons of Mumtaz Mahal – reached
adulthood, received their first mansabs, and were married: Dara Shukoh
(born 1615, mansab 1633), Muhammad Shah Shuja' (born 1616, mansab 1633), Aurangzeb (born 1618, mansab 1634), and Murad Bakhsh
(born 1624, mansab 1639). Without delay, virtually from the day they
reached adulthood and were allowed to build their own households, and
"animated by deadly hatred towards the others," each of the sons exerted
himself to the utmost to increase his political support at the expense of
the others, and of their father, who "trembled for his personal safety."[51]
The eldest son, Dara Shukoh, was the quasi-designated heir from 1632
onward, rising through the ranks more rapidly than any of his brothers, while in due course his own two sons, Sulayman Shukoh and the
younger, Sipihr Shukoh, both of the principal wife of royal blood, were
extended exceptional privileges and ranks as well. With all the ruthless
energy expended by Shah Jahan and his four sons in building up competing support networks and political capital for themselves throughout the imperial dominions, no significant territorial gains were made
anywhere on the northern peripheries of the empire. Approaching the
final decade of his reign, in 1646–1647, Shah Jahan attempted to realize
the Mughal dynasty's long-standing ambition of regaining its "hereditary cemetery" in Central Asia and occupy Balkh and Badakhshan.
But the year-and-a-half-long Mughal occupation and local resistance of
the Uzbek and Alman tribesmen merely devastated the province, and
the imperial frontier shifted no more than thirty-one miles further to

Figure 5.1 The Taj Mahal, Agra, India. The iconic building of the dynasty of the Great Mughals, the Taj Mahal was commissioned by Emperor Shah Jahan to house the tomb of his favorite wife, Mumtaz Mahal, and himself. James Gritz/Photographer's Choice RF via Getty Images.

the north of Kabul. Without advancing much in the north, the political and military frontier of the empire was, however, still wide open in the Deccan and further to the south. From as early as 1636, it was in the Deccan that Mughal dynastic politics and expansion, and indeed the future of the empire, were decided, when one prince of the dynasty, Aurangzeb, successfully leveraged its manpower and resources into a successful bid for the imperial throne. The contest began in 1636, when Aurangzeb became viceroy/governor of the Deccan for the first time and reached its dramatic climax in his victory over his brothers in the great war of succession of 1658–1659. Successfully availing himself of the rebellions of his brothers, and defeating and outmaneuvering his brother Dara Shukoh in two major battles, Aurangzeb besieged his father in the fortress in Agra and made him surrender, to become his son's prisoner. He then took possession of the immense treasures and armaments of the Agra fort and forced the emperor to abdicate. Aurangzeb proclaimed himself emperor eight months after his brothers did so, on July 22, 1658, with the title of ʿĀlamgir, or "world seizer." No coins were yet struck, nor were the Friday prayers read in his name, but he became master of a great army.

Alamgir, the "selected one of the dynasty of Timur," in the eleventh generation and the last of the Great Mughals, began his long reign of almost half a century by executing, imprisoning, or driving out every possible rival claimant to the throne in his entire family, foremost Dara Shukoh, with the exception of his own sons and some collaterals who were put on annual stipends.[52] He enthroned himself for a second time, with full paraphernalia and unprecedented ceremony, in Shahjahanabad, issuing coins and having the Friday prayers read in his name on June 15, 1659, at an astrologically auspicious time. With his usual consistency, Alamgir wreaked deadly vengeance on everyone who had laid hands upon the princes of the dynasty. Not even the slaves who had cut off the heads of his two brothers were spared. An Afghan who had turned in Dara Shukoh was assassinated under mysterious circumstances. And in 1663, Alamgir ordered his uncle Shaista Khan to punish the pirate king of Arakan for his cruel treatment of Shah Shujaʿ and his family, determined to avenge him, in Bernier's words "by a signal example, to teach his neighbors that princes of the blood, in all situations and under all circumstances, must be treated with humanity and reverence."[53]

Alamgir's victory over his brothers in the war of succession meant that the empire was never divided. What is more, Mughal dynastic legitimacy became unchallenged throughout the subcontinent. If, in Babur's time, the rulers of Gujarat, Bengal, Orissa, and South India were still regarded as sovereign powers in their own right, and throughout the sixteenth century and a large part of the seventeenth the Deccan Sultanates looked at Safawid Persia as the source of their legitimacy, in the course of the seventeenth century the Mughal dynasty gradually came to be seen more and more as the only true source of sovereignty in the Indian subcontinent, until by the latter part of Alamgir's reign even the idea of Vijayanagara had ceased to play a role. By then, even the rebellious Marathas of the Deccan fought "to protect the Sultan of Taimur." Beyond the subcontinent, Indo-Islamic rulers sometimes adopted seals that were patterned on that of the Great Mughals.

Yet dynastic feuding continued with a vengeance. Alamgir had a total of six sons, but only four get serious attention in the chronicles. He always kept all of these sons, and soon enough his grandsons and even great-grandsons as well, under a suspicious watch, rotating most of them throughout the empire in provincial and military assignments and keeping them geographically separate. His eldest son, born of a Rajput mother and briefly heir apparent, was Muhammad Shah. He was imprisoned early in the reign until brought to death in 1676 for defecting to Shah Shuja' during the war of succession and aiming for the throne "before his father's death." By the time of the captivity and death of the first son, the second son, Mu'azzam, also born of a Rajput mother, had twice became the nominal heir and entertained the same thoughts as the other had done, of destroying his father. His career is a record of almost constant obstruction, especially as viceroy of the Deccan, where he plotted with Golkonda, Bijapur, and the Maratha leader Shivaji, yet largely because of his connections in the Deccan among the Marathas and the Rajputs, as also among the Sikhs of the Panjab antagonized by his father, ultimately emerged victorious and succeeded his father in 1707 as Bahadur Shah I. The third son, Muhammad Azam Shah, was a descendant of the "royal blood of Persia" through his mother, the daughter of Shah Nawaz Khan, who descended from the kings of Muscat in Oman and was a son of Mirza Rustam Kandahari, a great-grandson of Shah Ismail, the Shah of Persia. Muhammad Azam was the only son of Alamgir who stayed out of prison. But he did not fail to play his part in plotting against his father with the king of Bijapur and also made plans in 1670 for independence with the governor of Allahabad. For some years he was the nominal heir, but he lost out in a dispute for precedence with Mu'azzam, the second son. And then there was Alamgir's fourth son, also born of Shah Nawaz Khan's daughter, whose name was Muhammad Akbar. More ambitious than all the others, the latter was sent to suppress an uprising of the Rajputs in 1680 by his father but joined them and rebelled with their support, then proclaimed himself emperor, issuing a manifesto deposing his father as a violator of Islamic law. In 1681 he advanced to give him battle but was defeated and had to flee to the Maratha king Sambhaji, then to Goa, and ultimately to Persia, where the Shah offered him men and money to fight his brothers but declined to support him in another attack against Alamgir himself. Akbar remained a threat until he died, a year before his father. As a result, by 1700, Alamgir had three politically competing sons in India and a fourth living in exile in Persia but ready to renew his claims to the throne at any opportune moment. And by 1707, the year of his death, he also had nine adult grandsons to consider, and adult great-grandsons who were at that time beginning to supplement the princely ranks. There thus emerged in Alamgir's reign an exceptionally crowded stage for the dynastic succession, and intergenerational tensions, while not new, rose higher than ever.

Unsurprisingly, the Mughal dynasty's fate was sealed in the Deccan. The continuing Deccan threat forced Alamgir to move south in 1682, with his entire court and with a large army that, in the course of the subsequent two decades, swelled to one hundred seventy thousand men, nearly five hundred thousand with noncombatants included, plus subsidiary armies. It was allegedly the "disobedience" of his princes and nobles that forced the emperor to remain in the Deccan and personally coordinate the Mughal conquests up to the very end of his life, in 1707. Secret alliances were formed, despite the emperor's countervailing presence, with factions at the Deccani courts or with the Sultans of Bijapur and Golkonda themselves or with the Marathas – always in opposition to Mughal factions that urged immediate annexation of the Deccan states to check such alliances. Rajput mansabdars were closely linked to the Marathas, Afghans to their compatriots at the Bijapur court, and Persian nobles easily appeased by the Shi'ite Qutub Shah of Golkonda. It became notorious that the Mughals did not fight hard, accepted bribes from the enemy to put off a battle, negotiated mock captures, and displayed cowardice and "loss of morale." Bernier observed that the generals sent against Bijapur "conduct[ed] every operation with languor, and avail[ed] themselves of any pretext for the prolongation of the war which [was] alike the source of their emoluments and dignity."[54] The subjugation of Bijapur and Golkonda occupied Alamgir until as late as 1686–1687. Bijapur was besieged for eighteen months, after which it surrendered; Golkonda was besieged for seven months and was finally taken by "treason." The two kingdoms were then turned into the Mughal subahs of Bijapur and Hyderabad, the two of them extending across the Karnataka, down to the extreme south of the peninsula. But these conquests could only be achieved through the most lenient and far-reaching concern for the assimilation of the Deccani nobles. Only the emperor himself stood to benefit from a final and definitive conclusion of the Deccan campaigns, but none of the other participants. With the end of the Deccan campaigns in sight, the Mughal nobility allowed the adversaries to reach a stalemate. Attempts to subdue the Marathas, most notably, failed spectacularly and only accelerated their rise. Natives of the Deccan, the Marathas were diffused in small

and mobile parties in the east in close conjunction with the Telugu
nayakas and zamindars and eluded a frontal assault, while remaining
an ever more indispensable lever for the Mughal nobles' and princes'
self-enhancement. During this time, in anticipation of the succession
struggle for the Mughal throne that would inevitably follow the death of
the aged emperor, an internecine contest for power convulsed the entire
Mughal Deccan. The Mughal commitment to open-ended princely
succession was now doomed to come to an end, as people across the
empire abandoned their allegiance to the dynasty in all but name and
gravitated toward newly rising regional elites, thus setting the stage for
the emergence of the post-Mughal successor states.

The Long Shadow of Chingiz Khan

None of the foregoing would be especially hard to understand or inter-
pret were it not for the unfortunate circumstance that the empire of the
Great Mughals has generally been described from the perspective of
the modern state. Recent scholarship in India depicts it as a more-or-
less successful or unsuccessful forerunner of the British Raj, a united
political structure with an all-powerful, even absolutist center. Thus,
the preeminent Indian historian of the Mughal empire, Irfan Habib,
asserted, "For a hundred and fifty years the Mughal empire covered
a whole subcontinent, united under a highly centralized administration. To what did it owe its great success? ... The unity and cohesion of
the Mughal ruling class found its practical expression in the absolute
power of the emperor."[55] Anglo-American scholarship has followed suit
in this belief. John F. Richards, in what has become the most widely
read standard work on the Mughal empire, similarly attributes its success to "autocratic centralism."[56] He stated as follows:

Buoyed by conquest and plunder, Akbar and his advisers built a centralizing
administration capable of steady expansion as new provinces were added to the
empire ... The emperor and his advisers were vigorous managers who creatively
adapted and responded to changing circumstances. Building on this foundation, Akbar's successors oversaw steady growth in imperial effectiveness,
power, and resources throughout the seventeenth century. [They] ... shaped
a vertebrate structure characterized by centralized, hierarchical, bureaucratic offices. Filling these offices were technically qualified officials, func-
tioning within standardized rules and procedures, who generated copious
written orders and records. At the apex of this system the emperor acted as a
vigorous and informed chief executive ... The service nobility's entrepreneur-
ial drive and spirit was of inestimable value to Akbar and his successors ...
Ranked nobles became reliable instruments of the imperial will ... Imperial

field commanders were virtually invulnerable to bribery or purchase. The Mughal system imposed strict accountability on its officials.[57]

Contemporary travelers to the Mughal empire never espoused this view. Most outspoken in this regard was, perhaps, Niccolao Manucci:

My third book will explain the way in which the generals and commanders behave in Hindustan. They aim only at their personal advantage, and ordinarily make no account of the royal commands, except only when it is necessary in order not to be expressly found out as traitors... This sort of thing is very common in the Mughal regime... I noticed that when vassals are in the royal presence they feign to be timid and afraid of His Majesty. These gestures please him, they being the custom. The combats and conquests made by both ancient and modern Mogul kings, it is to be noted, have for the major part been won rather by deceit and false oaths than by force of arms. Never does the Mogul attack any stronghold or give battle unless he is secure of having some traitor to help him.[58]

Manucci repeats this verdict throughout his work, with minor variations, as do others. According to Francisco Pelseart, "there are [in the Mughal empire] nearly as many rebels as there are subjects."[59] De Laet writes about "a spirit eager and ripe for insurrection and revolution... a revolutionary spirit among the subjects of the empire, a spirit which is readily inflamed and at any opportunity of revolt produces an insurrection... He [the emperor] can put little or no reliance upon their loyalty and obedience."[60] There is indeed not a single contemporary observer who does not describe Mughal politics as an unscrupulous double game. Observations to that effect are many.

As this chapter has aimed to show, Mughal politics was the politics of sedition (*fitna*), and our modern concepts of the state, justice, and the law are fundamentally incompatible with the earlier concepts of Mughal India. Here, the political process, conflicts over rights, and the pursuit of justice could be accompanied by a private resort to arms. A great number of feuds were waged by the sons of rulers, and by local powers against their rulers, and, when larger groups took part, such feuds were apt to take the form of uprisings or rebellions. This kind of "self-help" in conflict adjudication was radically delegitimized by the colonial/modern state of the nineteenth and twentieth centuries, which introduced the "polity of law" and dismissed the earlier dispensation as symptomatic of disorder, anarchy or chaos, and a nonstate or "law of the fist" – in contemporary terms, a "failed state." But behind this apparent disorder and violence of Mughal India there was a different kind of legal order: a synthesis of justice, rights, and law that was associated with the institutions of kingship, kinship, and custom and, while it had nothing to do with Islam as such, was not without some kind of conception of transcendental, religious, or divine justice. The political and legal foundations of the state were rooted in the matrix of clan rule and shared sovereignty in which feuding, sedition, self-help, and armed opposition were central and legitimate elements. The Mughal empire was, therefore, a "negotiated" state with a customary legal order that was based more on diplomacy and pressure than on formal rules and not a modern state – not quite at war, not quite at peace – like in some respects Pakistan and Afghanistan still are today.[61] From the point of view of the modern unitary and territorial state with its monopoly of legitimate violence, it is inconceivable that armed sedition could even be tolerated, let alone that it could be a source of strength, as in the succession struggles just described. Since it was rooted in unwritten customary law, the Tora of Chingiz Khan, which was passed down through the generations and constantly adapted to the changing circumstances in India, it is fruitless to search for an "imperial ideology" here. Sedition became the constitutional foundation of a system of rule that guaranteed the incorporative dynamism and success of the empire as a whole. The Mughals created a system of imperial rule on the basis of customary practices or rule, dynastic succession, and princely feuding that went back to the early medieval Turk Qaghanate and to Chingiz Khan and Timur; in other words, their constitution was an adaptation of the Mongol Yasa or Tora. If anything, this is what explains their "success," and it is what allowed them to transcend the limitations of their tribal culture in a way that their nomadic Afghan opponents never could.

Unsurprisingly perhaps, the dynasty came to consider itself as sacred or, better put, a spiritual resource in its own right. It became increasingly aligned with Sunni Islam and at times fostered certain forms of Islamic or Persianate millenarianism, such as the Mahdawiyya movement, and even notions of "divine" or "sacred" kingship, under the influence of Sufism, Mongol universalism, or messianism – including revelatory dreams, magic, and alchemy – and thus began to see itself (and was seen by others) as upholder of a divine dispensation.[62] Yet this was not a theocratic monarchy, and there is an obvious difference here with the theocratic conceptions of imperial rule that informed, for instance, the medieval Byzantine empire. The Byzantines held that promotion to rule came solely from God, and hence the imperial throne was open to anyone, peasant and noble, even scholars and unlearned men, as long as they were Christians. There was no absolute law regarding succession to the throne: all means of becoming emperor were legitimate, as long as they were successful, for what God had given he could also take away. The atmosphere of conspiracy and paranoia, of plot and counterplot, in Byzantine history is sometimes reminiscent of the Mughal politics of sedition. Byzantine rulers might be dethroned by murder or palace revolutions or riots, and "revolution" was incorporated into the body of constitutional practice – an autocracy tempered by the legal right of revolution, as Theodor Mommsen put it. But Mughal politics represented something quite different. In the Byzantine case it revolved around the institution of a theocratic monarchy, in the Mughal case around the customary code of law of the dynasty of Timur and Chingiz Khan. As the foundation of Mughal imperialism, the code of Chingiz Khan cast a long shadow. Irretrievably attached to this heritage, the Mughals would never entirely outgrow their origins as a nomadic war band and, in turn, were unable to make the transition to a modern state.

6   The Empire of the Great Mughals
       and Its Indian Foundations

It is difficult to understand how sovereigns who could not prevent
their own children from levying armies against them, should be so
absolute as some would like to make us believe.

Voltaire[1]

Horses have a long history in India. Having made their appearance
in Vedic times, they were soon put to military use. But they never
achieved a high standard of performance, and in ancient India elephants, not horses, became preeminent. There were two problems
with horses.

First was a problem of supply. The few horses that were bred in India
were mostly of poor quality, and imported horses did not do well there.
There was little room for horses, since the best soil was reserved for the
cultivation of agricultural crops to support a dense population. This
meant a scarcity of grazing grounds and a lack of appropriate fodder
grasses. Only in some parts of the subcontinent that were an extension
of the arid zone, in the northwest, could nutritious fodder grasses be
found. But even there, horse breeding, though viable, stood in tension
with arable farming.

Second, there was a problem of equipment and weaponry, particularly evident in the failure of the Indians to develop horse-mounted
archery. It was the Turkish and Mongol steppe nomads who developed
bow shooting on horseback and then established a quasi-monopoly
over it, thereby acquiring a qualified military superiority over their
sedentary neighbors in India – like they did in Persia, Byzantium, and
China. The Turko-Mongol armies penetrating into India from the late
tenth and early eleventh century onward were made up of light cavalry, with superior archery abilities, and also, to a lesser extent, heavy
cavalry trained as much in the cataphractarii or "armored" tradition
as in that of the typical steppe warriors. The main military advantage
always remained that mounted archers were more mobile than any

infantry and, in addition to being able to use the bow from horseback, were capable of making decisive charges with spears and swords in conjunction with heavy cavalry. Thus, in the medieval centuries, the growing reliance on horse archers, in combination with heavy cavalry, amounted to a genuine military revolution, and horses gradually drove elephants from their preeminent military position.[2]

A Farewell to Horses?

There is considerable confusion in the historical literature about what happened in the subsequent early modern centuries. Historians have rightly observed that by the fifteenth century the great age of Turko-Mongol nomadic conquerors – the likes of Chingiz Khan and Timur – was drawing to a close. Some have argued that the expansion of sedentary Moscovy into the territories of the nomadic Golden Horde is evidence that the historical relationship between nomads and peasants was beginning to be reversed, at least in some parts of Eurasia. But the actual causes of this alleged world-historical shift in power toward settled civilization have remained somewhat in the dark. There has been much speculation that horse warfare was rendered obsolete by the introduction of gunpowder weapons and infantry armies.[3] Likewise, it has often been speculated that early modern European maritime trade replaced or adversely affected the trans-Eurasian caravan trade and thereby further contributed to the decline of nomad power.[4] In the words of Andrew Hess, "Cannons, fire-arms, and galley fleets, together with all the urban-based organizational techniques necessary to command and sustain complex military units, heralded an end to the long dominance of the mounted archer."[5] More often than not, however, it has proved impossible to substantiate such assertions with hard facts.

Within the same framework of unsubstantiated speculation, the empire of the Great Mughals of India has long been cast as one of the "gunpowder empires" of the early modern Islamic world. The Russian Orientalist Vasilii Bartold, followed by world historians Marshall G. S. Hodgson and William H. McNeill, was among the first of many to assert that the diffusion of gunpowder weapons and siege artillery amounted to yet another military revolution (early modern "handgun" troops and artillery superseding medieval horsemanship) that went a long way toward explaining the increase and consolidation of central power in the three great sixteenth-century Islamic empires – the Ottomans, the Safawids, and the Mughals.[6] In Hodgson's view, it was most notably siege and field artillery that provided an increased advantage for these "gunpowder empires":

The implications of the changes in weapons were not restricted entirely to military organization. The relative expensiveness of artillery and the relative untenability of stone fortresses gave an increased advantage over local military garrisons to a well-organized central power which could afford artillery... Gunpowder was doubtless not the one great decisive factor in the political and social – and ultimately cultural – realignments that occurred in the three generations following 1450; but it played a distinctive role, and was perhaps the most easily identifiable single occasion for them.[7]

This emphasis on artillery as the distinctive element in an early modern military revolution seemed justified, according to a general understanding, because the introduction of similar technology had made possible the phenomenal expansion of Portuguese naval power in the Indian Ocean in the same century.[8] Moreover, in Europe, the diffusion of effective siege artillery had indeed made stone fortresses "untenable" – as was first demonstrated during the French invasion of Italy in 1494. While in Europe the situation was reversed within a matter of decades by the development of a new type of stone bastion, the *trace italienne*, which was an effective response against siege artillery, no such new developments in fortification took off in the Islamic world; thus here, the argument runs, artillery remained an advantage for those centralizing powers that "could afford to be abreast of the latest improvements."[9] Infantry was also thought to have played a major role, as in Europe again, to the extent that relatively small, undisciplined cavalry troops were replaced by larger, disciplined, and well-drilled infantry armies with gunpowder weapons.[10] In Egypt, most notably, the Mamluk cavalry was defeated by the more innovative Ottomans, who made effective use of infantry with modern matchlocks.[11]

The Ottomans, in effect, were major artillery producers at the time and used infantry on numerous major battlefields with proficiency. If any of the three great early modern Islamic empires could be called a gunpowder empire with some justification, it would be, without a doubt, that of the Ottomans.[12] The technology and skills of artillery and other gunpowder weapons were essentially passed on to the Mughals by the Ottoman rulers of "Rum" as well as by Europeans. In Hindustan, they made their appearance with Babur, and on the coasts with the Portuguese, in the early decades of the sixteenth century. Spurred on by opponents like Sher Shah Sur, the Mughals lost no time in building up their artillery park. None of the Hindu rulers that Akbar encountered – not even the preeminent Rajputs – appear to have possessed artillery, although some of the smaller Muslim rulers like the Arghuns of Sind and the Afghan warlords and their Hindu generals did. The Sultans of Gujarat had a grand park of artillery and mortars, some of which had been obtained directly from the Ottoman sultan Sulayman the Magnificent. Throughout much of the later sixteenth century there was intense competition for such technology and expertise among all the major states from the Horn of Africa (where Ottoman artillery emboldened a jihad against the Christian empire of Ethiopia) to the Deccan Sultanates and the Hindu empire of Vijayanagara in the Indian peninsula and to the emerging maritime Muslim powers of Johore and Aceh in the eastern Indian Ocean (who were also supported by the Ottomans). Akbar himself was trained in artillery shooting by a "Rumi Turk," and Rumi Turks and the "Firangis" (i.e., Franks – some of them converts) remained much in demand for their brilliant pyrotechnic skills throughout the sixteenth century and the early decades of the seventeenth, after which we see their pay drop commensurately with the decreasing rarity of their skills when these began to spread in India itself. Both groups, without a doubt, were a factor of significance in the success of Akbarian imperialism.

As it was originally formulated, however, the idea that the empire of the Great Mughals in India was a gunpowder empire in its early modern manifestations is no longer convincing. A growing number of critics have contended that, while there were indeed no technical improvements in fortification in India in the sixteenth and seventeenth centuries and in effect, the existing defenses continued to resemble medieval European castles, this is because Mughal artillery, while carried along with the moving camps, was not an important element of siege craft.[13] Most of the fortresses of Hindustan, Rajasthan, and the Deccan were located at sites that could not be reached by large guns, or only with the greatest difficulty, on steep, rocky hills and in the middle of dense, thorny forests. It appears that the siege technology that had reached India in the thirteenth and fourteenth centuries through the Mongols from China had already given fresh impetus to the building and rebuilding of Indian fortresses, with walls becoming much thicker and more solidly built already, and equipped with bastions, so that by the sixteenth century most Indian fortresses were better able than ever to sustain sieges, even if the besiegers deployed the cannon. If such strong hill fortresses as Chitor, Ranthambor, or Asirgarh were successfully besieged and taken by Mughal armies, it was not due to the use of artillery in breaching the stone walls. Fortresses, when taken, were not destroyed, either – quite the opposite. More fortresses were built by Akbar and later Mughal emperors on essentially the same pattern as previously. In Mughal hands, they became the seats of provincial governors, obstacles to rather than centers of revolt. In short, siege artillery was not the main and certainly never the only impetus toward centralization. It merely became one contributing factor among others and only for as long as the imperial center could maintain a monopoly in it. In later times, it could also undermine the central authority of the Mughals when regional forces became equipped with siege artillery as well.

Nor did the deployment of the cannon on the battlefield or "field artillery" in combination with infantry revolutionize Mughal warfare. Like siege craft, the deployment of artillery on the battlefield proved troublesome. Its mobility was hampered by primitive gun carriages, and the heaviness of Indian guns made rapid maneuvering in the field impossible. Field artillery remained unreliable and extremely inaccurate. There was a lack of standardization of both barrels and shot, and Indian gunpowder was less powerful by not being granulated. Above all, Mughal armies failed to adapt field artillery to their cavalry. If in sixteenth-century Europe, the rise of infantry signaled the decline of heavy cavalry and the beginning of a new gunpowder age, Indian foot soldiers or armed peasants, in spite of their sheer limitless availability, acquired only a marginal role on the battlefields of the sixteenth and seventeenth centuries. The numbers of infantry quoted are often remarkably high, but Indo-Persian chronicles hardly mention them in their battle accounts and continue to focus almost exclusively on horse warriors. The indigenously recruited units of infantry, with their matchlocks and primitive bows and spears, were held in such contempt that they were listed with litter bearers, carpenters, woodcutters, and cotton carders in the military payrolls. In Mughal India, the infantry held, in the words of William Irvine, "a very inferior position and was of little or no consideration."[14] As with artillery, its firearms and shot lacked standardization and it generally lacked body armor. Mounted archers could shoot three times as fast as matchlock musketeers – six aimed shots versus two per minute, without difficulty – and had a longer range as well as being more accurate. The bulk of the Indian infantry, in effect, served off the battlefield, as local militias or attendants of the cavalry, unlike the disciplined and drilled infantry that was successfully deployed in Europe, where cavalry lacked both numbers and sophistication. Relatively well-trained and regular infantry units, consisting mostly of peasants such as those recruited from among the Bundelas and the Baksariyas, were quite rare in Mughal India.

It was not until the second half of the eighteenth century, when European officers began to create and drill sepoy regiments equipped with flintlock muskets and socket bayonets, that the effectiveness of both artillery and infantry radically improved and came to revolutionize Indian warfare once more.[15] Even then it remained difficult to fully integrate the infantry units into the larger Indian armies, which remained emotionally attached to the horse. It would take another century and the Mutiny before advanced field artillery and drilled infantry broke the paramountcy of horse warriors. In the late eighteenth century, the armies of the indigenous Indian rulers that de facto succeeded the Great Mughals still ranged from cavalry without infantry or artillery, to cavalry supported by artillery, to mixed infantry and artillery, to infantry with irregular cavalry.

In this light, it is misleading to call the empire of the Great Mughals a gunpowder empire, since cavalry, not artillery or infantry, always was and remained its chief military asset. Not only was the key to the Mughals' military success to be found in the use of cavalry – and more specifically mounted archers – but the Mughals also controlled the regular supply of superior "Turki" warhorses from the steppe lands. This was another decisive advantage that they held over all Indian rulers, and also over the Afghans (who had lost control of Kabul, the major entrepôt of the horse trade), although less so over the Sultans of Gujarat, who had access to a supply of "seaborne" horses from Persia and Arabia that was of a similarly high quality but probably smaller.

The central importance of mounted archery in Mughal warfare is in evidence at all times. The Battle of Panipat in 1526, which first established Mughal power in India, was not decided by heavy artillery but instead by the traditional Turko-Mongol tactics of combining mounted archery with the defensive strategy of roping some seven hundred carts together in a park "in the Anatolian manner," behind which matchlock men took cover. These *Wagenburg* tactics had some impact at the beginning of the sixteenth century but did not mark the onset of a new gunpowder era in which infantry and artillery came to dominate warfare in India. When Humayun returned to India in 1555, his very first victory over the Afghans, in the Battle of Machiwara, on the banks of the Sutlej, was again entirely gained by mounted archers. Still later in the sixteenth century, Father Monserrate observed that "the strength of the Tartar [i.e., Mughal] armies lies in their cavalry... organized in accordance with the system of Cinguiscanus [Latin for Chingiz Khan]."[16] It was no different in the seventeenth century. The Battle of Dharmatpur in 1658, which brought Aurangzeb his decisive victory over his brother Dara Shukoh, was decided by thirty thousand Mongol mounted archers. Heavy cavalry also became increasingly important. Over all this time, the total number of Mughal cavalry had only increased – from about twelve thousand in the mid-sixteenth century to one hundred thousand in the later seventeenth century.

Cavalry warfare, furthermore, spread to other segments of Indian society that had previously been dominated by infantry. Under Akbar, the cavalry forces were still overwhelmingly made up of immigrant rather than Indian-born recruits. Later, in the seventeenth century, they were increasingly born in India, like much of their retinue. Subject Indian warrior castes like the Rajputs became increasingly important in the Mughal army to the extent that they adopted cavalry warfare. This took some time and required a profound transformation of earlier Rajput military practices. In the early sixteenth century, and in some places long afterward, the Rajputs carried only swords and short spears or lances into war, with light shields – nothing like bows and arrows or firearms that could kill from a dishonorable distance. Before the beginning of a battle, they were almost always heavily drugged with opium and strove to win or die with their archaic sense of honor intact. The Rajputs did not have access to large warhorses and often rode on ponies hardly as big as donkeys, dismounting for battle. Akbar immediately set out to change this pattern of Rajput warfare when he co-opted the leading Rajput warlords for his imperial service. Like the foreign Muslim amirs, these warlords then began to employ their own kinsmen as well as nonkin retainers and, with better horses, organized them into cavalry units that, already under Akbar, played a secondary but important role in Mughal warfare. Beyond the territories of the Rajputs, the Mughals understood and used everywhere to their advantage the enormous potential of the Indian countryside. During the seventeenth century, the practice and ethos of the horse service of Rajput kings and its symbols of honor spread further to populations never before associated with it and became a means of upward social mobility, as for instance in broad areas of tribal Central India and to the south of the Mughal empire, where it was the common traditions and symbols of cavalry service in the Deccan Sultanates that differentiated Marathas from relatives who were cultivators, ironworkers, and pastoralists.[17] These developments were only an extension of what had started much earlier. The Mughal cavalry under Akbar and his successors represented the culmination of a revolution in warfare begun under his Indo-Islamic predecessors, which had already replaced the disorderly infantries of hundreds of thousands as well as the related and logistically complex elephant warfare (suitable only for set battles) throughout the subcontinent in medieval times (Figure 6.1).

Figure 6.1 Portrait of Mughal emperor Alamgir on horseback. Heritage Images/Hulton Fine Art Collection via Getty Images.

If, then, horses remained central to warfare in India under the Great Mughals, and even in the successor states of the eighteenth century, it comes as no surprise to find that the horse trade held up equally well. One study after another has established that the Indo-Turanian caravan trade continued to flourish throughout the early modern era, even in the eighteenth century.[18] This bilateral trade was partly upheld by India's continued demand for Central Asian horses and partly by Central Asia's demand for Indian cotton textiles and dyes.[19]

Whereas Babur estimated that in his time seven, eight, or ten thousand horses came to Kabul to be sold in Hindustan, Tavernier in the second half of the seventeenth century observed that Uzbek merchants brought sixty thousand horses to Kabul per year and Manucci put the figure at over one hundred thousand and even one hundred fifty thousand.[20] This demand increased further in the eighteenth century and then became an important source of income for the emerging Indo-Afghan confederacy of the Durranis. Quantifying the value of this trade is not easy, but Jos Gommans has estimated that at any given time during that century the total number of horses in the Indian subcontinent amounted to between four hundred thousand and eight hundred thousand, and he put the annual value of the overland horse trade at around 20 million rupees, "more than three times the total of Bengal exports to Europe by the English and Dutch East India Companies together."[21]

The Culture of Chivalry

The term "chivalry" derives from the medieval French *cheval*, "horse," and denotes the ethos and practices of fully armed men fighting from horses. As such, chivalry became widely diffused from ancient and early medieval times onward among horse-mounted nobilities (also called aristocracies) and the societies they dominated across the world.[22] However, if in Europe and elsewhere infantry replaced cavalry from the sixteenth century onward and, in combination with radically new developments in gunpowder warfare, brought the age of chivalry to a close, in India it was essentially perpetuated until the age of European colonialism. What is more, together with the increased use of horses in warfare, chivalry was assimilated among ever broader segments of society.

The Timurids developed an elaborate culture of chivalry from their earlier nomadic roots in Samarkand, their great ancestor Timur's capital, and in Herat under the latter's son and successor, Shah Rukh (r. 1405–1447), that is reflected in the art, architecture, and literature of great sophistication that they patronized in the fifteenth century. Babur publicly identified with the Timurid culture of these and other urban centers of Mā warā' an-nahr and Khurasan rather than with that of the still-nomadic Mongol tribesmen of his Chingisid maternal relatives further to the north and east.[23] It was this Timurid heritage of chivalry that he brought to India and that flourished there for centuries, in various combinations, with both Persian and Indian elements. Of course, the old barbarian ways of the Mongol nomads that Babur tried to distance himself from continued to play a part as well. Babur's grandson Akbar had to crack down on the still-common Mongol practice, in times of war, of indiscriminately killing noncombatants, capturing women and children, and selling them as slaves. Akbar imposed a severe military discipline in order to curtail this kind of brutal and predatory behavior and, in another departure from the ways of his ancestors, tried to set himself up as an example of moderation, particularly in the consumption of alcohol and other intoxicants. None of Akbar's attempts to tame his nobility were entirely successful. In the 1580s, in the estimate of the Jesuit Rudolpho Acquaviva, the emperor "and all his men who are Mongols" still had "not a little of the barbarian."[24] Especially the warlike Uzbeks, who had been Babur's nemesis in Samarkand but were later absorbed in some numbers among the Mughal nobility in India, continued to be regarded as barbarian in the early seventeenth century. These were men of dirty and rustic habits who drank the blood of their horses and, with their Chingisid leadership, represented the closest approximation to the medieval Mongols. More generally, ghastly torturing and dismemberment practices were still condoned at that time, and the towers of skulls (and heads or bodies hung from trees) of vanquished opponents and rebellious peasants along the imperial highway from Agra to Delhi remained a potent reminder to all of the barbarian origin of India's newest ruling class. Even as the seventeenth century advanced, some of these practices (which were introduced in India by Akbar) remained in vogue. Nevertheless, the most brutal and devastating excesses of medieval Mongol ("Tartar") warfare and predation appear to have become much more restricted already by the turn of the century. In the subsequent decades, the Mughal courts at Delhi and Agra were to set new standards of good manners and good taste even for opponents and rebels. An extraordinarily complex courtly culture of chivalry had by then evolved in these Indian capitals. Moreover, the imperial sumptuousness of the Mughal courts of that time exceeded anything encountered in contemporary Europe. Manucci, with minor variations by virtually all other European authors on the subject, observed that "in the Mogul kingdom the nobles, and above all the king, live with such ostentation that the most sumptuous of European courts cannot compare in richness and magnificence with the luster beheld in the Indian court."[25] A powerful sense of aristocratic exclusiveness had taken hold that had few equals in the world. Nothing is more striking to the present-day reader of Jahangir's memoirs than the indifference toward European traders displayed by the king and his ministers. Jahangir's memoirs chronicle with precision and in minute detail the arrival of missions from Persia and other neighboring countries but make no direct allusion to the English ambassador Sir Thomas Roe, the representative of an obscure and distant country, a "nation of shopkeepers" that the Mughals held in such contempt that, when the English first arrived in Agra in 1613, it was considered derogatory to sign a treaty with them.[26]

This evolved Mughal culture of chivalry adopted remarkably little, at least directly, from the Arabs. According to a widely circulating account of the time, Alamgir resented the efforts of his private tutor to "turn him into a good Arab" and teach him the difficult and useless language of Arabic when he was a boy.[27] There were, obviously, distinguished and influential Arab Sayyids at the Mughal court, but their number was small. The many foreign Muslims recruited into the Mughal nobility were mostly Turks and Mongols, and nearly as often Persians. It was the latter who, at the Timurid courts of India, fostered the culture of chivalry most assiduously. The Persians were not necessarily an ethnically or racially distinct group at all, for many Persians were in fact of Turko-Mongol origin. Before coming to India, they were subjects of the Shiʿa dynasty of the Safawids of Persia, with whom the Timurid dynasty had long had a special relationship. The Safawids had been the imperial neighbor that provided the indispensable military support to Babur and Humayun. As a result, the Safawid Shahs thought themselves entitled to advance certain claims of imperial suzerainty over Mughal India. Akbar abrogated these claims in 1579, but even after that, Persian envoys at the Mughal court continued to enjoy the unique distinction of being received by one of the royal princes. And in the seventeenth century, a majority of the most powerful nobles in the empire of the Great Mughals continued to be of Persian origin. This was in spite of the fact that their Shiʿa orientation did not always sit well at the Mughal court, and their public rituals were eventually banned from court. Strongly attached to their Persian origins, they openly favored their own nation in the Mughal empire, especially in the wars for Kandahar and, more consequentially, those against the Deccan Sultanates of Bijapur and Golkonda. In the latter there was an even larger proportion of Persians, and Safawid-Persian overlordship continued to be recognized in the seventeenth century, while the customs of Shiʿa Islam were observed with the same strictness and freedom as in Persia itself. Throughout this time, the Persians continued to cultivate a strong sense of cultural superiority over the rest of the Mughal nobility and were apt to assume a lofty tone when they wished to impress an idea of their power and influence. They called the people of India "slaves" and "black men," and they made themselves resented for the many witticisms about the Indians, which they never tired of repeating. The Persians went to India for various reasons: because they had fallen out with the Shah of Persia, and were justly or unjustly persecuted, or, quite often, simply to seek their fortune in a land of infinitely greater resources and opportunities. Most important of all, they represented, or affected to represent, a culture of chivalry of unrivaled prestige. Their country of origin, as Pires observed in the early sixteenth century, was widely regarded as "the most ancient and noble [land] of all Asia."[28] Persia had the ancient imperial culture that India so conspicuously lacked. "It has always had monarchs [who are] great lords … It is they who obtained their Empire of Nabucudonosor and his son Cyrus and Darius and Ahasuerus and Xerxes and others. It was in this land that the great Alexander made his widespread conquests."[29] Persia abounded with "beautiful horses," and its people were "full of courtesy, well dressed, magnanimous and valiant in feats of arms" as well as "very fond of pleasure, very orderly in their dress, and us[ing] many perfumes."[30] The Persians in the Mughal empire of the seventeenth century are, thus, generally described as "more polite" and "ordinarily … of the most excellent judgment."[31]

The Mughal culture of chivalry adopted little from the Indo-Afghans. The ignominiously defeated Indo-Afghans, or Pathans, lingered as an ill-assimilated tribal element in the imperial body politic. Clustered across different parts of the empire, and once formidable in the eastern vicinities of the Ganges, they were not regarded as Mughals in the strict sense but in due course were able to make their way back into the imperial nobility. The Indo-Afghans absorbed a degree of Mughal court culture, not the other way around.[32] If they were not regarded as Mughals, or even as "people who are called Mughals" because they were white, foreign Muslims, it was because, together with the Rajputs, they were seen as a native bulwark against foreign dominance and domestic insurgence alike. As such, they held a uniquely ambivalent position. Although Muslims, they were regarded as "an intractable race."[33] And it was "the rule in the Mughal realm not to trust that race."[34] They were never allowed to hold fortresses, "for fear they may plot some treason, as they did to King Humayun."[35] On their part, they held "the Indians, both Gentiles and Mogols, in the utmost contempt; and, recollecting the consideration in which they were formerly held in India, they mortally hate[d] the Mogols."[36] From the time of the death of their great leader Sher Shah, they refused to bind on turbans, wearing in their place a fragment of cloth – a custom, they said, that was to endure until there would again be a Pathan king in India. The wives of Pathan nobles were the only ones not obliged to appear at the palace to make their compliments to the queens and princesses on birthdays and holidays like the Nauroz or New Year. Under the spell of their powerful code of honor of the Pashtunwali, even the menials and carriers of water belonging to that nation were "high-spirited and warlike." Like the tribal Uzbeks, they were prone temperament-wise to conflagration. There was always the possibility that they would unite with their fellow tribesmen to the west of the Indus – the "carnivorous brigands" who, in their strong positions, were a stumbling block on the way to Balkh and Turan – and the Mughal emperors always had to be very careful that these "most warlike" and "barbaric" people, whose fury could never be reduced and whose fierceness and persistence was unmatched, might collect eighty thousand horses and renew their claim to the throne of Hindustan.

Ambivalent as they were in their attitude toward the tribal Afghans of the frontier, and even the more assimilated Indo-Afghans, the Mughals had no difficulty recognizing the "nobility and high birth" of the other native ruling elite of their empire – the Hindu Rajput kings. Thus, unlike their own Indo-Islamic predecessors, the Mughals systematically integrated them into their imperial elite, treating them with the same consideration as the foreign Muslim nobility and appointing them to the same high ranks, army commands, and fortresses, in effect making them one of the foundations of Mughal rule.[37] The three most important Rajput kingdoms were those of the Kachwahas of Amber, the Rathors of Marwar (Jodhpur), and the Sisodias of Mewar (Udaipur). All three had royal pedigrees much longer than that of the Mughals themselves. In the sixteenth century, the Rana of Mewar was held to represent the oldest and most noble of the surviving Rajput houses, established by the Guhilots in Mewar's great fortress of Chitor around 728 CE, and not because members were descendants of an ancient Indian lineage but because they were allegedly descendants of the Sasanid-Persian emperor Nushirvan the Just (531–578 CE) through his daughter, herself born of a daughter of the Byzantine emperor Maurice of Constantinople (582–602 CE), who married into the Udaipur royal family.[38] The house of Mewar and the other two great Rajput houses ruled most of Rajasthan – or Rajwarra, as it was then known – a relatively isolated frontier region of marginal agricultural importance marked by great internal subdivision. Under the Mughals, all three could bring into the field at least twenty thousand cavalry, possibly fifty thousand, and a great number of infantry troops to boot. Raja Bharmal Kachwaha was the first Rajput king to enter Mughal service, under Akbar, with his sons and grandsons, and establish matrimonial relations with the Timurid dynasty.

Figure 6.2 The Rajput fortress of Chitor, Rajasthan, India. Braunger/
ullstein bild via Getty Images.

The Kachwahas, from the smallest of the states in the northeastern
plains of Rajasthan, remained the most favored and trusted of the
Rajput nobles under Akbar, and ever afterward found themselves dispersed all over the empire. By contrast, the Sisodia Rajputs, led by the
Rana of Mewar (or "the Rana," as he is usually called), never formally
submitted to Mughal rule, even though they accepted a limited military role in the empire. Abul Fazl describes the Rana as "this audacious and immoderate one, in whom the turbulence of ancestors was
added to his own haughtiness, [who] was proud of the steep mountains
and strong castles [he owned] and turned away the head of obedience
from the sublime court" (Figure 6.2).[39]

Akbar set off to conquer the Rana's citadel of Chitor in 1567, because
"His Majesty's dignity demanded that he should proceed in person to
chastise the Rana." In the ensuing conflict, "the price of life was low,
that of honor high." It was a bloody engagement out of which Akbar
emerged victorious but one that did nothing to bring about the Rana's
formal submission. In the seventeenth century, the Rana of Mewar
kept seven thousand horsemen in Mughal service at his own expense
but would never consent to put on the sarapa or robe of honor of the

Mughal, in order not to admit himself to be a subject, nor would he ever provide women for the imperial harem as all other Rajputs of distinction did. Alamgir also made war on the Rana but confirmed the latter's traditional privileges, including the shelter of an umbrella, an honor conceded to no one but the Mughal emperor himself. His seven thousand horsemen acquired such a bad name in the Mughal territories that they were commuted into a money payment.

There were perhaps another fifteen powerful Rajput kings in Hindustan, and another eighty smaller ones ensconced in the hills as well as the plains in other parts of the empire, all of whom paid tribute or provided soldiers for the imperial armies and were also specifically deployed to keep in check both each other or the Afghans or rebellious nobles, particularly the Persians in the Deccan. Lesser Rajputs were recruited even more widely. In the first half of the seventeenth century, about one of every six or seven nobles in the empire of the Great Mughals was a Rajput chief. The Maratha king Shivaji Bhonsle had himself proclaimed a Sisodia Rajput, a descendant of the royal house of Udaipur and Chitor, in a *rajyabhisheka* ceremony in 1674, and thus, when the Marathas entered Mughal service in the second half of the seventeenth and eighteenth centuries, the Rajputs' putative ranks swelled still further. In the course of the centuries that they were under Mughal rule, Rajput methods of warfare, as already mentioned, changed considerably and became much more cavalry-oriented, as a result of the acquisition of better warhorses and training (cf. p. 166). The top layer of Rajputs eventually closed ranks and began to articulate new norms of Rajput behavior that became more and more exclusively legitimized in the language of descent and kinship. By invoking Mughal support, these Rajput nobles were able to ignore traditional claims of the wider clans for a share of power and were thus given an opportunity to establish more autocratic and centralized regimes, while also adopting Mughal methods of more uniform and bureaucratic administration. Yet they always retained their own distinctive Rajput warrior code. In palaces or camps, they made less display than the Mughals or Indian Muslims. They had a special reputation for being bold and courageous people, especially so because they made a practice of heavily drugging themselves and their horses with opium for battle. They were determined and obstinate, as well as loyal to their own leaders, fostering a culture of self-sacrifice; and unlike the Muslims, they were keepers of their word. As part of the same Rajput code, kings and sometimes entire garrisons would immolate themselves with their wives and children or deliberately seek death in battle when faced with a particularly humiliating defeat. We find this custom in India as early as the eleventh century, and it survived among the Rajputs under the name of *jauhar* well into the seventeenth (with variants of the custom being encountered as far as the remote islands of Bali and Lombok as late as the nineteenth and twentieth centuries). Rajputs dyed their clothes with saffron and threw themselves on the enemy "like madmen."⁴⁰ De Laet states that "they advance furiously to the attack; but owing to their ignorance of military discipline and tactics, they become either victorious or are routed very quickly, and battles generally result in immense slaughter."⁴¹ The Shahjahannama refers to "the foolish obstinacy of the Rajputs."⁴² There was an especially strong religious dimension to Rajput warfare, with regard to which the Rajputs "call[ed] themselves lions of different idols."⁴³ Very few converted to Islam, and if they did it was mostly at the middle and lower rungs of the hierarchy. They would eat all kinds of meat except beef, and drink wine, but it appears that they ate separately, sitting bare-bodied, and did not eat anything cooked by Muslims.

What these horse-riding warrior elites of the Turks, Mongols, Persians, Afghans, and Rajputs had in common was a culture of chivalry, although it was far from homogeneous. An internally differentiated culture of chivalry is what one would expect in a multiethnic empire such as that of the Great Mughals. But for all this differentiation, it was in essential respects a single culture that was widely shared across ethnic and religious boundaries. As such, we can identify four characteristics of the culture of chivalry that permeated the Mughal empire in its entirety.

The first characteristic was a deeply rooted disdain for the petty details of daily administration, which the grandees dismissed as the domain of lowly shopkeepers. Akbar, to be sure, like the Indo-Afghan ruler Sher Shah, professed to subscribe to the idea that truly great kings did not confine their attention to great things only and declared himself a friend of good order and propriety in business, no matter how small. But it was an idea whose time had not yet come. Imperial statistics generally remained poor and unreliable in the extreme, but the Mughal nobility at all times displayed an obsessive precision with all issues of rank, precedence, and honor. The culture of chivalry drowned out utilitarian and practical considerations under the sheer weight of a formality that strikes modern observers as excessive and over-laborious. Paradoxically, it was Akbar himself who introduced many new elements of an imperial court etiquette that eventually became central to the culture of chivalry. Among these we find the display of largesse and the giving of gifts in acknowledgment of hierarchical status differences that had been absent from the dealings of the medieval Sultanates of

Delhi, and from the reigns of Babur and Humayun as well. Most conspicuously, the gift of a robe of honor by the emperor conveyed nobility at court, but the public giving of lavish gifts, the exact value of which was assiduously monitored and quantified in rupees, became a custom throughout the subcontinent and beyond. Gifts could be anything, even slaves and eunuchs or horses, but not money. The public display is what mattered, for, as Manucci observed, "they look on it as a distinction and an honor to receive presents in public, but as regards money they never take it but in secret."[44] Insofar as the etiquette of the court was concerned, the preservation of the dignity of the imperial family at the top of the noble hierarchy became the highest priority at all times, even during travel. When the king went on campaign, his personal camp, or *laskar,* covered an immense space of ground, and within four or five hours so many tents were pitched that a town would seem to have sprung up, and "the gradation of rank is so rigidly enforced that everyone in these camps, from the greatest to the least, knows precisely at what distance to pitch his own tents from those of the king."[45] At Agra, Manucci relates that when a noble with the title of Jafar Khan came to court, "he placed one foot farther forward than was allowed by the regulations" and therefore was reprimanded by the king, who later corrected himself and admitted to an error in not recognizing that Jafar Khan was a wazir.[46] It was ostensibly all about honor, not money, and none of it was considered too petty to be taken seriously. Ominous beyond measure, there was no greater crime than an affront to the honor of the Mughal emperor or any member of the royal family, an act for which no pardon was possible. But the nobility in general is presented in the chronicles as extremely touchy and sensitive to slights.

The second, and related, general characteristic of the culture of chivalry was its intimate connection with a distinctive noble lifestyle and pattern of consumption, with concomitant notions of polite society and dignified behavior. In the capitals as well as in the provinces, it was the great men's practice to spend lavishly on the extravagant display of elephants, horses, and servants, so that they themselves rode out more like kings than subjects. European observers took special note of the exclusive lifestyle of the nobles; "the indescribable luxury and extravagance" in which they lived; their indulgence in every kind of pleasure; how, for instance, only they would only eat basmati rice, which was "whiter than white"; and that they dressed their wives and concubines in the semitransparent muslin known as "flowing water" (*āb-i-ravān*) on hot summer nights. The nobles' mansions had several courts and flat rooftops to enjoy the fresh air, gardens, tanks, fountains, carpets, palatial halls, and many rooms.

In Agra...the waterfront is occupied by the costly palaces of all the famous lords, which make it appear very gay and magnificent...for a distance of 10.5 miles...including [those of the] Rajput nobles...Here the great lords far surpass ours in magnificence, for their gardens serve for enjoyment while they are alive, and after death for their tombs, which during their lifetime they build with great magnificence in the middle of the garden.[47]

The nobles and their women kept exceedingly large numbers of servants and slaves, according to their dignity and wealth. Meanwhile, all the business of bookkeeping and buying and selling was done by Hindu clerks and menials, "except for the sale of horses, oxen, camels, elephants, or any living creatures, which they will not handle as the Muslims do."[48] Inasmuch as they were freed from the practical preoccupations of running their large households, or indeed any manual work, the nobles strained to cultivate a dignified comportment. When in audience, the kings and princes displayed all imaginable gravity and majesty. An attitude of imperturbability and placidness was observed and greatly valued by all the great nobles. In conversation, according to De Thévenot, the nobles were "modest and civil, not using so many actions with their hands, not talking so loud as some Europeans do."[49] De Laet similarly emphasized that "in conversation they are very modest and polite (you would call them past masters of good manners): They never talk loudly or gesticulate."[50] Not only the nobility but the Indian people in general, according to Manucci, "esteem above everything else that moral virtue of gentleness and those who possess it...they abhor the bilious temperament which takes fire at once, a thing entirely unknown to their phlegmatic temperament, one very difficult to arouse."[51] Nonconfrontational to a fault, the vice of flattery pervaded "all ranks." Slow movement was the special mark of dignity. Nothing captures this better than Manucci's description of Shah Jahan's eldest daughter, Begum Sahib, proceeding to court:

When Begam Sahib leaves her palace to go to court, she proceeds in great pomp, with much cavalry and infantry and many eunuchs. The last named, who surround her closely, push on one side everyone they find in front of them, shouting out, pushing and assaulting everyone without the least respect of persons. The same is done by all the princesses of the blood-royal when they come out. Thus it is that, perceiving the approach of these princesses, everybody forthwith hastens out of the way. They proceed *very slowly* [italics added], men in front sprinkling water on the roadway to lay the dust. They are placed in a palanquin which has over it a rich cloth or net of gold, sometimes ornamented with precious stones or pieces of looking-glass. The eunuchs surround the palanquin, driving away the flies with peacock-feathers stuck into handles of enameled gold-work or adorned with precious stones. The men-servants hold sticks of gold or silver in their hands, and call out, "Out of the way! Out of the way!" Near the palanquin they carry various perfumes.[52]

The ideal of moving slowly, again, pervaded "all ranks" of Indian society. As Emily Eden observed about traveling in India in the 1830s, before "the curse of the railways," it was "the natives' mark of dignity to move as slowly as possible."[53] Only merchants and shopkeepers were concerned with "loss of time."[54]

The third characteristic of the culture of chivalry in Mughal India is that it regulated gender relations by investing honor in women in certain prescribed ways. At its most rarified level, this meant that the Mughal emperor had the *droit de seigneur*, which allowed him to requisition any woman in his realm, already married or not. Although far from purely theoretical, it had the potential to cause widespread resentment and was in practice restricted in its application. Especially in the beginning, it sent shockwaves through Rajasthan, and the Rana of Mewar successfully resisted it until the end. Shah Jahan became notorious for meddling with the wives of his nobles, who in the end avenged themselves by handing him over to Aurangzeb. The inviolability of the Mughal royal harems was, however, universally respected. It was said that since Timur, "in all generations of the Moguls, no queen has been made a prisoner in war, except Humayun's queen, who was taken by Sher Shah, the Pathan; and even that prince sent her back as far as Persia."[55] It was the same with the harems of the Mughal nobility. Furthermore, female seclusion, or *purda*, was universal among the nobility at large. The princesses (wives, daughters, and sisters of the emperor) would never leave the palace except on occasion with the emperor's special permission, and even then they were inaccessible to the sight of men. All nobles shut up their women and exercised the exact same supervision as the king did, not even trusting their own brothers. Noblewomen were committed to the custody of perhaps two or three eunuchs for each wife, usually purchased Bengali slaves, who would ensure that she was not seen by any man except her husband. In a desperate situation, Muslim noblewomen could be killed rather than exposed to the public gaze. The Mughal prince Shah Shuja', for instance, fleeing the troops of his brother Aurangzeb in Bengal, ordered a boat with one hundred fifty of his harem ladies to be sunk when, in the confusion, they just sat there in view of everybody – carried out without regard for the jewels they were wearing. And purda was by no means confined to the Muslim nobility. De Thévenot observed that in Mughal India it was the general practice that "the Mahometan women do not appear in public, except only the vulgar sort, and the leud Ones."[56] Even ordinary Muslims are on record for having killed their wives or daughters who were exposed to strangers or having confined them to burning homes rather than have them exposed to the view of strangers, and soldiers are known to have killed their wives amid the distress of famine when they could not carry them along without exposing them to public view. In the countryside and the towns of Afghanistan and Peshawar, if the early nineteenth-century evidence is anything to go by, the conditions of Muslim women varied more explicitly with their rank.[57] The Afghan peasant and nomad women went about unveiled, and among them there was less restraint in relations between the sexes, but it was regarded as indecent for women to associate with men with whom they were not intimate, except among Armenians, Persians, or Hindus, whom they counted as nothing. Women of the towns and noble houses were allowed to attend garden parties and go about the town but were entirely concealed, wrapped up in a large white sheet that covered them from head to foot and allowed them to see through a net in the white hood covering the face. Purda also prevailed among Hindus in an almost infinite number of ways, even though Hindu women were not normally entirely concealed by veils and clothes. Women of especially the upper castes were severely restricted in their freedom of movement, as it is manifested in the caste rules of commensality, prohibitions against travel abroad, taboos about entering port towns, and much more.

Polygamy was practically universal in the upper ranks of society, whether Muslim or Hindu. "Just as for other people more than one wife is not suitable," wrote Abul Fazl, "so for great persons more are necessary, so that their dwellings may be more splendid, and a large number of people may be supported; especially is this so with nobly-born persons who are the ornament of the age."[58] Islamic law allowed polygamy for those who could afford it, and as a rule the nobles had three or four wives, with each wife having her own apartments and ten to a hundred servants and slaves, but the very rich exceeded the legal number of four wives and kept crowds of female slaves besides. Some had over a thousand women in their harem, while emperors could have several thousand, if political wives and concubines free or slave are included in the count. Hindus, too, could have multiple wives either successively or simultaneously, according to their own customary law. It was uncommon and even quite rare among the poor. But there have been Hindu kings who have had as many as five thousand wives at once. Maintaining very large harems became more common among the great Rajput kings under Mughal rule. One such king, Man Singh, for instance, had fifteen hundred wives when he died in the Deccan.

Widow remarriage was universally restricted, although among Muslims the remarrying of widows was by no means prohibited, and there are instances of remarriage among the Mughal nobility and even the royal family. As a rule, "the wives of these great men do not marry again, though in no way prohibited."[59] The royal wives of Shah Jahan, for instance, were sent into retirement in a palace for royal widows. When great ladies came out, as a sign of their widowhood they covered their palanquins with green cloth and did not wear ornaments on their necks. Among the Hindu upper castes there was not even the option of widows getting remarried, even should they be four or five years of age. Their fates varied. They could become prostitutes, return to their parents' house as servants, sell rice door to door, or burn with the dead bodies of their husbands. It was imperative among the rajas that a wife burn with the dead husband, either voluntarily or not, thus becoming a goddess, for which statues were erected. Such self-immolation of widows, known as *sati* or *sahagamana*, was a tradition as old as the ninth century and became widespread in the subsequent centuries among upper-caste Hindus. It was found throughout the Indic realm under the medieval Indo-Islamic rulers, and even more so under the independent rajas, as well as in the great Hindu empire of Vijayanagara. It is frequently described by all European travelers to Mughal India. Jahangir described the practice in his memoirs: "It is the custom among the Hindus that after the death of their husbands women burn themselves, whether from love, or to save the honor of their fathers, or from being ashamed before their sons-in-law."[60] Indo-Islamic rulers turned against sati as early as the fourteenth century, and the Mughal government increasingly did so as well and ultimately prohibited it in the empire's territories. Yet the practice may actually have become more frequent in Mughal India. Since the great Rajput rajas became increasingly polygamous in the Mughal period, the number of women that "burnt themselves in the fire of fidelity" is likely to have increased drastically in the sixteenth and parts of the seventeenth century.

The fourth general characteristic of the culture of chivalry of Mughal India is that it was indissolubly linked to the world of privilege, institutionalized dissidence, and sedition (*fitna*) highlighted in Chapter 5 (pp. 156–9). Privilege means "private law," and the idea of a nobility or aristocracy without privilege is inconceivable. It was part of the code of honor. In Europe, too, privilege and honor provided license to defy the king and flout his laws in circumstances in which the nobleman himself was the sole judge.[61] The history of medieval and early modern European states, and indeed all chivalrous societies, is therefore made up of repeated clashes between kings and rebellious nobles and strewn with quarrels about precedence. It was no different in Mughal India, and here the culture of sedition perpetuated itself longer and with more vigor than perhaps anywhere else in the world. "Nothing can be more surprising than the way things go on in the Mogul Empire," to quote Manucci again, for "they flinch from nothing in their pursuit of wealth; they ignore even the loyalty to their sovereign ... no-one has the slightest hesitation in violating the fidelity he owes to the king."[62] Seen from this angle, Mughal chronicles are nothing but the annals of the procrastination, acts of "cowardice," and double-facedness of the nobility. Deceit was only matched by distrust:

Provided it suits their own interests, they trouble themselves little about those of the king or the honor of his arms. Thus what would be held in Europe as cowardice and open treason counts among them, if not for an act of high policy and the conduct of an able man, at any rate for a venial fault, and a proof that a man is acute enough to work things to his own advantage.[63]

Bernier referred to this predicament when he wrote about "the ungrateful conduct of nobles."[64] And when he observed that the Mughal nobles used every means at their disposal to prolong the war in the Deccan which was the source of their "emolument and dignity."[65] For all its wealth and power, therefore, "the vast bulk of the empire labors under many discomforts, both disorders within and assaults from without ... and is tormented by numerous intestine disorders and calamities."[66]

"The Greatest and Most Powerful Empire in the World"

The paradox of an empire riddled with dissent and sedition on all levels yet in De Thévenot's words "the greatest and most powerful empire in the world" should no longer confuse us. As we have seen, Akbar was able to invest dissent and sedition in the future of his dynasty by the adjustments he made to the Turko-Mongol succession practices that he inherited from his ancestors. The system of open competition and rivalry among the princes enabled the Great Mughals to absorb upwardly mobile elites, co-opt both imperial and nonimperial sources of dissent and sedition, and thereby reinforce the dynastic continuity of their empire and deepen their control in core as well as outlying territories.[67] It was this expanding and deepening dynastic control of an immense and virtually unrivaled human and agricultural resource base that explains the extraordinary wealth and power of the empire of the Great Mughals.

Thus, the Mughals not only managed to utilize dissent and sedition to their advantage but also captured the momentum of Indian economic and monetary growth associated with the influx of American silver through trade, which increased enormously in importance during Akbar's reign, especially after the conquest of Gujarat brought Portuguese trade within the Mughal orbit.[68] Everywhere the monetization of the economy fostered the development of an intermediary group of financiers and traders, converting land revenue into cash, extending credit, and transmitting funds and bills of exchange throughout the length and breadth of the subcontinent. Just as in early modern Europe, the increased demands for conscientious bureaucrats helped turn the bourgeoisie into the main agency of monarchical rule, in sixteenth-century Mughal India the same demands brought the Hindu banking and financier castes to power and prominence – notably the caste of the Khatris, of whom Akbar's finance minister Raja Todar Mal was the most illustrious representative (he had honed his skills under Sher Shah).[69] The new economy or cash nexus of the later sixteenth century, with its highly developed currency system and its ancillary monetary instruments such as the hundi, or bill of exchange, and short-term credit, drove fiscal reform and the establishment of a more effective bureaucracy. The dramatically enhanced circulation of money was a crucial factor that changed the conditions for deployment of power. Under Akbar this currency became the foundation of the land revenue settlement and the entire structure of remunerative entitlements and rewards, as well as ranks of the official bureaucratic and military institutions. By being computed in money values, these could acquire a greater degree of systematization than the far-less-monetized institutions of fiscal management and tributary flows in kind that had characterized the regimes of his predecessors.

By thus capitalizing on economic growth and expansion, Akbar was able to establish a new framework for his imperial service nobility – one that accommodated the leadership of the Hindu majority population in prominent positions and at the same time safeguarded its autonomy. In essence, this was again no more than an adaptation of the original institutional framework of the Mongol nomadic war band. The origins of this new and comprehensive framework, in effect, go back to the decimal system of military organization that Chingiz Khan deployed, in accordance with immemorial custom, to break the power of the Mongol nomad tribes.[70] Chingiz Khan divided his armies in units of ten, one hundred, one thousand, and ten thousand that he placed under the command of his own trusted followers and household officers. Subject peoples, whether nomadic tribes, city dwellers, or peasants, were enlisted as auxiliary troops under the same decimal system. Timur created his conquest army by a similar method, transforming a tribally organized society into a unified army subservient only to himself. In India, the actual vocabulary of the mansab system appears to have been introduced not by the Timurids but by Ibrahim Lodi (r. 1517–1526). That Indo-Afghan ruler introduced an early form of the mansab system among his nobility in an attempt – which ultimately failed – to undermine the Afghan custom of patrimonial sharing of revenue rights among clan members and with which he had become acquainted through his own numerous Mongol troops. Akbar, in the eighteenth year of his reign (1573), gave the system the comprehensive and systemic features it would retain during the remainder of the sixteenth century and throughout the seventeenth century, except that the numbers were corrected for inflation (by multiplying the ranks) at the beginning of the reigns of both Jahangir and Shah Jahan. The mansabs, or ranking system, of the less than two thousand men who constituted the top layer of the imperial nobility of the Mughal Raj represented a single, unified hierarchy that (unlike in Ibrahim Lodi's system) did not exclude the Rajputs, and excluded the Afghans as the representatives of the ancien regime only in the beginning. Mansabs were official places, usually of combined civil and military power, that did not differentiate between Hindus and Muslims as such.[71] They were perhaps the most striking aspect of the systematization that occurred under Akbar, in that they converted the rank, payment, and military and other obligations of their holders (mansabdars) into exact numbers. This system turned the political process into a form of political arithmetic. The numbers – ranging from ten to ten thousand, as had been the case with Chingiz Khan – indicated the number of men that the mansabdars were expected to bring in. Akbar did not maintain a large standing army paid from the treasury but relied on such mansabdars to raise and command their own contingents of (mostly) cavalry. The ranks and emoluments – which were obtained from centrally supervised jagirs, or "assignments," of revenue collection in particular localities and took up over 80 percent of the imperial budget – were not inheritable. Appointment, retention, promotion, and dismissal depended on the will of the emperor. The mansabdars were not an independently organized body and were not required to drill or observe uniformity in dress or arms. Here as everywhere, Akbar introduced regulations – including minutely descriptive rolls and the branding of horses – to ensure that the recruitment of the specified amounts of men, horses, provisions, and equipment took place. The jagirs in particular localities were normally assigned for a few years only, and they merely involved the rights of revenue collection. The higher mansabdars frequently held such land revenue assignments, large and small, in a number of noncontiguous villages and districts.

It was precisely the noninheritable nature of the revenue assignments that were made over to the mansabdars, and the practice of "revenue farming" (short-term leases of revenue rights that were sold to the highest bidder) with which it is often loosely associated, that fueled the argument that in the empire of the Great Mughals there was no room for a genuinely hereditary (which is to say landed) nobility with a lasting stake in the prosperity of the empire and therefore was ruinous to agricultural productivity and the prosperity of the peasants. In this estimate, the great wealth and power of the Mughal empire was basically achieved through plunder – by crushing any stable intermediary estates between the imperial household and an undifferentiated mass of subsistence-oriented peasants. Mughal imperial rule thus came to be seen as a form of "Oriental despotism." This view was widespread but is best known from François Bernier's letter to Jean-Baptiste Colbert, the French politician who served as the minister of finances from 1665 to 1683 under the rule of King Louis XIV, and accompanying travel accounts:

As the land throughout the whole [Mughal] empire is considered the property of the sovereign, there can be no earldoms, marquisates or duchies...From what I have said, a question will naturally arise, whether it would not be more advantageous for the King as well as for the people, if the former ceased to be sole possessor of the land, and the right of private property were recognised in the Indies as it is with us? I have carefully compared the condition of European states, where that right is acknowledged, with the condition of those countries where it is not known, and am persuaded that the absence of it among the people is injurious to the best interests of the Sovereign himself...The Timariots [Jagirdars], Governors, and Revenue contractors, on their part reason in this manner: "Why should the neglected state of this land create uneasiness in our minds? And why should we expend our own money and time to render it fruitful? We may be deprived of it in a single moment, and our exertions would benefit neither ourselves nor our children..." It is owing to this miserable system of government that most towns in Hindoustan are made up of earth, mud, and other wretched materials; that there is no city or town which, if it be not already ruined and deserted, does not bear evident marks of approaching decay...How happy and thankful should we feel, My Lord, that in our quarter of the globe, Kings are not the sole proprietor of the soil! Were they so, we should seek in vain for countries well cultivated and populous, for well-built and opulent cities, for a polite, contented, and flourishing people. If this exclusive and baneful right prevailed, far different would be the real riches of the sovereigns of Europe, and the loyalty and fidelity with which they are served. They would soon reign over solitudes and deserts, over mendicants and barbarians.[72]

Much has also been made in this context of a related doctrine known as *escheat* (from the Latin *ex-cadere*, to "fall out," via the medieval French *escheoir*), whereby property reverted to the ruler. In accordance with this doctrine, feudal lords in medieval Europe would sometimes resume the land of vassals, in particular in the absence of heirs but in certain other circumstances as well. In Europe it had ceased to play a role by the sixteenth century, as the revival of Roman laws of inheritance made private property rights almost absolute. It was, however, commonly believed by European authors of the sixteenth and seventeenth centuries that escheat in one form or another had become normal state policy (as an outgrowth of the theory that all land belonged ultimately to the ruler) in large parts of Asia – in the Mughal empire as much as in Thailand, Aceh, Bantam, Mataram, Laos, Burma, Cambodia, and elsewhere – at around the same time that it disappeared from Europe.[73] In the echo chamber of early modern European political theory, it contributed to the understanding that noble property in the East was "as unstable as the wind,"[74] that "no family can long maintain its distinction,"[75] and that "no family can for long remain great."[76] It is a widely held view still today; some recent authors have regarded the practice of escheat as a survival of Islamic corporate military slavery.[77]

In its broadest terms, it is not a view that has ever been entirely without some merit. Noble and princely fortunes, in effect, fluctuated wildly. The career of Babur, as described in vivid detail in his memoir, shows that even the fortunes of the emperors themselves could change overnight and sink very low indeed. Babur's son Humayun lost everything he had acquired by conquest and became a fugitive reduced to eating horsemeat boiled in a helmet in the desert. Under Akbar, fratricide became the sole road to survival for Mughal princes pitched against each other in merciless struggles for the succession to the Mughal throne. Careers could indeed be ruined as a result of trifling mistakes.

It is, of course, equally true that nobilities or aristocracies never stayed the same for long not only in the Mughal empire but anywhere in the world and that it was the normal state of affairs that imperial hierarchies were constantly overturned. As Vilfredo Pareto remarked, history is a "graveyard of aristocracies."[78] The Mughal nobility or aristocracy may have had an unusually high turnover for two reasons. For one, it was not clearly or legally defined as a closed status category. Just as the idea of the Mughal army as a distinct institution was a false one (because of the almost limitless proportions of the military profession in India), so the idea of a Mughal nobility as a distinct institution was a false one also. Whatever the hazards and pitfalls of noble existence at the top of the hierarchy, the ranks of the Mughal nobility were in fact very much open from below, and the Mughal empire throughout its history had to accommodate upwardly mobile elites and nobles or amirs of "low descent" and even "slave descent," such as the highly visible "eunuch grandees" (who invested all their money in their tombs). There were also no serious barriers preventing merchant-financiers from entering the ranks of the mansabdar nobility: Mir Jumla, the man who practically decided the fate of the Mughal empire at mid-century, as a Deccani ally and later court noble under Alamgir, started his professional life as a shoe salesman. In addition, there were constantly new conquests being made, and this, too, was a reason that "the number of nobles [omrahs] throughout the Empire [was] not settled."[79] Indeed, the Mughal nobility expanded in size all the time, while its composition was in constant flux, with new families and clans entering and older ones losing power and prestige or even disappearing altogether. There exist, therefore, countless lists of important amirs or nobles in the empire that have been drawn up at different times and that all varied. Some list forty, others only twenty-five amirs as the "pillars of the empire," and they have varying numbers of hundreds of other, lesser mansabdars at court and in the provinces where regional elites were being incorporated, especially in the later decades of Alamgir's reign. No one really knows how many nobles there were in the Mughal empire at any specific time, or even what exactly constituted "the nobility."[80] But how unusual was this really?

There is, at the same time, every indication that it was an almost invariable custom in the Mughal empire to make promotions gradual and for newcomers from outside the subcontinent to be paid in cash for some time, not jagirs, until they knew the affairs and customs of the people.[81] Similarly, demotion was far from random. The practice of escheat or confiscating (part of) the property of deceased mansabdars now appears to have been uncommon. It can be traced back to Akbar and appears to have been in existence under Jahangir and Shah Jahan, but not under Alamgir, who abolished it. The little that historians have found out about it in the Indo-Persian sources, however, is evidence that it was rarely applied in all reigns – in just seven or eight cases in total, and only among the highest ranks – in attempts to assert the ultimate authority of the crown, and that, unless there were no heirs, it did not affect the entire assets of any of these nobles but only the state's demand (*mutaliba*), which was usually a fraction of the nobles' wealth.[82] In the words of Muhammad Athar Ali, a historian who devoted a good part of his career to the study of the Mughal mansab system, "the escheat yoke was always very light."[83] What was vulnerable, especially in political crises, was the accumulated property of merchants – in other words, money obtained by people outside the ranks of the imperial hierarchy of the nobility who could be "squeezed like a sponge, not without danger to life itself."[84] While it is certainly true that the mansabdars were "reckoned by horses" and were not necessarily landowners, heredity was without question the most important factor determining noble status.[85] This is evident in the rise to prominence of an ever-expanding section of the nobility that became known as *khanazads*, "born to the house," and already by the early 1600s distinguished by familial hereditary service over three or four generations and actual residence at the imperial court or camp.[86] The khanazads could be both Hindus and Muslims, and included even some Afghans, and eventually counted for over half of the entire mansabdari corps, dominating the higher but also the middle and lower ranks until the Deccan wars of the latter seventeenth century. They enjoyed many unique privileges, such as never having to enter anywhere deprived of their arms.[87] They were without question the core of a hereditary nobility.

Heredity is equally in evidence among the native Indian nobles who were not khanazads. These comprised the most influential minority among the Mughal nobility – Rajputs, some Afghans, and Indian Muslims – and retained hereditary ties to landed patrimonial domains to which they would at times return. When Akbar came to the throne, a large part of the country (perhaps a third or half) of Hindustan was under the rule of numerous hereditary rajas or kings, mostly of small holdings but in places substantial ones, who were accommodated in this way. Irrespective of the size of their holdings, their Muslim overlords had long been referring to these potentates by the generic Indo-Persian name of *zamindars*, or "landholders." Akbar continued his predecessors' policy of demanding recognition for his claim of paramountcy by the provision of tribute and military aid but renewed their hereditary titles and left them with a large degree of autonomy in the internal administration of their domains. The great royal Rajput houses of Rajasthan and at least a hundred or a few hundred others became linked to the Timurid dynasty through matrimonial ties that were anything but transitory. Akbar's son Jahangir was born of one such marriage and therefore had Indian "blue blood." Jahangir's son Shah Jahan was three-quarters Indian himself – since both his mother and grandmother had been Rajput princesses – and did not marry any Indian wives, but his son Aurangzeb, the later emperor Alamgir, again did. Even more importantly than this matrimonial policy, many of these rajas, and some other influential Indians in key positions (like the Hindu finance minister Todar Mal), were accommodated into the imperial hierarchy of the mansabdari nobility, receiving lucrative and honorable employment on a hereditary basis, as well as jagirs, the revenue of which far exceeded that of their ancestral dominions. According to Athar Ali's calculations, in 1595, Rajputs held four of the twenty-five "highest mansabs," of 3,000 and above; Rajputs, other Hindus, and Indian Muslims held thirty-two of the ninety-eight "high mansabs," of 500–2,500, and forty-seven of one hundred sixty "medium mansabs," of 200–450. The proportions were not very different half a century after Akbar's death, although the total number of mansabs was higher then. In 1656 Rajputs and Marathas held four of the twenty-five "highest mansabs," of 5,000 and above; Rajputs, other Hindus, Marathas, and Indian Muslims held seventy-nine of two hundred twenty-three "high mansabs," of 1,000–4,500, and eighty-two of two hundred seventy "medium mansabs," of 500–900.[88] In the last decades of Alamgir's reign, the proportion of Indian mansabdars reached their highest levels in the Deccan wars. What mattered most, from the beginning until then, was that all ancestral dominions of the rajas were treated as *watan jagirs*, or "hereditary jagirs," under indirect Mughal rule. The Mughals thus intentionally promoted heredity. As a result, the institutions of hereditary rulership and clientele, as well as centralized administration, greatly developed in Rajasthan and beyond at the expense of the shared authority of the extended clan. The Mughal emperors, in fact, assumed the right to appoint successors to positions of hereditary rulership in Rajasthan by supporting them with arms and resources in the form of such watan jagirs and other revenue assignments outside their hereditary dominions.

In all the territories under direct imperial rule, including the bulk of the fertile plains of Hindustan, whether given out as jagirs or reserved as khalsa or "crown lands," the Mughal government from Akbar's time onward encountered another category of zamindars – a rural gentry of "landholders" with old, and vested, hereditary rights – who had historically arisen out of the agrarian function of colonization and settlement (which had a military dimension as well) and exercised customary jurisdiction across ill-demarcated stretches of inhabited countryside but were without rights of sovereignty like those of the rajas. These represented the mostly Hindu rural leadership, a class standing just above the peasantry. Ensconced in mud forts with local crack troops and commonly some low-breed horses and possessing detailed knowledge of and participating in rural society, these zamindars, with their ill-defined sub-sovereign powers, were indispensable in the preparation of the revenue assessment, the realization of the land revenue, and all the never-ending efforts to maintain and extend cultivation. They played a vital role in the political, economic, and cultural life of Indian rural society and on that level exercised tremendous power across generations.

Both categories of zamindars, whether the more-or-less autonomous royal or princely ones of the first type or the rural gentry of the second type, enjoyed hereditary rights that preceded the advent of the Great Mughals, often by centuries. To some extent, therefore, there was always an inevitable conflict of interest between the zamindars of both types and the Mughal government. Most of the administrative challenges the latter faced in rural society had to do with the recalcitrance of the zamindars of the second type. Although the Mughals granted the rajas a certain autonomy in internal affairs and did not concern themselves with their revenue collection, in the directly ruled territories they attempted to reduce the rural gentry, as well as the leadership of tribal populations (pastoralists, forest people, and the like, in the marginally cultivated parts of the empire), as much as possible to the position of official intermediaries between themselves and the peasants. As intermediaries, the zamindars were officially entitled to 10 percent of the land revenue as compensation for their services to the emperor; the rest went by right to him. Historians have been able to calculate that in reality more than half of the land revenue stayed in the hands of the zamindari rural gentry – although the Ain-i-Akbari, the great statistical gazetteer of Akbar's reign, is notoriously self-contradictory and unreliable especially here. Since these zamindars represented the invariably localist and parochial interests of rural society, the official representation of these minor magnates is highly misleading. Even the official Mughal chronicles cannot hide the fact that they were to a significant extent beyond the control of the imperial bureaucracy even in the best of times. "It is the general custom of the zamindars of Hindustan," writes Abul Fazl, "to leave wrongfully the path of single-mindedness and to have an eye to every side and to join anyone who is triumphant or stirring up sedition."[89] Well over two hundred distinct zamindari "uprisings" have made it into the official record of Akbar's reign alone, and there were similar numbers, as well as innumerable unrecorded ones, during the reigns of all later emperors, most often in the context of princely rivalry. The Mughal governors referred to the rural population and its leadership as *zulm-parast*, "adorers of tyranny," because in their eyes it was impossible to enlist their services unless enforced by harsh treatment and, indeed, torture. Fiscal docility had to be enforced and could never be taken for granted. The picture of these rural magnates as "officeholders" has therefore never been accurate. An eighteenth-century Maratha treatise on government, the *Ajñapatra*, makes it explicitly clear that the zamindars may be called "officeholders" but that this is only a term of convention, for they were in fact "sharers of the kingdom."[90]

The treatise explains that the zamindars were never satisfied with what they had and had no intention of being loyal to the sovereign but rather aimed to increase their power by encroachment on each other's lands and stir up sedition. They were an important and at times decisive factor in Mughal succession struggles and in the eighteenth century provided the underpinnings of the Mughal successor states across the subcontinent. Nevertheless, there was also, below all this, a level of cooperation that allowed the Mughal revenue machinery to remain operational. Akbar, in effect, succeeded in putting Mughal rule on a firm fiscal basis because he could secure the long-term collaboration of the zamindars. If they were not enrolled as mansabdars, like the Rajput princes, they always received the kinds of support from the Mughal government – financial, military, political – that allowed them to stay on top of their own numerous local rivals. The result was a new synergy between the imperial government and rural society that had as yet been unknown in the medieval Sultanate of Delhi and at best had been an incipient characteristic of the regional kingdoms.

Akbar's disciplinary drive and institution-building efforts were, thus, most in evidence in the realm of revenue collection and administration, as well as in his bureaucratic regulations. Before Sher Shah's and Akbar's time, the collection and expenditure of revenue had been a haphazard operation. Akbar, however, insisted that a radically scientific survey of the country's resources and products of all kinds be made, based on standardized measures and uniform criteria. He set up specialized daftars, or "offices" of records, that were to enable him to conduct audits and formulate and constantly adjust guidelines for future action, putting in place growing numbers of agents of the Hindu banking and financier castes who developed Akbar's conception of the state as a business enterprise. Mughal administration had to be made efficient and profitable; corruption had to be stamped out. In addition to the system of mansabs for the nobility, Akbar therefore became known for the introduction of revenue settlements, administrative regulations, and a never-ending series of revisions of these. Facilitated by the inflow of precious metals and the minting of prodigious quantities of coin, not a year went by without "good institutions" being devised. The results were limited, but they were nonetheless real, and they made Akbar an emperor with a reputation for frugality as much as for his extraordinary wealth.

It is perhaps ironic that the true excellence of keeping records was recognized by the illiterate emperor Akbar. But the *Ain-i-Akbari* contains copious amounts of detailed information about the fiscal affairs of the peasantry – about 85 percent of the 110 million or so people who lived in Mughal India by the end of Akbar's reign (of a total subcontinental population of perhaps 150 million). Medieval sources have nothing of the kind.

There is another body of evidence – corroborating the preceding information – that confirms beyond doubt that Akbar collected an immense amount of revenue from this vast peasantry. In effect, the collection of land revenue by the state appears to have been the dominant factor in the redistribution of wealth in the country. The proverbial amount of the "king's share" – reiterated by the *Ain-i-Akbari* – was 40 percent of the total production or virtually the whole of the moveable surplus. But there has been considerable conjecture about what exactly this figure represents, what the real "take" of the Mughal government might have been, and how it was collected. An analysis of the statistics in the *Ain-i-Akbari* of the total amounts of revenue actually remitted in combination with estimates of the population yields an average annual payment of less than one rupee per head of the population. Multiplied by 110 million, this amounts to an amount of revenue appropriately large for "the greatest and most powerful empire in the world," but, going by the prices in the *Ain-i-Akbari*, it was no more than the equivalent of the value of one-tenth of one acre when acreage cultivation per head was 1.08 acres. This weight may have become even less in the period after the 1590s.

The Mughal bureaucracy that collected this land revenue – whatever the exact amount – was in practice ramshackle at best, under Akbar and all later emperors, even if more effective than its medieval predecessors. Surveys once made would not be updated for years, until it was discovered by chance that the real wealth of a district was twice that indicated in the survey. There were enormous disparities between adjacent districts for no apparent reasons. Large parts of the empire, including the whole of Bengal – its most fertile and wealthy province – were never properly surveyed at all.[91] The author of the *Ain-i-Akbari* was Akbar's court historian Abul Fazl, and he was not a revenue expert and probably did not thoroughly understand the statistics he collected. British-Indian revenue authorities always displayed considerable skepticism about his statistical figures. Most unfortunately, the historical chronicles of the sixteenth and seventeenth centuries tell us hardly anything about the working of revenue legislation in actual practice, except that constant revisions were called for and remission of cesses. In 1585, for instance, the failure of previous administrative reforms was noted as follows: "The accountants have not rendered clear statements, and have not observed the sacred regulations … They have based this business – which rests upon inquiry and investigation – on conjecture and approximation."[92] Such observations abound in the historical record. Nevertheless, there was a clearly articulated memory in India of the standard measurement surveys executed in the directly ruled Mughal territories of Hindustan by Todar Mal in the late sixteenth century and, modeled on these, by the Nizam Shahi regent Malik Ambar, the Mughal diwan Murshid Quli Khan, and the Maratha king Shivaji in the Deccan in the seventeenth century.[93] They had in common that, after defining the king's share as a proportion of the total proceeds, they converted this proportion into fixed and invariable rates of assessment per uniformly measured unit of land of each quality *on paper*. After measuring and classifying the cultivated land, Todar Mal assessed it per bigha according to a uniform standard for each class. This standard assessment from Akbar's time penetrated into a part of Khandesh and Gujarat, and later to the Deccan, but not to Bengal.

We know that agriculture expanded quite considerably in the sixteenth and seventeenth centuries; in many areas it may well have increased by 50 percent or more during that time. Did it flourish? The Mughals certainly did not leave "solitudes and deserts" behind, as Bernier would have us believe (p. 184). French authors who came to India after Bernier, but before the consolidation of British rule, were often impressed with Indian agricultural skills and the prevailing passion for agriculture, and some were so taken with the prosperity of the Indian countryside, under Muslim Nawabs and Hindu Rajas alike, that they admonished the French to adopt their techniques.[94] Whether, in the wake of the reforms by Todar Mal and his successors, the condition of the peasantry improved or worsened under Mughal rule and whether it was better or worse than in British India we do not know. Scholars have argued all of these positions, generally without convincing evidence. Famines were frequent, widespread, and devastating in both Mughal India and British India, without the government doing much about it in either case. Poverty, even extreme poverty, was also widespread in both, although not universal by any means. Thanks to a large number of villages studies undertaken in the 1950s and 1960s, we now recognize the extraordinary complexity and variety of Indian rural society – something that should perhaps have been obvious all along. But we simply do not have such studies for Mughal India, or the required statistics, to answer such a question; and, under the circumstances, it is probably best to leave it open.

Religion and Politics

Paradoxically, from a religious point of view, the early modern Islamic world has routinely been described as "a liberal paradise compared with Europe."[95] Today we have the field of Mughal cultural historiography to present us a picture of the religious conditions in the India of the Great Mughals that looks positively benign in comparison. According to Rajeev Kinra, a brilliant and representative practitioner of this new field, the Great Mughals crafted "an empire of unprecedented dynamism, social harmony and "absolute civility" (*sulh- i-kull*)," while fostering a "distinctively liberal social, political and religious culture" and a "confident pluralism and the widespread accommodation of cultural diversity" that can be favorably contrasted with contemporary European attitudes of the Reformation.[96]

It is an attractive vision, and there is a good deal to be said for it. Yet it is hard to deny that religious attitudes and conditions across Mughal India varied a great deal and, taken in their entirety, were so mind-bogglingly complex and contradictory that it is difficult to generalize about them.

What, for instance, were the prevailing attitudes toward Christianity? Jahangir ordered three of his nephews to be converted to Christianity. This may seem to reflect an attitude of openness on the part of a Muslim emperor toward the Christian religion. But in fact Jahangir had this done only to render these three nephews politically ineffectual. The prevailing attitude toward Christianity in the Mughal empire was not at all encouraging. Jesuit priests traveling in India, even under Akbar, complained about the life-threatening hostility they encountered as Christians. It also seems as if the attitudes of some Mughal emperors toward other religions are better described as pragmatic acceptance rather than enlightened tolerance. The record is full of inconsistencies. If religious tolerance prevailed in some quarters, Muslim religious clerics did not commonly celebrate such a climate and more often than not denounced it as symptomatic of the poor state of Islam in the Indian subcontinent, especially if compared with that of *Mā warā' an-nahr* – a tradition that began with Babur and reached a climax with the blinkered Naqshbandi Sufi theologian Shaykh Ahmad Sirhindi a century later.

There is other evidence to show that, in important respects, imperial attitudes toward religion hardened over time. The more dominant the Timurid-Mughal dynasty became, the more its attitudes appear to have become infused with a reformist agenda, and in particular Mughal attitudes toward Hinduism changed decisively in the course of the seventeenth century, even when more and more Hindus came under Mughal imperial rule and entered the apparatus of government, often on honorable and lucrative terms. Partly as a result of the Mughals' deepening engagement with Hinduism on a theological level, increasingly self-conscious assertions about the superiority of Islam began to be made with increasing frequency. It can be shown that the Mughal regime, from Akbar's time onward, was indeed pluralistic and tolerant to a degree but that it also aimed, and successfully so, to set the terms of an ever more uniform Sunni Islamic culture that was sharply at odds with such pluralism and respect for diversity.

Although there is no question that the Mughal government did not normally interfere in the Hindu caste system, there were, in effect, attempts to reform Hinduism and undermine the power of the Brahmans. Like some of the medieval Indo-Islamic regimes that preceded it (in the subcontinent as well as in Java) and some contemporary Islamic governments (including Persia), the Mughal regime turned against the widespread practice of widow burning in the territories under its direct administration. It worked to terminate the practice, in both its voluntary and involuntary forms, and by the later seventeenth century had achieved at least a modicum of success in this effort in its directly ruled territories.

Imperial interference in Hindu religious life went well beyond this. While there is no denying that some of the Mughal emperors set themselves up as patrons of Indian literature (Sanskrit and vernacular), there is some indication that the intentional physical destruction of Hindu sacred manuscripts was not uncommon in Mughal India either.[97] Islamic iconoclasm and temple destruction was unmistakably on the increase in the Mughal period of Indian history, and unlike book manuscripts, only some movable icons and very few temples could be hidden from the iconoclasts. It was nothing new; already up to that point, we encounter blanket orders issued by Muslim rulers to destroy the temples of entire regions, which appear to have been carried out in, for example, medieval Gujarat and Kashmir.[98] All Mughal emperors from Babur to Alamgir engaged in iconoclasm and temple destruction at times, even those who are described as patrons of the arts and painting, and notwithstanding their simultaneous material support for Hindu religious institutions elsewhere. Among Indo-Islamic rulers, Akbar has the unique distinction of having ordered the reconversion of a mosque into a Hindu temple that had earlier been destroyed. But even Akbar, in his early career, after the conquest of Chitor in 1568, reportedly "destroyed temples in those places and also all over Hindustan."[99] Shah Jahan, at some point, ordered the destruction of all newly built temples throughout the imperial domains, prohibiting their construction entirely.[100] Shah Jahan is also on record for having destroyed some very old temples – in Kashmir, for example – for no particular fault of the inhabitants of the region (who were, moreover, Muslims). Yet it was under his successor Alamgir that the destruction of Hindu temples and icons reached its peak. There is overwhelming evidence for this, both in Indo-Persian and vernacular sources as well as European, and archaeological. It was even then not systematic. But among the most famous temples destroyed by Alamgir we count the great Keshava Rai temple of Mathura and the Vishwanath temple at Varanasi, which were both replaced by mosques (for the latter, see the cover of this book).

While this was going on, we are confronted in the sources with ever-higher levels of anti-Hindu rhetoric as a means of extolling the Islamic virtues of the Mughal rulers. The *Shahjahannama* praises Shah Jahan as the "infidel consuming monarch" and devotes an entire chapter to the "Manifestations of Signal Marks of Justice and Regard for the True Faith of Islam on the Part of the Emperor, the Bulwark of Religious Law."[101] An anti-Hindu climax was reached between 1678 and 1679, when Alamgir imposed a discriminatory fiscal policy by introducing the jiziya poll tax and other levies on Hindus. The theological engagements between Muslims and Hindus led to assertions of the superiority of Islam on a more rarefied level, but no less unambiguously, around the same time. Under the patronage of Shah Jahan's eldest son, Dara Shukoh (1615–1659), investigations into Hinduism took a decisive turn.[102] In his last work, the *Sirr-i-Akbar*, Dara Shukoh conclusively made the claim that the Upanishads were the source of all expressions of *tauhīd*, or Islamic monotheism. But this work can also be read as a call to all Hindu "believers in the unity of God" (*muwahhidān*) and "realizers of the truth" (*muhaqqiqān*) to accept their rightful place within the Islamic fold. In the words of Supriya Gandhi, "In general, his work reveals a pronounced commitment to the external forms of Islamic orthodoxy and piety, positioned as the dominant religious framework through which he integrates and ultimately subsumes his construction of Indic monotheism."[103] Accompanying the increasing commitment of the Timurid-Mughal dynasty to Sunni Islam as the sole religious legitimation of their rule, there was also an inevitable turn against Shi'ism. This is all the more remarkable because the dynasty had initially embraced it, if mostly per force. It was Akbar who repudiated Shi'ism by renouncing the claims of suzerainty of the Persian Safawid Shah in 1579. In Jahangir's time, we again witness an increasing influence of the Persian element and Shi'ism among the ruling nobility, largely due to the role played by the emperor's wife and regent Nur Jahan, herself of Persian extraction. For a short while the Twelve Shiʿa Imams came to be religiously revered even among Sunni Muslims, but this provoked a sharp backlash under Alamgir, and from then on the influence of Shiʿism was completely eclipsed and the public performance of Shiʿa rituals banned altogether among the Persian-Mughal court nobility.

Does this alignment with Sunni Islam mean that the Mughal dynasty introduced "Islamic law" or that it "upheld the Sharia"? The argument has often been made that before the British came to India "law followed religion." According to this argument, the Sharia was the official code of Islamic states and the Dharmashastra was the official code of Hindu states.[104] In British India, this conception was already enthroned by Warren Hastings (Governor-General, 1772–1785) during the time of the East India Company in his Plan for the Administration of Justice. The reality, however, is much more ambiguous and rather different. To be sure, our written sources do sometimes display a formal regard for what they call Islamic law or *sharʿ* (i.e., the Sharia). Thus, the *Shahjahannama* asserts unequivocally about Shah Jahan that "if His Majesty orders punishment, he does so in complete accord with Islamic law."[105] There is no denying that the constantly professed love of justice of all Mughal emperors is presented as a reflection of their dynastic commitment to Islam. Indeed, the pursuit of justice was made out to be the essence of Islam. And yet European travelers in India are in virtually unanimous agreement that the Mughal emperors were not bound by any written law and what is more, there was no written law in Mughal India anywhere.[106]

These European observations are not entirely wrong, and they should not come as a surprise, because Mughal governance and the administration of justice evolved within a matrix of customary law, not canonical or prescriptive texts. The formal religious codes always had few practical implications anywhere. In the towns and cities of Mughal India, the reach of the Sharia was mostly felt in the religious sphere. It prescribed sanctions against infractions such as adultery, drunkenness, blasphemy, and the consumption of pork or not fasting, violations of dress codes, and so on, as well as issues related to marriage and divorce among Muslims.[107] This was similar to how Hindus, Buddhists, Christians, Sikhs, Jains, and Zoroastrians applied their own religious or caste codes in the same spheres. In relevant cases, advice could be sought from religious experts or clergy, who might or might not consult scripture and whose advice might or might not be acted upon or be allowed to influence decision making. Outside these spheres the Sharia was an ambiguous system of law, characterized by a high degree of flexibility that allowed it to assimilate local norms and customs, and this ambiguity was always exploited by various social groups, who manipulated it to protect their interests.[108] In the "blessed" Mughal port city of Surat, as one recent study has demonstrated, what was alleged to be the code of the Sharia was "placed in the arena of local conflicts and struggles" and was for this reason not even restricted in its application to Muslims alone but came to be appropriated by all sections of society.[109] It was not until the British period that the Sharia was removed from local relations of power and became a rigid system of codified law. Until then it was a tool for vested interests, contested by political elites who treated the ʿulamā,ʾ or theologians, with indifference or used them for window dressing, if they did not ignore them altogether.

Wherever we encounter courts of justice, it was the emperor and the government officials with delegated authority who passed legal judgments in both civil and criminal cases, ostensibly in accordance with allegation and proof, and these courts might or might not include qazis, or "Islamic judges," but if they did, the qazis would always be appointed and dismissed at will by the government.[110] Payments of bribes decided the outcome of disputes, so poor people could not even get a fair hearing. Religion sometimes entered the picture. As Bowrey explains, it was especially difficult for Hindus to obtain fair treatment in Muslim courts because "even a Muhammadan villain in court is believed before others."[111] In other words, the powers that be had the legal means to retain that power. The number of qazis increased over time, especially under Alamgir, who aimed to increase their role in civil administration and affairs of state. But they soon became just another interest group, resented by other sections of the administrative apparatus. On the local level, Islamic judges transformed their offices into hereditary family property and merged into local society.[112] Islamic law was most often not even a veneer.

Legal practice and jurisprudence were further complicated by the fact that the joint or extended family household always remained the basic building block of society and the characteristic form of property enjoyment or hereditary rights in land, but the legal foundation of such property rights did not lie in religious law, whether Islamic or Hindu, but again in customary practice. The Islamic Sharia postulates a strictly freehold title to property, bypassing all the normal restrictions of customary or tribal conceptions of property in land. The Hindu Dharmashastra endorses separation and denies birthright in property, while the only form of collective property known to it is the religious endowment. Vernacular sources describe the incumbents of hereditary rights in lands, or zamindaris, as "sharers" of these rights and the patrimonial estates themselves as a form of "shared" sovereignty (cf. p. 189). In effect, they were the political community in any given locality. They consisted of the agnatic kin and a certain number of clients and supporters collectively holding landed estates. Their complex sharing arrangements were embedded in a polity of feuding clans and families who were armed and prone to erupt in small-scale violence, and they were guided by customary practices that had the force of law – in other words, by customary law and by political considerations, not by religious law. The imperial state itself operated within the same matrix of clan rule and shared sovereignty in which feuding and armed opposition were central and legitimate elements. As is still the case in parts of Pakistan and India today, the arbitration of justice and the law was really politics by other means.[113]

The traditional customary laws were of course very diverse and differed considerably across the different regions and populations of the Indo-Islamic world. But it was these customary laws that governed society and the punishment of a range of crimes as well as the conduct and resolution of a vast range of local disputes and feuds. Inasmuch as any official jurisprudence with abstract legal conceptions coming out of law books was remote and inconsequential, the customs of local society were immensely strong. Local people generally credited the customary laws with a degree of sanctity and, like in Pakistan today, even held them to be part of the Sharia. Simply put, customary law codes loosely associated with some degree of divine justice provided the legal framework for the conduct and regulation of tribal, ethnic, caste, and religious feuds and conflicts. Mughal India in this regard was always similar to many other heavily armed kinship-based societies. And since these kinship groups saw themselves as fundamentally independent sovereign groups, it is logical that the laws that grew out of these societies should resemble traditional international law more than modern national law. This is to say, again, that justice was really an extension of politics by other means, with the threat of violence always in the background. The customary legal order, in other words, has always been based more on diplomacy and pressure than on formal rules. Its aim was not so much to punish as to defend or restore collective honor and prestige, restore peace, maintain basic order, and provide compensation. It usually aimed at compromise. As such, these judicial codes were embedded in a negotiated state, not a modern state.[114]

Mughal India was thus largely governed by customary law on all levels, and politics took precedence over scriptural religion. With such tenuous links between politics and scriptural religion, wars of religion

such as those that convulsed Reformation Europe were hardly likely
to occur. Compromise, negotiation, tolerance, and diffuse rather than
schismatic conflict were the hallmarks of a society that was still three-
quarters pagan and hardly a quarter monotheistic. Still steeped in chivalrous ideals, the religious contours of this society were often blurred.

Even so, the difference with Europe was not absolute. The early
modern world was interconnected through trade and unprecedented
monetary flows. There were parallel developments of all kinds everywhere. Reformation-like developments occurred not only in Europe
but also in Mughal India and much of the rest of the Islamic world,
indeed throughout the world, in these same centuries. Many of Akbar's
imperial regulations, in particular, remind us of the new attitudes to
religious, social, economic, and political organization that emerged in
Europe during the Reformation era. For Akbar, the tools of bureaucracy, record keeping, information gathering, as also the enforcement
of court etiquette and of moderation in personal conduct, were primarily geared to the necessity of taming his post-nomadic conquest
nobility. His demand for methodical work habits, rational self-control,
and the efficient management of time (which in Reformation Europe
culminated in the idea that "time is money") was dictated by the same
imperial agenda. The result was a disciplinary revolution that was not
unlike the one associated with Protestantism.[115] Undeniably, it did
have its own spiritual underpinnings. In 1573, Abul Fazl summarized
Akbar's broader aims as follows: "The sovereign aims to enable the
inhabitants of every country...to establish harmony between their
outward and inward condition...[to abandon self-exaltation and]...to
become disciplined, so that while not deserving the appellation of
ignorant they may also not merit the description of being idle and
foolish."[116] He goes on to explain how before Akbar's reign the servants of the threshold paid no attention to time and season but lingered
around the court continually, while the rest of the people were lethargic
and slothful. But when Akbar came to the throne the slothful were
guided to activity, and fresh luster was brought to the court – things
were "knit together" – and the opportunity of service fell into the hands
of the energetic, while the slothful became depressed. Akbar became
obsessed with time, experimenting with schedules and revised schedules for the hours of the day, days of the week, and months of the year
throughout his later life – and especially when he was on tour. He never
decided on any fixed schedule. Rather, Akbar's spiritual drive for discipline went into overdrive. "Knowing the value of a lifetime," according
to Abul Fazl again, "he never wastes his time, nor does he omit any necessary duty, so that in the light of his upright intentions, every action

of his life may be considered as an adoration of God...He passes every moment of his life in self-examination or in adoration of God...in the morning, at noon...in the evening...[and] at midnight."[117]

Furthermore, scholars of religion have been able to show that the interconnected phenomena of Mughal imperial rule – improved communications and mobility, monetization and economic growth – did not fail to have a profound and comparable impact on Indian vernacular religious life as well. Early modern India did not have a printing press revolution, but there was a tremendous expansion of paper production, and these centuries saw the dissemination of a new kind of bhakti, or "devotional" literature, in many parts of the subcontinent.[118] The surge of bhakti textual production in the sixteenth and seventeenth centuries was facilitated by the patronage of a growing class of affluent patrons in Mughal India, even though some bhakti movements had their origins in the fifteenth century or even earlier, and historians of Jainism have likened a fifteenth-century reformist branch of their religion to Lutheran Protestantism and claimed it to be a forerunner of the many more devotional movements that were defining themselves in the early modern period.

In Mughal India, devotional communities with similar messages of salvation could develop bitter antagonisms in their competition for support from similar social groups and efforts to assert dominance over pilgrimage routes and sacred centers. Some were quite exclusive, others not at all.

The early Pushti Marg hagiographies elaborate primarily theological and eschatological modalities that advance religious exclusivity, offering just one path to salvation and no notion of toleration of even the somewhat like-minded, indeed of toleration as a virtue at all. The Sants, by contrast, were proud of having shown a "middle way" (madhī mārg) between Hinduism and Islam. The illiterate Kabir (1440–1518) attacked superstition and polytheism as well as the deadening influence of institutionalized religion in "the language of the Indian Reformation," stressing the importance of inner discipline.[119] In general, the devotionalist ethic of Mughal India was undeniably linked to the spirit of capitalism. Such interdependence between reformist devotionalism and capitalism has been particularly well documented in the case of Guru Nanak and the Sikh religion. But all bhakti reformers expressed the sentiments of the commercial classes and the artisan castes. As Chris Bayly has emphasized, the new culture of devotionalism that developed in the wake of early Sikhism and Kabir was built up through the institutions of the market and worked to strengthen the influence of corporations of merchants, gentry, and service people that had been emerging between state and agrarian society.[120] All such devotional movements represented the interests of townspeople, the merchant castes, artisans, and lower castes emerging from under imperial Mughal rule. In their denunciation of both Hinduism and Islam and their emphasis on inner discipline and personal piety, they offer parallels to the Protestant Reformation. Bhakti poems are about how one can simultaneously attain spiritual merit and material wealth.[121] They are perfect expressions of what Max Weber would later call "this-worldly asceticism" and amount to exhortations to spinners and weavers to abjure anything that might lessen productivity, including sleep, conversation, and daydreaming. But if, like the Protestant ethic, the devotionalist ethic of Mughal India established a link between piety and capitalism, in a milieu of increased monetization, it did not even come close to dislodging the still-dominant culture of chivalry.

Indian Summer

In the early years of the eighteenth century, proponents of a new prophecy wanted it to be known to all that the dynasty of Timur's descendants would cease to rule after the death of Alamgir and "once more the Hindus will reign over Hindustan as they did of old time."[122] This is not quite what happened, but there was some truth to it as well.

The dynasty of Timur's descendants continued to rule until 1858, albeit ever more nominally. Until 1818, there were no Indo-Islamic or Hindu rulers in the subcontinent (and arguably beyond) who asserted an imperial title or formal autonomy except the rulers of this dynasty, while even the invading Persian emperor Nadir Shah in 1739 acknowledged the reigning Timurid as emperor and the Afghan invaders under Ahmad Shah Abdali in 1748 and afterward did not formally subvert Timurid sovereignty entirely either. After the death of Alamgir, the last of the Great Mughals, in 1707, thus came the "Later Mughals" or the "Forgotten Mughals."[123] Through the reigns of Bahadur Shah (1707–1712), Muhammad Shah (1719–1748), Shah Alamgir II (1754–1759), Shah Alam II (1759–1806), and a small host of others in between, the dynasty was still honored by everyone, Hindus included, even if obeyed by almost no one.

In practice, there was a transition to a number of Mughal successor states, and these all differed from the preceding Mughal empire as well as from each other. Among the most important and largest of such successor states were the great Nawabis or "governorships" of Hyderabad, Awadh, and Bengal (essentially truncated provinces of the Mughal empire that became de facto independent); the sprawling Maratha-and-Brahman Raj of the Peshwas across much of the subcontinent;

and in the peninsula the Nawabi of Arcot, the Mysore Sultanate of Hyder Ali and Tipu Sultan, and Travancore. More often than not, these new states were founded on surging Hindu aspirations and close alliances with Hindu zamindari power or at least elements thereof. In a sense the eighteenth century is therefore when Indo-Islamic civilization most truly developed its hybrid potential. Only the Afghans positioned themselves as "saviors of Islam" from the infidels of the subcontinent (Figure 6.3).

To be sure, the transition to the Mughal successor states was often accompanied by war, and war on any appreciable scale meant economic catastrophe, but in recent decades it has been increasingly acknowledged that the eighteenth century was not just an age of bloodshed, devastation, and political chaos but also an era of continued economic prosperity. The economy continued to expand in many parts of the subcontinent, peasant agriculture often flourished in the new regional realms, even though there were major setbacks due to warfare and serious disruptions associated with regional famines, especially in the second half of the century – as for example in Bengal in 1769–1770 and Awadh in 1784, "in which even the well-to-do of the town were starving."[124] The economic picture was undoubtedly complex and varied. But it is clear that to a large extent these regional successor states represented newly accumulated wealth on the regional level rather than economic collapse on a subcontinental scale. The once-dominant idea that widespread peasant and zamindari revolts against the Mughal system of revenue extraction were the result of rapacious overexploitation and the workings of Oriental despotism has not held up well against new evidence. In some ways, the eighteenth century was, in fact, an Indian summer of the empire of the Great Mughals.

In the absence of good economic statistics, the eighteenth century is best described as a series of shifts in political power toward the regions. These political shifts were as complex and varied as the economic ones but also had elements in common with those of the preceding centuries. What impressed contemporary European observers in India was the impermanence of political power under the Great Mughals *and* under their successors. "India," according to Lefebvre, writing in 1802, "on account of her astonishing revolutions, has always – and more than any other country – offered a spectacle of the greatest interest to the political observer."[125] This was so, he thought, because the principles of Indian political organization and government were so utterly different from those of European countries. Most strikingly, India was always a vast continent without internal political boundaries. In 1795,

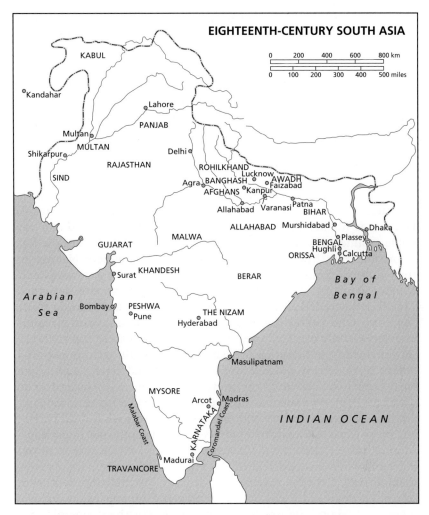

Figure 6.3 Map of eighteenth-century South Asia. Adapted from P. J. Marshall (ed.), *The Eighteenth Century in Indian History: Evolution or Revolution?* (Delhi, 2003).

as in 1757 or at any other time in her long history, the boundaries of its kingdoms had been fluid and were always shifting. To put it differently, as Law de Lauriston did in 1763, in India everybody was constantly on the brink of rebellion. "No one in India has ever had any idea of troops whose leaders did not pursue their own interests or which were employed solely in the service of 'the nation.'"[126] Powerful men had

many opportunities to rebel. The richest party always won, while lasting loyalty and patriotism were unknown virtues in India. Fear was the
only restraint on political ambition, while sedition and rebellion were
inherent in its political organization.

What did *not* happen in 1707, notably, was the partition of Mughal
India among Alamgir's sons. In effect, with the closing of the Mughal
frontier of conquest in the final decades of Alamgir's reign, the system
of open competition for succession among the emperor's sons, which
encouraged rebellion, was abandoned, and powerful nobles rose to the
fore who overshadowed the princes, in the peripheries of the empire as
much as in the capital of Delhi.[127]

Nizam al-Mulk Asaf Jah was the first of the Mughal governors who
detached a province from the empire, when he claimed the eastern
Deccan as his hereditary dominion in 1724. The scion of two elite
noble families, Nizam al-Mulk in that year completed a decade-long
transition from Mughal khanazad to semi-independent Nawab. All
the while maintaining the fiction that he was still a governor of the
Mughal emperor and never calling himself king until his death in
1748, he succeeded in large part because he made "peace with the
Marathas who [were] the landholders (zamindarān) of this region"
and successfully presided over the slow absorption of local elites. He
thus included the Marathas as well as Afghans, Telugus, Berads, and
others in the newly created and locally adapted state structures of
what came to be known as the Nawabi or Nizamate of Hyderabad, an
extensive Princely State that survived as such under his heirs throughout the eighteenth century and the subsequent British Raj. As Nawab,
Nizam al-Mulk successfully sponsored a great southward migration of
Mughal nobles from the old heartlands of the empire, while becoming more openly supportive of the Persian Shīʿa orientation among
them as well. Like the seventeenth-century Mughal emperors themselves, he deployed a normative Islamic vocabulary, patronizing all
manner of Islamic figures but, recognizing that the vast majority of
its subjects were not Muslims, pragmatically adopted a nonsectarian
attitude toward non-Muslim groups, extending religious patronage to
Marathi-speaking Brahmans as well as Khatris, Kayasthas, and other
Hindu groups.

A second important Mughal successor state, with a shifting realm
of comparable size and an even greater population, was the Nawabi of
Awadh.[128] According to contemporary British estimates, around 1774,
it had a greater size than England, Scotland, and Wales combined and
a population of at least 21 million, of whom probably 87 percent were
Hindus and 12 percent Muslims. Awadh emerged as a province with

that name under the Delhi Sultanate in the thirteenth century – on the Gangetic plain between the natural barriers of the Himalayas and the Ganges-Yamuna Doab – and a suba (administrative province) under the Mughals from Akbar's time onward. It became a de facto autonomous Mughal successor state during the period 1720–1754, under the two successive Nawabs Burhan al-Mulk and Safdar Jang. These Nawabs belonged to a family of recent immigrant nobles from Nishapur, Persia, and transformed their governors' charges into their hereditary dynastic rule of the province, with capitals at Lucknow and Faizabad, respectively. They did so in collusion with the Persian emperor Nadir Shah, who invaded India and sacked Delhi in 1739, in what proved to be a decisive event in the first half of the eighteenth century that catalyzed the emergence of Hyderabad as well, and in fact of all Mughal successor states of the subcontinent. Like those of Hyderabad, the emerging new rulers of Awadh leveraged Maratha power to their advantage, allied themselves with the restive local Rajputs and zamindars as well as other local groups and power holders, including the Afghans, whose wealth and power had increased under the previous Mughal dispensation and continued to do so in the eighteenth century. The Nawabs of Awadh also attracted a significant part, perhaps most, of the old Mughal nobility of Delhi. They thus reached their greatest autonomy under Shuja ad-Daula between 1754 and 1764, before they met defeat at the hands of the British in the Battle of Baksar in 1765. Nawab Sadat Ali Khan, on assuming the rulership of Awadh in 1798, presented half of his domain to the British and chose to live in Varanasi. His successor, Ghazi ad-Din Hyder, received the title of "emperor" (*padshah*) through British mediation, in an overt act of repudiation of Mughal sovereignty, in 1818. Virtually powerless, the dynasty would retain this title until it came to an end during the Sepoy Mutiny in 1856. "The final example of oriental refinement and culture in India," the Awadh court perpetuated much of the form and protocol, as well as the administrative practices, of the seventeenth-century Mughal court. It embraced an overtly Persian Shī'a identity – at a time when the religious climate in northern India became more tolerant toward Shī'ism in general and even the Mughal emperors themselves leaned more heavily in that direction – but not without, at the same time, patronizing Hindu religion among the Rajput zamindars and the other powerful elites entrenched in the hinterlands and towns throughout much of Awadh.

Still larger and wealthier than either Hyderabad or Awadh in the early eighteenth century was Bengal.[129] The Mughal suba of Bengal comprised the whole of eastern India, including Bihar and Orissa, and what is now Bangladesh. Its extensive river delta made this part of the subcontinent one of the most fertile of Indian regions. As a result, the highly productive economy of Bengal long embraced both food production and commercial crops (mulberry, cotton, opium, and sugarcane, among others) as well as manufacturing, especially textiles, and it retained an extremely vital trading sector, both internal and external. Moreover, its agriculture had been steadily expanding for centuries with the growth of the delta and the eastward shift of the river system – a process that accelerated in the final decades of the seventeenth century – while its trade and monetary resources were significantly boosted by the arrival of the Portuguese and the East India Companies. Throughout the rule of the first quasi-independent Nawab, Murshid Quli Khan (1700–1726), the land revenue collections continued to increase, and Hijli, the main port of Bengal, retained a substantial Shī'a-dominated Muslim trading community. Not until the later 1720s did the Muslim trade of Bengal begin to suffer. It then became adversely affected by the decline of Muslim shipping elsewhere and by the gradual takeover of trade and political power by the British East India Company. But the total volume of Bengal trade continued to increase almost continuously until the middle of the eighteenth century. Mobilizing this increased wealth of the province in the first half of the eighteenth century, Murshid Quli Khan and the succeeding Nawabs of Bengal leveraged the support of a relatively small number of very large zamindars who had also benefitted from this growth, and they promoted Hindus to high offices formerly filled by Muslims appointed from Delhi, while turning Hindu merchants and financiers like the Jagat Seths into the key intermediaries of their virtually autonomous and centralized but still tribute-paying and formally not independent provincial administrations. The Maratha invasions of the 1740s caused mere temporary disruptions of this picture. Conditions in the Mughal successor state of Bengal did not change until Clive defeated Nawab Siraj ad-Daula at Plassey in 1757, inaugurating the "Anglo-Mughal phase in Bengal history" – an infamous age of plunder but still a chapter in the history of the Timurids. The Timurids' coinage continued to circulate in Bengal, their names continued to be recited in the Friday prayers, and they remained "the sole fountainhead of honor" until Governor-General Cornwallis officially abolished the office of Nawab in 1791.

While the three Nawabis had fluctuating boundaries and checkered histories, the most continuously expansionist Mughal successor state throughout much of the eighteenth century was that of the Marathas.[130] If the rise of Hyderabad, Awadh, and Bengal was facilitated by and linked up with the expansion of Maratha power, in many other parts

of the subcontinent it is found that Mughal governors, after first inviting Maratha assistance, were eventually ousted by them. Such districts
were brought under complete Maratha control and then often flourished like never before. With their original home base in the western
Deccan and Maharashtra, the Marathas were also distinctive in that
they expanded their power both far to the north, the east, and into the
deep south. Quite at odds with their conventional image of a predatory horde, the Marathas had a long history of military and administrative or managerial service in Indo-Islamic states, dating back at
least to the fourteenth century, before rising to prominence in the
context of Mughal expansion in the Deccan in the later seventeenth
century, in particular through rapidly alternating alliances with con-
testing parties. In 1674, this rise to prominence was consummated in
the royal consecration of Shivaji Bhonsle, the great Maratha leader who
was a shudra by caste but now proclaimed himself a Sisodia Rajput, a
descendant of the royal house of Chitor and consequently of Kshatriya
lineage and a Chatrapati or "Lord of the Umbrella," with Satara, in
the western Deccan, as the capital of his own hereditary kingdom. The
small kingdom thus established remained the nucleus of the second
much-wider Maratha dominion continuously expanding to the north,
east, and south in the eighteenth century. Constitutionally it evolved as
a loose association or confederacy of military leaders denoted as *sardārs*
(Persian for "captains") who had the Bhonsle dynasty as their sovereigns. The sardārs were often titled and commanded stipulated quota
of troops, mostly cavalry, in the latter's service. At the same time, and
in conjunction with the mostly hereditary sardārs, Brahmans of the
Citpavan caste (originating in the Konkan), through the office of the
Peshwa (prime minister), turned the Maratha dominion into a veritable
*"brāhman rājya"*with a secondary capital at Pune. Appearances were
scrupulously maintained. Not only did the Peshwas always maintain
the fiction that they ruled on behalf of the Maratha rajas of Satara, but
from Shivaji's time onward the Maratha kings themselves never openly
challenged Mughal overlordship or Islam. Shivaji, in his relationship
with the Mughal emperor, spoke of his kingdom as a mere gentry or
zamindari right. As Malcolm has noted, among the eighteenth-century
rulers the Marathas most of all "affected a scrupulous sense of inferior-
ity in all their intercourse and correspondence with the Emperors, and
with their principal chiefs, particularly with the Rajput princes ... [and]
in hardly any instance considered the right of conquest as a sufficient
title to the smallest possession." Fastidious about rights and shares of
revenue and taxes, the Marathas left a detailed administrative record,
the largest single mass of extant indigenous material of the whole of

eighteenth-century India. They in many ways behaved like the zamindars they claimed to be. The Maratha rulers, wrote Jenkins, "have never
left the plain manners of their nation; they are connected by the ties of
blood and by constant familiar intercourse with every one of their principal officers, and born in the class of cultivators, consequently having
a hereditary respect for that order."

The Marathas campaigned extensively in the peninsular south, and
here they founded, among others, the independent Maratha principality of Tanjore – in the Tamil country, northeast of Madurai. The peninsular south, however, was never dominated by the Marathas. Instead,
it produced three important eighteenth-century states in its own right.

Of these three, the Nawabi of Arcot was a Mughal successor state
that was comparable to the Nawabis of Hyderabad, Awadh, and Bengal
in the sense that it had grown out of a governorship of the Mughal
empire.[131] But it was such a novel creation that it also stands apart from
the three others. The Tamil country, which was named the Lower
Karnataka or Payanghat – i.e., the region "below the Ghats from
Nellore to Kanyakumari" – was not declared a Mughal suba until the
very beginning of the eighteenth century, and it was initially subordinate to the adjacent Mughal suba of Hyderabad (created in the 1680s,
after the conquest of Golkonda). In 1710, the governorship of this new
Karnataka province went to a Navayat military man named Saadatullah
Khan, and it was he who made the first moves toward independent
dynastic Nawabi rule. The Nawabi court he presided over in the rough
garrison town of Arcot, inland from Madras, was the first Muslim-
ruled state in this part of the peninsula, which, from the Mughal point
of view, was still a new and unstable peripheral zone that had never
had secure links to the center or any tradition of Islamic statecraft to
speak of. Through local marriages; the recruitment of Afghan mercenaries from the north and the Deccan; the importation of new service
groups, Islamic scholars, poets, and clergy from elsewhere; and spon-
soring an extensive building program of mosques and market towns,
Saadatullah Khan attempted to turn Arcot into a princely capital with
its own distinctive Indo-Islamic culture. His dynastic ambitions were
cut short, however, when his son and successor, Dost Ali Khan, was
killed in battle in 1740 and replaced by a nominee of Nizam al-Mulk
Asaf Jah of Hyderabad. This created opportunity for a new line of
hereditary rulers who received their official title of Walahjahs directly
from the Mughal court itself, next to the more grandiloquent "Amir-
al-Hind," and also proclaimed themselves heirs and successors of the
Nayaka dynasty of Trichy. Initiating yet another large influx of Islamic
service people from North Indian qasba towns into the Tamil country,

Anwar ad-Din Walahjah and Muhammad Ali Walahjah thus ruled from 1744 to 1798 as the second dynasty of Nawabs of Arcot. Although originally appointees of the Nizam of Hyderabad, the fiction was maintained that the Karnataka remained a Mughal province throughout the eighteenth century. It was, as usual, entirely a facade, and in reality the Nawabs of Arcot had to contend on their own with a multitude of rajas and poligar chiefs in the localities, as well as with major rivals like the Nizams of Hyderabad, the Marathas, and the Mysore rulers Hyder Ali and Tipu Sultan. Anglo-French rivalry from the 1740s onward also brought a massive number of European troops into the Karnataka. This prompted the Walahjahs to move their court from Arcot to Madras in 1765. There they soon lost their independence to British arms and finance. Paradoxically, British protection allowed the Walahjahs to distance themselves from an eclectic and composite religious culture that they had initially patronized and in which a militant holy-man Islam of pirs was grafted onto the South Indian landscape of warrior divinities and martial cults of blood and power as well as great holy places of Hinduism, while also embracing a broad array of Sufi orientations and Shiʿism. It thus moved – albeit never more than partially – toward a more explicit association with a broadly based Islamic culture with links outside Karnataka and India, including recognition by the Ottoman Sultans; a heightening of Islamic identity and conspicuous piety; and the sponsorship of a more Persianate building style (shunning Hindu elements), in close association with the Naqshbandiya order of Sufism that denounced compromises with Hinduism, folk culture, and Shiʿism alike.

By contrast, the exploits of the militant Sultanate of Mysore under Hyder Ali (r. 1761–1782) and his son and successor, Tipu Sultan (r. 1782–1799), acquired heroic status in the annals of Indo-Islamic history above all from its implacable opposition to the territorial expansion of British rule.[132] This short-lived but renowned Muslim dynasty claimed Quraysh origins, consequently of the same tribe as the Prophet Muhammad, but was otherwise almost entirely undistinguished and parvenu, like so many eighteenth-century potentates, when it seized power from the post-Vijayanagara Wodeyar rulers of Srirangapattana (Seringapatam), the island-fortress capital of the predominantly Hindu kingdom of Mysore, in 1759–1761 through a military coup. Suffering a legitimacy gap, Hyder Ali affected throughout his reign to be merely a subordinate Nawab of this Brahman dynasty. In reality, the Sultans of Mysore did not leave the local Hindu elite even the semblance of any real independent power. In their continuous military campaign against the British, the Nawabs of Hyderabad and Arcot, the Marathas, and the Malabar rulers of Cochin and Travancore, Hyder Ali and Tipu Sultan relied on a standing army with hardly a role for the native elite beyond the ambit of their highly centralized military-fiscalist state. As early as 1755, Hyder Ali's brother appears to have been the first Indian who formed a corps of sepoys, equipped with matchlocks and bayonets and accompanied by a train of artillery served by Europeans. The Mysore rulers thus developed a formidable war machine, using European mercenaries, particularly French, and European methods of warfare throughout their reigns. For a while they were quite successful. Hyder Ali, although illiterate, presided over a court that, at its peak, was regarded as "the most brilliant in India." The Mysore plateau was a fertile region and provided a secure agricultural base for this state to develop. It was also quite large. The territory that Tipu Sultan inherited from his father encompassed almost two-thirds of the Indian peninsula, from the Krishna River and Dharwar in the north to beyond Dindigul in the south and bordered on the west by the Arabian Sea and to the east by the ghats that rose up from the Karnataka plains. These Mysore rulers first accepted titles from the Mughal emperor, then openly defied him as well as the Nizam of Hyderabad, by adopting titles like "Padshah" and "King of Islam" for themselves and seeking and obtaining endorsement from the Ottoman ruler Abdul Hamid I in Istanbul. Yet at certain opportune moments even they still evidenced a lingering sense of Mughal superiority, however tongue in cheek. Tipu Sultan was much more uncompromising than his father, Hyder Ali, in this regard and much more assertive of his independence. He completely eclipsed the Wodeyars, did away with Hindu figures on his coinage, and engaged in other forms of iconoclastic activity during much of his reign. Outside Mysore, Tipu Sultan became known as "a Brahman killer and despoiler of temples." But he always continued to employ Hindus in the high offices of his centralized administration, and in the Mysore realm in general, like in Arcot, a regional Islam developed that absorbed local belief and practice, with elements of a long-present Sufism and holy man veneration as well as a strong Shī'a orientation, accommodating itself to the warrior divinities of the Hinduism of the peninsula. Tipu Sultan also embraced a more militant form of Islam, especially after the humiliating treaty of Seringapatam in 1792 with the British, which resulted in a serious loss of territory. He then began to refer to his dominions as the "God-given realm," and he turned more and more to jihad, in thought as well as practice, attempting to raise support for the expulsion of the British with the Nizam, the French, the Afghan ruler Zaman Shah, and the Ottoman Sultan. In a letter to Istanbul, he stated that he did not want Mysore to suffer the same fate as Awadh, Bengal, and Arcot. But nothing came of it. Tipu Sultan was killed in the third Anglo-Mysore war in 1799.

With the rise of Travancore and Cochin, the political order of the Malabar coast went through an equally profound transformation in the eighteenth century.[133] These new kingdoms did not originate as Mughal successor states but resulted from some of the same pressures that shaped the emergent new militarized kingdoms of the eighteenth century elsewhere in the subcontinent. Until the 1740s, the Malabar coast was a loose congeries of some twenty to thirty small, shifting Hindu-dominated but multi-religious states, with a few larger ones assuming royal authority, that engaged in continual competition and confrontation for the proceeds of the pepper and spice trade as well as other forest products and controlled merely a river estuary entrepôt and its immediate hinterland. The founders of the state of Travancore, Raja Martanda Varma (r. 1729–1758) and his successor, Rama Varma (r. 1758–1798), set out to change all that. In response to Travancore, Cochin followed suit under its own Rajas, but Cochin was not nearly as powerful as Travancore and was encroached upon by its more powerful southern neighbor. The Hindu rulers who created these states brought about fundamental changes in military organization, political domination, caste leadership, and the structures of court culture and religious life of their domains. Engaging in a kind of warfare that was previously unknown in the region, Martanda Varma, in less than twenty years, between 1734 and 1752, swept away the old, fragmented order of chiefdoms in the southern half of Malabar and replaced it with a centralized war state with a large, modern standing army equipped with European weapons and trained by European mercenary officers. He was able to push deep into the Cochin domains and defeated the Dutch in a conflict over control of the pepper trade. In response to the threat of Mysore, he engaged in a ceaseless program of military fortification, recruitment, and training. At the same time, to pay for this military buildup, he launched the formation of a state trading system with a monopoly over pepper, cardamom, timber, and other export products, underwritten by a large bureaucracy. This was a time of rapid and sustained economic growth in Malabar, and the Travancore Rajas promoted the commercialization of the economy by founding new market towns and maritime entrepôts, enhanced the role of the Syrian Christians, patronized lavish temple building, and sponsored the wholesale importation of Brahmans from outside. It all came crashing down in the wake of the Mysorean invasion in which Tipu Sultan reduced Cochin to a client state and overran Martanda

Varma's lines of fortifications. This was followed by tributary alliances with the British East India Company in 1795.

In the early eighteenth century, finally, the Afghans too began to play a prominent role in Safawid Persia and again in Mughal India as well.[134] In Persia, the Afghans made their presence felt in the declining years of the Safawid dynasty, and it was here that Afghan imperial aspirations were reignited. The first to rise in this context were the Ghilzais, a large western tribe with many subdivisions. They ruled Persia until Nadir Shah expelled them in 1728. Then the Abdali Afghans, led by Ahmad Khan, became the principal Afghan tribe. Entirely nomadic, and scattered between Kandahar and Herat, the Abdali tribe had maintained close relations with Mughal India – especially with the Multan area, where some of its members made a living as camel traders – but its early rise to prominence was to a large extent the result of the intense Mughal-Safawid competition for Kandahar. The Safawid monarch Shah Abbas I (1588–1629) brought large numbers of nomadic Abdali tribesmen under his control by moving them from Kandahar to Herat and making Sado, of the Popalzai clan, the head of the Abdali tribe, with the title of *Mīr- i -Afāghina*. The Abdali tribe subsequently played off the two imperial parties against each other and as a consequence gained in power, status, and wealth, while competing for land with the Ghilzais. During the days of Ghilzai power in Persia, they were ousted by them from Kandahar. But, with the help of their Multani fellow tribesmen, they were able to take Herat from the Ghilzais in 1716, and their power rapidly increased after that, until they were forced, like the Ghilzais, to submit to Nadir Shah's numerous campaigns. With their aid, he took Herat in 1731, Kandahar in the next six years, Delhi in 1739, and soon afterward the suba of Kabul with all parts of the Panjab and Sind west of the Indus (down to the sea) as well as Thatta province and its ports. Nadir Shah removed the Abdalis from Herat and gave them back, in reward for their good services, their territory of Kandahar. He counted the tribe, when he was organizing their lands and the proportion of men they were to furnish for military service, and found sixty thousand families. During the remainder of his life, Nadir Shah was incessantly campaigning in western and Central Asia, with the aid of his Uzbek and Afghan supporters, while keeping up friendly relations with the Mughal emperor Muhammad Shah. Plotting the destruction of the Qizilbash (the former military supporters of the Safawid dynasty), he was murdered in 1747 and thus left the field open for Ahmad Khan Abdali.

Immediately upon Nadir Shah's assassination, Ahmad Khan Abdali crowned himself Shah or King of the Afghans. Ahmad Shah gave

himself the title of *Durr-i-Durrānī*, or "Pearl of Pearls," after which
the Abdalis, as the dominant tribe of the new monarchy, changed their
name to Durranis. He made Kandahar his new capital, surrounding
it with a wall, and from there expanded his empire from the west of
Khurasan to Sirhind and from the Amu Darya to the sea. It was the
first time the Afghans were ever united under a native king in their own
homeland. Notably, the forms of his royal government and court, as
well as the organization of his army, were exactly the same as those of
Nadir Shah. But whereas the Persians had long assented to the conven-
tions of an absolute monarchy, Ahmad Shah founded his over a warlike
and tribal people that had no attachment to that form of government.
Affecting a strong attachment to his nation, he adopted a policy of con-
ciliation among Afghans. Care was taken that the military divisions
were made to correspond to those of the tribes and that the authority of
the latter's hereditary chiefs was preserved.

If among Afghans the legitimacy of the Durrani empire to a large
extent derived from a compromise with tribal authority on all levels, it
was based on different premises everywhere else. Under Ahmad Shah,
the Afghans advanced a specifically Durrani form of Perso-Islamic universalism that superseded the imperial claims of all the older empires of
Persia, Central Asia, and India. In places like Herat and Kandahar, both
of which were now part of Persia, the Durranis avoided a clear commitment to fight Shi'ism and, like Nadir Shah, attempted to incorporate
the national Persian strand of Shi'ism into their own more universal-
istic mainstream Sunnism, seeking the Ottoman Sultan's recognition
of Twelver Shi'ism as the fifth Sunni school of law. Khurasan and the
whole of Persia were clearly seen as a Durrani client state. By contrast,
in Turkistan Ahmad Shah tried to legitimize his activities by taking
up the cause of Muslims endangered by the Chinese annexation of its
eastern territories. While in India, Ahmad Shah defied Mughal authority by reclaiming all the Indian provinces previously handed over to
Nadir Shah, even though, in the end, the Durrani territories extended
well beyond those of Nadir Shah and came to include Sirhind, Lahore,
Multan, Kashmir, Thatta, Sind, and the Derajat. In a letter written
to the Ottoman Sultan after his defeat of the Marathas at Panipat in
1761, Ahmad Shah commemorated the Afghan legacy in Hindustan,
pointing out that its conquest by Amir Timur had been facilitated by
numerous Afghans and that since then it had prospered and been well
governed by 29 Afghan rulers. Now, however, Islam was in danger in
Hind, prompting Ahmad Shah to declare a jihad against the infidel
Marathas and Sikhs in order to reestablish Mughal rule. As before,
geography positioned the ruler of Kabul as the last resource for Islam

in danger. Consistent with his stated aims, a few years earlier, during his fourth invasion of Hindustan, the Durrani emperor had read the khutba and issued coins (*sikka*) in his own name, while solemnly reinvesting Shah Alamgir II with the Sultanate of Hindustan in return for a considerable tributary payment. Ahmad Shah also repeatedly gave out that he had gone to India in order to support the Indo-Afghans whose territories were threatened by infidel Marathas and other such rebels, like the Jats. Rohilkhand, Shahjahanpur, Shahabad, Farrukhabad, and the other Afghan or "Rohilla" settlements benefitted from the process of regional centralization that accompanied the decline of Mughal power, but, flourishing as they were, on their own the Afghan communities of Hind were quite incapable of yet another imperial revival in the eighteenth century. As Ahmad Shah's allies, the Indo-Afghans were given new imperial titles and extensive territories in the Mian Doab in return for crucial military and financial support during the invasions. In effect, the Durranis and Indo-Afghans shared, apart from their common ethnicity, a powerful interest in the preservation of the extensive Afghan trading network that linked Central Asia and India and was the foundation of Durrani imperialism around the middle of the eighteenth century.

The new imperial system of Afghan states of the eighteenth century straddling Persia, Central Asia, and Hind was remarkable because it successfully deployed, for the last time, the resources of a mixed pastoral-nomadic and agricultural-sedentary economy. Combining stock breeding, raiding, trading, and agrarian management, it was the Afghans, above all others, who benefitted from the dual process of Chinese and Russian expansion that opened up new outlets for the Central Asian economy. The Durrani incorporation of Makran, Baluchistan, and Sind connected Central Asia with the Persian Gulf and its main port, Masqat. Emerging maritime trading links between Makran and the Sind ports of Karachi, Gwadar, Sonmiani, and Chach Bahar and Kachchh, Kathiawar, and the Malabar coast increasingly reduced the role of the once-dominant Mughal port of Surat. In the wake of Durrani expansion in India, the overland trade of the Persian Gulf and Khurasan was almost entirely redirected via Kandahar and Multan to Sind. Great numbers of Hindu bankers and merchants were drawn to Shikarpur, Multan, Dera Ghazi Khan, Kandahar, and Kabul.[135] Shikarpuri financial agents, carrying bills of exchange, moved across an area from Astrakhan to Calcutta and from Masqat to Samarkand. As Charles Masson put it, "From Shikarpur were supplied the funds which set on foot those successive [Durrani] inroads into, and invasions of the neighbouring countries ..."[136] In Hindustan itself, the traditional Mughal route from Bengal to the now-declining capitals of Agra and Delhi and, via Sirhind and Lahore, to Kabul was also completely redirected. The eastern leg of this route shifted northward, entering Rohilkhand via central Awadh and Farrukhabad, and from there could bypass Delhi (and the Sikh territories) altogether and continue south to Jaipur and the other cities of Rajasthan or, through Bareilly, along the hills, via Najibabad, Hardwar, and Laldong to Jammu and Kashmir, and from there to Peshawar and Kabul. Rohilkhand thus commanded the new crossroads of trade from the north, northwest, and east, while the Rajput states commanded the route from the north toward the Deccan and Sind and Afghanistan. Food grains, sheep, horses, and camels moved through the Thar desert routes to Bahawalpur, Multan, and Shikarpur. It was a configuration of imperial and commercial relations in which the horse trade remained central, lasting far into the second half of the eighteenth century. In the Durrani territories to the north of the Hindu Kush it even led to increased nomadic penetration in some areas and a shift away from crop cultivation to pasturage.

As was to be expected, Durrani expansion put the tribal institutions of Afghan society under severe strain. After Ahmad Shah's death in 1773, his son and successor, Timur Shah, like all earlier Afghan monarchs, was tempted to reduce, if not outright abolish, the power of his tribal constituency. Born in Mashad in 1746 and educated at his father's court and on expeditions, then stationed in the Panjab and appointed governor of Herat, a city with an overwhelmingly Persian population, Timur Shah was quite out of touch with Afghan tribal culture from the beginning and unable even to speak Pashto. Mistrustful of the Durranis, he moved his capital from Kandahar to Kabul. Although leaving the great dignities of the state in the hands of the same Durrani families on which Ahmad Shah had conferred them, he introduced new offices and changed the nature of the old ones, thereby in practice thrusting the entire government into the hands of his own dependents. Ensconced in Kabul, he relied on his own guard troops, the *ghulam-i-shah*, who were mostly Persian and Tajik and entirely devoted to him. Timur Shah attempted to set his finances on a new footing and make himself independent of military expeditions. But the result was a rapid reversal to the usual Afghan tribal fragmentation of power and a concomitant decline of the power of the monarchy. The remote provinces withdrew, and insurrections followed. Upon Timur Shah's death in Kabul in 1793, his successor, Zaman Shah, widened the breach between the Durranis and his court even further and made no serious effort to safeguard Khurasan, while his efforts to invade India were generally thwarted by the dangers that he had failed to attend to in the west. What is more, since Ahmad's time, Hind had changed as much as Persia. There were no longer any treasuries in Hind to be raided.

From about 1800 onward, then, the Afghan monarchy became more and more isolated. Afghan officials of the early nineteenth century were aware that the Mughal empire had declined, but they had, as Elphinstone put it, "a very imperfect knowledge of the numerous states that have been erected on its ruins."[137] Its tribal constitution still essentially intact, Afghanistan was now increasingly condemned to play a passive role in the Great Game between imperial Russia and Britain.[138] The other Mughal successor states were mostly defeated in wars with the British, while the last of the Mughal emperors, Bahadur Shah Zafar, was deposed after the Sepoy Mutiny in 1858, to die in 1862 in exile in Rangoon, Burma.

7 The Indian Ocean in the Age of the *Estado da India* and the East India Companies

He was a vagabond of the seas, a true Orang-Laut, living by rapine and plunder of coasts and ships in his prosperous days; earning his living by honest and irksome toil when the days of adversity were upon him ... He was brave and bloodthirsty without any affection, and he hated the white men who interfered with the manly pursuits of throat-cutting, kidnapping, slave-dealing, and fire-raising, that were the only possible occupation for a true man of the sea.

Joseph Conrad[1]

There is a long-held belief that, prior to the arrival of the Portuguese in 1498, the Indian Ocean was a zone of peaceful commercial and cultural interaction, existing outside the orbit of coercion of militarized states and their naval forces. According to K. M. Panikkar, writing almost a century ago, "Indian powers" were "accustomed to look only to dangers from land forces," and the Indian Ocean had enjoyed "complete freedom of trade and navigation," with "no interference of any kind with trade which was open to ships of all nations."[2] Fernand Braudel wrote in this same vein that "Indian maritime customs had [before the Portuguese] always been extremely pacific."[3] More recently, K. N. Chaudhuri wrote, "Indeed, the arrival of the Portuguese in the Indian Ocean abruptly ended the system of peaceful oceanic navigation that was such a marked feature of the region. The historian of 'catastrophe' theories in the Asian context is fortunate in being able to assign precise dates to the watershed."[4] Michael Pearson, over a long career, has also consistently written that "it was the Portuguese who introduced violence into what had been a peaceful maritime trading world."[5]

The persistence of this belief is remarkable, since the ancient, medieval, and early modern Portuguese accounts of the Indian Ocean – those of Pliny the Elder and Ptolemy, the Arab geographers Al-Mas'udi and Al-Idrisi, Marco Polo, Ibn Battuta, Nikitin, Ibn Majid, Tomé Pires, and Duarte Barbosa – do not provide a shred of support for it.

They unfailingly describe the Indian Ocean as a heavily militarized and violent frontier zone. On the strength of this evidence, we have argued earlier that the Indian Ocean was similar in essential respects to the frontier zone of deserts and steppelands, with their nomadic populations, to the north. Both the nomadic and the maritime frontier fell outside the orbit of settled societies and were inhabited by mobile populations that routinely combined livestock raising or fishing with armed trade, war, predation, "piracy," and slave raiding.[6] Due to the pervasive presence and activities of such "people of the sea" and "sea nomads," the medieval Indian Ocean became the crucible of countless maritime empires or thalassocracies spanning vast distances. They were often short-lived. Maritime empires, like nomadic steppe empires, did not have an elaborate, durable institutional infrastructure, and they were commonly ephemeral, amorphous entities. They typically did not leave behind historical accounts of their rise and fall. But a spate of new research supports the interpretation of a nonpeaceful Indian Ocean, and we have in recent years gained a much clearer picture of the area as a lawless and open frontier where armed trade and naval violence were the norm, not the exception.[7] We can now trace this back to ancient and early medieval times.

When the first Arab missionaries of the faith began to arrive in Madagascar, they found an island already colonized by Indonesian seafarers, the so-called Waqwaq (from *waqa*, an outrigger canoe) who had migrated from the "Zabaj islands" (most likely Sumatra) in the second and fourth centuries, after first landing on the African mainland, and again in the tenth century and possibly the twelfth also. The Arab geographers knew the Waqwaq for their piratical habits, because they raided Sofala and other towns and villages of the Zanj ("Africans"), up and down the Swahili coast of the African mainland, as well as on the Comoro islands. They besieged the island of Pemba, for instance, in 945, and obtained "ivory, tortoiseshell, panther skins, and ambergris" and captured and enslaved "Zanj people." But these seafaring Waqwaq maintained regular trading relations with Indonesia in the same centuries as well. We know, for instance, that they sold the Zanj slaves in Java. There thus emerge the contours of a Waqwaq maritime empire that extended across the Indian Ocean. It was underwritten by armed force; facilitated trade and the dissemination of Asian crops like rice, yams, and bananas up the Zambezi River and East African "banana corridor"; and left vestiges of Hinduism, Sanskrit, and the Batak languages (of north Sumatra) on the high plateau of the interior of Madagascar but produced no textual tradition, let alone historical writing, of its own.

Other notable maritime empires of these early centuries, with uncertain links to the Waqwaq but with the same basic characteristics, were those of the Colas of South India and Shrivijaya on the east coast of Sumatra. It was largely in the late tenth and eleventh centuries that the Cola dominion was established – beyond the Coromandel coast, in much of Malabar, in Sri Lanka, up the east coast of the peninsula, to Bengal, and across the Maldive Islands and then to Burma and Sumatra. Much of its expansion came in the form of armed raids and naval expeditions aiming to establish trading rights, particularly in the Sumatran maritime empire of Shrivijaya and over the Isthmus of Kra, in order to reach the Chinese market that was then rapidly expanding under the Sung dynasty. When the rival trading interests of the Cola empire and Shrivijaya erupted in armed conflict, both parties multiplied their missions to China. In particular, the Cola attack on Shrivijaya in 1025 was a brazen challenge to the Shrivijayan hegemony in the straits over the China trade. Shrivijayan hegemony in the archipelago did not survive for long after that point. For as long as it lasted, however, the Shrivijayan "kings of the islands" commanded an empire "without limits" that rested above all on the strength of their navies – the same Orang Laut that created the Waqwaq empire.

The expansion of the Umayyad and Abbasid Caliphates had a no-less-significant naval dimension, especially in Sind and the western Indian Ocean. In its wake, naval power developed almost entirely in the context of the steadily expanding maritime trade and increased commercial dynamism of the medieval Islamic world.[8] Indeed, it was in these centuries that superior naval power began to be perceived as an attribute of Islamic states. The Ayyubids in the Yemen (1174–1229), for instance, effectively provided armed naval support for their merchant shipping on the India route. Under their successors, the Turkish dynasty of the Rasulids of Aden (1229–1454), this support developed into a full-fledged "oceanic policy" to control the maritime expanse and conquer targeted ports between the Red Sea and the Indian peninsula in the late thirteenth century. Its oceanic policy had an empathically self-conscious religious dimension, involving as it did giving subsidies to Muslim clergy and bestowing robes of honor on Muslim merchants in a range of ports under Hindu rule, in return for having the names of its rulers recited in the Friday prayers at these ports.[9] Other Islamic dynasties with interests at stake in the Indian Ocean routinely did the same at different times. Some of the Sultans of Delhi, the Timurids, the Sultans of Bengal, and the Ottomans had their names read in the Friday prayers of Muslim communities on the seaboard in return for religious patronage, naval surveillance, and

security measures. Abyssinians or Habshis, many undoubtedly converts of slave origin, were particularly favored as men-at-arms on board
trading vessels on India's west coast, acquiring a special reputation
there as "protectors of the sea" in the employ of Muslim and Hindu
rulers. Abyssinians had a high profile as naval fighters in the domains
of the Samudri Raja (or Zamorin), the Ocean King of Calicut, in the
fourteenth century, when Ibn Battuta visited. Their formidable maritime reputation lived on in the sixteenth to eighteenth centuries when
the Abyssinian "Sidis" (i.e., Sayyids) of Janjirā (a Marathi corruption
of Ar. *jazīra*, "island"), near Mumbai on the Konkani coast, became
"lords of the sea" – then usually as auxiliaries of the Deccani Muslim
and Maratha powers. We find Habshi mercenaries, next to Turks and
Persians, among the naval forces – which prevented the construction of
rival local fleets – of Hormuz, the fifteenth-century maritime trading
kingdom in the Persian Gulf ruled by a dynasty of southern Arabian
origin under the suzerainty of the Ilkhanids and the Turko-Mongol
Qara-quyunlu and Aq-quyunlu. And a similar transition to Islamic
sea power occurred in the Malay-Indonesian archipelago. Succeeding
Shrivijaya, Majapahit maintained a naval force in Java's northern pasisir ports that maintained its hegemony through naval linkages with the
islands, and beyond with Yemen, Coromandel, and Bengal.[10] Melaka
became the most important Islamic maritime power in this region in
the fifteenth century, with important linkages to the rising naval powers
of the Javanese pasisir and recruiting the Orang Laut and Suku Galang
into its own naval forces from the amphibious Riau Daratan and the
Riau-Lingga archipelago (with nothing but the promise of loot) under
a Laseman, or "admiral," who served, when called upon, to destroy
the Siamese overlords in 1488 "on the open sea."[11] Subsequently, the
powerful pasisir states of Java's north coast destroyed what remained of
inland Majapahit and established an entire coastal civilization under
the aegis of Islam, similarly backed by naval force. In all early states
of mainland Southeast Asia and the Malay-Indonesian archipelago,
chronic warfare was to remedy low population densities. Here it was
especially common, as James Scott has recently emphasized again, for
both land-based and maritime states to accumulate people by war and
slave raiding, while political rivalries were a struggle more for men
than for land.[12] Another leading scholar of Southeast Asia, Victor
Lieberman, has it that "Southeast Asian port cities were constantly
subject to seaborne attack from within the region."[13]

Slave raiding, seaborne attack, naval escorts and patrols by warships,
armed merchant vessels, the enforcement of sea and port blockades,
protection rackets, piracy, taxes on maritime trade, coercive economic

diplomacy, enforced tribute payments, port rights, militarily enforced
monopolies of ship building, salvage rights, customary claims of maritime sovereignty against rivals – it all prevailed throughout the Indian
Ocean for many centuries prior to the arrival of the Portuguese.
Historians looking for antecedents of the Portuguese *cartaz* system of
naval passes that forced ships to call at specific ports in order to tax
them are now finding them everywhere, albeit usually on a smaller
scale. Even the word *cartaz* itself is likely a loanword from the Arabic
qirtās, which means "paper" or "document."[14] The Indian Ocean, in
short, was an open frontier of mobile wealth just as violent and militarized as the nomadic frontier, with archers on sailing ships every bit as
lethal as horse-mounted archers on land, in an arena of intense competition among a constantly changing cast of participants for the spoils
of its ever-increasing maritime trade. Like the nomadic frontier, the
maritime frontier was closed in the later seventeenth and eighteenth
centuries. How that happened is the subject of this final chapter.

China's Southern Ocean

The Chinese called this their Southern Ocean. On several occasions,
they interfered militarily in its maritime and coastal affairs, but the
Chinese never fundamentally changed or pacified the Southern Ocean.
In fact, they made no attempt to pacify it. The Chinese did not close
its southern maritime frontier, just as it did not close its northwestern
nomadic frontier, and, under the Manchus, lived in a kind of symbiosis
with both.

In ancient times, the Chinese did not yet engage in Southern Ocean
navigation and conducted their trade with the west largely over land,
along what has been called the "silk route." Even the first pepper
imports from India in the second century CE appear to have reached
China by the overland route. The southern coastal region of China
has been a source of wealth at least since the Chin dynasty, but China
did not have a powerful naval fleet at the time. At the other end, it
was not until the early centuries CE that Indians began to move eastward, prompted by emerging opportunities for trade with China and
the ambition to find new sources of gold. At first, the trade between
India and China went largely via a land portage on the Isthmus of
Kra and the Indianized state of Funan on the lower Mekong. When it
expanded, however, it shifted to entrepôts south and east of the Malay
Peninsula, while Funan was gradually bypassed. In the seventh century, Shrivijaya became the first major sea power in the eastern Indian
Ocean, to a large extent due to its involvement in the China trade.

Under the Tang, by the early eighth century, Chinese maritime trade had become a source of considerable wealth not only for overseas traders but for Chinese traders and the central government as well. The subsequent Sung empire, from the late tenth to the thirteenth century, was founded on the sea, attracting unprecedented numbers of foreign traders to coastal China, by the late eleventh century encouraging regular maritime trade among Chinese traders venturing to foreign ports in Southeast Asia and, by the twelfth century, into the Persian Gulf via India. Never before had Southern Ocean trade and the sale of overseas tribute articles played such an important role in the economy of China. There was a steady reinforcement of overseas Chinese communities, especially in the eastern parts of the Southern Ocean. After 1277, when the Mongol Khublai Khan, the founder of the Yuan dynasty, established his power over the coastal provinces of southeastern and southern China, the drain of China's precious metals accelerated and the Southern Ocean trade with China again received a big boost. By then, the trade with China had already become far more important than that with the Mediterranean. Moreover, Yuan diplomacy was underwritten by naval strength to safeguard China's expanded participation in Southern Ocean trade. Diplomats with military background were dispatched to kingdoms on the coasts of the Southern Ocean to demand recognition for the Yuan regime and preferential treatment for Chinese maritime traders. The ocean kingdoms that refused to submit to these demands were repeatedly threatened with military repercussions. Indeed, by the early fourteenth century, China had not only emerged as a major partner in Southern Ocean trade but had also developed a powerful naval fleet capable of enforcing its will far beyond the coastal towns – the open frontier of China. Yet apart from some incidental Mongol raids into the Indianized states of mainland Southeast Asia and Kublai Khan's naval expedition of an alleged force of twenty thousand soldiers and a thousand Chinese ships to Java in 1292, there were no conquests here, no permanent annexations, and no attempts to bring any part of the Southern Ocean under permanent and direct Chinese governmental control and pacify it.[15] China kept up brisk diplomatic exchanges with places like Calicut and Melaka under the Ming, and the immense naval expeditions with overwhelming military display to all parts of the Southern Ocean under Chwang Ho in the early fifteenth century (1405–1433) reflected a conception of Chinese maritime sovereignty that aimed to incorporate its coastal kingdoms into the tributary system of the empire and formally subject them to the Son of Heaven, while also guaranteeing commercial access, but such "Chinese imperialism in the age of discovery" was not aimed at territorial conquest or at monopolizing trade along any of its sea routes.[16] Ming China thus played a critical role in the rise and growing trade of Malabar, Melaka, and the pasisir polities that destroyed the Hindu-Javanese kraton of Majapahit, but mostly as a great market and military power in the background.

There is some evidence of the presence of a medieval Chinese trading diaspora in the Indian subcontinent, but it appears not to have lasted, and as a result Chinese communities of settlers came to be confined to the eastern parts of the Indian Ocean – which is what the Southern Ocean effectively became for the Chinese – by the sixteenth century. The first communities of Chinese settlers on the Coromandel coast can be traced to the later Cola period, but these appear to have vacated the region sometime between 1267 and the 1330s. China was the most important market for the black pepper of Malabar until at least the fifteenth century, and the treasure ships of Chwang Ho repeatedly visited both Calicut and Cochin between 1405 and 1433. Vital Muslim trading networks extending from Malabar to China survived well into the sixteenth century, even after the Portuguese attempted to disrupt them and even after pepper was introduced in Southeast Asia (a possible consequence of the Ming expeditions). We know from Ibn Battuta that there were Chinese traders in Calicut in 1341 and that the large Chinese junks that visited the coast and passed the winter monsoon there were the only vessels used at that time for travel between Malabar and China. Ming records fail to mention the existence of Chinese settlements in Malabar, or anywhere in India, but we learn from the Portuguese writers about a Chinese diaspora that withdrew from Calicut in the middle of the fifteenth century, apparently (although this is not certain) under violent attack from a coalition of Arabs and the Zamorin. In any event, there were no Chinese settlers left on the Malabar coast by the beginning of the sixteenth century.

By contrast, the Chinese presence was very significant in fifteenth-century Java as well as Melaka (much less so on Sumatra).[17] Like the resident Parsi, Kalinga, and other immigrants, most of the Chinese in the Malay-Indonesian archipelago at that time converted to Islam and assimilated to local Muslim society by marriage and the assumption of local leadership roles in the pasisir ports, while being heavily engaged in the booming spice trade with the Maluku islands. In other words, as overseas settlers, the Chinese, again, did not fundamentally transform the societies they encountered in the Southern Ocean.

Chinese trade, moreover, was the only sector of the long-distance trade of Asia largely unaffected by the Portuguese *Estado da India* and, at least until the last decades of the eighteenth century, by the

competition of the Dutch and English East India Companies as well.[18]
There was a minor Portuguese enclave at Macao, but other than that,
Europeans were denied trading access to China until 1684, when
Canton was finally opened to them. Even after 1684, discriminatory
tariffs were imposed against European trade, and Chinese junks continued to carry the overwhelming majority of Chinese trade for another
century. In addition, Japan was closed to all but the Dutch and Chinese
in 1635, with the latter greatly advantaged in the trade in Japanese min-
erals. Chinese trade with Southeast Asia recovered from the collapse of
the Ming dynasty, albeit after a long struggle of decades, and began to
expand again in the 1680s when the Manchus, who succeeded the Ming
in 1644, gained control of the southern maritime provinces. About the
same time, European trade was almost squeezed out of the mainland
states of Southeast Asia, but not Chinese trade. Over the course of the
seventeenth century, the port Chinese on the islands penetrated further and further into the hinterlands, began to dominate local shipping
networks that served the European enclave cities, and in the eighteenth
century also began to dominate the mining of tin and gold.[19] But as long
as the immigrant Chinese assimilated to local culture, the commercial
world of the Malay-Indonesian archipelago gained greatly from and
was invigorated by their presence and involvement. Denys Lombard
and Claudine Salmon have rightly warned that the ahistorical assumption that everything Chinese in Southeast Asia is foreign impedes our
understanding of the cosmopolitan societies of the Javanese pasisir
in the sixteenth and seventeenth centuries.[20] Chinese migration to
Southeast Asia gained further momentum in the last decades of the
seventeenth century, partly because of the legalization of foreign trade
in 1684 and the emigration of sea-based Ming loyalists, but by then the
trend toward assimilation was on the decline.[21] Assimilation became
a problem for several reasons. Unlike earlier movements of emigrants
from China, such as the one that accompanied the Chwang Ho expeditions, the Manchu legalization of overseas trade in 1684 meant that it
was now possible to return to China, and there was a constant flow of
new emigrants. There was now a new kind of legitimation of an overseas
Chinese identity outside China. As early as the second half of the seventeenth century in Mataram, the Chinese were acquiring an economic
grip over Javanese rulers and consequent legal privilege, while at the
same time establishing an alliance with the Dutch East India Company,
and they began acting as middlemen in the pepper trade of Bantam.
Chinese middlemen became responsible for the partial monetization of
the Javanese economy in the late seventeenth and early eighteenth centuries. Above all, the European port enclaves discouraged assimilation

and became dependent on such Chinese middlemen and compradors. Separateness was encouraged by the Dutch in Batavia and its satellite towns. Indeed, the Dutch deliberately tried to keep the Chinese a separate "nation." The *peranakan* category of assimilated Muslim Chinese disappeared. The Chinese now found an environment in which they could grow wealthy without ceasing to be Chinese. Batavia, Manila, and the satellite cities of Dutch Melaka, Makassar, and Semarang became centers of Chinese commercial activity that encouraged even the Chinese in Asian states of the region to maintain a separate Chinese identity. What tended to sharpen functional differentiation along ethnic lines and marginalize indigenous traders even further was the system of farming of state revenues to Chinese tax farmers.[22] This practice spread from Batavia to other ports in the archipelago, then to the impoverished Javanese rulers inland, and on to Thailand and Cambodia, and made it easier for rulers to withdraw entirely from commercial concerns, thus widening the gulf between the indigenous population and large-scale trade. But this new role of the Chinese overseas communities would have been unthinkable outside the structure of dominance that was being established by the Dutch East India Company in Melaka and Indonesia. It was a process that ran parallel to what happened in South Asia in the course of the eighteenth century. There, the traditional ports of Surat, Calicut, Hughli, and Masulipatnam gradually declined and gave way to the new port cities of Bombay, Madras, and Calcutta under the British East India Company. This happened concomitantly with a major overall reorientation of trade from the Persian Gulf and the Red Sea toward China. In the process, the indigenous trading and commercial classes that had developed the traditional centers of trade suffered great losses, or were subordinated to English interests, and parts of them were completely wiped out.[23]

The Closing of the Maritime Frontier

Without question, the Portuguese were the most formidable naval power to appear in the Indian Ocean subsequent to the great Ming expeditions in 1433. What they lacked in numbers, they made up for in the speed and agility of their caravels and the firepower of the deck-mounted artillery of their carracks. With these novel advantages in naval warfare, the Portuguese were not invincible (particularly small, oared vessels could effectively be deployed against them), but Carlo Cipolla's original assessment that "the gunned ship developed by Atlantic Europe in the course of the fourteenth and fifteenth centuries was the contrivance that made possible the European saga" remains substantially valid today, at least insofar as the early stages of Portuguese expansion are concerned.[24] They often used this power to devastating effect, with utmost brutality and ruthlessness, and hardly anything could resist them. What deserves to be stressed is the oceanwide scope of these Portuguese naval efforts, extending as they did from East Africa to the South China Sea, and the relatively systematic nature of these efforts to assert control over trade routes.[25] Calicut, where Vasco da Gama landed in 1498, was bombarded from Portuguese ships in 1500. It was never occupied but was attacked again in 1509 and then set on fire. A timber fortress was built at Cochin in 1503, a provisional first headquarters in India. On the Swahili coast, Kilwa was stormed in 1505, and here the Portuguese built their first stone fortress. There were naval engagements with combined Egyptian-Mamluk-Gujarati fleets off Diu in 1508 and 1509. The fanatical viceroy Afonso de Albuquerque took Goa from Bijapur in 1510; it became the capital of the Portuguese seaborne empire or what later was called the *Estado da India* in 1530. Melaka was captured in 1511, and Hormuz, at the entrance of the Persian Gulf, in 1515. The Portuguese made an effort to divert the entire pepper and spice trade around the Cape and force all non-Portuguese ships to buy sailing permits (cartazes), to secure safety from the Portuguese guns, but they suffered a great reversal in 1513 when their failure to take Aden put access to the Red Sea outside Portuguese control. Reversing its incipient decline to some extent, Goa successfully created an East Asian branch of trade in Macao, Nagasaki, and the Philippines between 1560 and 1600. For some time this was the most lucrative branch of Portuguese trade.

The vast network of Portuguese fortresses and factories between Kilwa and Amboina was stretched too thin to be able to enforce even a semi-monopoly of the spice and pepper trade. By the second half of the sixteenth century, the Red Sea route reemerged in full force, while new maritime port states, such as Aceh in north Sumatra, readily adopted the Portuguese gunpowder armaments. At the end of the century, the Portuguese had accepted a significant measure of accommodation with the local political and commercial environment of the different parts of the Indian Ocean, especially in the east, albeit often as private citizens and independent traders. The Portuguese seafarers, for all their pioneering successes, were by then vulnerable to attack by rival Atlantic powers. Their most serious challenge came from the much better capitalized and armed East India Companies: the Dutch East India Company or Vereenigde Oost-Indische Compagnie (VOC; 1602–1799), the British East India Company (1600–1858), and later the French East India Company or Compagnie Française pour le Commerce des Indes

Orientales (1664–1794).[26] Between 1605 and 1663, the *Estado da India* suffered catastrophic reverses specifically at the hands of the Dutch East India Company: the Portuguese fortress at Amboina was taken in 1605, Melaka in 1641, Colombo in 1656, Cochin in 1663. The Javanese port of Batavia became the Dutch capital in the Indian Ocean in 1619. Hormuz was taken from the Portuguese by the British East India Company in a joint endeavor with the Safawid Shah of Persia in 1622. Madras and Calcutta became the premier British strongholds in 1639 and 1698, respectively, while Bombay was acquired in 1668. The Dutch East India Company by and large succeeded in keeping the Portuguese as well as the British out of the Malay-Indonesian archipelago for most of the seventeenth and eighteenth centuries, but not East Asia. And while the practices of safe passes and armed trade were preserved by all three East India Companies, there were many parts of India, Persia, China, and Japan where, in the seventeenth century, coercive methods of trade could not be made to work. There was a great deal of armed rivalry between the Companies too. Not until the second half of the seventeenth century did the British Company begin to seize the dominating position in the Indian Ocean from the Dutch. Subsequently, after its reorganization in 1721, the French East India Company, with its capital at Pondicherry, became the main rival of the British, and with the rise of France to the position of leading Continental European power, maritime wars between these two nations in the 1740s and 1750s merged with dynastic wars in India that stemmed from the decline of the Mughal empire. The British-French contest for India was not just a commercial struggle but really about world dominance and was not finally decided until the defeat of Napoleon.

It was within this three-century-long period of European mercantile expansion between 1498 and 1800 that the tide turned against the indigenous, largely Muslim trading and seaboard societies all across the Indian Ocean. But it was by no means a simple story of Muslims not being able to compete with Europeans or a story of superior European naval force. As Ashin Das Gupta, more than anyone, made clear, many Indian Ocean ports and trading networks had held up quite well against European competition until the eighteenth century and then went into decline for complex reasons that varied across different parts of India and the Indian Ocean – in which European competition played a role but was not the sole factor.[27]

This is particularly well illustrated in Gujarat on the west coast. Gujarat had long been the subcontinent's most important maritime trading region, with vital links to Melaka and the Persian Gulf as well as the Red Sea. The Portuguese capture of Melaka in 1511 largely cut off Gujarat from the East Indies, their capture of Hormuz in 1515 from the Persian Gulf. Due to the Portuguese failure to take Aden, however, it still had the Red Sea. After the death of Afonso de Albuquerque in 1515, therefore, the first great long-term challenge for the emerging Portuguese maritime empire was how to deal with the competition on the Red Sea route of the Gujarati traders of Kambaya and Diu. A three-fold strategy was adopted: Annual naval blockades of the Bab al-Mandab, the entrance to the Red Sea; devastating coastal raids and the looting of ports and commercial centers (Surat was sacked in 1530, 1540, and 1547); and the gradual seizing of control of the fortified island port of Diu off the coast of Saurashtra. No permanent gains were made until 1534, when Sultan Bahadur Shah of Gujarat came under serious pressure from the Mughals and conceded the small port of Bassein to the Portuguese. From there, the Portuguese could impose their cartazes on Gujarati merchants trading with the Red Sea in exchange for military support. Subsequently, in 1535, Sultan Bahadur Shah allowed Goa to build a fortress on Diu. Not until 1540, however, did the Portuguese have possession of the whole island of Diu. And not until 1559 did they acquire complete naval control of the Gulf of Kambaya – by the acquisition of Daman. By then Portuguese maritime violence off Gujarat was largely a thing of the past, although their acts of piracy never entirely ceased.

Portuguese naval warfare and artillery supplies ultimately could not prevent the Mughals from conquering Gujarat and, from 1573 onward, making Surat the great port of the Mughal empire. Surat had already begun to overtake the increasingly inaccessible port of Kambaya by the 1530s and now became not merely the chief port of the most important maritime trading region in the Mughal empire but its "blessed port" – the gateway to Mecca. It was not an important center of production, and its chief exports of textiles came from the neighborhood of Gujarat's capital city of Ahmadabad, 140 miles to the north, northwest of Surat and near Broach, Baroda, and Kambaya. Surat was also the outlet for indigo, cloth, and a host of other items from the heartland of the empire, because it was the endpoint of continental land routes used by merchants from all over northern, central, and northwestern India, as well as the sea routes of the maritime regions to the west of India. The Portuguese never terminated this trade. They forced the Gujaratis out of the carrying trade of Indonesian spices, restricting them to Indian products such as textiles.[28] But the establishment of the Mughal empire coincided with a remarkable increase of trade in the western Indian Ocean, and Surat was at the hub of it. The Safawids also brought prosperity to Persia and, with the aid of the British East India Company, effectively liberated the

Persian Gulf from Portuguese control by taking back Hormuz in 1622. Last but not least, the rise of Surat was intimately linked to the promotion of Red Sea trade by the imperial Ottoman government.[29] Syria and Egypt fell to the Ottomans in 1516–1517, Mecca and the Yemen in 1536, and Aden in 1538. From the 1540s onward, the Ottoman government was directly involved in Indian Ocean trade, establishing factories in a number of ports and supporting Muslim trading activities as far as Aceh through diplomacy, religious patronage, and military support against the Portuguese, and targeting the latter's commercial interests as well.

By the opening years of the eighteenth century, the Portuguese had been active in Gujarat for two hundred years, and the British and Dutch East India Companies for about a hundred. Unlike the Portuguese, the Dutch East India Company had its principal establishment for western and northern India in Surat itself, with smaller ones at Broach, Ahmadabad, and Agra. The British East India Company had already moved its headquarters to Bombay but retained factories at Surat, Kambaya, and Ahmadabad, where they were involved in trading operations on a much smaller scale than the Dutch, and some British were resorting to piracy in the Arabian Seas. But Indian shipping was still doing extremely well at the time, and these years at the turn of the eighteenth century appear to have been especially good for trade at Surat, Surat's major trade to the Red Sea, trade in Gujarat in general, and that in much of northern India.[30] According to Das Gupta, "Northern European participation in Surat's trade had strengthened the local trading structure but had not altered it in any significant manner."[31] The rise to preeminence of Bombay did not begin until the middle of the eighteenth century and was more a response to than the cause of the decline of Surat.

Such decline occurred in the first half of the eighteenth century in the context of the disintegration of the Mughal empire and the conditions of turmoil and breakdown of security that accompanied the transfer of power to its successor states, particularly that of the Marathas, and of diminished Ottoman control of the Red Sea area, as well as the simultaneous collapse of the Safawid dynasty in Persia. Gujarat was then severed from the centers of production and the markets in north and central India – from Agra, Lahore, Delhi, and Varanasi. Surat's merchants lost access even to key cities of Gujarat itself, roads became insecure, and Mughal officials lost their customary restraint and began plundering the rich merchant houses, while the Abyssinian Sidis were no longer able to maintain security on the sea and became hopelessly divided among themselves, engaging in a deadly conflict with the Marathas.[32] Ottoman power had been weakening in the Red Sea area for a much longer period, but the merchants of Surat had built their trade anew in Yemen under the Zaidi Imams of Sana, who took over from the Ottomans in the 1630s. The second decade of the eighteenth century, however, saw the eruption of a protracted conflict among the Zaidis, and the trade at Mocha, on which Surat depended most, declined steeply. Gujarat then lost much of its trade in textiles and indigo, which had been channeled principally to the Red Sea. By the 1740s, Surat had moved steadily toward its destruction; its shipowners, who had been almost exclusively Muslims, were virtually wiped out, while three-quarters of Ahmadadad was laid waste as well. The total trade of Surat appears to have been reduced to a third of its previous volume, and the fact that one-third survived was to a large extent due to the expansion of English private trading. Bombay took its place but owed its rise entirely to the British East India Company. Powerful new networks of trade also emerged from the conquests of Nadir Shah and the rise of the Afghan Durrani empire, which linked India with Central Asia and there benefitted from Chinese and Russian expansion.[33] The new imperial system of the Durrani Afghans that emerged from the 1730s onward connected Central Asia with Makran and Sind, as well as with Kachchh and Kathiawar, the Persian Gulf and Masqat, and the Malabar coast. An entirely new network of trading routes thus arose to replace the traditional Mughal network centered on the declining capitals of Agra and Delhi. Until the end of the eighteenth century, this situation only served to marginalize the role of Surat even further.

Malabar suffered a strikingly similar outcome.[34] This coastal belt of about 400 miles, sealed off from the interior by the Western Ghats, was never part of the Mughal empire or, until the 1760s, of any other inland state (the nominal sovereignty of Vijayanagara aside) and was politically fragmented into small principalities dependent on transit fees on trade and not land revenue. Such political fragmentation fostered a vigorous merchant class, with Calicut as their most important port, but there were others of note, like Cochin, which periodically rose to importance as well. Its main export was pepper, but there was also some trade in other spices and agricultural products, next to timber and textiles. Malabar's sea trade was predominantly in the hands of Muslims, both local and foreign.

Ensconced at Cochin, not Calicut, the Portuguese pressed their claims on the Malabar coast with even greater ferocity than in Gujarat. Here they gradually imposed a complex system of coercion, of cartazes at sea and a series of treaties with the local princes on land, through which they could direct trade away from competitors, while their expansion and the construction of Portuguese fortresses went hand in hand with the targeted destruction of mosques. The impact of the Portuguese presence on the Malabar pepper and spice trade, however, is difficult to quantify. The pepper markets of China and West Asia were still far more important than those of Europe, and immense amounts of pepper ended up being traded by groups other than the Portuguese. Aceh and the Ottomans also had an important impact on Malabar in the sixteenth century. It is very unlikely that the Portuguese reduced the total volume of Malabar trade. Their attempt to seize control of the pepper trade resulted in the realignment – not the permanent displacement – of Muslim trade, production centers, markets, networks, and routes. Overland travel to the Coromandel ports became an important means of evading Portuguese surveillance and control. By bringing bullion, the Portuguese introduced a new liquidity to the Indian Ocean that inadvertently may have strengthened rather than weakened existing trading networks between Malabar and other Muslim communities of the Indian Ocean. New transoceanic alliances emerged.

Indisputably, in the face of Portuguese hostility, many Arabs and other paradesi or "foreign" Muslims of Malabar had relocated to Cairo, Aden, Hormuz, or Kambaya already by the second decade of the sixteenth century. As a result, the native Mappilla Muslims rose to greater prominence and found new economic opportunities, in both maritime and overland trade – by drawing "pirates" into their operations who would evade the cartaz system, by facilitating pepper purchases for the Portuguese (who regarded them with less hostility than they did the Arabs), and by drawing closer to indigenous rulers. Thus, in the sixteenth century, these local Muslims were not marginalized but instead assumed multiple, overlapping, and expanded roles in trade, piracy, privateering, and naval warfare. Especially dramatic was the increased involvement of Malabari Muslims in maritime violence. Soon enough, this acquired a religious dimension as well. Calls went out for other Muslim rulers to defend the Malabari Muslims in a wider jihad against the infidel Portuguese. In practice it came to little more than dogged localized resistance, numerous audacious and suicidal attacks by Mappilla seafarers in the name of Islam, and the spread of an ethos of individual Muslim martyrdom. Local conversion to Islam also intensified, in particular among the Hindu Mukkuvar corsairs, and was even promoted by some Malabar kings, including the Hindu Zamorins of Calicut, in order to increase manpower resources for their navies. Sea power became entirely a prerogative of the local Mappilla Muslims, and, with the departure of the Arabs, these were able to raise their profile in religious affairs, so that mosques became more significant in political life. Indeed, many of the oldest mosques on the coast are still standing today because they were restored or rebuilt in the sixteenth century. On the Malabar coast, the character of the Muslim community thus changed in that century. For the first time there emerged a Malabari Muslim identity and pan-Malabar Muslim institutions. The people who actually manned the boats, however, were not at all pious, let alone fanatical, and if they became involved in a jihad against the Portuguese, they were also known for their depredations against their fellow Muslims, as well as the attack and plunder of Hindu and Christian ships, which they regarded as their hereditary occupation. Wealthy Muslim merchants became involved in such pirate ventures, but local Hindu rulers as well, for the same maritime people became defenders of their ports and protected their shipping. Mappilla pirates had agreements with local lords of the Nayar caste, and the Zamorins themselves. Trade and warfare became indistinguishable.

Almost inevitably, the politicization of the Mappillas brought them into conflict not only with the Portuguese but at times with the very same Hindu rulers who had first sponsored them, including, again, the Zamorin of Calicut, as they sought to establish their own autonomous states. This happened on two occasions: With the Kunjali Marakkars of Calicut and then with the Ali Rajas of Cannanore. The Kunjali Marakkars were for four generations the hereditary "admirals of Calicut," with fleets manned by Mappilla sea raiders, and became the most formidable opponents of the Portuguese in all of western India. In 1573, the fourth Kunjali acquired his own stronghold at Putupattanam (later Kottakal), assuming the insignia of royalty and, in a direct challenge to the Zamorin, styling himself "King of the Malabar Muslims" and "Lord of the Indian Seas." But in 1600 the Zamorin joined with the Portuguese to defeat and execute him, after which the Zamorin began to exercise more direct control over the Mappilla pirates through his own officers. The other attempt to set up an autonomous Islamic state on the Malabar coast, by the Ali Raja dynasty of Mappillas of Cannanore, also was forged in a struggle over the sea trade (in this case, the profits of the horse trade) and the control over maritime violence. The Ali Rajas of Cannanore in the 1560s linked their naval and commercial resources with those of the Kunjalis in a loose alliance, evicting a Portuguese puppet from the Maldives and fighting the Portuguese in the Gulf of Mannar, between Tamil Nadu and Sri Lanka. This effort, too, ended in failure. But even though these attempts ultimately came to nothing, they indicate that the Portuguese involvement on the Malabar coast by no means brought indigenous naval warfare and trade to a halt; quite the opposite, it intensified the warfare in complex ways, exacerbating Malabar's frontier character.

The situation remained that way when, in 1663, the Portuguese stronghold of Cochin capitulated to the Dutch East India Company and then became, in turn, its headquarters on the Malabar coast. In the course of their struggle with the Portuguese, the Dutch took over their pass system, imposing it on the maritime trade of the same indigenous competitors and concluding a series of treaties with the various princes of the coast, that, like the Portuguese treaties, stipulated the obligatory and exclusive delivery of pepper, which amounted to monopolistic control over all the pepper and wild cinnamon produced in Malabar. In practice, the Dutch Company's capacity to enforce such claims was also limited, while the British carried on trade in Malabar like any other merchant with substantial capital, claiming no monopoly and imposing no restrictions. Throughout the remainder of the seventeenth century and well into the eighteenth, a vigorous Muslim trading community therefore continued to coexist with both companies. In a fundamental sense, the Dutch and the British, like the Portuguese before them, became part of the commercial order of Malabar and did not dominate it.[35]

By the 1720s, however, this was about to change for good. At first, the decline of Surat and the dispersal of its traders to Calicut and its other ports, the disruption of trade in the Persian Gulf by the overthrow of the Safawid dynasty, and the subsequent reordering of trade routes by the Indo-Afghan empire of the Durranis caused a dramatic surge in the demand for pepper in Malabar, and Calicut and the entire coast went through a last burst of commercial prosperity.[36] Muslim merchants from Surat and the coastal areas to the north of Gujarat, Sind, and Masqat relocated their trade from the Persian Gulf to Malabar. But this unanticipated boon for the merchants and princes of Malabar was soon threatened by a second dramatic development that followed almost immediately on the first and was linked to it. This was the transformation of the modest, southern principality of Travancore into a powerful kingdom that extended all along the coast, up to the environs of Calicut, and established a strict monopoly on the entire production and trade in pepper.[37] Two eighteenth-century kings of Travancore, Martanda Varma (1729–1758) and Rama Varma (1758–1798), built up this kingdom with the help of a standing army and a bureaucracy that were entirely maintained from the pepper trade. Travancore's monopoly of this trade meant the end of the political fragmentation of Malabar and the demise of its coastal Muslim mercantile elite as far as the kingdom stretched northward. Travancore turned the merchants into officials of its government, as its commercial department established control over both the production and the distribution of pepper throughout the state and took all the profits.

While this was happening on the Malabar coast dominated by Travancore, to the north of Travancore, in the area dominated by Calicut, developments followed a different and more familiar pattern. Between 1730 and 1770, the merchants of Calicut were able to exploit the new boom in pepper that resulted from the turning of the northern trade but then fell victim to the armies of Mysore, one of the successor states of the Mughal empire, which was hard-pressed for money and embattled, with most of its neighbors and the British East India Company alike. The first Mysorean Sultan, Hyder Ali (r. 1761–1782), conquered Calicut in 1766 but was financially compensated by its merchants to leave their trade alone. His son Tipu Sultan (r. 1782–1799), however, ruined trade by attempting to establish a monopoly on the model of Travancore, but without the availability of the requisite bureaucracy, and then resorting to a policy of concealed plunder, at times destroying the production of pepper and sandalwood with the intention of keeping it out of the hands of the British. By the 1770s, in effect, the days of the great Muslim merchants of Malabar were over, and the trade and maritime enterprise that had flourished in Malabar since the medieval centuries sounded their last retreat. By the end of the eighteenth century, the Dutch East India Company was still a countervailing force against the regulatory and monopolistic regimes imposed by Travancore and Mysore. But the departure of the Dutch doomed the independent Muslim merchants of Malabar.

As in Gujarat and Malabar, the presence in Bengal of the Portuguese – or "Firangis" ("Franks") as they are known in the Indo-Persian chronicles – went back to the early sixteenth century. They arrived in Satgaon as early as 1514, then fanned out to Bandar Hijli, the port of "Hugli," northwest of modern Calcutta/Kolkata, and Pipli, in Orissa. Long before the Mughal conquest, their numbers had greatly increased, and they built fortifications, obtained lands and villages, and, as in Goa, began converting the inhabitants to Christianity both by force and persuasion, while shipping them off to their own settlements and kidnapping others in the parganas bordering the seacoast.[38] Other than the Afghans, the Portuguese were the most predominant group of outsiders in Bengal. With their superior naval technology, they ensured themselves of a virtual monopoly over Bengal's export trade in cotton and other goods, while supplementing their trading activities with piracy, slave raiding, and levies on passing ships. As elsewhere in the Indian Ocean, the Portuguese thus accommodated themselves within the long-existing and normal patterns of life on the maritime frontier. By the first decade of the seventeenth century, they were entrenched in factories in a great number of settlements in Bengal and Arakan – in Satgaon,

Hijli, Chittagong, Sripur, Dhaka, Chandikan, Katrabhu, Midnapur, and Jessore, as well as on Sondip island in the delta. Ensconced in these settlements, they played the local rulers against each other and then for a while became an uncertain element in the emergent Mughal dispensation until they were drawn deep into the Mughal princely feuding of the later years of Jahangir's reign.[39] The Portuguese and their Christian Indian allies then decisively contributed to Khurram's defeat by the imperial forces. Just prior to Khurram's invasion of Bengal, the Mughal subadar Ibrahim Khan tried to assure himself of Portuguese naval support in return for a commitment to protect their trading interests against the Dutch and British East India Companies as well as the safeguarding of their control of the river trade between Patna and Hijli. The Portuguese subsequently supported Khurram against Ibrahim Khan, and a number of Portuguese officers joined his service, bringing along significant numbers of gunners and ships, and ferrying supplies for Khurram's troops as they advanced westward. On the eve of the pivotal battle of Tons, however, they were all lured back by the imperial forces with promises of money and goods, abandoning the rebel prince to a certain defeat. But Mughal succession politics in the end devoured them.[40] Taking revenge, in 1632, Emperor Shah Jahan ordered his subadar Qasim Khan to "suppress these heretics." The subadar released thousands of enslaved Bengali captives who had in many cases been forcibly detained by the Portuguese for up to forty years. With the aid of the local Afghans, he slew and captured thousands of Portuguese, deporting many of both sexes as slaves to Agra, where they were forcibly converted to Islam, their icons destroyed.[41] Eliminating in this way much of the Portuguese resistance against his rule, Shah Jahan assured himself of powerful allies among the many local landholders and trading groups that had suffered under Portuguese control in Bengal, allowing the Mughals to focus their expansionist ambitions further to the east. Other remaining Portuguese inhabitants of the province came over to his side and converted to Islam, while many chiefs of Arakan in 1638 returned to their own territories as part of a local Mughal coalition.

The pursuit of trade in rice and slaves had initially driven the Dutch East India Company toward eastern Bangal and Arakan, but Shah Jahan's expulsion of the bulk of the Portuguese from Bengal in 1632 motivated both the Dutch and the British East India Companies to shift their interests to West Bengal and send their agents to places like Pipli, Balasore, Hijli, Qasimbazaar, Patna, and Dhaka, the provincial capital.[42] Based in Hijli, the wholesale trade of the Companies is raw silk, opium, saltpeter, and various muslins grew rapidly. As much as the Mughals themselves, and in partnership with them, the two

Companies benefitted enormously from the spectacular expansion of the Bengal economy after 1660, which resulted from the accelerating expansion of agriculture that occurred in the wake of the still-ongoing eastward shift of the Ganges River system. The Dutch East India Company relocated to Chinsura in 1656, which it turned into the headquarters of a network of trading posts with linkages to Europe and China, while the British East India Company moved into Fort William in 1691, to the site of a then-obscure village called Calcutta, also on the banks of the Hijli River, about 22 miles to the south of Chinsura. For the Dutch East India Company, Bengal around 1700 was still by far its most important export economy. By the early decades of the eighteenth century, again, nothing fundamental had changed in the economy of Bengal. The large turnover of the two Companies provided an ever-increasing liquidity to the indigenous merchants and political elites of Bengal. The main port of Hijli, at the turn of the eighteenth century, was still home to a large number of Indian and other Muslim traders, among whom the Shī'a community, with connections to Persia, was predominant. And Muslim shipping continued on a substantial scale throughout the rule of Nawab Murshid Quli Khan (1701–1726).

The decline of Muslim shipping at Hijli and the steady impoverishment of the merchants of Bengal did not begin until the late 1720s.[43] It was not primarily due to the strains developing within Bengal itself or even the Maratha invasions that started in the 1740s. These internal factors should not be entirely discounted, but more important was the collapse of Surat and the virtual disappearance of Gujarati shipping in Bengal, as well as the decline of Muslim shipping elsewhere. The more decisive factor, in this case, was the competition and gradual takeover of trade and political power by the British East India Company. When Hijli declined, Calcutta became prosperous. The decline in Muslim shipping, and Gujarati shipping from the west in particular, was beginning by the 1750s to be made up by British private shipping and a turn toward the east. Only those merchants continued in business who did not challenge English domination. Many began to freight their goods on British ships. There was the switch from the manufacture and trade in textiles to one in agricultural products. Then, from the 1780s onward, the Industrial Revolution destroyed the remaining trade with Europe and forever changed India's home market. All this was felt most acutely in Bengal.

The Coromandel, or "Colamandalam," was the second great coastal trading hub of the Bay of Bengal. It was named after the eleventh- to thirteenth-century Cola dynasty at the center of a maritime empire that

stretched from the Maldives to Sumatra.[44] Unlike Malabar, it did not
have an economy of pepper and spices but was known for its cotton
textile manufacturing industries in and around the northern Krishna-
Godavari and southern Kaveri deltas as well as in the Tondaimandalam,
the area around Pulicat, in between. Throughout the medieval centuries, the Coromandel traded these textiles against the spices of the
Indonesian archipelago, and it maintained close trading and diplomatic
links with China as well. After the Colas, it became part of the powerful Hindu empire of Vijayanagara (1346–1565), but by the time the
Portuguese and the Dutch and British East India Companies began to
settle on this coast, the entire southern peninsula to the east of Malabar
and the Ghats had become fragmented among a number of Nayaka
kingdoms dominated by the warlike Telugus from the north. These
kingdoms included Senji (Gingee), Thanjavur, and Madurai in the east;
Mysore and Ikkeri in the west; and a number of new coastal states, such
as Chandragiri, in shifting constellations – all heirs of Vijayanagara.
At that time, the coast was still an open frontier zone with a maritime
trading culture of remarkable dynamism that meshed naturally with
the highly militarized, post-nomadic Telugu states. Like elsewhere in
the Indian Ocean, the Portuguese did not fundamentally change this
situation on the Coromandel coast. They founded a small settlement
at Meliapur, which became known as Sao Tomé, and later Madras,
just south of Pulicat, from where they participated in, and to some
extent redirected but never disrupted, the long-going trade in printed
South Indian textiles with Java and the Spice Islands. The Dutch and
British Companies first settled in Masulipatnam, the leading port of
the Coromandel, in the delta between the Krishna and the Godavari.
Masulipatnam had land routes to Surat and Dabhol, giving access to
Golkonda and Bijapur as well as the northern markets of the Mughal
empire, and, at the turn of the seventeenth century, it was at the center of
an especially influential network of Persian nobles and great merchants
with important trading links with Arakan, Pegu, Mergui-Tenasserim,
and Thailand in the east as well as the Red Sea and the Persian Gulf
in the west. The Dutch Company concluded a treaty for a settlement
in Masulipatnam in 1605 with Golkonda, then in Teganapatnam
and Thiruppapulyar in 1608 with Senji, and in Pulicat in 1610 with
Chandragiri. Political frictions at Golkonda and the disruptive conditions resulting from the almost-uninterrupted military campaigns
conducted by the Deccan Sultanates, the Marathas, and the Mughals –
which resulted in recurrent famines in the area as well as constantly
changing relationships among the various regional Nayaka courts –
induced both the Dutch and the British to set up further down the

coast. Innumerable Indian traders, such as the Muslim Maraikkayars, followed them to the more peaceful south, as the growth of trading centers like Porto Novo and Nagore testifies. Masulipatnam always remained important for the two Companies, but in 1658 the Dutch wrested Nagapatnam from the Portuguese and, abandoning Pulicat, turned it into their new headquarters on the southern Coromandel in 1690. With its abundant rice fields, and away from military operations and famines, Nagapatnam was close to Sri Lanka, another recent Dutch conquest from the Portuguese. The British made Madras their capital on the coast. And by 1674, the French East India Company had established itself at Pondicherry, about 85 miles to the south of Madras and linked to subsidiary factories at Surat, as well as at Chandarnagar, on the Hijli, by the end of the century. At Masulipatnam, Nagapatnam, Madras, and Pondicherry, the trade of the three Companies flourished, its textile products finding their way to markets from Amsterdam and London to West Africa and Spanish America. The Company settlements, foremost Madras, acquired an importance on the Coromandel coast in the seventeenth century that elsewhere they did not obtain until the eighteenth, and prosperity was maintained, while trade continued to expand in sync with the development of Indo-Muslim trade on the coast throughout the century. Historians have referred to this circumstance as "the Coromandel miracle," as it has been hard to explain. The Dutch Company records, however, do suggest some favorable circumstances that may have played a role in making the seventeenth-century Coromandel trade such a resounding success. The officials of the Dutch Company specifically maintained tight control over the textile production process and very close symbiotic ties with the numerous Indian intermediary trading groups (Indo-Muslim and Persian "portfolio capitalists"), while penetrating, as "white Mughals," deeply into local networks of political power and acquiring access to influential coalitions – far more so than in North India – by offering maritime protection to indigenous trade. These were also some of the reasons, apparently, that the Dutch Company did not begin to lose out decisively to British competition until 1780.

On the Coromandel, as in Gujarat, Malabar, and Bengal, however, the symbiosis with Indian trade was not sustained in the eighteenth century.[45] The reasons for this adverse change are not as well understood as for the other coastal regions. Increased military activity in the region and widespread devastation, leading to the flight of weavers and official oppression of merchants, combined with droughts and bad harvests resulting in still more famines and epidemics, probably played a big part in the first half of the eighteenth century. The British and the French intervened decisively in the confused fighting on the Coromandel coast and in the 1740s to early 1760s – the age of "Nabobism" – drew on local conflict to gain the upper hand in what essentially became a European conflict for the control of the coast, and ultimately India. The trade of the Indians was unable to weather this crisis and ultimately gave in to British domination. Only those elements of Indian trade that found refuge at Madras, the capital of an emergent and victorious British India, continued to flourish. Das Gupta summarized the fate of independent Muslim trade in the subcontinent:

Whether at Bombay, Calcutta or Madras, prosperity was possible only in cooperation with the Englishmen…Exclusion of all independent trade, which competed with the trade of the English, was a fact, and so was the ultimate English control over the general directions of trade…But the trading security structure which grew under English dispensation lacked the quality of freedom…The class which appears to have been wholly swept out in the process was that of the Muslim shipowners of Surat, Calicut, Masulipatnam and Hugli…Thus much of Muslim trade disappeared along with Muslim administration in 18C India.[46]

In Melaka and the Malay-Indonesian archipelago, athwart one of the world's most vital maritime trading corridors, the historical trajectory was again different from that of any of the coastal regions of the subcontinent, but the eventual outcome was the same. In the sixteenth century, the Portuguese boosted the demand for pepper and spices, and production in the archipelago increased, and with it the trade of the Muslims. Due in part to shortages of shipping and manpower, from about 1560 onward, the Portuguese lost their grip on the spice trade monopoly, the route through the Red Sea and the Mediterranean revived, and the traffic in the spice islands reverted to the Javanese. The quantity of spices and pepper reaching Europe by Acehnese exports on Gujarati ships, via Jiddah and Alexandria, now surpassed that at the end of the fifteenth century. Moreover, it is worth recalling here that the vast bulk of Indian Ocean trade was not bound for Europe. On the coastal routes, basic foodstuffs, like rice, were carried in bulk by local traders, as were cloth, horses, and dyes. Most of the spice distribution in the Indian Ocean and China was also completely out of Portuguese control. And the Indonesian spices that were controlled by the Portuguese were resold at Melaka, Goa, and Hormuz to Muslim traders. Throughout the Indian Ocean, interport trading by the Portuguese also grew greatly in importance when new and more profitable opportunities opened up in the Far East by the rupture of relations between China and Japan. This was enhanced by the monetary situation of the time. By the 1560s, the *Estado da India* traded

Figure 7.1 Banda Api volcano, Banda Islands. Drawing by Hubert Clerget (1818–1899), from The Malay Archipelago, 1861–1862, by Alfred Russell Wallace (1823–1913). DEA/Biblioteca Ambrosiana/ De Agostoni via Getty Images.

in Japanese silver, Chinese silks, Indonesian spices, Persian horses, Indian pepper, cotton textiles, dyes, jewelry, African gold, Sumatran gold, and the silver from Peru and Mexico. But with the increased production of spices and their increased consumption in Europe, their prices doubled or tripled in the second half of the sixteenth century, and until tea, coffee, and tobacco were introduced in the seventeenth century, pepper and spices remained the leading merchandise from South India, Sri Lanka, and the Indonesian archipelago to reach Europe (Figure 7.1).

Overall, then, the Muslim trade of the Malay-Indonesian archipelago did not suffer but instead was boosted, and, like elsewhere, its networks adjusted to the Portuguese presence. The fall of Melaka to the Portuguese in 1511 was followed by the rise of a number of Islamic maritime states that lost no time in adopting Portuguese techniques of naval warfare and capturing their offensive ordnance. Aceh took over the role of chief emporium of the transit trade to the Red Sea, West Asia, and South Asia. The Acehnese market was almost completely in the hands of Arab traders (and until 1614 also of Gujaratis), and Aceh's harbor became "the gate to the Holy Land," drawing to itself a fair number of Islamic scholars as well.[47] In addition to Aceh, the fall of Melaka spurred the rise of the coastal kingdom of Johore, on the Malay peninsula, as well as Bantam in West Java; Japara, Demak, Tuban, Gresik,

Surabaya, and other ports in North Java; Brunei in Kalimantan; and Ternate. There was also Tidore, controlling a large part of the clove and nutmeg production, its Islamic ruler becoming hegemonic in eastern Indonesia, "lord of seventy-two islands" after 1575, when Portuguese power in the Maluku islands was on the wane. All of these kingdoms participated in the global Islamic upsurge of the late sixteenth century, but Aceh was the most truly international among them. As the principal emporium of the transit trade to the west, it maintained official relations with the rulers of Calicut, Sri Lanka, Bengal, and numerous others. Only in Aceh have written accounts been found of historic contacts with the Ottomans. The first Acehnese attack on Melaka in 1537, in effect, coincides with the one major Ottoman enterprise in the Indian Ocean, the abortive expedition to Diu. After the Ottoman occupation of Aden in 1538 and the revival of the Red Sea trade, which owed so much to Acehnese involvement, there continued to be substantial material support from the Ottomans for Aceh, and a new burst of expansion was the result. Soldiers and weapons kept arriving from Ottoman Egypt, and Aceh, at the peak of trade, became the focal point of a formidable jihad effort directed against the Portuguese. Alliances were effected with some of the pasisir states of Java, with Johore, and with Calicut. But the Acehnese attacks on Melaka, even when supported by Turkish and Abyssinian soldiers, remained as inconsequential as the Portuguese attacks on Aden, and solidarities soon faded. These Islamic trading cities were divided by the commercial rivalries typical of the open frontier. Especially Bantam and Brunei hardly ever opposed the Portuguese, owing to their competition with Aceh. No clear-cut line of division existed between the Islamic and Portuguese/Catholic forces, not even in the sixteenth century. The link with the Ottomans was largely severed after 1580, when their power east of Aden collapsed (the Yemen fell away in 1635). Even so, the Portuguese remained on the defensive, and Aceh continued to dominate the Strait of Melaka, while the pasisir ports inexorably rose to power in Java, and Ternate in the eastern archipelago.

Aceh in the sixteenth century was and always remained a harbor principality – like Melaka in the fifteenth century. A creation of the Orang Laut, it thrived under the essentially unchanged conditions of medieval trade and maritime enterprise. Thus, Banda Aceh had Arabian-Islamic underpinnings derived directly from the Holy Land or indirectly via the South Indian peninsula, in particular Malabar; then and afterward its kings were either Arabs or Malayans and sometimes Buginese. In times of prosperity, its fleets managed to control the trading emporia in coastal regions on all sides. For a while Aceh became fairly successful in manipulating the pepper production of Sumatra, and contemporaries sometimes referred to Aceh and Sumatra as identical. As a result of the great demand for pepper, its cultivation spread to the west coast of Sumatra during the sixteenth and seventeenth centuries, and it was due to the Acehnese that this region converted to Islam. Yet Banda Aceh never directly ruled much of Sumatra. In central Sumatra, it was the Minangkabau king who remained "lord of the pepper and the gold," and here, by the mid-seventeenth century, the centers of the gold trade and the villages with a high percentage of gold traders had all converted to Islam, but the Acehnese could not establish effective territorial lordship over these regions. Among the Minangkabau, Acehnese rule did not go beyond paper edicts, and soon the Dutch East India Company was on its way to becoming the sole trading partner of the gold-producing Minangkabau.[48] Even the immediate hinterland of Banda Aceh was not ruled by the Muslim harbor king but rather by the *adat* lords, who were called *uleëbalangs*. The latter derived their titles from the court at Banda Aceh, but not their authority, which preceded that of the harbor king and was merely confirmed by him. For most of the seventeenth century the Acehnese Sultan was a *primus inter pares* of the *uleëbalangs*. By the turn of the century, he was entirely under their tutelage. If Aceh survived the seventeenth century with its redoubtable maritime reputation intact, inland it could only catalyze Islamic sentiment. According to Denys Lombard, the relative decline of Aceh in the later seventeenth century was partly caused by its earlier success, since the city grew to such size that it could not properly be supported (Figure 7.2).[49]

A century later, Aceh still exported half of the world's pepper. By then the British and Dutch East India Companies had practically taken over the Bay of Bengal, and the Malay Peninsula as well. Aceh remained independent. It did not become part of the Dutch East Indies until the final decades of the nineteenth century. The "Aceh war" against the Dutch (1873–1904) – also known as the "Dutch War" and the "Infidel War" – was the last great, desperate fight for survival of the Orang Laut.

The other development of momentous importance for the archipelago was the shift and decline of maritime power that occurred in Java in the century after about 1680. By comparison, the mainland of Southeast Asia was better able to harness its Muslim-dominated maritime trade, largely because its resources were less sought after by Europeans and because its geography, territorial consolidation, and political integration around the Buddhist Sangha in three great imperial systems (Burma, Thailand, and Vietnam) made it much more difficult to penetrate.[50] In the archipelago, the Portuguese attempts to obtain the spice monopoly failed, but they stimulated spice production, intensifying

Figure 7.2 Slave market in Aceh, Sumatra, Indonesia, 1873. Illustration by Smeeton Tilly from L'Illustration, Journal Universel, No. 1571, Volume LXI, April 5, 1873. De Agostine Picture Library via Getty Images.

links between Java and the Spice Islands, where Muslim trading activity and pan-Islamic sentiment coalesced in Ternate.[51] At first, one coastal town, Demak, attempted to establish a claim over the whole of Java and conquered the Hindu-Buddhist state of Majapahit in 1527, setting itself up as its successor. The remains of the Majapahit dynasty lingered on in eastern Java (Pasuruan, Panuruhan, Balambangan) until 1639 and were then transferred to Bali. Demak's expansion brought other important ports to submission and reached into as yet un-Islamized inland regions of East Java. In West Java, the expansion spurred on Bantam and Cirebon; these coastal states conquered Sunda Kalapa, the port of the Hindu-Buddhist state of Pajajaran in the inland Sundanese area in the same year that Majapahit fell to Demak. The second ruler of Bantam, Hasan ad-Din (1552–1570), spread his authority to South Sumatra and established Bantam as a pepper port. In 1579, Demak conquered Pajajaran, the last significant Hindu-Buddhist inland state in Java, after the demise of which the Sundanese elite appears to have embraced Islam. Superseding Demak, two new powers emerged in the central Javanese interior, at Pajang and Mataram (located at the present-day cities of Surakarta and Yogyakarta) in the second half of the sixteenth century. These regions, with rich agricultural economies but with little involvement in seaborne commerce, at sites where no extensive kingdoms had fixed their kratons since the tenth century, were soon to eclipse the dominant role of the coastal states of Java. In the sixteenth century, however, the power of the inland states over towns like Japara, Tuban, Gresik, and especially Surabaya (which became the leading coastal power in the early seventeenth century) was still entirely nominal. It was under Sultan Agung (1613–1646) that Mataram established its hegemony in east and central Java and in Madura. Surabaya was conquered in 1625. From this period onward, up to the early nineteenth century, central Java was once again the heartland of an all-Javanese state and of a specifically Javanese courtly culture. Surrounded by the monumental Hindu and Buddhist relics of Borobudur and Prambanan, Mataram remained rooted in Indic and Old Javanese patterns. The commercial interlude of Javanese history was now despised, and a sense of continuity with the medieval past came easy. With the Dutch East India Company as the dominant naval power in the archipelago, Javanese society turned inward and became relatively closed to Indian and Chinese influence from overseas.

The kingdom of Mataram was the last Indo-Islamic state to emerge on Java. It was not founded on Islamic law; again, like other Indo-Islamic states, including the Mughal empire and the Sultanates of Aceh and Melaka, it was rooted in customary (*adat*) law. Islam's abrogation of the identification of king and god (usually Vishnu) did not by any means strip it of its non-Islamic sacral qualities of majestic and awesome power. The law codes of Java, in Mataram as much as in the northeast Islamic centers, owed almost nothing to Islam.[52] In Raffles' words, in some cases rulers "considered it a point of honor to profess adherence to Islamic law," but they were always "vested with a discretionary power of adapting the Mahometan law to the circumstances of society, a prerogative liberally exercised." It was by means of this discretionary power that all legal innovations appear to have been introduced and justified, in Mataram as everywhere in the Indo-Islamic world. The laws gained their authority from having been laid down by the ruler. Moreover, the administration of law was the ruler's responsibility. Where qazis existed, they appear to have been royal appointees. In many regions, however, legal administration was carried out by the nobles of the court rather than Islamic officials. The centrality of kingship was the dominant characteristic of Mataram and had deep roots in the pre-Islamic past.[53] The very process of Islamization occurred in the idiom of kingship. In Mataram, the insignia and rituals of kingship, even the religious and spiritual importance of the institution, were largely of pre-Islamic, Indic origin. Its formal arrangements of administration bore the mark of Indic cosmological principles.

This is not to deny that the arrival of Islam did lead to a reorientation of the culture of Java and the archipelago. Many archipelago rulers, of Java and elsewhere, displayed a vigorous interest in Islamic matters. Monarchs are sometimes credited with introducing Islam and sometimes assumed the role of Islamic teachers. Learned Muslims from Arabia and other parts of the Islamic world were welcomed at the Javanese courts. Such interaction over wide geographical distances is very impressive. Yet it inspired few innovations in political organization. What the Javanese kings and the other kings in the archipelago took from Islam was the Indo-Persian tradition of kingship that flourished in the Mughal empire, as also the Sufi ideal of the Perfect Man – both features that concern leadership rather than the doctrines of the Sharia. In Java, as elsewhere in the archipelago, it was not until the later eighteenth and nineteenth centuries that the Sharia-minded clergy and its following took on a more important political role. The conversion of the countryside was also very partial. Conversion to Islam proceeded steadily in these centuries, but it has to be kept in mind what that meant. Among the largely illiterate peasants of Java, the dominant religious belief system was one of deep ritual concern for the propitiation of the dead, not the brahmanism and caste system sanctioned by the scriptural high tradition of the Hindu dharmashastra (which, in Indonesia, has always remained largely confined to the courts, even in Java). Islam spread in the same form of "holy-man Islam" as in Sind, East Bengal, and elsewhere in the Indian subcontinent. In the Malay-Indonesian archipelago it did not inspire a radically different political culture and mode of political organization or a new social order. Here again, law did not follow religion. To be sure, in Aceh and the rest of the Malay-Indonesian archipelago, there are indications of the presence of Islamic law and legal administration prior to the era of colonial rule. But the presence of elements of Islamic law and of officials known as qazis does not in itself indicate that Islam inspired a political and institutional transformation, or that Islamic legal institutions were the articulating features of a new political structure.[54] The Sharia played a role, but mostly in the religious sphere, by regulating prayer, dietary codes, dress codes, personal piety and conduct, gender relations, the treatment of widows (widow burning disappeared), funerary practices, and family and inheritance issues. Of far greater importance, in Aceh and the archipelago as a whole, were the legal codes or digests that were called *Undang* and contained few or no elements of Islamic law. It is the customary, or *adat*, aspect of these digests that conforms most closely to foreign accounts of Malay-Indonesian legal arrangements. Overwhelmingly, these legal texts are concerned with the institution of kingship rather than the explication of Islamic law.

The great Dutch colonial historian Bernard Schrieke thought that Hindu Majapahit and Muslim Mataram had basic characteristics in common: both were presiding over mainly goods economies, both were politically fragmented due to geography (isolated plains and valleys dissected by volcanic mountain ranges), they had equally primitive military techniques and no standing armies (not to mention slave armies), and in both cases virtually autonomous and chivalrous regional lords were only loosely integrated in the state and broke away whenever the patrimonial mechanisms of control faltered.[55] Like Majapahit, but with even less justice, Mataram claimed hegemony of the entire archipelago. The dynasty of Mataram lasted longer than any other post-Majapahit Javanese dynasty. It reigned for almost four centuries, first at Mataram itself, then in Pajang (Kartasura, Surakarta), and finally, bifurcated, in both Surakarta and Yogyakarta.[56] The Dutch Company propped up Mataram's rulers from the 1670s to the later eighteenth century and was responsible for the final partitioning of the realm among Surakarta and Yogyakarta – with the Mangkunegara as a third part. But the Dutch presence in Java also plunged the dynasty into chronic crisis. If Sultan Agung consolidated the power of Mataram, it was by destroying much of the rice lands and the irrigation system in the coastal towns and forcing a large part of the seafaring Javanese to take up new positions at Bantam, Palembang, Macassar, and Banjarmasin. Dutch power in Maluku added to the isolation of the Mataram polity from the outer islands. Macassar began to attract "all the strange and Moorish nations." It became the center of the "smuggling trade" and a notable disseminator of Islamic propaganda once the Dutch attempted to obtain the monopoly of the spices and Ternate had been terminally weakened. Maluku put itself under Macassarese instead of Javanese protection – until Speelman conquered Macassar in 1669. Javanese shipping was destroyed completely by Agung's successor Amangkurat I (1646–1679), after his final attempt to control the pasisir had failed. The Dutch East India Company intervened for the first time in central Java when Amangkurat II (1677–1703) faced widespread rebellion, arising from the loss of consensus of the Javanese nobility and supported by Islamic and pasisir opposition and a rival Madurese claimant to the throne. The pasisir was formally ceded to the Dutch in payment of debts. Five successive rulers followed in Surakarta in the sixty years from 1680 onward. In the west of Java, Bantam underwent a crisis that resulted in *Kumpeni* intervention and the loss of independence in 1683; Cirebon and the Priangan highlands were ceded to the Dutch.

Throughout the Kartasura period, the Dutch presence remained disruptive. While formerly no succession to the throne could be achieved without the support of the nobles, now Dutch support could tip the scales in favor of almost any pretender they chose to put forward. Javanese kings had normally maintained power by balancing aristocratic interests. But in the seventeenth to the mid-eighteenth century, the mere possibility of a Dutch military action was sufficient to spoil the system and bring candidates to the throne who, feeding upon pasisir discontent and Arabian-Islamic reactions (emanating from Aceh) against the Javanistic Islam of the agrarian interior, could not avoid upsetting this balance. Not before the mid-eighteenth century did princes emerge who had fought against the Dutch. Sultan Mangkubumi (1749–1792) was able to marshal both Javanese and Dutch support. But the Dutch supported a second candidate at the same time and thus again prevented the traditional resolution of dynastic crisis. This ultimately led, after the Giyanti pact of 1755 and the peace of Salatiga in 1770, to the permanent division of Java. The coast – the maritime frontier – was now entirely in Dutch hands, the colonial era about to begin.

Epilogue

> The impulse that drew an Alexander, a Timur, and a Baber eastwards to the Indus was the same that in the sixteenth century gave the Portuguese that brief lease of sovereignty whose outworn shibboleths they have ever since continued to mumble; that early in the last century made a Shah of Persia for ten years the arbiter of the East, that all but gave to France the empire which stouter hearts and a more propitious star have conferred upon our own people; that to this day stirs the ambition and quickens the pulses of the Colossus of the North.
>
> G. N. Curzon (1892)[1]

Recent events in the East – from the Islamic Revolution and the Soviet invasion of Afghanistan in 1979 to the development of global jihadism or "terrorism" and the rise of Osama bin Laden and the Taliban, then ISIS – have taken almost everyone by surprise. These events have also sparked a new and intense interest in the historical evolution of a region with which most Americans were quite unfamiliar and regarded as of little relevance for themselves. In the daily press, in foreign policy journals, and in academic books, what came to be called the "new great game" for empire became a hotly debated subject. Parallels have thus been drawn between the Cold War engagements of the twentieth century and the contest between Russia and Great Britain for power and influence in the same region in the nineteenth century. As the quotation from Lord George Nathaniel Curzon (1859–1925; Viceroy of India, 1899–1905) illustrates, the struggle for empire in South Asia has been depicted as something that was historically inevitable and of all ages – proof, if any were needed, of the old adage that "geography is destiny." But this, of course, even in Curzon's time was no longer true.

Today some argue that a sense of displacement has taken root among the Muslim population living in India and the other countries covered in this book. The argument has its origin in the perception that the Islamic culture of these countries is somehow derivative of the real

Islam of the Arabs and therefore deeply alienated. This perception is perhaps best articulated by V. S. Naipaul in his travelogue *Beyond Belief: Islamic Excursions among the Converted Peoples* (1998):

Islam is in its origins an Arab religion. Everyone not an Arab who is a Muslim is a convert. Islam is not simply a matter of conscience or private belief. It makes imperial demands. A convert's world view alters. His holy places are in Arab lands; his sacred language is Arabic. His idea of history alters. He rejects his own; he becomes, whether he likes it or not, a part of the Arab story. The convert has to turn away from everything that is his. The disturbance for societies is immense, and even after a thousand years can remain unresolved; the turning away has to be done again and again. People develop fantasies about who and what they are; and in the Islam of converted countries there is an element of neurosis and nihilism. These countries can be easily set on the boil.[2]

Naipaul saw conversion to Islam as "a kind of crossover from old beliefs, earth religions, the cult of rulers and local deities, to the revealed religions – Christianity and Islam principally – with their larger philosophical and humanitarian and social concerns."[3] In the West this process has had a parallel in late antiquity, in the conversion to Christianity. In the East, however, for Naipaul, the crossover to Islam is still going on: "It is the extra drama in the background," he writes, "... the steady grinding down of the old world."[4]

Naipaul has argued that there has never been anything like a final conquest of India. This was why, in the eighteenth century, the peoples who rose to power after the Mughal decline – the Marathas, the Sikhs, and so on – were still able to champion their own faith against the Muslims.[5] The British period then came to be a time of Hindu regeneration. This was the beginning of the intellectual distance between the two communities. That distance has grown with independence. In the end, it was "Muslim insecurity" that led to the call for the creation of Pakistan.[6] But the creation of Pakistan "went at the same time with an idea of old glory, of the invaders sweeping down from the northwest and looting the temples of Hindustan and imposing the faith on the infidel."[7] And in the school history books, writes Naipaul, the history of Pakistan would become only an aspect of the history of Islam. The Muslim invaders, and especially the Arabs, would become "the heroes of the Pakistan story."[8] "It is a dreadful mangling of history. It is a convert's view; that's all that can be said for it. History has become a kind of neurosis."[9]

In an interview with the *New York Times* on October 28, 2001 – published shortly after the September 11 terrorist attacks on the World Trade Center and just after having won the Nobel Prize in Literature – Naipaul was asked, "Are you surprised by Osama bin Laden's support in Pakistan, Indonesia, Malaysia and Iran – countries you wrote about in your travel books on Islam?" His answer was "No, because these are the converted peoples of Islam. To put it brutally, these are the people who are not Arabs. Part of the neurosis of the convert is that he always has to prove himself. He has to be more royalist than the king, as the French say."[10]

The vision of history that goes with this idea is in fact much older than Naipaul and has long had wide currency as a literary theme. In *Lord Jim* (1900), for instance, Conrad brings up a wandering stranger, an "Arab half-breed," Sherif Ali, who, "on purely religious grounds, had incited the tribes of the interior (the bush-folk, as Jim himself called them) to rise, and had established himself in a fortified camp on the summit of one of the twin hills. He hung over the town of Patusan like a hawk over a poultry yard, but he devastated the open country."[11]

The same perception has been widespread as a theme in the imagination of both the Dutch and the British colonial governments. Around 1889, the Dutch Islamicist and influential adviser to the Dutch colonial government, Christiaan Snouck Hurgronje, wrote that "the credulity of the masses in Java enables foreign Muslims too easily to induce them into religious-politics movements and if the agitators are Arabs, they can always be sure of a certain amount of success."[12] Snouck Hurgronje observed in Mecca that

most Javanese lack in an international gathering of Muslims the necessary self-respect which partly explains the contemptuous treatment they often receive ... They start by regarding their own home as a dunghill in comparison with pure, holy Mecca, because the outer forms of life here (in Mecca) bring to mind the Muslim faith; there often the heathen past ... [And] at the same time they sacrifice without inner strife every patriotic feeling, every inclination to native custom, to the uplifting consciousness of solidarity with the great Muslim Empire ... [T]hey look down on the "impure" society to which they once belonged.[13]

Like the Dutch government in the East Indies, the British government in India was haunted by the idea that its Muslim subjects could be "easily set on the boil." Recent research by Chandra Mallampalli has revealed in considerable detail how fears of a Muslim conspiracy in British India emerged as early as 1839, when the British prepared for war in Afghanistan and colonial officials became convinced that itinerant preachers of jihad, under the influence of "Wahhabism" emanating from Arabia, were collaborating with Russian and Persian armies and inspiring Muslim princes as far as the Deccan to revolt.[14] In another recent study, Seema Alavi describes the role of itinerant Arabs in the aftermath of the 1857 Rebellion, whose mobility and spiritual convictions served their goal of forging an alternative "Arabicist" empire that called for the global unity of Muslims to fill the vacuum created by the fall of the Mughal empire and presented Muslims with an alternative to Western imperialism.[15] Events of this kind during the First World War have drawn considerable attention. In November 1914, upon entering the war, the Turkish Sultan, the spiritual head of all Sunni Muslims, gave in to German prompting by declaring a jihad on Britain and her allies. A jihad manifesto was issued that was particularly aimed at *Indian* Muslims. The German foreign ministry hoped that the Sultan's proclamation would "awaken the fanaticism of Islam" and might lead to a large-scale revolution in India.[16] The British worried about this possibility a great deal. For Kitchener, the war minister, already traumatized by the 1898 uprising in the Sudan and with the Indian Rebellion (Mutiny) of 1857–1858 in mind, the possibility that a jihad might be hurled against Britain was a recurrent nightmare. Over half the world's Muslims were under British rule: 70 million in India alone, constituting a disproportionately large part of the Indian army; millions more in Egypt and the Sudan, along the Suez canal route to India, policed by tiny British garrisons that would be swept away in a revolt. These wartime fears became the subject of a novel, *Greenmantle*, by the director of information, John Buchan, in which Germany makes use of a Muslim prophet, "of the Koreish…the tribe of the Prophet himself," who appears in Turkey and instigates a jihad against Britain's empire.[17] The novel dramatizes the fear that the jihad would ignite the Indian Muslims: "There is a dry wind blowing through the East, and the parched grasses wait the spark. And the wind is blowing toward the Indian border…There is a Jehad preparing…There will be hell let loose in those parts pretty soon. Hell which may spread. Beyond Persia, remember, lies India."[18]

To be sure, when the Turkish jihad was proclaimed in 1914, nothing happened, no parched grasses were ignited. But it is striking that fears of a German-instigated jihad persisted for a number of years. If they eventually subsided during the 1920s and 1930s, it was not least because Adolf Hitler was an outspoken opponent of the strategy of mobilizing India's Muslims against the British empire.[19] And in the Second World War, Hitler resorted to a quite different strategy to subvert the British empire in India. Rather than instigate a jihad among Indian Muslims, he relied on the Japanese to do the job, by planning an invasion of India from the East.

And yet, only a few decades later, it was the Arabs again who turned up on the Indian frontier and instigated yet another jihad against the infidels. Supported this time by the United States as well as by Saudi Arabia, they became involved in proxy warfare against the Soviets in Afghanistan. In the final days of the Cold War, it was the Arabs and their leader Osama bin Laden who pulled the strings of the Taliban regime in Afghanistan and Pakistan, as well as their offshoots in Indian Kashmir, and were the driving force behind the destruction of the Buddhas of Bamiyan, "the grinding down of the old world."

This book was completed around the time Naipaul died. Over a fifty-year career, few post-colonial writers emerging from the sub-continent escaped his influence, or indeed his shadow. Many wrote about the alienation between India and Pakistan, the dilemma of Islam in Indonesia, the danger of becoming strangers to their own history. "To build Pakistan," wrote Salman Rushdie, "it was necessary to cover up Indian history, to deny that Indian centuries lay just beneath the surface of Pakistani Standard Time. The past was rewritten; there was nothing else to be done."[20] Aatish Taseer wrote at length about how "the idea of Pakistan came to be expressed not so much on its own terms, but as a negation of India: not so much by what it was, but what it wasn't."[21] Taseer wrote about the time since independence when

the Islamic Republic set itself the task of erasing its association with the subcontinent, an association which many in Pakistan came to view as a con-tamination ... [and] its mixed language, an incredible amalgam of Sanskrit, Persian, Arabic, and Turkic words, was cleansed of its Sanskrit vocabulary; history, even when Islamic, was taught in such a way that the connection to India was edged out; all things regional and cultural – dress, customs, festivals, marriage rituals, literature, ideas of caste – that had been common to Muslim and non-Muslim alike in pre-Partition India fell under suspicion.[22]

He views this process as tantamount to a "systematic historical and cultural denuding." According to the same writer, in an obituary of Naipaul, "At a time when the West was full of apology, and the non-West a sense of grievance, his [Naipaul's] great theme was the harm countries like mine would do themselves if they did not take respon-sibility for their histories."[23] Historians must take note and share this responsibility. It is hoped that this book, too, whatever its shortcom-ings, will contribute something to the will to face up to that history. It is a confrontation that has barely begun.

Glossary

Adat, customary law
Al-Hind, India
Bhakti, devotional religion
Brahmans, priestly/upper caste
Dharmashastra, Hindu law code
Dhow, sailing boat of the Indian Ocean
Estado da India, the Portuguese maritime empire in India
Fitna, rebellion, sedition
Habshis, Abyssinians
Jagir, revenue assignment
Jihad, Islamic holy war
Khalsa, crown land
Khanazads, 'born to the house,' hereditary nobility
Khutba, Islamic Friday prayer
Kraton, court
Kshatriyas, Hindu warrior caste
Madrasa, Islamic school, seminary
Mamluk, slave soldier or officer
Mansab, rank
Mansabdar, rank-holder
Mā warā' an-nahr, 'What is beyond the river (Amu Darya),' ancient Transoxania
Mirza, from Amirzada, 'Offspring of the Amir [Timur]'
Nawab, governor
Nawabi, governorship
Nökör, retainer
Noyan, Mongol military commander
Orang Laut, 'People of the Sea'
Padshah, emperor
Pashtunwali, customary/tribal law of the Pashtuns/Afghans
Pasisir, coast
Pathans, Afghans
Pir, holy man, saint
Powindas, Afghan nomads
Purda, concealment of women
Qazi, Islamic judge

Rajputs, 'Kings' Sons,' Hindu warrior caste, ruling elite or nobility of Rajasthan
    and North India
Sangha, Buddhist monastic order
Sayyid, (alleged) descendant of the Prophet Muhammad
Sharia, Islamic law
Sharif, magistrate, religious leader
Shaykh, Islamic scholar, theologian
Shudras, peasant caste
Stupa, Buddhist shrine
Suba, province
Subadar, provincial governor
Sufis, members of religious/mystical orders of Islam
Ta'ifa, (Sufi) order
Törü, Tora, Turko-Mongol customary law
Tuman, Mongol military unit of ten thousand
Turan, Central Asia
ʿUlamāʾ, scholars, theologians, jurists of Islam
Ulus, Mongol dynastic or tribal realm
Vedas, earliest literature in Sanskrit, c. 1500–500 BCE
Wilayat, province
Zamindar, 'land-holder,' landed magnate

Chronological Table

Pre-historic: from the Neolithic or agricultural revolution in the fifth or sixth
    millennium BC to the end of the Indus Valley civilization (3000–1500
    BCE)
Vedic, Vedic Aryan: the period between 1500 BCE and 500 BCE during
    which the so-called Vedic texts were composed in Sanskrit and much of
    North India came to be dominated by an Aryan ruling elite expanding its
    sway from the north-west
Ancient: approximately 500 BCE to 600 CE
Medieval: approximately 600 CE to 1500 CE
Early modern: approximately 1500 CE to 1800 CE
Modern: approximately 1800 CE to the present

Notes

Preface

1   A. Wink, *Al-Hind: The Making of the Indo-Islamic World, 5 vols.* (Leiden, 1990, 1997, 2004; vols. IV and V forthcoming).

Chapter 1

1   See note 9.
2   See note 19.
3   A. Wink, *Al-Hind: The Making of the Indo-Islamic World,* 3 vols. (Leiden, 1990, 1997, 2004), passim, especially Vol. III, pp. 1–78.
4   Cf. W. H. Arden Wood, "Rivers and Man in the Indus-Ganges Alluvial Plain," *The Scottish Geographical Magazine*, XL (1924), pp. 1–16.
5   A rare study of the impact of historical tsunamis is Anthony Reid, "Two Hitherto Unknown Indonesian Tsunamis of the Seventeenth Century: Probabilities and Context," *Journal of Southeast Asian Studies*, 47, 1 (2016), pp. 88–108.
6   R. F. Burton, *Sindh and the Races That Inhabit the Valley of the Indus* (1851) (Karachi, 1973), pp. 3–4.
7   According to Madhuri Desai in a lecture presented on January 26, 2017, at the Center for South Asia, Madison.
8   S. Winchester, *Krakatoa: The Day the World Exploded: August 27, 1883* (New York, 2003); G. D'Arcy Wood, *Tambora: The Eruption That Changed the World* (Princeton, 2014); N. F. Cantor, *In the Wake of the Plague: The Black Death and the World It Made* (New York, 2001), pp. 171–83.
9   *BN*, f. 274b.
10 C. Defrémery and B. R. Sanguinetti (eds. and trans.), *Voyages d'Ibn Batoutah*, 4 vols. (Paris, 1853–58), Vol. III, pp. 145–6.
11 Ibid., pp. 315–16.
12 S. Sen (ed.), *Indian Travels of Thevenot and Careri* (Delhi, 1949), p. 60.
13 A. Ghosh, *The City in Early Historical India* (Simla, 1973), pp. 49, 52, and passim.
14 Ibid., p. 11.
15 Ibid., p. 64.
16 F. Bernier, *Travels in the Mogul Empire, A. D. 1656–1688* (Delhi, 1989), pp. 246–7: "It is because of these wretched mud and thatch houses that I always represent to myself Dehli as a collection of many villages, or as

a military encampment with a few more conveniences than are usually found in such places." The recent secondary literature (in contrast to the older colonial one) is often misleading on this subject. For instance, C. Asher and C. Talbot, *India before Europe* (Cambridge, 2006), has it that "The Frenchman François Bernier compared [Delhi] to Paris in terms of its beauty, extent, and number of inhabitants" (p. 197). If so, Bernier actually suggested that it was very much unlike Paris. Similarly, Y. Sharma and P. Malekandathil (eds.), *Cities in Medieval India* (Delhi, 2014), sets out to present Indian cities as comparable to Mediterranean/European ones, only to run into constant problems with the evidence.

17   The term "rurban" was introduced in R. G. Fox, "Rurban Settlements and Rajput 'Clans' in Northern India," in R. G. Fox (ed.), *Urban India: Society, Space and Image* (Durham, 1970), pp. 167–85.

18   Murari Kumar Jha, "Migration, Settlement, and State Formation in the Ganga Plain: A Historical Geographic Perspective," *Journal of the Economic and Social History of the Orient*, 57 (2014), pp. 587–627; D. Chakrabarti, *Archaeological Geography of the Ganga Plain: The Lower and Middle Ganga* (Delhi, 2001); T. N. Roy, *The Ganges Civilization: A Critical Archaeological Study of the Painted Grey Ware and Northern Black Polished Ware Periods of the Ganga Plains of India* (Delhi, 1983); B. Prasad Sahu (ed.), *Iron and Social Change in Early India* (Delhi, 2006); N. Sengupta, *Land of Two Rivers: A History of Bengal from the Mahabharata to Mujib* (Delhi, 2011); L. Gopal and V. C. Srivastava (eds.), *History of Agriculture in India, up to 1200 A. D.* (Delhi, 2008).

19   As G. Fussman points out, "Le concept d'empire, en effet, n'a guère de sens pour les théoriciens indiens" ("Le concept d'empire dans l'inde ancienne," in M. Duverger (ed.), *The Concept d'Empire* (Paris, 1980), p. 386). For Georges Duby's statement that serves as the second epigraph of this chapter, see the discussion of this volume's article by Fussman on p. 391.

20   B. Madhab Barua, *Asoka and His Inscriptions*, 2 vols. (Calcutta, 1946), and R. Thapar, *Asoka and the Decline of the Mauryas* (Oxford, 1961), are among early examples of this view that has been repeated endlessly in subsequent works. In the political discourse of the Indian republic, it is a standard assumption that the Mauryan empire was highly centralized and politically unified the Indian subcontinent. Western Indologists and historians often followed suit (cf. note 21).

21   A. L. Basham, *The Wonder That Was India: A Survey of the History and Culture of the Indian Sub-continent before the Coming of the Muslims* (first published 1954; Delhi, 1987), p. 55.

22   T. R. Trautmann, *Kautilya and the Arthashastra: A Statistical Investigation of the Authorship and Evolution of the Text* (Leiden, 1971); D. Ali, *Courtly Culture and Political Life in Early Medieval India* (Cambridge, 2004), pp. 71–2.

23   J. W. McCrindle, *Ancient India as Described by Megasthenes and Arrian* (Calcutta, 1877).

24   G. Fussman, "Pouvoir central et régions dans l'Inde ancienne," *Annales ESC*, 37, 4 (1982), pp. 621–41; U. N. Ghoshal, *A History of Indian Political Ideas* (Oxford, 1966), pp. 77–8.

25 These edicts greatly appealed to mid-twentieth-century Europeans traumatized by the world wars. Basham calls Ashoka "the greatest and noblest ruler India has known, and indeed one of the great kings of the world," solely on the merit of his inscriptions (*The Wonder That Was India*, p. 53). American scholars and intellectuals have continued fantasizing about Ashoka. Basham's student Thomas R. Trautmann writes that "Ashoka, at once the head of a powerful state and a Buddhist, directed the state once again toward a transcendental object… the active principle of compassion, and for once in human history it became the guiding spirit of political life" (T. R. Trautmann, *India: A Brief History of a Civilization* (Oxford, 2011), p. 61). One American journalist, Chris Hedges, writes, "One of the first known legal protections of basic human freedoms and equality was promulgated in India, in the third century B. C. by the Buddhist emperor Ashoka. And, unlike Aristotle, he insisted on equal rights for women and slaves" (C. Hedges, *The World as It Is: Dispatches on the Myth of Human Progress* (New York, 2009), p. 264).

26 F. Virkus, *Politische Strukturen im Guptareich (300–550 n. Chr)* (Wiesbaden, 2014).

27 H. Bechert (ed.), *When Did the Buddha Live? The Controversy of the Dating of the Historical Buddha* (Delhi, 1994), p. 286.

28 Cf. R. Thapar, *From Lineage to State* (Bombay, 1984), pp. 16–17.

29 J. Keay, *India: A History* (New York, 2000), p. 102.

Chapter 2

1 G. Deleury, *Les Indes Florissantes: Anthologie des Voyageurs Français (1750–1820)* (Paris, 1991), p. 119.

2 Wink, *Al-Hind*, Vol. I, pp. 144–89.

3 I. Habib, "Jatts of Panjāb and Sind," in H. Singh and N. G. Barrier (eds.), *Punjab Past and Present: Essays in Honour of Dr Garda Singh* (Patiala, 1976), pp. 93–7; Wink, *Al-Hind*, Vol. I, pp. 162–3; Vol. II, pp. 239–46.

4 M. A. Stein (ed.), *Kalhana's Rājataranginī* (Delhi, 1960); M. A. Stein (trans.), *Kalhana's Rājataranginī: A Chronicle of the Kings of Kashmir*, 2 vols. (Delhi, 1961); Wink, *Al-Hind*, Vol. I, pp. 231–54.

5 S. Sheikh, *Forging a Region: Sultans, Traders and Pilgrims in Gujarat, 1200–1500* (Delhi, 2010); V. K. Jain, *Trade and Traders in Western India (AD 1000–1300)* (Delhi, 1990); Wink, *Al-Hind*, Vol. II, pp. 269–75.

6 Murari Kumar Jha, "Migration, Settlement, and State Formation in the Ganga Plain: A Historical Geographic Perspective," *Journal of the Economic and Social History of the Orient*, 57 (2014), pp. 600, 612–13.

7 Ibid., pp. 588–90, 593, 598, 608, 616.

8 G. Roerich (trans.), *Biography of Dharmasvamin* (Patna, 1959), p. 73.

9 Jha, "Migration, Settlement, and State Formation in the Ganga Plain," p. 618; J. N. Asopa, *Origin of the Rajputs* (Delhi, 1976); V. B. Mishra, *The Gurjara-Pratiharas and Their Times* (Delhi, 1966); Wink, *Al-Hind*, Vol. I, pp. 277–302.

258 Notes to pages 34–42

10 R. M. Eaton, *The Rise of Islam and the Bengal Frontier, 1204–1760* (Berkeley, 1993); P. L. Paul, *The Early History of Bengal*, 2 vols. (Calcutta, 1939–40); B. M. Morrison, *Political Centers and Cultural Regions in Early Bengal* (Tucson, 1970); Wink, *Al-Hind*, Vol. I, pp. 254–77.

11 B. Stein, *Peasant State and Society in Medieval South India* (Delhi, 1980), pp. 45–66; Wink, *Al-Hind*, Vol. I, pp. 311–27.

12 R. Lingat, *Royautés Bouddhiques* (Paris, 1989), pp. 61–239.

13 C. Higham, *The Archaeology of Mainland Southeast Asia: From 10.000 B. C. to the Fall of Angkor* (Cambridge, 1989); G. Coedès, *The Indianized States of Southeast Asia* (Honolulu, 1968), pp. 1–45; G. Coedès, *The Making of South-East Asia* (Berkeley, 1983), pp. 1–56; A. Reid, *A History of Southeast Asia: A Critical Crossroads* (Oxford, 2015), pp. 8–13; V. Lieberman, "Local Integration and Eurasian Analogies: Structuring Southeast Asian History, c. 1350–c.1830," *Modern Asian Studies*, 27, 3 (1993), pp. 475–572; Wink, *Al-Hind*, Vol. I, pp. 342–58; Vol. II, pp. 365–80; Vol. III, pp. 5–63.

14 Coedès, *Indianized States of Southeast Asia*, pp. 36–8, 40–2; Coedès, *Making of South-East Asia*, s. v.; G. Coedès, *Angkor* (Singapore, 1963); Reid, *History of Southeast Asia*, pp. 6, 16, 31, 37, 40–1; I. Mabbett and D. Chandler, *The Khmers* (Oxford, 1995).

15 M. Aung-Thwin, *Pagan: The Origins of Modern Burma* (Honolulu, 1985); Wink, *Al-Hind*, Vol. I, pp. 346–51; Vol. II, pp. 374–7.

16 Wink, *Al-Hind*, Vol. III, pp. 39–40; B. Gosling, *Sukhothai: Its History, Culture, and Art* (Singapore, 1991).

17 B. Schrieke, *Indonesian Sociological Studies*, 2 vols. (The Hague, 1955–7); Wink, *Al-Hind*, Vol. III, pp. 58–63.

18 W. H. McNeill, *Plagues and Peoples* (New York, 1976), pp. 83, 95, 126; M. H. Green (ed.), "Pandemic Disease in the Medieval World: Rethinking the Black Death," *The Medieval Globe*, 1 (2014); M. H. Green, "The Globalisations of Disease," in N. Boivin, R. Crassard, and M. D. Petraglia (eds.), *Human Dispersal and Species Movement: From Prehistory to the Present* (Cambridge, 2017), pp. 494–520; G. D. Sussman, "Was the Black Death in India and China?" *Bulletin of the History of Medicine*, 85 (2011), pp. 319–55.

19 For the European figures, see J. Le Goff, *Medieval Civilization, 400–1500* (Oxford, 2006), p. 59; more on the subject in Wink, *Al-Hind*, Vol. II, pp. 162–7.

20 The literature on this subject is vast; see the special issue of *The Journal of the Royal Asiatic Society*, 22, 1 (March, 2012); H. C. Ray, *The Dynastic History of Northern India*, 2 vols. (Delhi, 1973; or 1931–36); Wink, *Al-Hind*, Vol. I, pp. 219–358.

21 J. Tod, *Annals and Antiquities of Rajasthan*, 2 vols. (Delhi, 1983), Vol. II, p. 356; Wink, *Al-Hind*, Vol. I, pp. 277–302.

22 Wink, *Al-Hind*, Vol. I, p. 158 ff.

23 Ibid., pp. 231–54.

24 Ibid., pp. 254–77.

25 Ibid., pp. 303–9.

26 Ibid., pp. 309–34.

27 Ibid., s.v.; *II*, s.v.

28 R. S. Khare, "The Kānya-Kubja Brahmins and Their Caste Organization," *Southwestern Journal of Anthropology*, 16 (1960), pp. 348–67.

29 M. Reinaud, *Fragments Arabes et Persans inédits Relatifs à l'Inde, antérieure-ment au Xe siècle de l'ère Chrétienne* (Paris, 1895), pp. 1–24.

30 Sheikh, *Forging a Region*, pp. 47–9.

31 Y. Bronner, "From Conqueror to Connoisseur: Kalhana's Account of Jayāpīda and the Fashioning of Kashmir as Kingdom of Learning," *The Indian Economic and Social History Review*, 50, 2 (2013), pp. 161–77.

32 S. Bhattacharya, *Landschenkungen und Staatliche Entwicklung im Frühmittelalterlichen Bengalen (5. bis 13 Jh. N. Chr)* (Wiesbaden, 1985); P. L. Paul, "Brāhmana Immigration in Bengal," *Proceedings of the Indian History Congress*, III, (1939), pp. 575–6.

33 Wink, *Al-Hind*, Vol. I, s. v. Malabar; Vol. II, s.v. Malabar.

34 Stein, *Peasant State and Society in Medieval South India*, pp. 4, 52–3, 66, 100; M. Liceria, "Emergence of Brāhmanas as Landed Intermediaries in Karnataka: A. D. 1000–1300," *The Indian Historical Review*, I, 1 (March, 1974), p. 29; Wink, *Al-Hind*, Vol. I, pp. 311–13.

35 Lingat, *Royautés Bouddhiques*, pp. 89–107.

36 Coedès, *Indianized States*, pp. 17–18, 30, 32, 37, and s.v. Kaundinya Brahmans.

37 V. B. Mishra, *Religious Beliefs and Practices of North India during the Early Mediaeval Period* (Leiden, 1973); R. Inden, "Imperial Purānas: Kashmir as Vaisnava Center of the World," in R. Inden, J. Walters, and D. Ali (eds.), *Querying the Medieval: Texts and the History of Practices in South Asia* (New York, 2000), pp. 29–98; P. Bisschop, "Shaivism in the Gupta-Vākātaka Age," *Journal of the Royal Asiatic Society*, 20, 4 (2010), pp. 477–88; A. Sanderson, "The Shaiva Age: An Explanation of the Rise and Dominance of Shaivism during the Early Medieval Period," in S. Einoo (ed.), *Genesis and Development of Tantrism* (Tokyo, 2009), pp. 41–350.

38 G. Michell, *The Hindu Temple: An Introduction to Its Meaning and Forms* (Chicago, 1988); S. Kramrisch, *The Hindu Temple* (Delhi, 1980); M. Willis, *The Archaeology of Hindu Ritual: Temples and the Establishment of the Gods* (Cambridge, 2009).

39 G. Bühler (trans.), *The Laws of Manu* (1883; Delhi, reprint 1975), V.96, VII.5–6, 8; *Mahabharata*, 12.68.40, 12.59.128 ff, 12.67.4.

40 Schrieke, *Indonesian Sociological Studies*, Vol. II, pp. 10, 77–8, 99.

41 J. C. Heesterman, "The King's Order," *Contributions to Indian Sociology*, new series, 20, 1 (1986).

42 S. Pollock, "The Sanskrit Cosmopolis, 300–1300: Transculturation, Vernacularization, and the Question of Ideology," in J. E. M. Houben (ed.), *Ideology and Status of Sanskrit: Contributions to the History of the Sanskrit Language* (Leiden, 1996), pp. 197–247; S. Pollock, *The Language of the Gods in the World of Men: Sanskrit, Culture, and Power in Premodern India* (Berkeley, 2006).

43 Tod, *Annals and Antiquities of Rajasthan*; S. Settar and G. D. Sontheimer (eds.), *Memorial Stones: A Study of their Origin, Significance and Variety* (Dharwad, 1982); Ali, *Courtly Culture and Political Life in Early Medieval India*; Wink, *Al-Hind*, Vol. II, pp. 172–82.

44 Le Goff, *Medieval Civilization*, p. 315; J. Huizinga, *The Autumn of the Middle Ages* (Chicago, 1996), p. 250.
45 M. D. Bailey, *Magic and Superstition in Europe: A Concise History from Antiquity to the Present* (Lanham, 2007), pp. 148, 170–1, 175–6.
46 Wink, *Al-Hind*, Vols. I–III, s.v. caste.
47 C. Defrémery and B. R. Sanguinetti (eds. and trans.), *Voyages d'Ibn Batoutah*, 4 vols (Paris, 1853–1858), Vol. IV, pp. 71–87; Wink, *Al-Hind*, Vol. I, pp. 69–78.
48 Lingat, *Royautés Bouddhiques*, pp. 89–117.
49 T. Pigeaud, *Java in the Fourteenth Century*, 4 vols. (The Hague, 1960–63), Vol. I, p. 62; Vol. IV, p. 259; D. Lombard, *Le Carrefour Javanais: Essai d'Histoire Globale*, 3 vols. (Paris, 1990), Vol. III, pp. 55–6.
50 J. L. Swellengrebel (ed.), *Bali: Studies in Life, Thought and Ritual, Selected Studies on Indonesia by Dutch Scholars, No 5* (The Hague, 1960), pp. 287–9.
51 S. C. Levi, *The Indian Diaspora in Central Asia and Its Trade, 1550–1900* (Leiden, 2002), esp. 261–2; C. Markovits, *The Global World of Indian Merchants, 1750–1947: Traders from Bukhara to Panama* (Cambridge, 2000), pp. 4, 12, 27, 64, 68, 109, 139, 168; C. D. Ley (ed.), *Portuguese Voyages, 1498–1663: Tales from the Great Age of Discovery* (London, 1947), p. 22.

Chapter 3

1 B. Schrieke, "Ruler and Realm in Early Java," in B. Schrieke (ed.), *Indonesian Sociological Studies*, Vol. II (The Hague, 1959), pp. 78, 99.
2 M. G. S. Hodgson, *The Venture of Islam*, 3 vols. (Chicago, 1974), Vol. II, p. 71; X. De Planhol, *Le monde islamique: essai de géographie religieuse* (Paris, 1957); J. J. L. Gommans, "The Silent Frontier of South Asia, c. A.D. 1000–1800," *Journal of World History*, 9, 1 (1998), pp. 1–23.
3 V. B. Lieberman, *Strange Parallels: Southeast Asia in Global Context, c. 800–1830*, 2 vols. (Cambridge, 2003–2009), esp. Vol. II, pp. 85, 97–114.
4 G. Rawlinson (trans.), *Herodotus: The Histories* (London, 1992), pp. 300, 303, 323–5, 346.
5 L. Casson (ed. and trans.), *The Periplus Maris Erythraei* (Princeton, 1989), pp. 74–5, 86.
6 P. B. Golden, *An Introduction to the History of the Turkic Peoples: Ethnogenesis and State-Formation in Medieval and Early Modern Eurasia and the Middle East* (Wiesbaden, 1992), pp. 46–9.
7 F. W. Thomas, "Sakastana: Where Dwelt the Sakas Named by Darius and Herodotus?" *Journal of the Royal Asiatic Society*, 38 (1906), pp. 181–200, 460–4.
8 Wink, *Al-Hind*, Vol. II, pp. 54–9.
9 B. Fagan, *The Great Warming: Climate Change and the Rise and Fall of Civilizations* (New York, 2008), esp. pp. xi–xiii, 33–8, 47, 51–6.
10 T. Barfield, "Nomadic Pastoralism," in J. H. Bentley (ed.), *The Oxford Handbook of World History* (Oxford, 2012), pp. 164–6.
11 T. Barfield, *Afghanistan: A Cultural and Political History* (Princeton, 2010), pp. 58–60, 78–9; cf. Chapter 4, pp. 82–4; Chapter 5, pp. 124–36.

12 G. Clauson, *Turkish and Mongolian Studies* (London, 1962), pp. 1–3, 6, 8–9, 11, 14.
13 Ibid., pp. 26, 28.
14 Wink, *Al-Hind*, Vol. I, p. 43; Vol. II, pp. 62–7.
15 O. Pritsak, *The Origin of Rus*, Vol. I (Cambridge, MA 1981), pp. 15–16.
16 P. B. Golden, "Imperial Ideology and the Sources of Political Unity among the Pre-Cinggisid Nomads of Western Eurasia," *Archivum Eurasiae Medii Aevi*, Vol. II (1982), pp. 39, 42–61; O. Turan, "The Ideal of World Dominion among the Medieval Turks," *Studia Islamica*, 4 (1975), pp. 77–90.
17 I. De Rachewiltz, "Some Remarks on the Ideological Foundations of Chingis Khan's Empire," *Papers on Far Eastern History*, 7 (1973), pp. 21–36; A. F. Broadbridge, *Kingship and Ideology in the Islamic and Mongol Worlds* (Cambridge, 2008); T. T. Allsen, *Mongol Imperialism: The Politics of the Grand Qan Möngke in China, Russia, and the Islamic Lands, 1251–1259* (Berkeley, 1987); B. F. Manz, *The Rise and Rule of Tamerlane* (Cambridge, 1989).
18 D. R. Hill, "The Role of the Camel and the Horse in the Early Arab Conquests," in V. J. Parry and M. E. Yapp (eds.), *War, Technology and Society in the Middle East* (London, 1975), pp. 36–42; Wink, *Al-Hind*, Vol. I, p. 203; Vol. II, p. 86.
19 Wink, *Al-Hind*, Vol. I, pp. 115–16; Vol. II, pp. 68–76.
20 A. Wink, "India and the Turko-Mongol Frontier," in A. M. Khazanov and A. Wink (eds.), *Nomads in the Sedentary World* (London, 2001), pp. 211–33.
21 Cf. Chapter 4, pp. 94–108.
22 P. Jackson (trans.), *The Mission of Friar William Rubruck: His Journey to the Court of the Great Khan Möngke 1253–1255* (Introduction, Notes, and Appendices by P. Jackson and D. Morgan; London, 1990), p. 142.
23 Cf. W. H. Auden, *The Enchafèd Flood or the Romantic Iconography of the Sea* (London, 1949), pp. 25–6.
24 S. K. Nambiar (ed. and trans.), *Prabodhacandrodaya* (Delhi, 1971), pp. 49, 127.
25 A. L. Basham, "Notes on Seafaring in Ancient India," *Art and Letters: The Journal of the Royal India and Pakistan Society*, 23 (1949), p. 26.
26 F. W. Clothey, "Pilgrimage Centers in the Tamil Cultus of Murukan," *Journal of the American Academy of Religion*, 40 (1972), pp. 91–2.
27 Wink, *Al-Hind*, Vol. III, pp. 100–2.
28 D. Lombard, "Le thème de la mer dans les littératures et les mentalités de l'archipel insulindien," *Archipel*, 20 (1980), pp. 317–28; B. Schrieke, "De Javanen als zee- en handelsvolk," *Tijdschrift van het Bataafsch Genootschap*, LVIII (1919), pp. 424–8.
29 M. N. Pearson, *Port Cities and Intruders: The Swahili Coast, India, and Portugal in the Early Modern Era* (Baltimore, 1998), p. 39.
30 H. Yule (ed. and trans.), *The Book of Ser Marco Polo*, 2 vols. (New York, 1903), Vol. II, p. 389.
31 Wink, *Al-Hind*, Vol. III, pp. 170–243.

32 W. W. Rockhill, "Notes on the Relations and Trade of China with the Eastern Archipelago and the Coast of the Indian Ocean during the Fourteenth Century, Part I," *T'oung Pao*, XV (1914), pp. 418–66.

Chapter 4

1   Qur'ān 9.33.

2   M. Lombard, *L'Islam dans sa première grandeur, VIIIe–XIeme siècle* (Paris, 1971).

3   M. Lombard, "Les bases monétaires d'une suprématie économique: L'or musulmane du VIIe au Xie siècle," *Annales*, 2 (1947), pp. 143–60.

4   Lombard, *L'Islam*; Lombard, "Bases monétaires"; M. G. Morony, "Economic Boundaries? Late Antiquity and Early Islam," *Journal of the Economic and Social History of the Orient*, 47, 2 (2004), pp. 166–94; T. Daryaee, *Sasanian Persia: The Rise and Fall of an Empire* (London, 2009); P. Pourshariati, *Decline and Fall of the Sasanian Empire: The Sasanian-Parthian Confederacy and the Arab Conquest of Iran* (London, 2009); G. Fisher, *Between Empires: Arabs, Romans, and Sasanians in Late Antiquity* (Oxford, 2011); D. Morgan, "Sasanian Iran and the Early Arab Conquests," *Journal of the Economic and Social History of the Orient*, 54, 4 (2011), pp. 528–36.

5   Al-Biruni, *Kitāb fī Tahqīqī mā li-l-Hind* (Hyderabad, 1958), p. 16.

6   Al-ʿUtbi, *Tārīkh al-Yamīnī* (Delhi, 1847); M. Nazim (ed.), *Zayn al-Akhbār of Gardīzī* (Berlin, 1928); *Taʾrīkh-i-Firishta* (Lucknow, 1864); W. H. Morley (ed.), *Taʾrīkh-i-Baihaqī* (Calcutta, 1862); *Tabaqāt-i-Nāsirī of Jūzjānī* (Lahore, 1954); C. E. Bosworth, *The Ghaznavids: Their Empire in Afghanistan and Eastern Iran, 994–1040* (Edinburgh, 1963); C. E. Bosworth, *The Later Ghaznavids: Splendour and Decay: The Dynasty in Afghanistan and Northern India* (Edinburgh, 1977); Wink, *Al-Hind*, Vol. II, pp. 112–35.

7   It was H. L. O. Garrett who identified "military conversion" as perhaps the most common form of conversion and identity in the context of the Indian military labor market (cf. D. H. A. Kolff, *Naukar, Rajput, and Sepoy: The Ethnohistory of the Military Labour Market of Hindustan, 1450–1850* (Cambridge, 1990), pp. 57–8, 67).

8   Wink, *Al-Hind*, Vol. II, pp. 138–40.

9   J. J. L. Gommans, "The Silent Frontier of South Asia, c. A.D. 1000–1800," *Journal of World History*, 9, 1 (1998), pp. 17–22.

10 B. H. Auer, *Symbols of Authority in Medieval Islam: History, Religion, and Muslim Legitimacy in the Delhi Sultanate* (London, 2012); A. Anooshahr, *The Ghazi Sultans and the Frontiers of Islam: A Comparative Study of the Late Medieval and Early Modern Periods* (New York, 2009).

11 S. Ahmad Khan (ed.), *Taʾrīkh-i-Fīroz Shāhī of Ziāʾ ad-Dīn Baranī* (Calcutta, 1888), pp. 454–66.

12 C. Defrémery and B. R. Sanguinetti (eds. and trans.), *Voyages d'Ibn Batoutah*, 4 vols (Paris, 1853–1858), Vol. III, pp. 184–5.

13 A. Khan, *Taʾrīkh-i-Fīroz Shāhī of Baranī*, pp. 189–90, 211–2.

14 *Tabaqāt-i-Nāsirī*; Wink, *Al-Hind*, Vol. II, pp. 135–49.

15 *Tabaqāt-i-Nāsirī*; Wink, *Al-Hind*, Vol. II, pp. 150–211; S. Kumar, *The Emergence of the Delhi Sultanate* (Delhi, 2011).
16 Wink, *Al-Hind*, Vol. III, pp. 127–30.
17 C. Masson, *Narrative of Various Journeys in Balochistan, Afghanistan and the Panjab, 1826 to 1838*, 4 vols. (Karachi, 1974–1977), Vol. II, pp. 204, 207, 212.
18 P. Jackson, *The Delhi Sultanate: A Political and Military History* (Cambridge, 1999), pp. 178–82; Defrémery and Sanguinetti, *Ibn Batoutah*, Vol. III; Wink, *Al-Hind*, Vol. III, pp. 130–4.
19 S. Digby, "Before Timur Came: Provincialization of the Delhi Sultanate through the Fourteenth Century," *Journal of the Economic and Social History of the Orient*, 47, 3 (2004), pp. 298–356; F. Orsini and S. Sheikh (eds.), *After Timur Left: Culture and Circulation in Fifteenth Century North India* (Delhi, 2014); Wink, *Al-Hind*, Vol. III, pp. 122–5.
20 Wink, *Al-Hind*, Vol. III, p. 134.
21 Ibid., pp. 134–8; A. Wink, "On the Road of Failure: The Afghans in Mughal India," *Cracow Indological Studies*, XI (2009), pp. 267–339.
22 See Chapter 5.
23 S. Sadiq Ali, *The African Dispersal in the Deccan* (Delhi, 1996), p. 3.
24 B. De (trans.), *The Tabaqāt-i-Akbarī: A History of India from the Early Musulman Invasions in the 38th Year of the Reign of Akbar by Khwajah Nizamuddin Ahmad* (Delhi, 1990), pp. 414–46; *Ta'rīkh-i-Firishta*, Vol. II, pp. 292–304; R. M. Eaton, *The Rise of Islam and the Bengal Frontier, 1204–1760* (Berkeley, 1993); Wink, *Al-Hind*, Vol. III, pp. 139–40.
25 De, *Tabaqāt-i-Akbarī*, pp. 632–761; *Ta'rīkh-i-Firishta*, Vol. II, pp. 333–67; R. K. Parmu, *A History of Muslim Rule in Kashmir, 1320–1819* (Delhi, 1969); S. C. Ray, *Early History of Kashmir* (Delhi, 1970); N. K. Zutshi, *Sultan Zain-ul-Abidin: An Age of Enlightenment* (Jammu, 1976); Wink, *Al-Hind*, Vol. III, pp. 140–2.
26 Wink, *Al-Hind*, Vol. III, pp. 142–4.
27 *Ta'rīkh-i-Firishta*, Vol. II; R. M. Eaton, *Sufis of Bijapur, 1300–1700: Social Roles of Sufis in Medieval India* (Princeton, 1978); H. K. Sherwani and P. M. Joshi (eds.), *History of Medieval Deccan (1295–1724)*, 2 vols. (Hyderabad, 1973–4); Wink, *Al-Hind*, Vol. III, pp. 144–8.
28 C. Talbot, *Precolonial India in Practice: Society, Region, and Identity in Medieval Andhra* (Delhi, 2001); Wink, *Al-Hind*, Vol. III, pp. 148–51.
29 V. Narayana Rao (trans.), *Shiva's Warriors: The Basava Purāna of Pālkuriki Somanātha* (Princeton, 1990).
30 B. Stein, *Vijayanagara* (Cambridge, 1989); C. M. Sinopoli, "From the Lion Throne: Political and Social Dynamics of the Vijayanagara Empire," *Journal of the Economic and Social History of the Orient*, 43, 3 (2000), p. 376.
31 P. Hardy, "Modern European and Muslim Explanations of Conversion to Islam in South Asia: A Preliminary Survey of the Literature," in N. Levtzion (ed.), *Conversion to Islam* (New York, 1979), pp. 68–99.
32 Wink, *Al-Hind*, Vol. III, p. 164; *Al-Hind*, Vols. I–III, passim.
33 Wink, *Al-Hind*, Vol. III, p. 164.
34 Ibid.

35 See especially Eaton, *The Rise of Islam and the Bengal Frontier*; R. M. Eaton, "The Political and Religious Authority of the Shrine of Baba Farid," in B. D. Metcalf (ed.), *Moral Conduct and Authority: The Place of Adab in South Asian Islam* (Berkeley, 1984), pp. 333–56; R. M. Eaton, "Approaches to the Study of Islam in India," in R. C. Martin (ed.), *Approaches to Islam in Religious Studies* (Tucson, 1985), pp. 106–26; R. M. Eaton, *Islamic History as Global History* (Washington, DC, 1990).

36 Eaton, "Approaches to the Study of Islam in India," p. 111.

37 Masson, *Narrative of Various Journeys*, Vol. IV, pp. 326–7.

38 Ibid., Vol. I, p. 218.

39 G. S. Robertson, *The Kafirs of the Hindu-Kush* (1898; Delhi, 1998); G. Fussman, *Atlas Linguistique des Parlers Dardes et Kafirs* (Paris, 1972); Masson, *Narrative of Various Journeys*, Vol. I, pp. 193–235; M. Elphinstone, *An Account of the Kingdom of Caubul*, 2 vols (Karachi, 1992), Vol. II, pp. 373–89.

40 S. Vryonis, Jr., *The Decline of Medieval Hellenism in Asia Minor and the Process of Islamization from the Eleventh through Fifteenth Century* (Berkeley, 1971).

41 Ibid., p. 194.

42 Ibid., pp. 143, 351.

43 Ibid., p. 143.

44 A. K. S. Lambton, *Continuity and Change in Medieval Persia: Aspects of Administrative, Economic and Social History, 11–14th Century* (New York, 1988); D. O. Morgan, *Medieval Persia, 1040–1747* (London, 1988); D. O. Morgan, *The Mongols* (Oxford, 2007).

45 V. Minorsky (trans.), *Hudūd al-ʿālam: The Regions of the World, A Persian Geography, 372 A.H.–982 A. D.* (Karachi, 1980), p. 122 (f. 26a).

46 Wink, *Al-Hind*, Vol. II, pp. 202–11, 239–44; Vol. III, pp. 118, 120–2; S. A. Rashid (ed.), *Inshā-i-Māhrū* (Lahore, 1965), pp. 9, 19–22, 100–3, 186–8, 229–35; Masson, *Narrative of Various Journeys*, Vol. IV, p. 388; K. R. Pandit (trans.), *A Chronicle of Medieval Kashmir* (Calcutta, 1991), pp. 17, 27–9.

47 M. Wahid Mirza, *The Life and Works of Amir Khusrau* (Lahore, 1962), p. 55.

48 *Tārkhān-nāma* (British Museum, ms. Or.1814), f. 72; *BN*, ff. 125b, 128, 131, 135b, 136, 137b, 140, 144b, 145, 154–155b, 160, 162–162b, 172b, 184b, 187b, 195–202, 209–211b, 215b–216, 237b; J. Humai (ed.), *Habīb as-siyar fī akhbār-i-afrād-i-bashar* of Khwandamir, 4 vols. (Teheran, 1333/1954), Vol. III, pp. 150, 276, and Vol. IV, pp. 170, 293; Shams-i-Siraj ʿAfif, *Tārīkh-i-Fīrūz Shāhī* (Calcutta, 1888), p. 51; M. S. Akhtar, *Sind under the Mughals: An Introduction to, Translation of and Commentary on the Mahzar-i-Shahjahani of Yusuf Mirak (1044/1634)* (Karachi, 1990), p. 246; M. H. Siddiqi, "Baluch Migration in Sindh," in G. M. Lakho (ed.), *The Samma Kingdom of Sindh* (Historical Studies) (Jamshoro, 2006), pp. 99–104; Wink, "On the Road to Failure."

49 Wink, *Al-Hind*, Vol. II, pp. 202–1; Vol. III, pp. 119–25.

50 Quoted ibid., Vol. II, p. 205.

51 Quoted ibid., Vol. II, p. 207.
52 'Isāmī, quoted in Wink, *Al-Hind*, Vol. II, pp. 120–1.
53 Rashid, *Inshā'-i-Māhrū*, pp. 9, 19–22 (no. 8), 100–3 (no. 46), 186–8 (no. 99), 229–35 (no. 134).
54 K. Jahn, "A Note on Kashmir and the Mongols," *Central Asiatic Journal*, II (1956), pp. 176–80; K. Jahn, *Rashid Al-Din's History of India* (The Hague, 1965), pp. xiii, lxxxvii–xci; K. Jahn, "Zum Problem der Mongolischen Eroberungen in Indien (13.-14 Jahrhundert)," *Akten des 24. Internationalen Orientalisten Kongress* (Munich, 1957), pp. 617–19; A. Stein, "Marco Polo's Account of a Mongol Inroad into Kashmir," *The Geographical Journal*, LIV (1919), pp. 92–103; Pandit, *Chronicle of Medieval Kashmir*, p. 17; Wink, *Al-Hind*, Vol. I, pp. 207–8; Vol. II, p. 122.
55 S. L. Sadhu (ed.), *Medieval Kashmir: Being a Reprint of the Rajataranginis of Jonaraja, Shrivara and Shuka, as Translated into English by J. C. Dutt and Published in 1898 A. D. under the Title "Kings of Kashmira,"* Vol. III (Delhi, 1993), p. 28.
56 *Malfūzāt-i-amīr tīmūr: BM. Or. 158*; B. F. Manz, *The Rise and Rule of Tamerlane* (Cambridge. 1989); Wink, *Al-Hind*, Vol. III, pp. 123–5.
57 Wink, *Al-Hind*, Vol. III, p. 160.
58 *Tārkhan-nāma*, f. 71.
59 Ibid., f. 72.
60 M. Irving, "The Shrine of Baba Farid Shakarganj at Pakpattan," *Journal of the Panjab Historical Society*, 1 (1919–1920), pp. 70–6; A. O'Brien, "The Mohammedan Saints of the Western Panjab," *The Journal of the Royal Athropological Institute of Great Britain and Ireland*, 41 (1911), pp. 509–20; K. de Vries, "Islamitische heiligen en heiligentomben in Multan: De rol van heiligen in ontginning, sedentarisatie and Islamisering (1320–1901)" (unpublished master's thesis, Department of Indian Studies, Instituut Kern, University of Leiden, 1997); S. F. D. Ansari, *Sufi Saints and State Power: The Pirs of Sind, 1843–1947* (Cambridge, 2003); N. Green, "Blessed Men and Tribal Politics: Notes on Political Culture in the Indo-Afghan World," *Journal of the Economic and Social History of the Orient*, 49, 3 (2006), pp. 344–60; J. Howard-Johnston and P. A. Hayward (eds.), *The Cult of Saints in Late Antiquity and the Middle Ages: Essays on the Contribution of Peter Brown* (Oxford, 1999).
61 E. Gellner, *Saints of the Atlas* (London, 1969), applies this terminology to Muslim saints in Morocco.
62 O. G. S. Crawford (ed.), *Ethiopian Itineraries, circa 1400–1524* (Cambridge, 1958).
63 Tome Pires, *The Suma Oriental of Tomé Pires: An Account of the East, from the Red Sea to Japan, Written in Malacca and India in 1512–1515*, 2 vols. (Delhi, 1990), Vol. II, p. 10.
64 Wink, *Al-Hind*, Vol. III, p. 177.
65 Ibid., p. 185.
66 Ibid., pp. 192–3.
67 Ibid., p. 194.
68 Ibid., p. 205.

69 Ibid., p. 233.
70 Ibid., Vol. II, p. 291.
71 S. Bayly, "Islam in Southern India: 'Purist' or 'Syncretic'?" in C. A. Bayly and D. H. A. Kolff (eds.), *Two Colonial Empires: Comparative Essays on the History of India and Indonesia in the Nineteenth Century* (Leiden, 1986), pp. 37–59.
72 Wink, *Al-Hind*, Vol. I, pp. 25–33; Vol. III, pp. 179–87.
73 J. Aubin, "Le royaume d'Ormuz au début du xvi siècle," *Mare Luso-Indicum*, II (1973), pp. 77–137.
74 Wink, *Al-Hind*, Vol. II, pp. 273–5.
75 Wink, *Al-Hind*, Vol. I, pp. 67–104; Vol. II, pp. 276–8; Vol. III, pp. 203–7.
76 M. Longworth Dames, *The Book of Duarte Barbosa: An Account of the Countries Bordering on the Indian Ocean and Their Inhabitants, Written by Duarte Barbosa and Completed about the Year 1518 A. D.*, 2 vols. (Delhi, 1989), Vol. II, pp. 135, 140, 148; *Suma Oriental of Tomé Pires*, Vol. I, pp. 90–1.
77 Longworth Dames, *Duarte Barbosa*, Vol. II, pp. 135, 142.
78 Ibid., pp. 93, 147–8.
79 Ibid., p. 149.
80 Ibid., pp. 153–7; cf. *Suma Oriental of Tomé Pires*, Vol. I, pp. 97–101.
81 V. B. Lieberman, "Local Integration and Eurasian Analogies: Structuring Southeast Asian History, c. 1350–1830," *Modern Asian Studies*, 27, 3 (1993), pp. 477–80; M. Aung-Thwin, "Lower Burma and Bago in the History of Burma," in J. J. L. Gommans and J. Leider (eds.), *The Maritime Frontier of Burma: Exploring Political, Cultural and Commercial Interaction in the Indian Ocean World, 1200–1800* (Leiden, 2002), pp. 25–57.
82 Wink, *Al-Hind*, Vol. III, pp. 215–22.
83 *Suma Oriental of Tomé Pires*, Vol. II, p. 253.
84 Ibid., p. 240.
85 Ibid., p. 242.
86 J. V. G. Mills (ed. and trans.), *Ma Huan, Ying-yai Sheng-lan [The Overall Survey of the Ocean's Shore]* (Cambridge, 1970), p. 110.
87 *Suma Oriental of Tomé Pires*, Vol. II, p. 245.
88 Ibid., p. 269.
89 Longworth Dames, *Duarte Barbosa*, Vol. II, p. 175.
90 G. W. J. Drewes (ed.), *Hikajat Potjut Muhamat: An Acehnese Epic* (The Hague, 1979).
91 J. Von Hammer-Purgstall, *Geschichte Wassaf's, Persisch herausgegeben und Deutsch überstzt, I Band* (Vienna, 1856), text, p. 45.
92 *Suma Oriental of Tomé Pires*, Vol. I, pp. 166–8, 173.
93 Ibid., pp. 182, 199–200; and see M. C. Ricklefs, "Six Centuries of Islamization in Java," in M. Levtzion (ed.), *Conversion to Islam* (New York, 1979), pp. 104–5.
94 Mills, *Ma Huan*, p. 93.
95 *Suma Oriental of Tomé Pires*, Vol. I, p. 197; P. J. Veth, *Java, Geografisch, Ethnologisch, Historisch*, 4 vols. (Haarlem, 1896–1907), Vol. IV, p. 89.
96 *Suma Oriental of Tomé Pires*, Vol. I, p. 197.
97 Mendez Pinto, quoted in A. Reid, *Southeast Asia in the Age of Commerce*, 2 vols. (New Haven, 1988–93), Vol. II, p. 175.

Chapter 5

1 S. Sen (ed.), *Indian Travels of Thevenot and Careri* (Delhi, 1949), p. 5.
2 See pp. 82–84.
3 For this section, see especially *BN*; J. T. Arlinghaus, "The Transformation of Afghan Tribal Society: Tribal Expansion, Mughal Imperialism and the Roshaniyya Insurrection, 1450–1600" (unpublished PhD dissertation, Duke University, 1983); M. Elphinstone, *An Account of the Kingdom of Caubul*, 2 vols. (Karachi, 1992); A. Wink, "On the Road of Failure: The Afghans in Mughal India," *Cracow Indological Studies*, XI (2009), pp. 267–339. Wink, *Al-Hind*, Vol. IV, ch. 1.
4 M. Hidayat Hosain (ed.), *Tārīkh-i-Shāhī of Ahmad Yādgār* (Calcutta, 1939), p. 99.
5 S. Digby, "Dreams and Reminiscences of Dattu Sarvani, a Sixteenth-Century Indo-Afghan Soldier," *The Indian Economic and Social History Review*, 2, 1 (January, 1965), pp. 52–80, & 2 (April, 1965), pp. 178–94.
6 Ibid., p. 62.
7 Ibid., p. 64.
8 S. M. Imam al-Din (ed. and trans.), *The Tā'rīkh-i-Sher Shāhī of 'Abbas Sarwānī*, Vol. I (Persian text) and Vol. II (English translation) (Dacca, 1964).
9 Ibid., Vol. I, p. 68 (Vol. II, p. 50).
10 Ibid., Vol. I, p. 54 (Vol. II, p. 41).
11 Ibid., Vol. I, p. 72 (Vol. II, p. 52).
12 Ibid., Vol. I, p. 127 (Vol. II, p. 91).
13 Ibid., Vol. I, p. 116 (Vol. II, p. 81), p. 135 (Vol. II, p. 96), pp. 148–9 (Vol. II, p. 109).
14 Ibid., Vol. I, p. 96 (Vol. II, p. 69).
15 Ibid., Vol. I, p. 231.
16 Ibid., Vol. I, pp. 224–5 (Vol. II, p. 178).
17 Hidayat Hosain, *Tārīkh-i-Shāhī*, p. 301.
18 *MT*, Vol. I, p. 436.
19 Wink, *Al-Hind*, Vol. IV, ch. 2.
20 For this contrast, see especially K. E. Meyer, *The Dust of Empire: The Race for Mastery in the Asian Heartland* (New York, 2003), pp. 176, 180–1.
21 J. Fletcher, "The Mongols: Ecological and Social Perspectives," *Harvard Journal of Asiatic Studies*, 46, 1 (1986), pp. 16, 21.
22 I. de Rachewiltz, "Some Remarks on the Ideological Foundations of Chingis Khan's Empire," *Papers on Far Eastern History* (1973), pp. 21–36; A. F. Broadbridge, *Kingship and Ideology in the Islamic and Mongol Worlds* (Cambridge, 2008).
23 P. B. Golden, "Imperial Ideology and the Sources of Political Unity among Pre-Cingissid Nomads of Western Eurasia," *Archivum Eurasiae Medii Aevi*, II (1982), p. 72.
24 T. T. Allsen, *Mongol Imperialism: The Politics of the Grand Qan Möngke in China, Russia, and the Islamic Lands, 1251–1259* (Berkeley, 1987); B. F. Manz, *The Rise and Rule of Tamerlane* (Cambridge, 1989), pp. 3–4.
25 Manz, *The Rise and Rule of Tamerlane*, p. 4.
26 Ibid., p. 5.

27 Cf. p. 62; D. O. Morgan, "The 'Great Yasa of Chinggis Khan' Revisited," in R. Amitai and M. Biran (eds.), *Mongols, Turks and Others: Eurasian Nomads and the Sedentary World* (Leiden, 2005), pp. 291–308; D. Aigle, "Le Grand Jasaq de Gengis-Khan, l'empire, la culture Mongole et la Shari`a," *Journal of the Economic and Social History of the Orient*, 47, 1 (2004), pp. 31–79.
28 W. M. Thackston, *Tarikh-i-Rashidi* (Cambridge, 1996), p. 24.
29 Ibid., p. 226, ff (f. 205a, f); *BN*, 1a.
30 *AN*, Vol. I, 85.
31 Thackston, *Tarikh-i-Rashidi*, p. 93 (f. 62b).
32 Ibid., pp. 90–2 (f. 60b).
33 Ibid., f. 58a.
34 Manz, *Rise and Rule of Tamerlane*, p. 64.
35 Ibid., pp. 41–64.
36 Ibid., pp. 74, 77–80, 84.
37 M. E. Subtelny, "Babur's Rival Relations: A Study of Kinship and Conflict in 15th–16th Century Central Asia," *Der Islam*, LXVI, 1 (1989), pp. 102–3, 106–7.
38 T. Barfield, *Afghanistan: A Cultural and Political History* (Princeton, 2010), pp. 71–3.
39 *BN*, 1–5b, 102b–103, 108b, 126–126b, 144–144b–152, 156b–158b, 159–60, 162, 183–87, 202b–203b, 212–215b, 216b–221, 226b, 237b–248b, 252, 266–266b, 269, 293b–294, 299, 301, 307b, 316, 318, 319b, 321b, 329b, 351, 356b, 358b–359b; *HN*, 2b, 4b, 6b–7a, 8b, 11a, 19b–20a, 71b, 78b; *AN*, Vol. I, 87, 90, 93, 102; *TA*, Vol. II, 38, 44; G. R. Hambly, "The King's Affinity in Early Mughal India: The Chaghatayid Connection," Paper presented at the Annual Conference on South Asia, Madison, 1992; Subtelny, "Babur's Rival Relations," pp. 113–15; M. D. Faruqui, *Princes of the Mughal Empire, 1504–1719* (Cambridge, 2012), pp. 20, 47.
40 A recent example of such a portrayal of Babur is S. F. Dale, *The Garden of the Eight Paradises: Bābur and the Culture of Empire in Central Asia, Afghanistan and India (1483–1530)* (Leiden, 2004).
41 *HN*, 15b, 19b.
42 *MT*, Vol. I, 335, 344–55, 443–5, 452–3; *AN*, Vol. I, 120–72, 174, 178–82, 185, 188–94, 197–231, 238–41, 255–331, 334–51; *TA*, Vol. II, 44–74, 78, 126–9; *HN*, 3b–40b, 45b–48b, 50b–52a, 56a–60a, 63b, 82b; Ch. Stewart, *The Tezkereh al Vakiāt, or Private Memoirs of the Moghul Emperor Humāyūn, Written in the Persian Language by Jouher* (London, 1832); Thackston, *Tarikh-i-Rashidi*, f. 185; *BL: MS 2182*; Faruqui, *Princes of the Mughal Empire*, pp. 60–3; S. Ray, *Humayun in Persia* (Calcutta, 1948).
43 A. Wink, *Akbar* (Oxford, 2009); Faruqui, *Princes of the Mughal Empire*, pp. 7, 9, 17–18, 20, 29, 65, 143, 158, 237, ff.
44 Faruqui, *Princes of the Mughal Empire*, p. 7 and passim.
45 Ibid., p. 17 and passim.
46 Ibid., pp. 10, 144, 149–53.
47 *AN*, Vol. III, 773; Faruqui, *Princes of the Mughal Empire*, pp. 33–5.
48 Faruqui, *Princes of the Mughal Empire*, pp. 33–4; A. Rogers (trans.), *Tuzuk-i-Jahangiri or Memoirs of Jahangir* (Delhi, 1989), Vol. I, p. 57.
49 Rogers, *Tuzuk-i-Jahangiri*, Vol. I, pp. 58, 61–2, 64–9, 72, 111, 131, 173–7, 394–7, 401; Vol. II, pp. 234–5, 237–9, 244, 246–76, 289–94; *SJN*, 5–15;

MU, 521–7; V. Ball and W. Crooke (trans. and eds.), *Travels in India by Jean-Baptiste Tavernier* (or. 1676; Delhi, n.d.), Vol. I, p. 268; H. Nelson Wright, *Coins of the Mughal Emperors of India* (Delhi, 1975; or 1908), p. 93; F. Bernier, *Travels in the Mogul Empire, A.D. 1656–1688* (Delhi, 1989), p. 5. Mutamid Khan, "Iqbalnama-i-Jahangiri," *ED*, Vol. VI, pp. 420–34; B. Prasad, *History of Jahangir* (Delhi, 1930), p. 404; Faruqui, *Princes of the Mughal Empire*, pp. 208–15, 224.

50 *SJN*, 2, 18–21, 26–36, 40–1, 49–51, 56, 61–2, 82–7, 90, 92, 117–19, 143, 149–66, 154, 190, 206–8, 219–66, 273, 276–95, 298, 302–3, 313–400, 405–6, 411–93, 499–516, 525, 529, 542–6, 552–4; Rogers, *Tuzuk-i-Jahangiri*, Vol. I, pp. 87–9, 128, 139, 372; Vol. II, pp. 191, 233, 281; *MU*, Vol. I, 795–803; *ML*, 4–23, 31, 44–5, 66–9; "Amil-i-Salih of Muhammad Salih Kambu," *ED*, Vol. VII, 124–8; "Adab-i-Alamgiri," in J. Scott (trans.), *Tales, Anecdotes and Letters* (Shrewsbury, 1800), pp. 400–5; W. Irvine (trans.), *Niccolao Manucci: Mogul India (1653–1708), Storia Do Mogor*, 4 vols. (Delhi, 2005), Vol. I, pp. 208, 210, 214–16, 218–21, 224–39, 241–8, 251–80, 285–92, 360, 362–3; Vol. III, p. 182; F. Bernier, *Travels in the Mogul Empire, A.D. 1656–1688* (Delhi, 1989) pp. 6–22, 25–36, 42, 58–66; Ball and Crooke, *Tavernier*, Vol. I, pp. 262–4; D. H. A. Kolff, *Naukar, Rajput, and Sepoy: The Ethnohistory of the Military Labor Market of Hindustan, 1450–1850* (Cambridge, 1990), p. 120; Faruqui, *Princes of the Mughal Empire*, pp. 38–9, 149–50, 159–60, 215–17; R. Foltz, "The Mughal Occupation of Balkh, 1646–1647," *Journal of Islamic Studies*, 7, 1 (1996), pp. 49–61; J. Sarkar, *History of Aurangzeb*, 5 vols. (Calcutta, 1912–1919), Vol. I, pp. 54, 76–8, 170–205, 216–28, 304–5; Vol. II, pp. 1–100, 130.

51 Bernier, *Travels*, pp. 6–7, 14–15; Irvine, *Manucci*, Vol. I, pp. 214–15, 220–1, 280, 360; Vol. III, p. 182.

52 *ML*, 1, 4, 47, 49–92, 96–105, 112–15, 137–75, 188–92, 210–49, 262, 266–8, 270, 288–93, 297–555; *MA*, 4–18, 24–7, 125–8, 137–323; *SJN*, 554–6, 558–63; *ED*, Vol. VII, 131; V. G. Khobrekar (ed.), *Tarikh–i–Dilkasha of Bhimsen (English Translation by Jadunath Sarkar)* (Bombay, 1972), p. 208; Sen, *Travels of Thevenot and Careri*, pp. 227–30, 237–9; Bernier, *Travels*, pp. 70–99, 103–4, 107–8, 114–15, 126–7, 144, 169–83, 187, 196–7; Irvine, *Manucci*, Vol. I, pp. 181–2, 292–7, 304–43, 348–58, 360–2, 378–81; Vol. II, pp. 52, 58, 91, 109–10, 118, 186–208, 218–21, 225, 227–35; Vol. III, passim; Vol. IV, p. 461, and passim; Ball and Crooke, *Tavernier*, Vol. I, pp. 276–8, 281, 286–9, 292–4; Sarkar, *History of Aurangzeb*, Vol. II, pp. 137–220, 237–88; Vol. III, pp. 43–61, 146–247, 300–81, and passim; Vol. IV, passim; Faruqui, *Princes of the Mughal Empire*, pp. 41–4; M. Alam and S. Subrahmanyam (eds.), *The Mughal State, 1526–1750* (Delhi, 2001), "Introduction," p. 33; L. Balabanlilar, *Imperial Identity in the Mughal Empire: Memory and Dynastic Politics in Early Modern South and Central Asia* (London, 2012); A. Wink, *Land and Sovereignty in India: Agrarian Society and Politics under the Eighteenth-Century Maratha Svarajya* (Cambridge, 1986), pp. 4, 59–66; B. Schrieke, *Indonesian Sociological Studies*, 2 vols. (The Hague and Bandung, 1955–1957), Vol. I, p. 44; G. P. Badger, *History of the Imams and Seyyids of `Oman, Translated from the Original Arabic* (London, 1871); J. S. Grewal and S. S. Bal, *Guru Gobind Singh: A Biographical Study* (Chandigarh, 1967),

pp. 29, 44–7; R. C. Hallissey, *The Rajput Rebellion against Aurangzeb: A Study of the Mughal Empire in Seventeenth-Century India* (Columbia, 1977), pp. 29–30, 42, 219; M. N. Pearson, "Shivaji and the Decline of the Mughal Empire," *Journal of Asian Studies*, 35, 2 (1976), p. 233.

53 Bernier, *Travels*, pp. 179–80.
54 Ibid., pp. 196–7.
55 I. Habib, *The Agrarian System of Mughal India, 1556–1707* (2nd rev. ed., Delhi, 1999), pp. 364, 366.
56 J. F. Richards, *The Mughal Empire* (Cambridge, 1993), pp. 58–78.
57 Ibid., pp. 59–60, 65.
58 Irvine, *Manucci*, Vol. II, pp. 297, 418, 436.
59 W. H. Moreland and P. Geyl (trans.), *Jahangir's India: The Remonstrantie of Francisco Pelsaert* (Cambridge, 1925), p. 58.
60 J. S. Hoyland (trans.), *The Empire of the Great Mogol: A Translation of De Laet's "Description of India and Fragment of Indian History"* (Delhi, 1975), pp. 241–3.
61 Cf. A. Lieven, Pakistan: A Hard Country (New York, 2011), p. 87 ff; *The Wall Street Journal*, August 29–30, 2015.
62 A. A. Moin, *The Millenial Sovereign: Sacred Kingship and Sainthood in Islam* (New York, 2012); A. Strathern, "Drawing the Veil of Sovereignty: Early Modern Islamic Empires and Understanding Sacred Kingship," *History and Theory*, 53 (2014), pp. 79–93.

Chapter 6

1 Voltaire, *An Essay on Universal History, The Manners, and Spirit of Nations: From the Reign of Charlemaign to the Age of Lewis XIV* (Miami, 2017) (*Essai sur les moeurs et l'esprit des nations*), ch. 14.
2 Cf. Chapter 3, pp. 64–5, and Chapter 4, pp. 75, 90.
3 See, for instance, J. Fletcher, "Integrative History: Parallels and Interconnections in the Early Modern Period, 1500–1800," *Journal of Turkish Studies*, 9 (1985), pp. 54–5.
4 S. Levi, "India, Russia and the Eighteenth Century Transformation of the Central Asian Caravan Trade," *Journal of the Economic and Social History of the Orient*, 42, 4 (1999), pp. 519–24.
5 A. C. Hess, "The Ottoman Conquest of Egypt (1517) and the Beginnings of the Sixteenth-Century World War," *International Journal of Middle East Studies*, 4, 1 (1973), p. 58.
6 V. Bartold, *Sochineniia (Collected Works)*, Vol. VI (Moscow, 1966); M. G. S. Hodgson, *The Venture of Islam, Vol. 3: The Gunpowder Empires and Modern Times* (Chicago, 1974), esp. pp. 59–98.; W. H. McNeill, *The Pursuit of Power* (Chicago, 1982), pp. 95–9, 148.
7 Hodgson, *Venture of Islam*, Vol. 3, pp. 17–18.
8 C. Cipolla, *Guns, Sails and Empires: Technological Innovation & European Expansion, 1400–1700* (New York, 1996).
9 Hodgson, *Venture of Islam*, Vol. 3, p. 18.
10 M. Roberts, *The Military Revolution, 1560–1660* (Belfast, 1956); J. Black, *A Military Revolution? Military Change and European Society* (London, 1991).

11 D. Ayalon, *Gunpowder and Firearms in the Mamluk Kingdom: A Challenge to Medieval Society* (London, 1956).

12 G. Agoston, *Guns for the Sultan: Military Power and the Weapons Industry in the Ottoman Empire* (Cambridge, 2005).

13 J. J. L. Gommans, *Mughal Warfare* (London, 2002); J. J. L. Gommans, "Warhorse and Gunpowder in India, c. 1000–1850," in J. Black (ed.), *War in the Early-Modern World, 1450–1815* (London, 1999), pp. 113–15; J. J. L. Gommans, *The Indian Frontier: Horse and Warband in the Making of Empires* (Delhi, 2018), pp. 21–2; C. Duffy, *Siege Warfare* (London, 1979), pp. 9–13; D. E. Streusand, *The Formation of the Mughal Empire* (Delhi, 1989), pp. 12–13, 66–8.

14 W. Irvine, *The Army of the Indian Moghals: Its Organization and Administration* (Delhi, 1994), p. 161.

15 Gommans, "Warhorse and Gunpowder in India," pp. 115–19; S. Gordon, "The Limited Adoption of European-Style Military Forces by Eighteenth Century Rulers in India," *The Indian Economic and Social History Review*, 35, 3 (1998), pp. 229–37; P. Barua, "Military Developments in India, 1750–1850," *The Journal of Military History*, 58 (1994), pp. 599–616.

16 J. S. Hoyland (trans.), *The Commentary of Father Monserrate, S. J. on His Journey to the Court of Akbar* (Oxford, 1922), p. 68.

17 Gordon, "Limited Adoption of European-Style Military Forces," pp. 235–6.

18 S. Dale, "Indo-Russian Trade in the Eighteenth Century," in S. Bose (ed.), *South Asia and World Capitalism* (Delhi, 1990), pp. 140–56; S. Dale, *Indian Merchants and Eurasian Trade, 1600–1750* (Cambridge, 1994); M. Alam, "Trade, State Policy and Regional Change: Aspects of Mughal-Uzbek Commercial Relations, c. 1550–1750," *Journal of the Economic and Social History of the Orient*, 37, 3 (1994), pp. 202–27; Levi, "India, Russia and the Eighteenth-Century Transformation of the Central Asian Caravan Trade," pp. 522–32.

19 J. J. L. Gommans, "Mughal India and Central Asia in the Eighteenth Century: An Introduction to a Wider Perspective," *Itinerario*, 15, 1 (1991), pp. 51–70; J. J. L. Gommans, "The Horse Trade in Eighteenth-Century South Asia," *Journal of the Economic and Social History of the Orient*, 37, 3 (1994), pp. 228–50; J. J. L. Gommans, *The Rise of the Indo-Afghan Empire, c. 1710–1780* (Leiden, 1995).

20 V. Ball and W. Crooke (trans. and eds.), *Travels in India by Jean-Baptiste Tavernier* (or. 1676; Delhi, n.d.), Vol. II, p. 63; W. Irvine (trans.), Niccolao Manucci, *Mogul India (1653–1708), Storia Do Mogor*, 4 vols (Delhi, 2005), Vol. I, p. 307; Vol. II, p. 366.

21 Gommans, *Indo-Afghan Empire*, p. 89.

22 For medieval India, see Chapter 2, pp. 39–42, 49; Chapter 4, passim; Wink, *Al-Hind*, Vol. II, pp. 170–82. For medieval Europe, e.g., Georges Duby, *The Chivalrous Society* (Berkeley, 1980).

23 Cf. Chapter 5, pp. 143–4.

24 J. Correia-Afonso (ed. and trans.), *Letters from the Mughal Court: The First Jesuit Mission to Akbar, 1580–1583* (Bombay, 1980), Letter 56.

25 Irvine, *Manucci*, Vol. II, p. 308. For similar comments, see ibid., Vol. I, p. 92; Vol. II, pp. 69, 320–1; S. Sen (ed.), *Indian Travels of Thevenot and Careri*

(Delhi, 1949), pp. 218, 242; F. Bernier, *Travels in the Mogul Empire, A.D. 1656–1688* (Delhi, 1989) pp. 205, 222, 373; W. Foster (ed.), *The Embassy of Sir Thomas Roe to the Court of the Great Mogul, 1615–1619*, 2 vols. (London, 1909), Vol. I, p. 120.

26   Foster, *Roe*, Vol. I, pp. ix, xxviii, xxix.
27   Irvine, *Manucci*, Vol. II, p. 28.
28   Tome Pires, *The Suma Oriental of Tomé Pires: An Account of the East, from the Red Sea to Japan, Written in Malacca and India in 1512–1515*, 2 vols (Delhi, 1990), Vol. I, p. 23.
29   Ibid.
30   Ibid.
31   Bernier, *Travels*, p. 232; Irvine, *Manucci*, Vol. IV, p. 244.
32   Cf. Chapter 5, pp. 124–36.
33   Bernier, *Travels*, p. 206.
34   Irvine, *Manucci*, Vol. II, p. 241.
35   Ibid., p. 419.
36   Bernier, *Travels*, p. 207; Irvine, *Manucci*, Vol. II, pp. 186–91, 322, 425; Vol. IV, p. 56; *AN*, Vol. III, 110.
37   A. Rogers (trans.), *Tuzuk-i-Jahangiri or Memoirs of Jahangir* (Delhi, 1989), Vol. I, p. 296; Bernier, *Travels*, pp. 39–40, 210; J. S. Hoyland (trans.), *The Empire of the Great Mogul: A Translation of De Laet's "Description of India and Fragment of Indian History"* (Delhi, 1975), p. 40.
38   H. Blochmann (trans.), *The A'in-i-Akbari*, 3 vols (Delhi, 1971), Vol. II, 273.
39   *AN*, Vol. II, 443, 462, 244–5.
40   Irvine, *Manucci*, Vol. II, p. 411.
41   Hoyland, *De Laet*, p. 115.
42   *SJN*, 316.
43   Irvine, *Manucci*, Vol. II, p. 410, and cf. p. 414.
44   Ibid., Vol. III, p. 368.
45   Foster, *Roe*, Vol. I, p. 116.
46   Irvine, *Manucci*, Vol. II, p. 416.
47   W. H. Moreland and P. Geyl (trans.), *Jahangir's India: The Remonstrantie of Francisco Pelsaert* (Cambridge, 1925), pp. 1, 2, 5, 35, 54–5.
48   Ibid., p. 78.
49   Sen, *Thevenot and Careri*, p. 247.
50   Hoyland, *De Laet*, p. 91.
51   Irvine, *Manucci*, Vol. III, p. 303.
52   Ibid., Vol. I, p. 212.
53   E. Eden, *Up the Country: Letters from India* (London, 1983), p. 368.
54   Foster, *Roe*, Vol. I, p. 65.
55   Irvine, *Manucci*, Vol. II, p. 366.
56   Sen, *Thevenot and Careri*, p. 248; and cf. Irvine, *Manucci*, Vol. II, p. 163.
57   M. Elphinstone, *An Account of the Kingdom of Caubul*, 2 vols (Karachi, 1992), Vol. I, pp. 239, 241–3.
58   *AN*, Vol. III, 969.
59   Irvine, *Manucci*, Vol. III, pp. 118, 145.
60   Rogers, *Tuzuk-i-Jahangiri*, Vol. I, p. 142.
61   W. Doyle, *Aristocracy* (Kindle, 2010), pp. 15, 33, 35.

62 Irvine, *Manucci*, Vol. III, pp. 256–7.
63 Ibid., pp. 392–3.
64 Bernier, *Travels*, p. 65.
65 Ibid.
66 Hoyland, *De Laet*, p. 241.
67 Cf. Chapter 5, esp. pp. 147–9.
68 J. F. Richards (ed.), *Precious Metals in the Later Medieval and Early Modern Worlds* (Durham, 1983).
69 R. Kinra, *Writing Self, Writing Empire: Chandar Bhan Brahman and the Cultural World of the Indo-Persian State Secretary* (Berkeley, 2015); M. Alam and S. Subrahmanyam, *Writing the Mughal World: Studies on Culture and Politics* (New York, 2011).
70 Cf. Chapter 5, p. 137; W. H. Moreland, "Rank (*mansab*) in the Mughal State Service," in M. Alam and S. Subrahmanyam, *The Mughal State, 1526–1750* (Delhi, 1998), pp. 213–33.
71 M. Athar Ali, *The Apparatus of Empire: Awards of Ranks, Offices and Titles to the Mughal Nobility, 1573–1658* (Delhi, 1985).
72 Bernier, *Travels*, pp. 5, 226–7, 232.
73 Bernier, *Travels*, pp. 65, 211–14, 230, 232; Hoyland, *De Laet*, pp. 103, 107; Moreland and Geyl, *Jahangir's India*, p. 55; Foster, *Roe*, p. 110; Irvine, *Manucci*, Vol. I, p. 198; Ball and Crooke, *Tavernier*, Vol. I, pp. 15, 44; Sen, *Thevenot and Careri*, pp. 218, 241; for Southeast Asia, see A. Reid, *Southeast Asia in the Age of Commerce*, 2 vols (New Haven, 1988–1993), Vol. II, pp. 258–9.
74 Moreland and Geyl, *Jahangir's India*, p. 64.
75 Bernier, *Travels*, p. 211.
76 Sen, *Thevenot and Careri*, p. 241.
77 E.g., J. F. Richards, "The Formulation of Imperial Authority under Akbar and Jahangir," in: Alam and Subrahmanyam, *The Mughal State*, pp. 158–9.
78 As quoted by Jonathan Powis, *Aristocracy* (Oxford, 1984), p. 1.
79 Sen, *Thevenot and Careri*, p. 243.
80 Cf. MU; Bernier, *Travels*, pp. 211, 215; Irvine, *Manucci*, Vol. II, pp. 342–5; M. Athar Ali, *The Mughal Nobility under Aurangzeb* (Aligarh, 1966); J. F. Richards, *The Mughal Empire* (Cambridge, 1993) p. 63; Afzal Husain, *The Nobility under Akbar and Jahangir: A Study of Family Groups* (Manohar, 1999); Firdos Anwar, *Nobility under the Mughals (1628–1658)* (Delhi, 2001).
81 S. Moinul Haq, *Khafi Khan's History of Alamgir: Being an English Translation of Muntakhab al-Lubab with Notes and an Introduction* (Karachi, 1975), p. 190; Irvine, *Manucci*, Vol. I, p. 143; Bernier, *Travels*, p. 212.
82 Anwar, *Nobility*, pp. 46–8; Athar Ali, *Mughal Nobility*, p. 65.
83 Athar Ali, *Mughal Nobility*, p. 65.
84 Hoyland, *De Laet*, p. 90. See also Bernier, *Travels*, p. 255.
85 Foster, *Roe*, p. 110; Athar Ali, *Mughal Nobility*, p. 65.
86 Richards, "Formulation of Imperial Authority," pp. 159–60; Richards, *Mughal Empire*, p. 148; Anwar, *Nobility*, pp. 24–5, 44, 46, 89–92, 191; Athar Ali, *Mughal Nobility*, pp. 11–12.
87 *MA*, 124.

88 Ali, *The Apparatus of Empire,* Vol. I, p. xx.
89 *AN,* Vol. II, 96.
90 A. Wink, *Land and Sovereignty in India: Agrarian Society and Politics under the Eighteenth-Century Maratha Svarajya* (Cambridge, 1986), p. 186.
91 There is a vast literature on the "agrarian system" of Mughal India dating back to the early works by W. H. Moreland of the 1920s. See especially I. Habib, *The Agrarian System of Mughal India, 1556–1707* (2nd rev. ed.; Delhi, 1999).
92 *AN,* Vol. III, 687–93.
93 Wink, *Land and Sovereignty,* p. 272 and s.v.
94 Cf. G. Deleury, *Les Indes Florissantes: Anthologie des Voyageurs Francais* (1750–1820) (Paris, 1991).
95 Y. N. Harari, *Homo Deus* (Kindle edition, 2017), p. 197.
96 R. Kinra, "Handling Diversity with Absolute Civility: The Global Historical Legacy of Mughal Sulh-I Kull," *The Medieval History Journal,* 16, 2 (2013), pp. 251–95; Kinra, *Writing Self, Writing Empire.*
97 Cf. Bernier, *Travels,* pp. 335–6.
98 Wink, *Al-Hind,* Vol. III, pp. 160–1. My conclusions on this subject, here and elsewhere, do not confirm those of R. M. Eaton, "Temple Desecration and Indo-Muslim States," *Journal of Islamic Studies,* 11, 3 (2000), pp. 283–319. Contrary to Eaton, I hold that Islamic iconoclasm always has both a political and a religious dimension, that it was far more widespread than he allows, and that it is not just a phenomenon of the political frontier.
99 According to a fathnama of March 9, 1568, quoted in Wink, *Akbar,* p. 89.
100 *SJN,* 89–90.
101 Ibid., p. 139.
102 Munis D. Faruqui, "Dara Shukoh, Vedanta, and Imperial Succession in Mughal India," in V. Dalmia and M. D. Faruqui (eds.), *Religious Interactions in Mughal India* (Delhi, 2014), pp. 30–64.
103 S. Gandhi, "The Prince and the Muvahhid: Dara Shukoh and Mughal Engagements with Vedants," in ibid., p. 70.
104 J. F. Holleman (ed.), *Van Vollenhoven on Indonesian Adat Law: Selections from Het Adatrecht van Nederlandsch Indië* (Vol. I, 1918; Vol. II, 1931) (The Hague, 1981), p. 8.
105 *SJN,* 571.
106 Hoyland, *De Laet,* p. 93; Sen, *Thevenot and Careri,* p. 240; Foster, *Roe,* Vol. I, pp. 110, 120; Irvine, *Manucci,* Vol. I, p. 353; Vol. III, p. 46.
107 See in particular *SJN,* passim; *MA,* 73–7; T. Bowrey, *A Geographical Account of Countries Round the Bay of Bengal, 1669 to 1679* (Calcutta, 1993), p. 94; Sen, *Thevenot and Careri,* p. 26.
108 F. Hasan, *State and Locality in Mughal India: Power Relations in Western India, c. 1572–1730* (Cambridge, 2006), pp. 71–2; K. M. Ewing, *Shari`a and Ambiguity in South Asian Islam* (Berkeley, 1988); K. S. Vikør, *Between God and the Sultan: A History of Islamic Law* (Oxford, 2005).
109 Hasan, *State and Locality,* p. 72.
110 Hoyland, *De Laet,* p. 93; Moreland and Geyl, *Jahangir's India,* p. 57; Sen, *Thevenot and Careri,* p. 240.
111 Bowrey, *Geographical Account,* pp. 94, 126.

112 S. Guha, *Beyond Caste: Identity and Power in South Asia, Past and Present* (Leiden, 2013), p. 71.

113 Cf. A. Lieven, *Pakistan: A Hard Country* (New York, 2011), pp. 113–18; M. A. Chaudhary, *Justice in Practice: Legal Ethnography of a Pakistani Punjabi Village* (Oxford, 1999); M. Hayat Khan, *Customary Law of the Pakpattan and Dipalpur Tahsils of the Montgomery District* (Lahore, 1925); A. Dundes Renteln and A. Dundes (eds.), *Folk Law: Essays in the Theory and Practice of Lex Non Scripta*, Vol. I (Madison, 1995).

114 Lieven, *Pakistan*, p. 87 ff.; Guha, *Beyond Caste*, pp. 70–1; according to O. Brunner, *Land und Herrschaft: Grundfragen der territorialen Verfassungsgeschichte Österreichs im Mittelalter* (Darmstadt, 1973), this is fundamental to "all pre-modern forms of political life" (p. 91).

115 Cf. Philip S. Gorski, *The Disciplinary Revolution: Calvinism and the Rise of the State in Early Modern Europe* (Chicago, 2003).

116 *AN*, Vol. III, 86.

117 Blochmann, *A'in*, Vol. I, 162–3.

118 See in particular the editorial "Introduction" in Dalmia and Faruqui (eds.), *Religious Interactions in Mughal India*, pp. xii–xiv.

119 C. Vaudeville, *Kabir*, Vol. I (Oxford, 1974), pp. 49–50, 53, 66.

120 C. A. Bayly, *Rulers, Townsmen and Bazaars: North Indian Society in the Age of British Expansion, 1770–1870* (Cambridge, 1983), pp. 7, 10, 21–3, 34, and passim.

121 B. Larocque, "Trade, State and Religion in Early Modern India" (unpublished PhD dissertation, Department of History, UW-Madison, 2004).

122 Irvine, *Manucci*, Vol. IV, p. 219.

123 W. Irvine, *The Later Mughals* (Delhi, 1995 reprint); G. S. Cheema, *The Forgotten Mughals: A History of the Later Emperors of the House of Babur (1707–1857)* (Delhi, 2002).

124 A. H. Sharar, *Lucknow, The Last Phase of an Oriental Culture (Translated and edited by E. E. Harcourt and Fakhir Hussain)* (1913 and after; Delhi, 1989), p. 47.

125 Deleury, *Les Indes Florissantes*, p. 122.

126 Ibid., pp. 346–52.

127 Munis D. Faruqui, "At Empire's End: The Nizam, Hyderabad and Eighteenth-Century India," *Modern Asian Studies*, 43, 1 (2009), pp. 5–43.

128 Richard B. Barnett, *North India between Empires: Awadh, the Mughals, and the British, 1720–1801* (Berkeley, 1980); M. Alam, *The Crisis of Empire in Mughal North India: Awadh and the Panjab, 1707–1748*, 2nd ed. (Delhi, 2013); M. H. Fisher, *A Clash of Cultures: Awadh, The British and the Mughals* (Delhi, 1987); J. R. I. Cole, *Roots of North Indian Shī'ism in Iran and Iraq: Religion and State in Awadh, 1722–1859* (Berkeley, 1988); Sharar, *Lucknow*.

129 P. B. Calkins, "The Formation of a Regionally Oriented Ruling Group in Bengal, 1700–1740," *Journal of Asian Studies*, 29, 4 (1970), pp. 799–806; P. J. Marshall, "Introduction," in P. J. Marshall (ed.), *The Eighteenth Century in Indian History: Evolution or Revolution?* (Delhi, 2005), pp. 1–49; A. M. Khan, "Introduction: The Twilight of Mughal Bengal," in Marshall, ibid., pp. 359–73; M. Alam, "The Mughals and the 18th Century Transition in Bengal: A Note," (unpublished paper, n.d.); O. Prakash, "Trade and

Politics in Eighteenth-Century Bengal," in S. Alavi (ed.), *The Eighteenth Century in India* (Delhi, 2002), pp. 136–64; J. R. McLane, *Land and Local Kingship in Eighteenth-Century Bengal* (Cambridge, 1993); A. Rahim, "The Rise of a Hindu Aristocracy under the Bengal Nawabs," *Journal of the Asiatic Society of Pakistan*, 6 (1961), pp. 104–18; K. Chatterjee, *Merchants, Politics and Society in Early Modern India: Bihar 1733–1820* (Leiden, 1996).

130 Wink, *Land and Sovereignty in India*.

131 M. Alam and S. Subrahmanyam, "Exploring the Hinterland: Trade and Politics in the Arcot Nizāmat (1700–1732)," in R. Mukherjee and L. Subramanian (eds.), *Politics and Trade in the Indian Ocean World: Essays in Honour of Ashin Das Gupta* (Delhi, 1998), pp. 113–64; S. Bayly, "The South Indian State and the Creation of Muslim Community," in *Saints, Goddesses and Kings: Muslims and Christians in South Indian Society, 1700–1900* (Cambridge, 1989), pp. 151–86.

132 M. Wilks and M. Hammick, *Historical Sketches of South Indian History from the Earliest Times to the Last Muhammadan Dynasty*, 4 vols. (1817) (Delhi, 1980); Maistre De La Touche, *The History of Hyder Shah Alias Hyder Ali Khan Bahadur or New Memoirs Concerning the East Indies, With Historical Notes* (Delhi, 1996); K. Brittlebank, *Islam and Kingship in a Hindu Domain: Tipu Sultan's Search for Legitimacy* (Delhi, 1996).

133 S. Bayly, "Hindu Kingship and the Origin of Community: Religion, State and Society in Kerala, 1750–1850," *Modern Asian Studies*, 18, 2 (1984), pp. 177–213.

134 M. Axworthy (ed.), *Crisis, Collapse, Militarism & Civil War: The History & Historiography of 18th Century Iran* (Oxford, 2018); Gommans, *Rise of the Indo-Afghan Empire*; Wink, "On the Road to Failure," pp. 331–9; Elphinstone, *Caubul*, Vol. II, pp. 95–105, 129–45, 298–9.

135 On this see also S. C. Levi, *The Indian Diaspora in Central Asia and Its Trade, 1550–1900* (Leiden, 2002), esp. pp. 27, 55, 59, 114–17, 147–8, 161–3, 176–8, 207.

136 C. Masson, *Narrative of Various Journeys in Belochistan, Afghanistan and the Panjab, 1826 to 1838*, 4 vols (Karachi, 1974–1977), Vol. I, p. 355.

137 Elphinstone, *Caubul*, Vol. II, p. 249.

138 A. Ghani, "Islam and State-Building in a Tribal Society: Afghanistan, 1880–1901," *Modern Asian Studies*, 12, 2 (1978), pp. 269–84; F. Ahmed, *Afghanistan Rising: Islamic Law and Statecraft between the Ottoman and British Empires* (Cambridge, MA, 2017).

Chapter 7

1 Joseph Conrad, *An Outcast of the Islands* (1896; Penguin Modern Classics, Middlesex, 1975), p. 50.

2 K. M. Panikkar, *Malabar and the Portuguese* (1929; Delhi, 1997), p. 33; K. M. Panikkar, *India and the Indian Ocean: An Essay on the Influence of Sea Power on Indian History* (London, 1945), p. 35.

3 F. Braudel, *Civilization & Capitalism, 15th–18th Centuries*, 3 vols. (London, 1984), Vol. III, p. 492.

4 K. N. Chaudhuri, *Trade and Civilisation in the Indian Ocean: An Economic History from the Rise of Islam to 1750* (Cambridge, 1985), p. 63, and passim for similar assessments.

5 M. N. Pearson, "The Portuguese and Violence in the Indian Ocean: Some Second Thoughts," *Oriente*, 12 (2004), pp. 11–23.

6 Chapter 3, pp. 65–70; Chapter 4, pp. 108–23. More on this in Wink, *Al-Hind*, Vols. I–III, passim.

7 See, e.g., the following books and articles, with extensive bibliographies: S. R. Prange, "A Trade of No Dishonor: Piracy, Commerce, and Continuity in the Western Indian Ocean, Twelfth to Sixteenth Century," *American Historical Review*, 116, 5 (2011), pp. 1269–93; S. R. Prange, "The Contested Sea: Regimes of Maritime Violence in the Pre-modern Indian Ocean," *Journal of Early Modern History*, 17, 1 (2013), pp. 9–33; S. R. Prange, *Monsoon Islam: Trade and Faith on the Medieval Malabar Coast* (Cambridge, 2018); P. Risso, "Cross-Cultural Perceptions of Piracy: Maritime Violence in the Western Indian Ocean and Persian Gulf Region during a Long Eighteenth Century," *Journal of World History*, 12, 2 (2001), pp. 293–319; Lakshmi Subramanian, *Medieval Seafarers* (Delhi, 1999); L. Subramanian, *The Sovereign and the Pirate: Ordering Maritime Subjects in India's Western Littoral* (Oxford, 2016); J. Kleinen and M. Osseweijer (eds.), *Pirates, Ports, and Coasts in Asia: Historical and Contemporary Perspectives* (Leiden, 2010); and the partial retraction and *mea culpa* (which does not go far enough) by Pearson in *Oriente* (quoted in note 5).

8 Cf. Chapter 4.

9 E. Vallet, *L'Arabie Marchande: Etat et commerce sous les sultans rasūlides du Yémen (626–858/1229–1454)* (Paris, 2010), pp. 541–623; E. Vallet, "Yemeni 'Oceanic Policy' at the End of the Thirteenth Century," *Proceedings of the Seminar for Arabian Studies*, 36 (2006), pp. 289–96; E. Vallet, "Les sultans rasūlides du Yémen: Protecteurs des communautés musulmanes de l'Inde, VIIe-VIIIe/XIIIe-XIVe siècles," *Annales Islamologiques*, 41 (2007), pp. 149–76.

10 Cf. *supra*, pp. 120–1.

11 Cf. *supra*, pp. 117–19.

12 J. C. Scott, *The Art of Not Being Governed: An Anarchist History of Upland Southeast Asia* (New Haven, 2009), p. 67.

13 V. B. Lieberman, *Strange Parallels: Southeast Asia in Global Context, c. 800–1830*, 2 vols (Cambridge, 2003–2009), Vol. II, p. 769, note 11.

14 L. F. F. R. Thomaz, "Precedents and Parallels of the Portuguese Cartaz System," in P. Malekandathil and J. Mohammed (eds.), *The Portuguese, Indian Ocean, and European Bridgeheads, 1500–1800: Festschrift of Professor K. S. Mathew* (Tellicherry, 2001), pp. 67–85.

15 Cf. Chapter 3, p. 70; Chapter 4, pp. 119–20.

16 R. Finlay, "The Treasure-Ships of Zheng-He: Chinese Maritime Imperialism in the Age of Discovery," *Terrae Incognitae*, 23 (1991), p. 8.

17 Cf. Chapter 4, pp. 118–19, 122.

18 A. Reid, *Southeast Asia in the Age of Commerce*, 2 vols (New Haven, 1988–1993), Vol. II, p. 311.

19 Ibid., pp. 311–14.

20 D. Lombard and C. Salmon, "Islam et sinité," *Archipel*, 30 (1985), pp. 73–94; and see A. L. Kumar, "Islam, the Chinese, and Indonesian Historiography – A Review Article," *Journal of Asian Studies*, 46, 3 (1987), pp. 603–16.

21 Reid, *Southeast Asia in the Age of Commerce*, Vol. II, pp. 314–19.

22 Ibid., pp. 318–19.

23 A. Das Gupta, "Trade and Politics in 18th Century India," in D. S. Richards (ed.), *Islam and the Trade of Asia* (Oxford, 1970), p. 181.

24 C. Cipolla, *Guns, Sails & Empires: Technological Innivation & European Expansion, 1400–1700* (New York, 1965), p. 137.

25 S. Subrahmanyam, *The Career and Legend of Vasco da Gama* (New York, 1997), pp. 109–12; Pearson, "Portuguese and Violence." For the history of Portuguese expansion, see C. R. Boxer, *The Portuguese Seaborne Empire, 1415–1825* (London, 1969); M. N. Pearson, *The Portuguese in India* (Cambridge, 1987); S. Subrahmanyam, *The Portuguese Empire in Asia, 1500–1700: A Political and Economic History* (London, 1993); Chaudhuri, *Trade and Civilisation*, pp. 63–79.

26 For the Dutch East India Company, see F. S. Gaastra, *De geschiedenis van de VOC* (Zutphen, 2002); for the English East India Company, see K. N. Chaudhuri, *The English East India Company: The Study of an Early Joint-Stock Company, 1600–1640* (London, 1965); K. N. Chaudhuri, *The Trading World of Asia and the English East India Company, 1660–1760* (Cambridge, 1978); on the French in India, see G. J. Ames, *Colbert, Mercantilism, and the French Quest for Asian Trade* (De Kalb, 1996).

27 See the introduction by P. J. Marshall to A. Das Gupta, *India and the Indian Ocean World: Trade and Politics* (Delhi, 2004), p. ix.

28 Das Gupta, "Indian Merchants and the Decline of Surat, c. 1700–1750," ibid., p. 5.

29 G. Casale, *The Ottoman Age of Exploration* (Oxford, 2010).

30 Das Gupta, "Indian Merchants and the Decline of Surat," p. 17; Das Gupta, "Trade and Politics in 18th century India," pp. 187–8.

31 Das Gupta, "Indian Merchants and the Decline of Surat," p. 74.

32 Ibid.; Das Gupta, "Trade and Politics in 18th Century India," pp. 189–96.

33 Cf. Chapter 6, p. 214.

34 This section relies mostly on Prange, *Monsoon Islam*; S. F. Dale, *Islamic Society and the South Asian Frontier: The Mappilas of Malabar, 1498–1922* (Oxford, 1980); A. Das Gupta, "Malabar in Asian Trade, 1740–1800," in *India and the Indian Ocean World* (Delhi, 2004), pp. 1–204; P. Malekandathil, "From Merchant Capitalists to Corsairs: The Response of the Muslim Merchants of Malabar to the Portuguese Commercial Expansion (1498–1600)," *Portuguese Studies Review*, 12, 1 (2004), pp. 75–96.

35 Das Gupta, "Malabar in Asian Trade," p. xiii.

36 Ibid., p. 19; Chapter 6, p. 214.

37 Das Gupta, "Malabar in Asian Trade," pp. 197–9.

38 *SJN*, p. 85.

39 M. D. Faruqui, *Princes of the Mughal Empire, 1504–1719* (Cambridge, 2012), p. 216.

40 Cf. above, p. 150.
41 *SJN*, 85–7, 117, 249.
42 O. Prakash, *The Dutch East India Company and the Economy of Bengal, 1630–1720* (Princeton, 1985); O. Prakash and D. Lombard (eds.), *Commerce and Culture in the Bay of Bengal, 1500–1800* (Delhi, 1999).
43 Das Gupta, "Trade and Politics in 18th Century India," pp. 199–202.
44 For the later history, see S. Subrahmanyam, *The Political Economy of Commerce: Southern India, 1500–1650* (Cambridge, 1990); S. Arasaratnam, *Merchants, Companies and Commerce on the Coromandel Coast 1650–1740* (Delhi, 1986); S. Arasaratnam, *Maritime India in the Seventeenth Century* (Delhi, 1994); S. Arasaratnam, "Coromandel's Bay of Bengal Trade, 1740–1800: A Study of Continuities and Changes," in O. Prakash and D. Lombard, *Commerce and Culture in the Bay of Bengal* (Delhi, 1999), pp. 307–28; P. Emmer and J. Gommans, *Rijk aan de Rand van de Wereld: De Geschiedenis van Nederland Overzee, 1600–1800* (Amsterdam, 2012), pp. 345–54; D. Havart, *Op- en ondergang van Coromandel* (Amsterdam, 1693); L. Bes, *The Heirs of Vijayanagara: Court Politics in Early-Modern South India* (PhD dissertation, Radboud University, Nijmegen, 2018).
45 Das Gupta, "Trade and Politics in 18th Century India," pp. 204–7.
46 Ibid., p. 206.
47 B. Schrieke, *Indonesian Sociological Studies*, 2 vols (The Hague and Bandung, 1955–1957), Vol. II, pp. 235, 246–7.
48 Schrieke, *Indonesian Sociological Studies*, Vol. I, pp. 50, 52, 55; Ch. Dobbin, *Islamic Revivalism in a Changing Peasant Economy: Central Sumatra, 1784–1847* (London, 1983), pp. 64–5, 119; C. Snouck Hurgronje, *De Atjehers*, Vol. I (Batavia, 1893), pp. 8–9, 50, 91–2, 132, 138–9, 142, 155.
49 D. Lombard, *Le Sultanat d'Atjéh au temps d'Iskandar Muda, 1607–1636* (Paris, 1967).
50 V. B. Lieberman, "Local Integration and Eurasian Analogies: Structuring Southeast Asian History, c. 1350–1830," *Modern Asian Studies*, 27, 3 (1993), pp. 475–572; J. J. L. Gommans and J. Leider (eds.), *The Maritime Frontier of Burma: Exploring Political, Cultural and Commercial Interaction in the Indian Ocean World, 1200–1800* (Leiden, 2002).
51 See especially H. J. De Graaf and Th. G. Th. Pigeaud, *De Eerste Moslimse Vorstendommen op Java* (The Hague, 1974); H. J. De Graaf and Th. G. Th. Pigeaud, *Islamic States in Java, 1500–1700* (The Hague, 1976); Reid, *Southeast Asia in the Age of Commerce*, Vol. II.
52 A. C. Milner, "Islam and the Muslim State," in M. B. Hooker (ed.), *Islam in South-East Asia* (Leiden, 1983), pp. 23–49.
53 Ibid., pp. 29–34.
54 Ibid., pp. 26–8.
55 Schrieke, *Indonesian Sociological Studies*, Vol. II, pp. 217–18; and see on this issue S. Moertono, *State and Statecraft in Old Java: A Study of the Later Mataram Period, 16th to 19th Century* (Ithaca, 1968).
56 M. C. Ricklefs, *Jogjakarta under Sultan Mangkubumi, 1749–1792: A History of the Division of Java* (London, 1979), p. 11.

Epilogue

1   G. N. Curzon, *Persia and the Persian Question*, 2 vols. (1892; London, 1966), Vol. I, p. 4.
2   V. S. Naipaul, *Beyond Belief: Islamic Excursions among the Converted Peoples* (London, 1998), p. 1.
3   Ibid., pp. 2–3.
4   Ibid., p. 3.
5   Ibid., p. 265.
6   Ibid.
7   Ibid.
8   Ibid., p. 239.
9   Ibid.
10   *The New York Times, Sunday Magazine*, October 28, 2001, p. 14.
11   Joseph Conrad, *Selected Works* (New York, 1994), p. 219.
12   C. Snouck Hurgronje, *Mekka in the Later Part of the 19th Century* (Leiden, 1970), p. 219. For an Indonesian novelistic account of Snouck Hurgronje's immense influence in the Dutch East Indies around the turn of the nineteenth century, see P. Ananta Toer, *Bumi Manusia* (Jakarta, 1981).
13   Snouck Hurgronje, *Mekka*, p. 233.
14   C. Mallampalli, *A Muslim Conspiracy in British India? Politics and Paranoia in the Early Nineteenth-Century Deccan* (Cambridge, 2017).
15   S. Alavi, *Muslim Cosmopolitanism in the Age of Empire* (Cambridge, MA, 2015); S. Alavi, "'Fugitive Mullahs and Outlawed Fanatics': Indian Muslims in Nineteenth Century Trans-Asiatic Imperial Rivalries," *Modern Asian Studies*, 45, 6 (2011), pp. 337–82.
16   For these events, see D. Fromkin, *A Peace to End All Peace: The Fall of the Ottoman Empire and the Creation of the Modern Middle East* (New York, 1989), esp. p. 96 ff; C. Snouck Hurgronje, *Verspreide Geschriften*, 6 vols. (Bonn & Leipzig, 1923–27), Vol. III, pp. 257–92, 327–54.
17   J. Buchan, *Greenmantle* (London, 1916), p. 23.
18   Ibid., p. 6.
19   A. Hitler, *Mein Kampf* (New York, 1971), p. 658.
20   S. Rushdie, *Shame* (New York, 1983).
21   A. Taseer, *Stranger to History: A Son's Journey through Islamic Lands* (Minneapolis, 2012), Kindle edition, Introduction.
22   Ibid., p. 109, ff.
23   A. Taseer, "V. S. Naipaul, My Wonderful, Cruel Friend," *The New York Times*, August 12, 2018.

Suggested Reading

Chapter 1

W. H. Arden Wood, "Rivers and Man in the Indus-Ganges Alluvial Plain," *Scottish Geographical Magazine*, 40 (1924), pp. 1–16.

G. Fussman, "Le concept d'empire dans l'Inde ancienne," in M. Duverger (ed.), *Concept d'Empire* (Paris, 1980).

G. Fussman, "Pouvoir central et régions dans l'Inde ancienne," *Annales ESC*, 37, 4 (1982), pp. 621–41.

R. Thapar, *From Lineage to State* (Bombay, 1984).

A. Wink, *Al-Hind: The Making of the Indo-Islamic World*, Vol. III (Leiden, 2004), pp. 1–78.

Chapter 2

J. N. Asopa, *Origin of the Rajputs* (Delhi, 1976).

M. Kumar Jha, "Migration, Settlement, and State Formation in the Ganga Plain: A Historical Geographical Perspective," *Journal of the Economic and Social History of the Orient*, 57 (2014), pp. 587–627.

V. B. Lieberman, "Local Integration and Eurasian Analogies: Structuring Southeast Asian History, c. 1350–c. 1830," *Modern Asian Studies*, 27, 3 (1993), pp. 475–572.

R. Lingat, *Royautés Bouddhiques* (Paris, 1989).

G. Michell, *The Hindu Temple: An Introduction to Its Meaning and Forms* (Chicago, 1988).

A. Reid, *A History of Southeast Asia: A Critical Crossroads* (Oxford, 2015).

A. Wink, *Al-Hind: The Making of the Indo-Islamic World*, Vol. I (Leiden, 1990), pp. 144–89.

Chapter 3

P. B. Golden, *An Introduction to the History of the Turkic Peoples: Ethnogenesis and State-Formation in Medieval and Early Modern Eurasia and the Middle East* (Wiesbaden, 1992).

J. J. L. Gommans, "The Silent Frontier of South Asia, c. A. D. 1000–1800," *Journal of World History*, 9, 1 (1998), pp. 1–23.

V. B. Lieberman, *Strange Parallels: Southeast Asia in Global Context, c. 800–1830*, 2 vols. (Cambridge, 2003–2009).
D. Lombard, "Le thème de la mer dans les littératures et les mentalités de l'archipel insulindien," *Archipel*, 20 (1980), pp. 317–28.
B. Schrieke, *Indonesian Sociological Studies*, 2 vols. (The Hague, 1955–1957).

Chapter 4

S. Bayly, "Islam in Southern India: 'Purist' or 'Syncretic'?" in C. A. Bayly and D. H. A. Kolff (eds.), *Two Colonial Empires: Comparative Essays on the History of India and Indonesia in the Nineteenth Century* (Leiden, 1986), pp. 37–59.
R. M. Eaton, *The Rise of Islam and the Bengal Frontier, 1204–1760* (Berkeley, 1993).
P. Jackson, *The Delhi Sultanate: A Political and Military History* (Cambridge, 1999).
M. Lombard, *L'Islam dans sa première grandeur. VIII-XI siècles* (Paris, 1971).
V. G. Mills (ed. and trans.), *Ma Huan, Ying-yai Sheng-lan* [The Overall Survey of the Ocean's Shore] (Cambridge, 1970).
A. Reid, *Southeast Asia in the Age of Commerce*, 2 vols. (New Haven, 1988–1993).
B. Stein, *Vijayanagara* (Cambridge, 1989).
C. Talbot, *Precolonial India in Practice: Society, Region, and Identity in Medieval Andhra* (Oxford, 2001).

Chapter 5

T. T. Allsen, *Mongol Imperialism: The Politics of the Grand Qan Möngke in China, Russia, and the Islamic Lands, 1251–1259* (Berkeley, 1987).
M. Elphinstone, *An Account of the Kingdom of Caubul*, 2 vols. (Karachi, 1992).
M. D. Faruqui, *The Princes of the Mughal Empire, 1504–1719* (Cambridge, 2012).
B. F. Manz, *The Rise and Rule of Tamerlane* (Cambridge, 1989).
S. Sen (ed.), *Indian Travels of Thevenot and Careri* (Delhi, 1949).

Chapter 6

M. Alam and S. Subrahmanyam (eds.), *The Mughal State, 1526–1750* (Delhi, 2001).
J. J. L. Gommans, *Mughal Warfare* (London, 2002).
I. Habib, *The Agrarian System of Mughal India, 1556–1707*, 2nd ed. (Delhi, 1999).
P. J. Marshall (ed.), *The Eighteenth Century in Indian History: Evolution or Revolution?* (Delhi, 2005).
J. F. Richards, *The Mughal Empire* (Cambridge, 1993).
A. Wink, *Akbar* (Oxford, 2009).

Chapter 7

C. R. Boxer, *The Portuguese Seaborne Empire, 1415–1825* (London, 1969).

K. N. Chaudhuri, *The Trading World of Asia and the English East India Company, 1660–1760* (Cambridge, 1978).

C. Cipolla, *Guns, Sails and Empires: Technological Innovation and European Expansion, 1400–1700* (New York, 1996).

A. Das Gupta, *India and the Indian Ocean World: Trade and Politics* (Delhi, 2004).

H. J. De Graaf and T. G. T. Pigeaud, *Islamic States in Java, 1500–1700* (The Hague, 1976).

D. Lombard, *Le Sultanat d'Atjéh au temps d'Iskandar Muda, 1607–1636* (Paris, 1967).

S. S. Prange, *Monsoon Islam: Trade and Faith on the Medieval Malabar Coast* (Cambridge, 2018).

M. C. Ricklefs, *Jogjakarta under Sultan Mangkubumi, 1749–1792: A History of the Division of Java* (London, 1979).

Index